Peace with Justice?

The New International Relations of Europe
Series Editor: Ronald H. Linden

Forthcoming

Peace with Justice?

War Crimes and Accountability in the Former Yugoslavia

PAUL R. WILLIAMS AND MICHAEL P. SCHARF

ROWMAN & LITTLEFIELD PUBLISHERS, INC.
Lanham • Boulder • New York • Oxford

ROWMAN & LITTLEFIELD PUBLISHERS, INC.

Published in the United States of America
by Rowman & Littlefield Publishers, Inc.
A Member of the Rowman & Littlefield Publishing Group
4720 Boston Way, Lanham, Maryland 20706
www.rowmanlittlefield.com

PO Box 317, Oxford, OX2 9RU, United Kingdom

British Library Cataloguing in Publication Information Available

Library of Congress Cataloging-in-Publication Data

Williams, Paul R.
    Peace with justice? : war crimes and accountability in the former Yugoslavia / by
Paul R. Williams & Michael P. Scharf.
        p.   cm. — (New international relations of Europe)
    Includes bibliographical references and index.
    ISBN 0-7425-1855-8 (cloth : alk. paper) — ISBN 0-7425-1856-6 (pbk. : alk. paper)
    1. Former Yugoslav republics—Politics and government. 2.War crime trials—
Former Yugoslav republics. I. Scharf, Michael P., 1963– II. Title. III. Series.

    DR1318 .W55 2002
    949.705—dc21

                                                                            2002069689

Printed in the United States of America

⊖™ The paper used in this publication meets the minimum requirements of American
National Standard for Information Sciences—Permanence of Paper for Printed Library
Materials, ANSI/NISO Z39.48-1992.

To Kathy and Samantha Nicole Williams
and
Trina and Garrett Scharf
for their inspiration and support

And in memory of our dear friend and mentor,
Monroe Leigh
(1919–2001)

Contents

Abbreviations

ACTORD	NATO Activation Order
Bosnia	Bosnia and Herzegovina
EU	European Union
FRY	Federal Republic of Yugoslavia
G7	Group of Seven
G8	Group of Eight (G7 plus Russia)
GAO	U.S. Government Accounting Office
IFOR	Implementation Force
IPTF	International Police Task Force
JNA	Yugoslav National Army
KDOM	Kosovo Diplomatic Observer Mission
KFOR	Kosovo Force
KLA	Kosovo Liberation Army
KVM	Kosovo Verification Mission
NAC	North Atlantic Council
NATO	North Atlantic Treaty Organization
NGO	Nongovernmental Organization
OHR	Office of the High Representative
OSCE	Organization for Security and Cooperation in Europe
SFOR	Stabilization Force
UN	United Nations
UNHCR	United Nations High Commission for Human Rights
UNMIK	United Nations Mission in Kosovo
UNPREDEP	United Nations Preventative Deployment
UNPROFOR	United Nations Protection Force
U.S.	United States
WEU	West European Union
World Court or ICJ	International Court of Justice
Yugoslav Tribunal (or Tribunal)	International Criminal Tribunal for the Former Yugoslavia

Preface

No matter how rigorous the methodology adopted by authors who are writing on topics as controversial as the dissolution of the former Yugoslavia and the role of justice in peace-building, the life experiences of the authors will invariably permeate the work. With this in mind, we believe it is necessary to share with the readers a brief identification of our involvement with matters relating to the dissolution of the former Yugoslavia and efforts to use justice as a tool of peace-building, and how our contemporary perspectives were shaped by these experiences.

While we both were exposed to the debate concerning notions of justice and their utility in peace-building during our legal education, we began our professional engagement with peace-building and the former Yugoslavia when we served as attorney-advisers in the Office of the Legal Adviser for the U.S. Department of State. As a lawyer with the European and Canadian Affairs Division of the Legal Office, Dr. Williams was deeply involved in the legal aspects of the U.S. response to the dissolution of Yugoslavia and the accompanying widespread commission of ethnic cleansing and attempted genocide, as well as the efforts of the United Nations and European Union to mediate the conflict, including the proposed Vance/Owen Peace Plan. Professor Scharf, as an attorney-adviser for United Nations affairs, was intensely involved in U.S. government efforts to utilize the United Nations to promote a resolution of the conflict and produced first drafts of resolutions adopted by the Security Council relating to the imposition of economic and diplomatic sanctions, the authorization of "all necessary means" to protect humanitarian convoys, the imposition of the no-fly zone and safe areas, and the establishment of the commission of experts to investigate the Yugoslav atrocities. While at the Department of State the authors served as co-counsel on the Inter-Agency Serbian Sanctions Task Force, and they actively participated in United States efforts to bring about the creation of the International Criminal Tribunal for the Former Yugoslavia.

After leaving the Department of State, Professor Williams began to provide pro bono legal assistance to the government of Bosnia-Herzegovina, and he served as its legal adviser and member of its delegation during the Dayton negotiations. He subsequently advised the Kosovo Albanian government and served as its legal and policy adviser during the Rambouillet/Paris negotiations, and he advised the Macedonian Albanians during the Skopje/Lake Ohrid negotiations. After leaving the Department of State, Professor Scharf established a program for the provision of pro bono public international legal assistance to both the Yugoslav and Rwanda Tribunals. At the request of the Office of the Prosecutor, Professor Scharf's program has to date provided over ninety legal memoranda on issues pending before the International Tribunals. In addition, both authors have been involved in advocacy efforts designed to enhance the incorporation of justice into the peace-building process, and to enhance international support for the efforts of the Yugoslav Tribunal.

Having had access to the resources and analysis available to State Department officials, we both firmly hold the view that the crisis in the former Yugoslavia was not the result of the bubbling over of ancient ethnic hatreds, or economic deprivation, but rather was caused by an ethno-centered nationalist response to the erosion of public support for a communist regime characterized by totalitarianism. The response of Serbian political elites to efforts by Yugoslavia's constituent republics to reconfigure the structure of government and provide for greater republic level autonomy included a calculated policy of nationalism designed to tap into deeply held convictions about ethnic superiority in order to retain political and economic power, the use of force to change internal boundaries, and the provision of ethnic cleansing of non-Serb populations and, where necessary, genocide to create Serbian-dominated territory, which then could be incorporated into a greater Serbia. In Croatia, the political elites relied upon similar forms of ethno-nationalism to rally support for an independent Croatia and to signal to the Croatian-Serbian population that they would be unwelcome in the new Croatian state. Importantly, the Yugoslav Tribunal has found that the Serbian nationalist regime orchestrated the commission of systematic and widespread atrocities, and these acts reflected an official policy of the Serbian regime. The Tribunal has also found the atrocities committed by the Bosnian Serb army constituted genocide. The matter of Croatian policy is also the subject of a number of cases before the Yugoslav Tribunal, and it has found the Croatian regime similarly culpable for orchestrated atrocities. According to Tribunal experts, the Bosnian government forces, while responsible for some atrocities, committed fewer than ten percent, and these were not part of an organized policy of ethnic cleansing as was the case with Serbian and Croatian forces.

Concerning the nature of Western and international foreign policy institutions, we hold great respect for the professional diplomats and operational personnel who are responsible for the formulation and implementation of complex political arrangements. We are also keenly aware, however, of the focus on near term political victories, protection of institutional turf, and, in the case of governments, attention to the reaction of domestic constituencies, which grips most administrations and international organizations. Our time in government service has led us to acknowledge a general unwillingness or inability among most governments to make the tough choices that may lead to greater peace in the long run, but will not generate short-term accolades. Where social scientists tend to see grand foreign policy designs, and diplomats see the nitty gritty of daily policy trade-offs, we see an imperfect, yet functional, process of peace-building. Although plagued by disorganization, a lack of coherency, the pursuit of short-term interests, and the willingness to settle for perceived foreign policy successes and the establishment of a "process" rather than meaningful developments, this process was nevertheless able to create the first ad hoc War Crimes Tribunal, produce the Dayton Accords, structure the use of legitimate force to stop ethnic aggression, and provide for the deployment of tens of thousands of international peacekeepers to secure strategic interests, promote the protection of human rights, and begin to reverse the gains of ethnic cleansing.

Having participated in mediation and negotiation from the perspective of a third party (the United States), and from the perspective of primary parties (the Bosnians, Kosovars, and Macedonian-Albanians), we similarly hold neither an idealistic nor a completely academic view of mediation and negotiation, nor of the primary players and peace builders. For instance, we do not perceive Slobodan Milosevic as a silver fox who adeptly manipulated Western governments, but rather as a pragmatic nationalist who took advantage of the generally disparate and contradictory efforts of Western peace builders and played on Russia's desire to project itself as a great power.

Finally, as what might be called advocates of justice, we are inclined to look favorably upon the role of justice in peace-building, but believe it is important that, before one can advocate for justice, one must precisely understand the role of justice. In this book we undertake to accurately portray the role of justice, warts and all, because we believe it is necessary to tell the true story of the role of justice. All too often human rights and peace advocates treat the norms and institutions of justice as a panacea for conflict, ethnic violence, and orchestrated crimes against humanity, while self-proclaimed realists and professional diplomats dismiss justice as at best mere moral window dressing and at worst an impediment to peace. We believe the truth lies somewhere in between, and if peace builders possess a proper understanding of its role, the norm of justice may better serve to bring about peaceful relations among both states and peoples.

Paul R. Williams

Michael P. Scharf

Acknowledgments

This project was made possible by a generous grant of the United States Institute of Peace and research support from the American University and the New England School of Law. In addition, several people deserve special recognition for the assistance they have furnished us in writing this book.

Foremost among those are the officials of the Office of the Prosecutor of the International Criminal Tribunal for the Former Yugoslavia, who opened their doors to us and provided incredible insights into the workings of the Tribunal and its role in peacemaking and implementation in the former Yugoslavia. In particular, we thank Richard Goldstone, the former prosecutor of the International Criminal Tribunal, Graham Blewitt, the Tribunal's deputy prosecutor, Grant Niemann, senior trial attorney, and Payam Akhvan, legal adviser to the International Prosecutor for meeting with us and providing on-the record comments for use in this book.

Additionally, we express our deep gratitude to Major General (ret.) William Nash, who had commanded the United States IFOR troops, for providing us a candid picture of the military's perceptions of the role of justice in peace enforcement in Bosnia. We are also grateful to the invaluable insights and assistance provided by Jim Hooper and Marshall Harris—two former U.S. State Department officials who have dedicated much of their recent professional careers to advocacy efforts designed to imbue U.S. policy toward the former Yugoslavia with a sense of justice; by Mohamed Sacirbey, Bosnia's ambassador to the United Nations; and by Nina Bang-Jensen of the Coalition for International Justice.

We are also indebted to a number of other lawyers, diplomats, and foreign policy practitioners working with the U.S. government, the United Nations, the European Commission, and the Yugoslav Tribunal, who provided innumerable valuable insights into the peace-building process, and who for valid reasons requested their remarks be treated as background and not for attribution, but agreed to allow us to use their insights to draw conclusions, or to confirm factual information which could only accurately be attested to by someone "on the inside" of the peace-building process.

Finally, we would like to thank the Carnegie Endowment for International Peace, the American University's School of International Service and Washington

College of Law, and the New England School of Law, for providing institutional support, as well as the following young professionals who provided research assistance: Sabrineh Ardalan, Rose Park, Omar Vargas, Monika Pohlmann, Karina Michael, Megan Akers, Cassandra Capobianco, Ramzi Nemo, Leslie Kurshan, Amjed Atallah, Michael Staconis, Jennifer Harris, Erica Bomsey, Adam Hill, Kathleen Kelly, Teresa Taylor, Samantha Williams, Bethany McAndrew, Scott Worden, and Karen Glasgow. We also thank Abigail Taylor for her crucial assistance with copyediting and for her patience in tolerating our many changes and corrections.

Introduction

If you want peace, work for justice.

—Pope Paul XI on January 1, 1972, in a homily
on World Peace Day.[1]

In the late 1980s, Yugoslavia began its bloody disintegration, igniting over a decade of ethnic fighting marked by systematic war crimes, crimes against humanity, and acts of genocide committed in Croatia, Bosnia, and Kosovo. In total, close to half a million civilians would be killed, and four million driven from their homes as a result of Slobodan Milosevic's reliance on ethno-nationalism and ethnic cleansing as tools for accumulating and retaining political power in order to pursue his dream of a greater Serbia.[2] To the major powers and the United Nations organization, the effort to halt atrocities and restore peace to this troubled part of the world would constitute the last great foreign policy challenge of the twentieth century.

This study examines and explores the role of the norms and institutions of justice in the process of peace-building during this time of conflict in the former Yugoslavia. The specific task of this study is not to argue for a greater or lesser role for justice, but rather to evaluate the extent to which the norms and institutions of justice have played and continue to play a role in the peace-building process in the former Yugoslavia, and to assess the extent to which the approach of accountability conflicts with and/or serves concomitantly with other normative approaches such as accommodation, economic inducement, and the use of force. Based on this evaluation and assessment, the study seeks to promote an understanding of the relationship between the approach of accountability and other relevant approaches so they may be properly balanced by diplomats and foreign policy agents in their future attempts to build peace out of conflict.

The norm of justice applied through the approach of accountability may be a useful tool for the diplomat or peace builder, and given the limited number of tools in the diplomatic bag, a detailed understanding of the norm of justice and the approach of accountability can only help to foster a better and more lasting peace. Traditionally, the peace builders have relied upon the approach of either accommodation or the use of force, and more recently the approach of economic inducement, in an effort to accomplish desired ends. In most of these cases the peace structure is fatally flawed and the tool of justice/accountability is often neglected, and, when used, not employed in an efficient or constructive manner. Recently, however, there has been an increasing use of the tool of justice/accountability in the peace-building process, including in South Africa, Sierra Leone, Rwanda, East Timor, and Cambodia.

On the whole, the investigation into the role of accountability and its relationship to other approaches indicates that state and substate actors lack both an in-depth understanding of the utility of the accountability approach and a realization of the necessity of incorporating the norm of justice into the peace-building process. Where the norm of justice has been incorporated and institutions established, they have frequently failed to meet realistic expectations, and have been improperly balanced with other salient norms and approaches. In large part the peace builders are uncomfortable and unskilled in giving adequate effect to the norm of justice as they have been reared in the school of realism, and they have been perplexed by the mantra of human rights advocates claiming there can be no peace without justice, when in fact there appear to be many instances of peace based on injustice. The utilization of the norms and institutions of justice is further hampered by the entrenched interests supporting other approaches such as accommodation (which may slide into appeasement), use of force, and economic inducements, as well as the lack of suitably functioning institutions of justice.

The story of the role of justice in the crisis in the former Yugoslavia is important to tell for a number of reasons. First, if the norms and institutions of justice do in fact play a positive role in building peace, then it is necessary to make the case for their further incorporation into the peace-building process and to understand the real utility of justice as well as its practical limits so that it may be most effectively applied in future conflicts. To date, foreign policy practitioners and international relations scholars generally have held three views of the role of justice. Some perceive justice as playing no productive role whatsoever. The most telling example of this group would be David Owen, co-chair of the UN/EU mediation efforts from 1992-1995, who declared, "the search for a juster peace than was obtainable at the negotiating table has inflicted hardship and havoc on innocent civilians within the former Yugoslavia and exacted a heavy price from the already weak economies of the neighboring states."[3] The second group ascribe a narrow and well-defined role for justice and primarily concern themselves with the contribution to reconciliation provided by truth and reconciliation commissions. The third group, in contrast, assert that there can be "no peace without justice" and justice is the keystone to any lasting peace. This study will add to a more refined understanding of the actual role of justice, which lies somewhere between the second and third perspectives.

The second reason for telling the story of the role of justice and the approach of accountability in the Yugoslav conflict is that in no other peace-building process in history has there been so much political emphasis placed on the need to employ the norm of justice, and so much energy devoted to creating and utilizing justice based institutions. The Yugoslav conflict is a particularly fertile research ground for accurately assessing the role of justice in peace building given the UN Security Council's creation of the United Nations War Crimes Commission for Yugoslavia and the subsequent creation of the Yugoslav Tribunal; the utilization of the World Court by the government of Bosnia to allege genocide by the government of the Federal Republic of Yugoslavia (FRY), and the FRY's counterclaim; the utilization of the World Court by the FRY to allege a violation of sovereignty, territorial integrity, and the commission of genocide by ten NATO member states for the Kosovo air campaign; the application of a plethora of minor institutions such as human rights rapporteurs, domestic truth commission and criminal prosecutions; and the extensive deployment of human rights monitors to prevent violations of international humanitarian law.

Third, in the case of Yugoslavia, as in most other cases, the norm of justice and the approach of accountability had to compete for a role in the peace-building process with other approaches, and at times the approaches were mutually supportive or contradictory in their purposes and application, thus providing a relatively rare opportunity to evaluate the relationship between the approach of accountability and other salient approaches. In particular, the interested third party states imposed UN and EU-sponsored, as well as unilateral, sanctions on certain parties; then provided financial assistance to those and other parties; posted rewards for the capture of indicted war criminals; engaged in acts of accommodation, which sometimes led to instances of appeasement; invoked the politics of moral equivalency; deployed tens of thousands of lightly armed UN peacekeepers and delivered pin prick air strikes; and then employed more strategic air strikes and deployed over 50,000 heavily armed ground troops.

Fourth, in large part because of the significant effort and high-level official endorsement of the norms and institutions of justice, and the perceived failure of the peace-building process in the former Yugoslavia, many foreign policy practitioners and international relations scholars are coming to view the role of justice with significant skepticism.[4] The examination conducted in this study will help to properly target this skepticism by ascertaining how the norms and institutions of justice have been misapplied, as a result of (1) the pursuit of short-term interests by states and substate actors, (2) the unfocused application of the norm, (3) the lack of a commitment to make the politically tough choices necessary for lasting peace, (4) the difficulty of conceiving justice as a long-term process, and (5) the occasional inability of international personnel to adequately and competently perform necessary tasks associated with the approach of accountability. With this focus, it is possible to assess whether a role for justice is salvageable and to determine how it might be best applied in future conflicts.

Part I of the book sets the intellectual foundation for structuring this inquiry into the role of justice. Chapter 1 reviews the suitability of various legal and social science methodologies for structuring an inquiry into the role of justice, and settles on a hybrid approach designed by the authors specifically for this task. This approach, which we refer to as "cognitive contextual process," is then relied upon to deduce ten questions which frame the study of the role of justice. Chapter 2 familiarizes the reader with the definition and functions of the norm of justice, the approach of accountability, and various institutions associated with that approach. Chapter 3 examines the definitions of the other relevant approaches—accommodation, economic inducement, and use of force—and the institutions associated with those norms. That chapter further examines the traditional conflict between the norm of justice and the approach of accommodation and explains the manner in which the approach of accommodation interacts with other approaches during the peace-building process.

Part II seeks to familiarize the reader with the background to the conflict, beginning with chapter 4, which briefly reviews the causes and consequences of the conflict in the former Yugoslavia, followed by chapter 5, which identifies the interests of the primary stakeholders in the conflict, including the United States, Great Britain, France, Russia, the European Union, and the United Nations. These two chapters are intended to serve as a factual primer for readers not well versed in the Yugoslav conflict, and they are not designed to serve as a comprehensive account of all pertinent events.

To examine the process whereby institutions of justice are created and utilized in the peace-building process, Part III begins in chapter 6 with an account of the political and other circumstances giving rise to the establishment of the Yugoslav War Crimes Commission and the creation of the Yugoslav Tribunal. Chapter 7 then evaluates the operation of the Yugoslav Tribunal, contrasts its accomplishments with its expectations, and identifies both the extent to which it influenced the peace process (positively and negatively) and the extent to which it may have been more effective had the peace builders and the officers of the Tribunal better understood its peace-building role and capabilities. Chapter 8 then assesses the role of the International Court of Justice in the Genocide Case brought by Bosnia-Herzegovina against the FRY, charging the FRY with responsibility for crimes of genocide committed against the people of Bosnia-Herzegovina, and the case brought by the FRY against ten NATO member states, charging NATO with the unlawful use of force against the FRY. This chapter pays particular attention to the reluctance of the peace builders to support utilization of the Court as an instrument to build peace, and assesses how, if they had chosen to do so, they might have more adeptly used the Court to further their interests.

To evaluate the role of justice in the negotiation phase of the peace-building process, Part IV begins in chapter 9 with an examination of the Vance/Owen mediation efforts and the subsequent Dayton negotiations, which highlights the limited extent to which justice influenced the negotiation process and the extent to which the peace builders sought to limit the reference to the norms and institutions of justice within the Accords. Chapter 10 conducts a similar evaluation of the international mediation prior to the Rambouillet/Paris negotiations, with particular attention paid to the conflict between accommodation and the use of force and accountability approaches, noting how different stakeholders advocated different approaches. Chapter 11 then explores in detail the Rambouillet/Paris negotiations and the subsequent NATO strategic air campaign launched against the FRY, assessing the extent to which the norms and institutions of justice were invoked by the peace builders to influence the behavior of the parties, and tracking the ebb and flow of the peace builders' interest in these norms and institutions.

To appraise the relationship between justice and the approaches of economic inducements, use of force and accommodation, Part V begins in chapter 12 with a review of the limited efforts of the NATO led Implementation Force to arrest indicted war criminals in Bosnia-Herzegovina, discussing the motivations for those arrests, and indicating the positive and negative effects of those arrests on the peace process. Chapter 13 then examines the relationship between economic inducements and justice, exploring both how economic inducements may be used to promote the role of justice, as well as the competition between the two approaches and how this influenced the peace-building process. This chapter also examines how economic inducements ultimately led to the surrender of Serb leader, Slobodan Milosevic, for trial before the Yugoslav Tribunal.

The concluding section then returns to the ten questions articulated in the first chapter and, drawing from the discussion throughout the text, provides a concise answer to each question. Taken together, these answers illuminate the role played by justice in the peace-building process, and explain its relationship to other more predominate approaches. They also validate the utility of the cognitive contextual process method for the study of similar conflicts and questions concerning the relationship between various norms and approaches during the peace-building process.

Part I

Structuring an Inquiry into the Role of Justice during the Peace-Building Process

Chapter 1

The Cognitive Contextual Process: Melding International Relations and International Legal Theory

As the most powerful nation committed to the rule of law, we have a responsibility to confront these assaults on humankind. One response mechanism is accountability, namely to help bring the perpetrators of genocide, crimes against humanity, and war crimes to justice. If we allow them to act with impunity, then we will only be inviting a perpetuation of these crimes far into the next millennium. Our legacy must demonstrate an unyielding commitment to the pursuit of justice.

— David Scheffer,
U.S. Ambassador for War Crimes Issues[1]

To structure an inquiry into the role of justice in peace-building, it is necessary to select a theoretical framework, or what lawyers might call a method, to guide the investigation. As most of the research to date has involved advocacy for or against the incorporation of justice into the peace-building process there is no pre-existing method which can be employed to investigate the role justice has actually played. Moreover, as this project undertakes a multilayered inquiry, no single existing general theoretical framework comprehensively fits the needs of this project. The quote by Ambassador Scheffer above is illustrative, in that he invokes the constructivist principle of a unique responsibility to prevent atrocities, the realist principle of deterrence, the legal process principle of rule of law, the institutionalist principle of accountability through the Yugoslav Tribunal, the game theory axiom of learned behavior, and the liberalist notion of legacy.

To meld the relevant axioms of the various applicable international relations and international law methods into an approach suitable for investigating the role of justice, this chapter develops a novel method termed the cognitive contextual process. This method was specifically developed by the authors for the

3

purpose of structuring inquiries into the role of legal norms in the conduct of international relations. As a hybrid method which melds international relations and international law approaches to understanding state behavior, the primary tenets of the cognitive contextual process are drawn from the methods of realism, game theory, institutionalism/regime theory, liberalism, constructivism, traditional legal theory, legal process, and the liberal approach to legal theory.[2]

The cognitive contextual process method is designed to serve two functions. The first is to aid the reader in understanding the social and political process in which states and substate and nonstate actors interact, and how this process influences their selection of particular courses of action as opposed to other equally viable options. Second, the cognitive contextual process method can be employed to deduce a series of guiding questions used to structure an inquiry into the role of justice (and other norms and approaches) in the peace-building process to ascertain why states may or may not employ the norm, and the effect of its application or nonapplication on the peace-building process.[3]

Constructing a Hybrid Method: The Cognitive Contextual Process

This is a conflict between the rule of law and politics, and the rule of law has lost.

—OSCE lawyer commenting on mission leader Ambassador Robert
Frowick's decision to overrule the disqualification of fifty
pro-Karadzic municipal candidates in Pale.[4]

The cognitive contextual process holds that during a peace-building endeavor, self-aware and learning capable states interact within a context of circumstances that influence the course of their political interplay. During this interaction, states generate, test, and modify peace-building approaches, norms, and regimes in a manner designed to achieve their interests.[5]

As such, the cognitive contextual process is built upon three key premises. First, the decision to utilize a particular approach or a combination of approaches, and the manner in which it is employed is the result of a series of cognitive developments relating to the perceived identity and interests of a state or nonstate actor, the perceived value of the approach, and the perceived obligation to apply such an approach.

Second, the manner in which a particular approach is applied and the degree to which it effectively achieves its objectives is influenced by a number of domestic and international factors, including the application of other approaches and the existence of regimes relevant to a particular approach, which constitute the context in which that norm operates.

Third, the utilization of the various approaches is the result of a continual process of learning, rule development, self-identification, contexualization, and competition among states, in which approaches and norms are applied, evolved, and modified. With these three premises in mind, the following narrative description and narrative model seeks to describe the cognitive contextual process as applied to the utilization of the approach of accountability and the application of the norm of justice.

The Cognitive Factor

States are cognitive actors which possess a self-identity based upon their form of government, their political history, the relative power and influence of various substate actors, the perceptions of individual political leaders, the state's perceived role in the international community, and their material and other resources which may enable them to influence the behavior of other states and institutions consistent with their perceived role.[6] States are aware their interests may coincide or conflict with the interests of other states, and purposefully seek to manage these conflicts through the creation of alliances, regimes, and de facto balances of power.[7] As cognitive actors, states act based on their perceived interests, tested methods, and perceived rules of interaction (norms).[8]

The concerns of states are seldom narrow, and they frequently encompass the spectrum of interests from power to morality.[9] These interests are most frequently defined by the ordered aggregation of subsystematic interests through a bureaucratic system operating within a political system, be it a democratic, oligarchic, or totalitarian form of governance.[10] Notably, the identification of state interests may be influenced by substate and nonstate actors depending on the type of political system charged with aggregating a state's interests.[11] Moreover, state interests are not static and may transform with a change in the form of government, change in government personnel, or increased influence of substate and nonstate actors.[12]

To promote their interests, states will employ a variety of methods of interstate interaction, be it cooperative or adversarial, seeking first to use those that have yielded results in previous instances of conflict resolution.[13] States will generally first employ methods they believe hold the lowest risk of endangering or affecting other interests of that state, and for which political will and domestic stakeholder support is easily generated, for example, first accommodation and then weak economic sanctions, only later followed by the threat of the use of force. If and when these methods prove inadequate, states will consider the employment of relatively untested methods, such as the creation of a war crimes tribunal, the creation of safe havens, or the use of methods with high political risk, such as the use of force.

States further create and employ rules designed to promote their interests and create and utilize institutions built around these rules in order to further promote the achievement of those interests.[14] Binding rules are identified by an examination of bilateral and multilateral treaties and customary international law. Nonbinding, but authoritative rules are identified by declarations, resolutions, codes of conduct, and social and diplomatic custom between states.[15] Through a pattern of perpetual interaction with other states and with institutions, states learn which rules and institutions work best to promote their interests.[16] States may also learn through a pattern of interaction which rules are generally enforced, and which are not.[17]

The Context

State action and the accompanying rule development are influenced by the context in which states interact.[18] This context involves the facts of a given dispute, the historical prism through which states perceive the conflict, the relative involvement of other states, the existence of applicable formal and informal regimes, and the involvement of nonstate and substate actors, including individuals.[19] The influence of these various actors and circumstances can be assessed according to their power, access, and claim to legitimacy.

The most important factual elements of the context relate to the perception of who is doing what to whom and why, who is allied with whom and why, and who is uncommitted and why. Similarly, the effect of the historical prism is dictated by the perception of who did what to whom and why, who was allied with whom and why at relevant historical points in time, and who might be perceived as neutral or objective and thus a potential arbiter of the conflict.[20]

The involvement of other states in the peace-building process affects the context of the process as each state possesses its own self-identity (e.g., that of a peace builder, superpower, victim, avenger), its own interests (e.g., justice, money, power, hegemony, territorial expansion/consolidation, status, reestablishment of national identity), an established pattern of political discourse with other states, and a particular form of government, which may affect its interaction with other states.

The existence of formal and informal regimes, with various overlapping functions, further influences the context of state interaction.[21] Although regimes are created by states and often operated by states, they can take on a self-identity separate from the states which created them (as with the Yugoslav Tribunal), and in some instances separate from the states which operate them (as with the office of the United Nations Secretary-General, and possibly even NATO). Regimes may serve the function of a means for dispute resolution (e.g., the United Nations Security Council and the OSCE), they may serve as a means of alliance building and coordination (e.g., the Contact Group and NATO), and they may seek to promote a particular interest that may affect the peace-building process (e.g., the Yugoslav Tribunal, the UN Human Rights Commission, and OSCE monitors).

The operation of the regimes themselves are influenced by the existence of previously created rules such as those relating to the laws of war, crimes against humanity, sovereignty, and territorial integrity. Moreover, the operation of regimes, in addition to being influenced by the state parties to the regime, are greatly influenced by individuals holding executive positions within those institutions.

Each substate and nonstate actor possesses its own self-identity and self-interests, thereby influencing the peace-building process. These groups may also increase or dilute public pressure to take action, and in some instances may become directly involved in the peace-building process by providing humanitarian assistance and reporting on crimes against humanity. Certain substate and nonstate actors may even provide capacity building to the parties during the conflict. Importantly, individual peacemakers often have a significant impact on the context of the peace-building process and invariably possess their own self-identity and self-interests which affect the nature of the peace sought. Moreover, individual peace builders meld their self-interest and that of their sponsoring state, which do not necessarily perfectly correspond.

The Process

The peace-building process may be characterized by a perpetual and predictive process of social and political interaction among states, substate, and nonstate actors. This process generates an established pattern of practice, which in turn generates norms such as justice, which may be translated into rules, such as laws of war, regulations pertaining to economic sanctions, and justifications for the use of force.[22] During this process new and existing norms compete for influence and primacy.[23]

This pattern of practice and norm creation may then generate formal and informal regimes, such as the Yugoslav Tribunal, UN Sanctions Committee, ICFY Peace Process, which then influence additional social and political interaction. These regimes will also influence the context of the peace-building process as they become part of it, create an opportunity for substate and nonstate actors to influence the process, and advance cognition in that states evaluate themselves in light of their response to the regimes—both in terms of support of and compliance with the regimes. Regimes will also affect the selection of approaches by their mere existence, and by the possibility of their independent and sometimes unpredictable interaction.

As the process of state interaction proceeds through its cycles, either throughout the same crisis, or with the addition of new crises, the parties engage in further social and political interaction. Further interaction will be influenced by the previous cycle of interaction and may lead to a reassessment of identity, interests, and perception of appropriate methods. The additional interaction may also be constrained or enhanced by norms and regimes developed in previous cycles of interaction. These subsequent cycles of interaction may also entrench existing norms and regimes, modify existing norms and regimes, and/or generate additional norms and regimes. This normative modification, evolution and creation, together with regime evolution and regime creation will affect subsequent cycles of interaction within the peace-building process.[24]

Illustrating the Cognitive Contextual Process

The above narrative description of the cognitive contextual process of peace-building may be illustrated by the following narrative model.

Initial Cycle: State, substate and nonstate actor self-identification → Identification of state and substate actor interests and objectives → Identification of other state, substate and nonstate actors with which actors must interact in order to accomplish their objectives → Social and political interaction among state, substate and nonstate actors who establish patterns of practice—for example, use of force, use of economic sanctions, humane treatment of non-combatants, establishment of peace talks → The development of norms and expectations about behavior—for example, when is the use of force or economic sanctions legitimate and effective, how should non-combatants be treated → The creation of informal regimes and formal institutions to perpetuate norms that promote self interest by influencing the pattern of social interaction—for example, convening UN/EU sponsored peace talks, establishing no-fly zones and safe havens, creating the Yugoslav Tribunal.

Subsequent Cycles: Reassessment of state, substate and nonstate actor self-identification → Identification of state, substate and nonstate actor interests and assessment of existing norms and regimes that may be used to achieve those interests → Modified social and political interaction among state, substate and nonstate actors entailing the repetition of established patterns of practice and the further development of new patterns broadly consistent with established norms—for example, proportional use of force, targeted economic sanctions with humanitarian exemptions → The modification, evolution, and creation of norms resulting in the confirmation and possible modification of existing expectations about behavior, and the creation of new expectations—for example, humanitarian intervention, mass sexual assault as a war crime, and prohibition on negotiating with indicted war criminals → The continuation, modification, or discontinuation of established regimes and creation of additional regimes to better promote the use of norms to achieve state and substate actor interests—for example, discontinuance of the UN/EU Peace Initiative and creation of the Contact Group and convening of the Dayton negotiations, enhanced funding for Tribunal and adoption of policy of sealed indictment.

This repetitive cyclical relationship explains this study's relevance and importance to policymakers. From the foregoing discussion, we can see that if outcomes change, they do so by using some element of the previous normative structure to change the salience of different norms. In this way, formal institutions like the United Nations, NATO, and the Yugoslav Tribunal reflect certain types of normative consensus. As such, international social institutions and the state and substate actors' employment of certain combination of norms plays a crucial role in shaping outcomes in international society.

In the case of the former Yugoslavia, this interactive cycle was repeated many times with the norm of justice identified in the initial cycle as imbedded in over fifty years of international humanitarian law. In the initial cycle, and to a certain extent in subsequent cycles, the norm of justice did not necessarily produce the desired or expected outcomes despite the fact the interested states created and modified regimes and institutions to promote the norm. The extent to which the norm of justice produced the desired outcomes can be assessed in terms of whether the norm of justice is inherently capable of producing such outcomes, whether the norm was inherently flawed, whether the institutions created to implement the norm were inherently limited or flawed, whether the operation of other norms interfered with or inhibited the operation of the norm of justice, or whether there was a failure to adequately and appropriately utilize other approaches in cooperation with the norm of justice.

Framing Questions for Study

In the back seat with the window open, the [IPTF] monitors saw one of the most wanted men on the planet, Radovan Karadzic, enjoying the view.

—Alexander Ivanko,
UN spokesman[25]

As evidenced by the quote above, the norm of justice played an indeterminate role in the Yugoslav peace-building process. While Mr. Karadzic, the former president of the Republika Srpska, was indicted for crimes of genocide by an international tribunal—an unprecedented act in the midst of an ongoing conflict, for a significant period of time he was nonetheless relatively free to travel about the Republika Srpska (the NATO-patrolled Bosnian-Serb territorial entity) and to influence political developments. In order to understand the complicated and often constrained role of justice, the cognitive contextual process method can be relied upon to deduce a series of guiding questions, which if investigated can help to identify the role of justice in the Yugoslav peace-building process—in particular how the norm of justice operated to promote or inhibit peace, and why it was or was not effective in promoting a meaningful and durable peace.

1. Who are the primary state, substate and nonstate actors, what are their geopolitical interests, and how did these interests influence their view of the norm of justice and its utility in the Yugoslav crisis?
2. Which approaches to peace-building did interested states initially employ to promote their objectives, and how did these evolve during the course of the conflict?
3. During the peace-building process, to what extent did the competing interests of relevant actors influence the selection of peace-building approaches and the application of other approaches in relation to the norm of justice? In what manner did states and

substate stakeholders act to promote the role of justice and the other approaches?

4. To what extent did preexisting rules and norms influence the behavior of the relevant actors and the choice of peace-building approaches, and did the influence of specific rules and norms fluctuate over the course of the conflict?

5. Which formal and informal regimes did the relevant states invoke to promote peace-building, and how did the nature of these regimes influence the ability of states to employ and evolve certain methods and norms?

6. What regimes and institutions were created to aid in the incorporation of justice into the peace-building process and were they effective?

7. During the peace-building process, to what extent did the various approaches and norms compete for primacy, and to what extent were certain approaches and norms compatible?

8. To what extent did competition between the various approaches and norms influence the development of new regimes, in particular during the Dayton and Rambouillet/Paris negotiations?

9. To what extent did states "learn" during the process of peace-building, in particular to what extent did states reevaluate the approaches of peace-building and the applicability of various norms?

10. To what extent did the eventual combination of approaches incorporated in the peace-building process create an effective foundation/framework for postsettlement implementation in Bosnia and Kosovo?

Chapter 2

Justice and Anti-Justice: The Functions of Accountability in the Peace-Building Process

You cannot forget justice. And justice has to be patient because you have to deal with the realities of the day. You have to try to get people to think about the future more than they think about the past.

—Major General William Nash, IFOR commander[1]

The norm of justice, while frequently invoked, is seldom defined. Before investigating the role of justice in peace-building it is necessary to precisely define the norm as well as articulate its functions. This chapter therefore begins with a detailed definitional description of the justice norm and articulates the variety of functions performed by the norm of justice and the approach of accountability during the peace-building process, including denying collective guilt by establishing individual responsibility, enabling the dismantlement of institutions responsible for perpetuating the commission of atrocities, establishing an accurate historical record, providing a cathartic process for victims, and deterring further instances of violence in the current conflict as well as deterring atrocities in similar conflicts. Importantly, depending on a state's or institution's strategic interest and self-identity it will ascribe varying values to each of these functions. Over time, these values will be reevaluated as the mechanisms of justice become more efficient and are improved with use.

Defining Justice

Justice being done, and being seen to be done, is the difference between a lasting peace and an interval between hostilities.

—Ed Vulliamy, correspondent for
the *Guardian*[2]

The word "norm" refers to collectively established guides for action; it originates from a Greek word referring to a carpenter's square. When the norm of justice is applied to the peace-building process, it operates as a carpenter's square in that it constrains the actions of state and substate parties to the dispute, including the actions of third-party actors. The norm of justice also guides and in some cases dictates the actions to be taken by the parties, and may in some instances dictate specific terms to be included in a peace agreement or actions to be undertaken to aid the peace-building process. The sides of the carpenter's square of justice are comprised of truth, fairness, rectitude, and retribution/requital.

As important as understanding the definition of justice, it is essential to understand the nature of certain acts which undermine the effectiveness of the norm of justice, or acts which may be deemed to constitute the norm of anti-justice. These would be intentional falsehoods and propaganda, perpetual impartiality and moral equivalence, the active erosion of the moral imperative to take action, and impunity and de facto or de jure immunity.

The Essence of Justice

In the context of peace-building, truth relates to an accurate understanding and recording of the causes of a conflict, as well as which parties are responsible for which actions, and which parties, including individuals, may be characterized as the victims or the aggressors (including the possibility both parties are the aggressors). Truth also requires an understanding and articulation of the objectives of the various parties, including those of third parties, and an assessment of those interests in light of generally accepted rules of international behavior—in particular those set forth in the UN Charter and other legal instruments.[3]

An example of the use of truth to influence the peace process is the report of the War Crimes Commission created by the United Nations in 1993 to assess the nature of the conflict in Yugoslavia and the extent to which the various parties were responsible for war crimes. This report, consisting of over 3,000 pages, paints a fairly accurate portrayal of the nature and extent of the crimes committed by all the parties, finding that although representatives of each party had committed crimes, warranting the creation of an international tribunal, it was clear the Serbian forces were acting as aggressors and they had committed the vast majority of crimes.[4] This may be contrasted with what the authors were told were efforts of David Owen, the co-chair of the UN/EU peace process, to persuade the chairman of the War Crimes Commission to find all three of the parties had committed a roughly equal number of crimes and all were therefore equally culpable.

Fairness relates to an initial approach of impartiality—which can and must be adjusted in light of the truth about the conflict. Thus, while fairness requires that at the initiation of the conflict third parties approach peace-building in an impartial manner, it also requires that once elements of truth are ascertained, they not be misrepresented in order to maintain artificial impartiality, but rather that they be incorporated into the decision-making process, and policy be adjusted accordingly. An example of the use of fairness to guide the peace process is the State Department's attempts in the spring of 1999 to provide extensive detail to the public as to the nature of the crimes being committed by the Serbian regime in Kosovo, even to the extent of naming names of suspected war criminals.[5]

Fairness also requires that third parties do not seek to apply undue pressure on the victims of a conflict in order to achieve an expedient political objective. This application is best exemplified by the U.S. efforts at the Rambouillet/Paris negotiations to openly acknowledged the victim status of the Kosovars. Thus, although the United States sought to persuade the Kosovar delegation to accept major concessions sought by the Serbian side, it did not initially seek to exploit their victim status. This can be contrasted with the approach of the United States four years earlier in the Dayton negotiations, where the United States threatened to close the talks and blame their failure on the Bosnian delegation if the Bosnians failed to agree to a number of concessions, which the Bosnians thought might undermine any serious effort to build peace—knowing that if the Bosnians were blamed for the failure of the negotiations, this would erode international support for protecting them from the continued campaign of genocide.

Rectitude encompasses a sense of moral virtue, integrity, and righteousness, requiring the parties to "do the right thing" based in part on their assessment of the truth and the application of fairness, but also including the legitimate interests of the third-party states and institutions—the legitimacy of which is defined by principles of international law and generally accepted norms of state behavior. Although rectitude may seem subjective, in matters of armed conflict involving ethnic aggression and crimes against humanity it is usually possible to draw certain boundaries around the behavior of state and substate actors.

A peace process influenced by rectitude, for example, would likely find states reluctant to substantially accommodate or appease those responsible for orchestrating crimes against humanity as this legitimizes those actors and their methods, while also providing an opportunity for them to ratify at the negotiating table the fruits of their crimes. Moreover, the likelihood of building a meaningful peace on the promises and commitments of individuals and institutions responsible for crimes against humanity is greatly diminished, as evidenced by the multitude of failed cease-fires negotiated by various UNPROFOR generals with Serbian leaders Mladic and Karadzic, who were indicted by the Yugoslav Tribunal for genocide.[6]

The guide of rectitude may also lead third parties to adopt appropriate policy responses to the conflict. For instance, in the Bosnian conflict and the early stages of the Kosovo conflict, the United States and its allies sought a negotiated settlement with those directly responsible for orchestrating the ethnic aggression. Failing to heed the guide of rectitude resulted in five atrocity-filled years of conflict, and a peace settlement in Bosnia many critics believe ratifies the gains of ethnic cleansing, widespread war crimes, and crimes against humanity. In contrast, when in the case of Kosovo the United States and its allies ascertained negotiations with the perpetrators would no longer suffice as a viable policy, they embarked on the use of force to defeat the Serbian military forces operating in Kosovo. As a result, the gains of ethnic cleansing were reversed, and there appears to be a greater likelihood for a meaningful peace in Kosovo.

Retribution/requital comprises notions of compensation for victims, punishment of aggressors, recompense for physical damage, delegitimization of responsible institutions, and reimposition of the rule of law. It does not encompass notions of revenge, retaliation, or reprisals. Institutions frequently associated with this norm include war crimes tribunals and truth commissions. Retribution/requital is particularly important in peace building as, according to one notable commentator, "in the fragile political climate that exists following a settlement, the temptation for retribution and revenge are considerable." [7] Retribution/requital and associated institutions "bring an element of impartiality that is necessary to restore faith in the judicial process and in the rule of law," something the parties and their domestic institutions are unlikely to accomplish on their own.[8]

An example of the influence of retribution/requital on the peace process is the establishment of the Yugoslav Tribunal to try those responsible for war crimes within the territory of the former Yugoslavia. Other examples include the case against the FRY brought in the World Court by Bosnia and a similar case pending by Croatia, the Dayton Accords' creation of a property restitution commission, and discussions about a possible Bosnian Truth Commission.

The Essence of Anti-Justice

The antithesis of truth is falsehood, often spread by propaganda. For example, as detailed in U.S. Department of State cables, and a number of more recent publications, Slobodan Milosevic relied upon a highly capable propaganda machine to at first stir the nationalist feelings of the Serbian population into support for his objective of an ethnically pure greater Serbia and then to promote recruitment into the paramilitary forces responsible for many of the brutal acts of ethnic cleansing.[9] As noted by Ambassador Zimmermann, through a barrage of propaganda via the state-owned media,[10] Milosevic played on Serb fears and feelings of victimization, going back to their defeat by the Ottomans at Kosovo in 1389, and emphasizing their treatment at the hands of the Ustasha during World War II. "The virus of television," Ambassador Zimmermann recounts, "spread ethnic hatred like an epidemic." [11]

Slobodan Milosevic then turned his propaganda enterprise toward the international community and successfully imbued Western foreign policymakers with falsehoods such as the war was caused by the bubbling over of "ancient ethnic hatreds," all the parties were in effect "warring factions" equally responsible for the commission of atrocities, the conflict was a "civil war" not involving Serbia, and the Bosnian government was prone to killing its own civilians in order to garner international sympathy and intervention.[12] The adoption of these falsehoods greatly undercut the influence of the norm of justice. [13]

While the U.S. embassy in Belgrade accurately reported on the efforts of the Serbian regime to use propaganda to influence the international community,[14] a number of foreign policymakers succumbed to these efforts.[15] In particular, David Owen readily adopted the notion of warring factions equally responsible for atrocities as it promoted his objective of a negotiated settlement of the conflict without the complicated involvement of the norm of justice. Similarly, Secretary of State Christopher adopted Milosevic's notion of ancient ethnic hatreds along with the notion of warring factions,[16] to create the impression the conflict was inevitable and the American government could therefore not be faulted for failing to prevent the conflict or the continuing atrocities.[17] And the propensity for UNPROFOR commander General Janvier to "believe Serb propaganda," according to his aides, was in part responsible for his rejection of close air support to defend the UN declared safe area of Srebrenica, and the subsequent massacre of 7,000 civilians.[18]

Not all those involved in seeking a resolution of the conflict fell victim to Milosevic's propaganda ploys, as illustrated by General Clark's assessment that "above all, I recognized that fundamentally, quarrels in the region were not really about age old religious differences but rather the result of many unscrupulous and manipulative leaders seeking their own power and wealth at the expense of ordinary people in their countries."[19]

The antithesis of fairness is artificial impartiality and moral equivalence. An example of moral equivalence created through falsehoods occured when, immediately after the Sarajevo market was struck by an artillery shell in 1995 killing 68 Bosnians, General Michael Rose threatened that, unless the Bosnian government signed up to yet another cease-fire, the general would disclose to the media the Bosnian government had killed its own people in an attempt to gain international sympathy. General Rose's threat was made with the full knowledge that a UN investigation had determined the shell had in fact been fired by Serbian forces, and that the U.S. embassy in Belgrade had reported the conspiracy theory of Bosnian government responsibility had in fact originated in Belgrade as part of its propaganda effort.[20]

The antithesis of rectitude is behavior intended to erode the moral imperative to take action. For example, Secretary Christopher sought to erode the moral imperative to use force or take other aggressive action, when he testified before the U.S. Congress in the spring of 1993 that all parties to the conflict were equally responsible for the atrocities, which did not amount to a campaign of genocide. At the time internal CIA and State Department reports—subsequently leaked to the *New York Times*—indicated over 90 percent of the atrocities were being committed by Serbian forces, and the campaign very likely constituted attempted genocide.

The antithesis of retribution/requital is political legitimization and de facto or de jure immunity. Political legitimization occurs when individuals responsible for war crimes are embraced by the international mediators or others as "partners in peace," and essential to the peace process. For instance, David Owen repeatedly legitimized Radovan Karadzic by embracing him as a legitimate partner in the ICFY negotiations in Geneva, despite Karadzic's clear culpability at the time for attempted genocide. Similarly, Richard Holbrooke's now famous quote just before the negotiation of the Dayton Accords, "you can't make peace without President Milosevic,"[21] reestablished Milosevic as a legitimate partner in peace despite his orchestration of genocide against non-Serbs. De facto immunity is best represented by NATO's initial reluctance to apprehend indicted war criminals at large in Bosnia and what may be perceived as Slobodan Milosevic's immunity, until the spring of 1999, from his international crimes.

Articulating the Functions of Justice

[The Serbs are] going to have to come to grips with what Mr. Milosevic ordered in Kosovo [and] . . . they're going to have to get out of denial. And then, they're going to have to decide whether they support his leadership or not, whether they think it's OK that all those tens of thousands of people were killed. And all those hundreds of thousands of people were run out of their homes and all those little girls were raped and all those little boys were murdered. . . . They're going to have to decide if they think that is OK.

—William Jefferson Clinton,
U. S. President[22]

Within the context of creating stable, peaceful societies out of war-torn states, the norms and institutions of justice may serve several functions. These include establishing individual responsibility and denying collective guilt, dismantling and discrediting institutions and leaders responsible for the commission of atrocities, establishing an accurate historical record, providing victim catharsis, and promoting deterrence.

Establishing Individual Responsibility and Denying Collective Guilt

The first function of justice is to expose the individuals responsible for atrocities and to avoid assigning guilt to an entire people. As illustrated by the above quote, if foreign policymakers fail to grasp the notion of individual responsibility, they are likely to assign collective responsibility to an entire population. Not only is such an assignation of guilt inappropriate and unfair, but it will likely skew the policy options under consideration for managing the crisis.

Importantly, by assigning guilt to specific perpetrators on all sides, the Tribunal was designed to avoid the assignment of collective guilt which had characterized the years following World War II and in part laid the foundation for the commission of atrocities during the 1990s Balkan conflict. "Far from being a vehicle for revenge" the president of the Yugoslav Tribunal, Antonio Cassese explains, by individualizing guilt in hate-mongering leaders and by disabusing people of the myth that adversary ethnic groups bear collective responsibility for the crimes, "the Yugoslav Tribunal is an instrument for reconciliation."[23]

The assignment of individual guilt to government leaders would also serve the purpose of providing the justification for any use of force to prevent the continued commission of atrocities. As noted by Michael Walzer, "the assignment of responsibility is the critical test of the argument for justice. . . . If there are recognizable war crimes, there must be recognizable criminals. . . . The theory of justice should point us to the men and women from whom we can rightly demand an accounting, and it should shape and control the judgments we make of the excuses they offer (or that are offered on their behalf). . . . There can be no justice in war if there are not, ultimately, responsible men and women."[24]

While this function requires prosecution of responsible leaders, where the norms and institutions do not attach individual liability to a significant number of the individuals responsible for the commission of war crimes, they run the risk that they will be unable to perform the function of denying collective guilt, as many victims and observers will still believe that large or important sections of the group associated with the atrocities are still at large and will thus tend to blame the entire group rather than risk inadvertent impunity. Moreover, those persons who escape individual responsibility will feel emboldened by their impunity and are more likely to commit future crimes or interfere with the peace-building process in other ways. This risk is particularly acute in the former Yugoslavia where the Office of the Prosecutor has indicted only approximately 100 individuals of the over 7,000 it estimates are indictable.

Dismantling Institutions and Discrediting Leaders Responsible for Atrocities

The second function of justice is to provide a foundation for dismantling institutions and discrediting leaders and their ideology that have promoted war crimes. When a government pursues policies of ethnic cleansing or systematically denies human rights, it is often done through legal structures. South Africa's apartheid government used its constitution to oppress, and special government forces to torture and murder, members of black opposition groups. The South African Truth and Reconciliation Commission was later given the task of documenting the full extent of government involvement in racial killings and incidents of torture to help remove the stigma of past wrongs from new governmental institutions. In Yugoslavia, too, government leaders and government forces were a driving force behind much of the ethnic killing.

Through the work of various justice-based institutions, in particular the Tribunal, it becomes possible to promote the dismantling of the institutions and a discrediting of the leaders who encouraged, enabled, and carried out the commission of humanitarian crimes. Drawing on his experience as the head of South Africa's Goldstone Commission (a predecessor to the South African Truth and Reconciliation Commission), Justice Goldstone observes that "exposure of the nature and extent of human rights violations frequently will reveal a systematic and institutional pattern of gross human rights violations. It will assist in the identification and dismantling of institutions responsible [for these crimes] and deter future recurrences."[25]

In the case of Serbia, there is particular benefit to laying bare to Serbs unscathed in Belgrade the consequences of nationalistic rhetoric.[26] Even for those who continue to support Bosnian Serb leader Radovan Karadzic and former Serb president Slobodan Milosevic, "it will be much more difficult to dismiss live testimony given under oath than simple newspaper reports," the Tribunal's deputy prosecutor, Graham Blewitt points out. "The testimony will send a reminder in a very dramatic way that these crimes were horrendous,"[27] and presumably aid in the continued democratic transformation of Serbia. A notable effect to date of the norm of justice has been to discredit the concept that it is permissible to commit atrocities in the effort to create a greater Serbia. For instance, the Serbian Orthodox Patriarch Pavle, speaking in Kosovo in June 1999 declared, "if the only way to create a greater Serbia is by crime, then I do not accept that, and let that Serbia disappear. And also if a lesser Serbia can only survive by crime, let it also disappear. And if all the Serbs had to die and only I remained and I could live only by crime, then I would not accept that, it would be better to die."[28]

By failing to make sufficient information available about the individuals, institutions, and ideologies associated with the commission of atrocities, there is a significant risk that these individuals, institutions, and ideas may in fact attain some degree of de facto legitimization. For instance, the Office of the Prosecutor's prolonged failure to publicly indict the leaders of the Serbian political and military regime responsible for the atrocities in Bosnia and the failure of the United States to consistently identify certain political leaders as suspected war criminals—and in fact publicly rehabilitating them—served the purpose of legitimizing the Serbian regime, which then committed nearly identical atrocities in Kosovo. Moreover, the failure of the United States and its allies to provide the Tribunal with the resources and evidence to indict Slobodan Milosevic prior to the Dayton negotiations enabled him not only to substantially influence the institutional structure of postwar Bosnia in a manner which furthered his objectives but also legitimized him as a partner in peace.

The need for the mechanisms of justice to delegitimize the perpetrators of international crimes is all the more crucial given the propensity of international peace negotiators to either avoid assigning responsibility for such crimes or to actually praise the behavior and personal characteristics of war criminals. A telling example is a previously classified State Department demarche to Radovan Karadzic in April 1994 concerning the commission of war crimes in Banja Luka and the UN safe area of Gorazde, which declares, "those responsible for committing these crimes should be apprehended and punished. We expect you to do so."[29] As noted in the Tribunal's indictment of Karadzic for genocide, he was in fact the individual known to be responsible for orchestrating these crimes. More damaging to the peace process and the operation of the norm of justice may be frequent accolades, such as David Owen's description of Radovan Karadzic (later indicted for genocide) as a "gracious host," with "excellent English." Other examples of this include Warren Christopher's characterization of Slobodan Milosevic (later indicted for crimes against humanity and genocide) as "though unscrupulous and suspected of war crimes, Milosevic has a rough charm and he appealed to some Western European leaders as a bulwark against an Islamic tide."[30] Richard Holbrooke similarly characterized Milosevic as willing to walk the extra mile for peace in Dayton. One of the more vivid journalistic accounts, according to Carol Hodge, was a Milosevic-friendly BBC program aired during the Kosovo air campaign titled "In the Mind of Milosevic," which portrayed him as a man who "talks, laughs, is a good singer, and likes a drink occasionally, and, unlike President Clinton, does not cheat on his wife."[31] Finally, a senior British army officer characterized General Mladic (indicted for genocide) in the following terms, "he has presence, and when he had power he wielded it ruthlessly. That brought him some grudging respect, if not admiration."[32]

Establishing an Accurate Historical Record

The third function served by justice is to establish an accurate accounting of the actions of all parties and to create an accurate historical record. If, to paraphrase George Santayana, a society is condemned to repeat its mistakes if it does learn the lessons of the past, then a reliable record of those mistakes must be established if we wish to prevent their recurrence. Michael Ignatieff recognizes that the "great virtue of legal proceedings . . . [is] that their evidentiary rules confer legitimacy on otherwise contestable facts. In this sense, war crimes trials make it more difficult for societies to take refuge in denial—the trials do assist the process of uncovering the truth."[33] The chief prosecutor at Nuremberg, Supreme Court Justice Robert Jackson, underscored the logic of this proposition when he reported to President Truman that one of the most important legacies of the Nuremberg trials following World War II was that they documented the Nazi atrocities "with such authenticity and in such detail that there can be no responsible denial of these crimes in the future and no tradition of martyrdom of the Nazi leaders can arise among informed people."[34]

In both Guatemala and El Salvador, truth commissions were established to resolve disputes between the former combatants as to who was responsible for which atrocities. In each case an objective historical record led to the establishment of credible judicial systems that then helped to sustain peace.[35] The problems of accurately assessing blame for war crimes in the former Yugoslavia is especially acute. In Richard Goldstone's words, "It doesn't take hours after human rights violations for the denials to begin. . . . Justice plays a vital role in stopping that fabrication, in stopping that cover-up, which is inevitable."[36]

The need for an accurate accounting of the conflict is all the more compelling in the case of the former Yugoslavia as according to Natasha Kandic, head of the Humanitarian Law Fund in Belgrade, "when I tried to talk about what I had seen and experienced [concerning atrocities in Kosovo], people would get impatient and change the subject. It's as if people here simply don't want to know the truth about what happened in Kosovo. Even the intellectuals are under the influence of official propaganda."[37]

If the institution of the Yugoslav Tribunal operates as designed, the Tribunal should generate a comprehensive record of the nature and extent of crimes against humanity and genocide in the Balkans, how they were planned and executed, the fate of individual victims, who gave the orders and who carried them out. By carfully proving these facts one witness at a time in the face of vigilant cross-examination by distinguished defense counsel, the international trials would produce a definitive account that can pierce the distortions generated by official propaganda, endure the test of time, and resist the forces of revisionism.

Failure to create a comprehensive record will undermine many, if not all, of the benefits associated with creating an accurate record. This risk is heightened when only one institution of justice is employed, or where others are minimized. For instance, although the Yugoslav Tribunal is capable of creating a lengthy record for cases on its docket, there is no official process for summarizing findings, and no process for including facts not relevant to the specific cases before the Tribunal. In addition, where a defendant is not present before the Tribunal the indictment and Rule 61 hearing provide only a minimal basis for assessing the truth of the alleged actions. In other cases, the death of defendants prior to judgment led to a dismissal of their case, thereby erasing the official history of atrocities.

Victim Catharsis

The fourth function of justice is to acknowledge the victims of crimes— an often overlooked but equally important element to the success of any peace process as is punishing the offenders. Offering victims an opportunity to state their injuries publicly can "provide victims with a sense of justice and catharsis—a sense that their grievances have been addressed and can more easily be put to rest, rather than smoldering in anticipation of the next round of conflict."[38]

In South Africa, the Truth Commission heard tearful testimony from thousands of victims as well as the confessions of many who played a role in brutal killings for the apartheid regime. Although some of this testimony was offered in exchange for amnesty, the overall effect was to purge the national consciousness of past racial killings so that the society may be rebuilt. In Yugoslavia the same logic was used in the International Criminal Tribunal's creation. According to the Yugoslav Tribunal's first president, Antonio Cassese, the pursuit of justice "is essential to the restoration of peaceful and normal relations especially for people who have had to live under a reign of terror [because] [i]t breaks the cycle of violence, hatred, and extra judicial retribution."[39]

As Richard Goldstone noted, "the Nuremberg Trials played an important role in enabling the victims of the Holocaust to obtain official acknowledgment of what befell them."[40] Such acknowledgment constitutes a partial remedy for their suffering and a powerful catharsis that can discourage acts of retaliation. According to Antonio Cassese, the "only civilized alternative to this desire for revenge is to render justice" for otherwise "feelings of hatred and resentment seething below the surface will, sooner or later, erupt and lead to renewed violence."[41] As confirmed by Munira Subasic, who lost two sons in the Srebrenica massacre, "if we are deprived of the right to justice, then we shall seek the right to revenge."[42]

If the norm of justice is employed, but not effectively, it can have the disadvantage of raising the expectations of victims, and then causing them additional psychological trauma as they come to perceive themselves as abandoned, or worse, used by the international community to clear its own conscience. As Justice Goldstone noted in response to the persistent failure of the international community to arrest indicted war criminals Radovan Karadzic and Ratko Mladic, "imagine [the victim's] disappointment at the failure of the international community to follow through with the arrest of those indicted. If this situation is not corrected, the establishment of the Yugoslav Tribunal will have caused more harm than good to the persons it was intended to benefit."[43]

Deterrence

Finally, in the case of criminal prosecutions, the execution of justice ideally acts as a deterrent against future humanitarian crimes, or at least sets a precedent for accountability. As observed by David Scheffer, the U.S. ambassador at large for war crimes issues, "we know from experience in Bosnia that local authorities—camp commanders and temporary local officials—sometimes do what they can to improve the circumstances of those under their care once they know that the international community will investigate and punish those who fail to respect human rights standards."[44] Richard Goldstone adds that the existence of the Tribunal may have deterred widespread human rights violations during the Croatian army offensive against Serb rebels in August 1995. "Fear of prosecution in the Hague," he said, "prompted Croat authorities to issue orders to their soldiers to protect Serb civilian rights when Croatia took control of the Krajina and Western Slavonia regions of the country."[45]

Unfortunately, as the Tribunal was not at the time perceived to be a meaningful threat, these "orders" were generally ignored with the consequence that the Serbian population was subject to numerous atrocities. Goldstone also argued that by broadcasting televised highlights of the trials throughout Bosnia and Serbia, that message could get through directly to the citizenry, "people don't relate to statistics, to generalizations. People can only relate and feel when they hear somebody that they can identify with telling what happened to them. That's why the public broadcasts of the Tribunal's cases can have a strong deterrent effect."[46]

Moreover, the international prosecution of responsible individuals can become an instrument through which respect for the rule of law is instilled into the popular consciousness.[47] As judge Gabrielle Kirk McDonald, who presided over the Tribunal's first trial, succinctly put it, "we are here to tell people that the rule of law has to be respected."[48] The establishment of the rule of law is particularly important since a dominant characteristic of the post-Cold War era in international affairs is that conflicts occur among peoples of different ethnic and religious backgrounds *within* states, not between them. In war-torn societies, one of the most basic obstacles to reconciliation is a lack of trust on the part of citizens between each other and with their government. And one of the most effective ways to institutionalize that trust is to establish a stable legal system and the rule of law.[49]

Although the punishment of crimes committed in the Balkans would send the message, both to potential aggressors and vulnerable minorities, that the international community will not allow atrocities to be committed with impunity, if a Tribunal is established and is unable to indict those responsible for orchestrating the campaign of terror—as the case with the inability to indict Mr. Milosevic for war crimes in Bosnia, then it may in fact encourage them to feel free to commit atrocities in a future conflict—as in Kosovo, believing they possess some degree of de facto immunity.

In many cases, however, the nature of injustice and internal pressures militate toward the establishment of a truth commission often accompanied by grants of amnesty to bring the dark practices of civil violence into the light without necessarily prosecuting the guilty.[50] Versions of this system has been adopted in South Africa, El Salvador, Chile, and Argentina, where the calculation was made that the benefits of healing wounds through the establishment of the truth outweighed the benefits of retributive justice.[51] But the particular circumstance of the crimes committed in the former Yugoslavia required the formation of an ad hoc criminal tribunal for both moral and practical reasons. First, the genocide, rape, and torture that occurred was of a nature and scale so horrific that nothing short of full accountability for those responsible would provide justice.[52] Second, the domestic legal systems in some of the republics of the former Yugoslavia had been so thoroughly corrupted that they were not competent to conduct a fair trial of the war's perpetrators, many of whom are still in power.

Given that the norm of justice is based upon near universally accepted principles and serves a variety of policy relevant functions ranging from deterrence to victim catharsis, one might expect that it would play a central if not determinative role in the peace-building process. The norm of justice must, however, compete for influence with other highly relevant and practicable approaches such as accommodation, economic inducement, and the use of force, which are based on equally compelling principles, and which have a longer history of use by peace builders. To establish the necessary background to understand the relationship between the norm of justice and these other approaches in the Yugoslav peace process, the next chapter will define these normative approaches and discuss their traditional relationship to the justice-based approach of accountability.

Chapter 3

Peace versus Justice: The Relationship between Accountability and Other Relevant Peace-Building Approaches

The cardinal lesson of Srebrenica is that a deliberate and systematic attempt to terrorize, expel or murder an entire people must be met decisively with all necessary means, and with the political will to carry the policy through to its logical conclusion.

—UN report on the Srebrenica massacre[1]

As with the approach of accountability, the approaches of accommodation, economic inducements, and use of force, when used appropriately, serve valuable roles during the peace-building process. At times, however, the overreliance on a particular approach, or a lack of understanding of the risks associated with its application to the exclusion of others, may undermine the peace-building effort. Moreover, there is an unfortunate tradition of conflict between the norm of accountability and the approach of accommodation, and the Yugoslav crisis proved no exception to this history. To promote lasting peace, it will be necessary for foreign policymakers and scholars to understand the mutually supportive roles that may be played by the various approaches, and how best to integrate them into the process of peace-building.

This chapter therefore briefly describes the approaches of accommodation, economic inducement, and use of force. It then discusses the traditional conflict between accountability and accommodation—noting that this conflict proved central to many policy debates during the Yugoslav crisis. The chapter concludes by discussing the need for heightened efforts to apply a hybrid mix of normative approaches, particularly in light of the Srebrenica massacre report quoted above.

Defining the Approaches of Accommodation, Economic Inducements, and the Use of Force

[Serb] leaders engaged in high-level negotiations with representatives of the international community while their forces on the ground, executed and buried thousands of men and boys within a matter of days. . . . At various points during the war, these negotiations amounted to appeasement.

—UN report on the Srebrenica massacre[2]

Accommodation

The approach of accommodation seeks to reduce conflict by accommodating the interests of adversarial states or parties. In most instances, the approach of accommodation instructs a negotiator to seek to end the conflict by meeting as many of the objectives of each party as possible, thereby accommodating their interests and satiating their appetite for more conflict. If applied appropriately, the norm can lead to the creation of win-win gaming situations where each party is able to attain its objectives without unduly prejudicing the interests of the other party. Such an outcome is most probable in a prisoners' dilemma and related situations, and least possible in deadlock situations. If applied recklessly or forced on a deadlock situation, such as the situation in the former Yugoslavia, the norm can ratify illegitimate actions of a party and enhance its appetite for similar gains through further conflict.

Institutions and individuals most frequently associated with the approach of accommodation tend to be those most closely associated with peace negotiations and thus include special envoys such as Yasushi Akashi and Richard Holbrooke; and UN/EU peace conference co-chairs Lord Carrington, Cyrus Vance, David Owen, Carl Bildt, and Thorvald Stoltenberg. Accommodation is frequently the approach of choice because it is the approach around which it is the easiest to build political will, and it is the approach most likely to lead to a formal agreement among the parties.

The brokering of the Washington Agreement between Croatia and Bosnia represents an example of the appropriate utilization of the accommodation norm in that it was used to craft a relationship between Bosnia and Croatia which sought to meet the needs, as far as possible, of both parties while creating a system of democratic government capable of preserving those interests. Unfortunately the system has in practice proven difficult to implement, and may have represented too much of an accommodation of minority interests.

One of the more committed applications of the accommodation norm was the proposed Vance/Owen Peace Plan which intended to bring peace by essentially partitioning Bosnia into ethnically based cantons and permitting the Serbian cantons to de facto confederate with Serbia proper. The proposal thus sought to achieve peace at the expense of ratifying the aims of the campaign of ethnic cleansing and legitimizing the anti-multicultural nationalism propagated by the Serbian and Croatian combatants. In fact, earlier David Owen had proposed that as EU mediator he actively engage the parties in redrawing their territorial boundaries. When this was rejected by eleven of the EU states he believed "[t]he refusal to make these borders negotiable greatly hampered the EC's attempt at crisis management in July and August 1991 and subsequently put all peacemaking from September 1991 onwards within a straitjacket that greatly inhibited compromises between the parties in dispute."[3]

As it was, the Vance/Owen Peace Plan was widely perceived as the catalyst for the conflict between Bosnian Croats and the Bosnian government as the Bosnian Croats sought to capture land "promised" them under the peace plan.[4] Similarly, with the aim of peace, the peace negotiators embarked on an approach until 1995 of continually redrafting peace plans to offer more and more favorable terms to the Serbian party when it rejected earlier "take it or leave it" offers by the Contact Group.[5] Some critics have even argued UNPROFOR commander General Janvier deliberately denied close air support to the UN Dutch defenders of Srebrenica in order to make a negotiated settlement more feasible.[6] Other commentators note air strikes were also blocked by the French government as it had promised General Mladic it would seek to prevent air strikes in exchange for the release of two French pilots and several hundred UNPROFOR peacekeepers held hostage by Bosnian Serb forces in the spring of 1995.[7]

The perspective of those supporting unfettered accommodation when faced with the criticism that the approach of accommodation might reward the use of force and ethnic cleansing, is typified by Canadian general Lewis MacKenzie, the former head of the UN forces in Bosnia when he testified before the U.S. Congress that "[n]ow obviously the critics will say this rewards force and sets a bad example. I can only say to them, read your history. Force has been rewarded since the first caveman picked up a club, occupied his neighbor's cave, and ran off with his wife."[8]

Unfortunately, the overreliance on the approach of accommodation can create situations where once diplomacy alone fails, policymakers are reluctant to move onto or incorporate other norms, creating even more intractable conflicts. As noted by Former British defense minister Sir John Nott in 1994, "[w]e will not bring about a diplomatic solution. Even if there is peace obtained, it cannot hold. We have given these diplomats, these committees . . . two and a half years to bring about peace, and they have failed. . . . I would remove the arms embargo [on the Bosnian government] straight away because it is only a military balance now in that part of the world that can restore stability."[9] Similarly, Ed Vulliamy, the correspondent for the *Guardian* during the Bosnian conflict, argued that an early use of force against Serb military targets designed to neutralize their artillery and destroy their communications system would have brought them to the negotiating table, and then "the Serbs would have been required to dismount the sieges and to accept international supervision in a complete reversal of ethnic cleansing. This would have been infinitely easier in 1992 than the imposition of the Dayton plan—with its pledge to return all refugees—is now."[10] This assessment was supported by Manfred Worner, the then NATO Secretary-General.[11]

In the end, the primary risk associated with the approach of accommodation is that it can become one of appeasement, and possibly even coercive appease-ment. While accommodation may be a useful and valuable tool, appeasement is characterized by an artificial moral equivalence, neutrality in the face of aggres-sion, active efforts to erode the moral imperative to become involved, and the total exclusion of the use of force and the norm of justice, with the effect of of-ten encouraging further violence and atrocities.

The approach of coercive appeasement is more nuanced and entails ap-peasement within the context of the perceived use of force and the perceived incorporation of the norm of justice. Coercive appeasement is characterized first by a general diplomatic deficit which entails the failure to create the conditions for effective leadership or the articulation of a clear policy objective coupled with the inability to structure a coordinated or capable diplomatic process for peace-building. This diplomatic deficit is augmented by a failure to adequately undergo institutional and personal "learning" during the peace-building process. Often the diplomatic deficit encompasses the unintentional misuse of diplomatic signaling, and the readily transparent articulation of intentions by the peace builders. Coercive appeasement is also characterized by aggressive accommo-dation, which entails the pursuit of actions designed to meet the needs and inter-ests of the aggressor, coupled with intentional or unintentional obfuscation of the aggressor's true objectives.

Moral duplicity is also an element of coercive appeasement, consisting of the application of pressure on the victims designed to compel their acquiescence to the primary demands of the aggressor, coupled with intentional and uninten-tional actions designed to create division among the political representatives of the victim state. Moral duplicity also frequently entails declarations and actions designed to create the perception of moral equivalence among the parties, thereby eroding the distinction between aggressor and victim and spreading cul-pability among all parties. Frequently these official pronouncements are de-signed to actively erode the moral and strategic imperative to adopt approaches other than that of accommodation. Finally, coercive appeasement may be char-acterized by constrained use of force, which entails activities designed to con-strain and minimize the use of legitimate force, and marginalized justice, which entails actions designed to minimize and obfuscate the role of justice, including the political resurrection of culpable partners in peace.

Economic Inducement

The approach of economic inducement entails the notion that it is legitimate to seek a modification of a party's behavior through the employment of financial incentives and/or economic sanctions. Institutions and entities generally associ-ated with the approach of economic inducement include states themselves, the United Nations Security Council, which has the authority to impose economic sanctions, and international financial institutions, which, although mandated to operate in a nonpolitical manner, can provide or deny assistance and member-ship in order to effect state behavior. Other relevant institutions include state export-import banks and overseas development funds.

Financial incentives may take the form of direct financial assistance, preferential trade practices, and financial rewards for certain actions—such as the apprehension of indicted war criminals. Economic sanctions include a spectrum of sanctions ranging from the denial of air travel and trade preferences to the imposition of a full scale economic embargo prohibiting any type of trade, investment or financial transactions other than those necessary for humanitarian purposes. In the Yugoslav conflict, for instance, in 1992, the UN and EU enacted a wide range of sanctions against all of the parties to the Yugoslav conflict. As the nature of the conflict became more apparent, the UN and EU suspended their economic sanctions against all the parties except the FRY, and they began to provide financial assistance to Croatia and Bosnia. Subsequently, economic inducements in the form of hundreds of millions of dollars in conditional aid prompted Croatia to turn dozens of indicted citizens over to the Yugoslav Tribunal, and ultimately compelled Serbia to surrender Slobodan Milosevic for trial at The Hague.

Use of Force

The use of force approach provides that in certain narrowly defined circumstances (such as individual and collective self-defense, humanitarian intervention to prevent crimes against humanity, or where authorized by the UN Security Council as a necessary act to promote peace and security) states and regional organizations may use military force to affect the behavior of another state or substate entity.[12] According to some scholars, force may be used against an aggressor state in order to deter further aggression or to protect a civilian population from massive human rights abuses.[13] The use of force approach also embodies principles of necessity, proportionality, and respect for the laws and customs of war.

The institutions associated with the use of force approach include each state's Ministry of Defense, regional military organizations such as NATO, and the United Nations Security Council, which possesses the authority to authorize the "use of all necessary means" to resolve a dispute and to deploy UN peacekeepers.

Examples of the appropriate application of the use of force approach in the former Yugoslavia include NATO air strikes in August 1995 to prevent further Serbian aggression against Bosnia; the deployment of an International Force (IFOR) on the territory of Bosnia following the Dayton negotiations; the spring 1999 air campaign conducted against Serbian forces in Kosovo and Serbia proper in order to deter Serbian aggression in Kosovo;[14] and the deployment of Kosovo Force (KFOR) to provide security during the implementation of UN Security Council Resolution 1244 providing for the interim international management of Kosovo.

There exist a number of counterexamples where the use of force approach was either misapplied, such as in 1993-1995 when NATO was limited to striking only those specific military assets which had fired on civilian targets, rather than any asset in the unit engaged in the attack; or where it was not applied at all, as in the case where UNPROFOR commanders failed to act upon the request for close air support by UNPROFOR forces defending the safe areas of Srebrenica and Zepa, the citizens of which were subsequently ethnically cleansed or massacred.[15] The norm was also distorted when the United Nations maintained an arms embargo against Bosnia even though it was being subjected to territorial aggression and genocide, on the basis that this would help prevent an escalation of the conflict.[16]

In many instances the use of force approach is misapplied as key actors fail to understand the role of "diplomacy backed by force" (as enunciated by Secretary of State Albright) or misconstrue the extent of force that must be used to accomplish an objective. For instance, at the height of the atrocities in Bosnia Senate Majority Leader Bob Dole and House Speaker Newt Gingrich called for the withdrawal of UNPROFOR, the arming and training of Bosnian government forces, and extensive air strikes against the Bosnian Serbs if they continued to commit atrocities. President Clinton, however, ruled out "a military solution," and Secretary of State Warren Christopher labeled the plan a "war strategy," and argued the only two options for the United States in Bosnia were either to stick to diplomacy alone or to send in more than a hundred thousand U.S. ground troops.[17] It subsequently required only a meaningful ground offensive by combined Croat/Bosnian forces and NATO air strikes to compel the Serbian forces to end their attacks and negotiate the Dayton Accords.

As confirmed by a complex time-series statistical analysis conducted by Joshua Goldstein and Jon Pevehouse, the threat or actual use of force by NATO produced compliance and cooperation by Serbian forces. The research further demonstrated that "Serb forces were more responsive to American actions than European ones."[18] According to the authors, "the results thus support the assumptions of the aggressor-victim school of thought that the international use of force could induce Serbian cooperation in this regional conflict." Importantly, the authors also note, "by contrast, the warring-factions school of thought, with its preferred policy of using international cooperation to elicit Serbian cooperation toward Bosnia, receives little support."[19] As put concisely in lay terms by Serbian human rights lawyer Srdja Popovic, "from the very beginning, I thought that only a military defeat could put an end to Slobodan Milosevic's regime. As far as I am concerned, what happened in Kosovo actually confirms that. Until Milosevic was militarily defeated, there was no chance to remove him." [20]

The lack of an understanding of the parameters of the use of force approach and the capabilities of military institutions led to contradictory outcomes, such as when the United States agreed to use force only to support the withdrawal of UNPROFOR troops, but not to protect civilians subjected to atrocities. As proclaimed by Richard Hass, "I don't know if it's tragic or ironic or both that the only time we're now considering to use meaningful force in Bosnia is for the purpose of a pull-out."[21]

In other instances the use of force approach can be complicated when two or more institutions are responsible for the employment of the norm. In Bosnia, for instance, UNPROFOR officials exercised control over UN troops on the ground, while NATO exercised control over air assets. When the safe area of Bihac was under attack, NATO sought to respond with extensive air strikes, while UNPROFOR objected, arguing that such strikes would provoke the Serbs into killing UNPROFOR troops.[22] Thus, UNPROFOR commanders limited the NATO strike against the strategic Udbina airfield in Serb-held Croatia to inflict only cosmetic damage to the runway—in fact the planes responsible for attacks on the safe area were specifically exempted from attack. UNPROFOR even later criticized the independent action of NATO in destroying Serbian anti-aircraft installations after British warplanes were fired upon near Banja Luka, and subsequently denied permission to NATO to attack other Serbian anti-aircraft installations, which NATO officials said had to be destroyed before any meaningful action could be taken to defend the Bihac safe area from the air.

Forcing a False Choice between Justice and Accommodation

The "peace-makers" primary responsibility is to end the war—but not to call for justice.

—anonymous UN official[23]

The Tradition of Conflict between Justice and Accommodation

Traditionally, many foreign policy practitioners and scholars have perceived of justice and peace in conflicting terms. The choices are often cast in terms of either working toward peace and ignoring justice or seeking justice at the price of jeopardizing any chance for peace.[24] Proponents of peace are typically characterized as "more aware, more worldly," while those in favor of justice are characterized as "living in an unreal world, shall we say, a metaphysical or idealistic realm."[25]

While this distinction is overly artificial, historically, amnesty or de facto immunity from prosecution has often been the price for peace. The Turks, who many considered responsible for the genocidal massacre of over one million Armenians during World War I were given amnesty in the 1923 Treaty of Lausanne;[26] the French and Algerians responsible for the slaughter of thousands of civilians during the Algerian war were given amnesty in the Evian Agreement of 1962; and Bangladesh gave amnesty in 1973 to Pakistanis charged with genocide in exchange for political recognition by Pakistan.[27]

During the 1980s, in order to facilitate a transition to democracy the governments of Argentina, Chile, El Salvador, Guatemala, and Uruguay each granted amnesty to members of the former regime who commanded death squads that tortured and killed thousands of civilians within their respective countries.[28] To this list must be added the modern practice of the United Nations, which in the early 1990s worked to block inclusion of provisions in the Cambodia peace accords providing for the prosecution of former Khmer Rouge leaders for their atrocities, pushed the

Mandela government to accept an amnesty for crimes committed by the apartheid regime in South Africa, and helped negotiate, and later endorsed, a broad amnesty for the leaders of the Haitian military regime in order to induce them to relinquish power.[29]

Even the Nuremberg experience eventually involved the bartering away of accountability as the cost for German support of the Western alliance during the beginning of the Cold War. Within ten years of the conclusion of the Nuremberg Trials, all 150 of the convicted German war criminals (including several who were serving life sentences and a few who were sentenced to death) were released from Landsberg prison pursuant to a controversial clemency program.[30] While this program removed a "diplomatic pebble from the State Department's shoes," it had the effect of undermining the purpose of the Nuremberg trials. In a nationwide survey conducted by the U.S. State Department, West Germans overwhelmingly indicated their belief that the reason for American leniency was that "they realize the injustice of the trials."[31]

As explained by an anonymous UN official, the quest for justice and retribution is traditionally believed to hamper the search for peace, which in turn prolongs the conflict, enables the continuation of atrocities, and increases human suffering. The UN official also asserts that the intrusion of fact-finding missions seeking to investigate crimes committed by one side may complicate the task of peace negotiations to the point where they become prolonged or impossible.[32]

Efforts to build peace in the former Yugoslavia were not exempt from the conflict between justice and accommodation.[33] According to Payam Akhvan of the Office of the Prosecutor of the Tribunal, "from its very inception in 1993, the International Criminal Tribunal for the former Yugoslavia was surrounded by the so-called 'peace versus accountability' controversy." According to Akhvan, "It was argued indicting political and military leaders such as Radovan Karadzic and Ratko Mladic would undermine the prospects of a peace settlement because they were indispensable to on-going negotiations, and because they would have no incentive to put an end to the fighting without assurances of immunity or amnesty."[34] In fact, during his tenure as co-chairman of the Yugoslav Peace Conference, David Owen expressly opposed the prosecution of Serbian officials engaged in the peace negotiations on the basis that this would undermine his efforts to craft a settlement.[35]

Even after the massacre in Srebrenica and the clear pattern of genocide, policymakers doubted the compatibility of justice and accommodation. As noted by Richard Goldstone, "particularly at the time of the negotiations at Dayton, Ohio, in September 1995, there were many astute politicians and political commentators who suggested that, in fact, peace and justice were in opposition, and that the work of the Yugoslav Tribunal was retarding the peace process in the Balkans."[36] Some commentators even noted that with Radovan Karadzic's alleged approval rating among Bosnian Serbs of 79 percent, any NATO efforts to capture him would undermine the implementation of the Dayton Peace Accord and foster the Serbian people's belief that they were subject to perpetual injustice and persecution.[37] Goldstone rightly expressed surprise at this view, especially in light of the atrocities which had been committed over four years.[38]

In some cases, the existence of a mechanism of justice, such as a tribunal, may be used to further the efforts of those pursing an approach of accommodation by indicating that the norm of justice plays a role outside the peace process and that questions of culpability belong solely with that mechanism. For instance, in February 1994, when Secretary of State Warren Christopher was under pressure by the media to identify those responsible for the commission of war crimes in Bosnia, which would have limited his ability to accommodate the interests of those individuals, his standard press guidance was: "I would like to emphasize that no conclusion can or should be drawn at this stage as to the culpability of particular individuals. This is a question that should be reserved for the War Crimes Tribunal or other court, where the question of culpability will be considered on a case-by-case basis."[39]

Still others, like Richard Holbrooke, asserted that in order to achieve the aims of justice, it was necessary to negotiate with and if necessary accommodate/appease those who were responsible for the commission of atrocities.[40] As such, the insistence on a role for justice was characterized as something which undermined the effectiveness of the negotiator. When asked by Senator Smith during his confirmation hearing why he had systematically declined to ever indicate Milosevic's guilt for the war and atrocities in the former Yugoslavia, Holbrooke responded, "This is tough slogging, and my job was not to make moral judgments. I leave that to moralists and political pundits and columnists, most of whom think they're moralists anyway. . . . I was well aware of the fact that I might have to continue to be engaged on other issues. And the highest goal here was to avoid war, bring peace."[41]

Many peace builders also assert that the conflict between accommodation and justice reflects the perspectives of those on the ground trying to save lives versus those more distant from the conflict. For instance, during his confirmation testimony, Ambassador Holbrooke responded to criticisms of his persistent failure to acknowledge Milosevic's culpability as made "by people who haven't been there, who haven't tried to end wars and prevent wars."[42] Similar statements were made by numerous generals serving in UNPROFOR, who also invoked the mantra of "saving lives" over pursuing justice.[43] In fact, as reported by Cambridge historian Brendan Simms, many of the actual troops on the ground in the safe areas, and particularly SAS troops were keenly aware of the failings of accommodation and urged for a stronger use of force in the pursuit of justice.[44]

The "saving lives" rationale while encapsulated in only two words, is a powerful tool used by the negotiators to undermine the influence of the norm of justice. By characterizing accomodation/appeasement of war criminals in the cloak of "saving lives," it automatically infers that those interested in justice are not interested in saving lives, or at least are willing to permit more killing in order to accomplish an idealistic objective. This view is succinctly stated by an anonymous UN official who criticized the then Yugoslav Tribunal prosecutor and president at the time for their public pressure on the Dayton negotiators. The UN official argues that "their 'ill-considered statements' could have led to a breakdown of delicate negotiations in Dayton. . . . Everyone who was at the

Dayton proximity talks knew that if this issue [mandatory cooperation with the Tribunal] were pressed it could have ruined the talks."[45] He declared that they were acting "irresponsibly" and asked, "in the name of what moral principle would one be able to defend those [further] deaths?"[46] As evidenced by the subsequent conflict in Kosovo, it was in fact the act of accommodation at Dayton that resulted in further deaths, and that only the use of force, coupled with the indictment of Milosevic, brought an end to ethnic cleansing perpetrated by Serbian forces.

Some scholarly commentators assert that the tension between justice and accommodation is inherent in that "the need to establish power sharing structures that accommodate rival factions and interests may well clash with the desire to punish perpetrators of human rights abuses [and] the need to reform the police and the military may be at odds with the practical need to bring those powerful groups into the peace process."[47] In their eyes, the inherent tension "prompt[s] the question of which model works best in a given situation, the power-sharing conflict manager's model, or the democratizer's political justice model? Empirical evidence suggests that a concern for justice must be tempered by the realities of negotiation and by the parties' interests in reaching a political settlement."[48]

In response, defenders of the justice norm have argued, "in short, there is a grudging but emerging widespread acceptance—even among the so-called 'realists'—that regional peace and stability, democratization and multiethnic coexistence in Bosnia-Herzegovina are at best precarious without the arrest and prosecution of indicted persons," and that "the [Yugoslav Tribunal] demonstrates that far from being irreconcilable, peace and accountability, realities and ideals, are inextricably interlinked."[49] According to Richard Goldstone, "if one is talking about short term cease-fires, short term cessation of hostilities, it could be that the investigation of war crimes is a nuisance. But if one is concerned with real peace, enduring and effective peace, if one is talking about proper reconciliation, then, in my respectful opinion, there is and can be no contradiction between peace and justice."[50]

Despite the tradition of an apparent overwhelming preference for accommodation over justice, there is no clear evidence that this approach promotes lasting peace.[51] In fact, the opposite may be the case. For example, history records that the international amnesty given to the Turkish officials responsible for the massacre of the Armenians during World War I encouraged Adolf Hitler some twenty years later to conclude that Germany could pursue his genocidal policies with impunity.[52] In 1939, in relation to the acts of genocide and aggression committed by German forces, Hitler remarked, "Who after all is today speaking about the destruction of the Armenians?"[53] As David Matas, a Canadian expert on international law, observed, "nothing emboldens a criminal so much as the knowledge he can get away with a crime. That was the message the failure to prosecute for the Armenian massacre gave to the Nazis. We ignore the lesson of the Holocaust at our peril."[54]

Richard Goldstone declared that in the case of the former Yugoslavia the failure of the international community to prosecute Pol Pot (Cambodia), Idi Amin

(Uganda), Saddam Hussein (Iraq), and Mohammed Aidid (Somalia), among others, encouraged the Serbs to launch their policy of ethnic cleansing with the expectation that they would not be held accountable for their international crimes.[55] When the international community encourages or endorses an amnesty for human rights abuses, it sends a signal to other rogue regimes that they have nothing to lose by instituting repressive measures; if things start going badly, they can always bargain away their crimes by agreeing to peace. The apprehension of Slobodan Milosevic in the spring of 2001 may be the first step in the reversal of this long history of accommodation and de facto immunity.

Given the poor track record for accommodation, there has been increasing demand for an inclusion of the norm of justice in peace-building since the end of the Cold War.[56] For example, since 1989, some level of justice, in the form of international tribunals and truth commissions, has been pursued in Argentina, Cambodia, Chile, East Timor, El Salvador, Ethiopia, Guatemala, Honduras, Rwanda, Sierra Leone, and South Africa, as well as the former Yugoslavia. As discussed in the next section, there is a role for each of the approaches of accountability, accommodation, economic inducement, and use of force in the peace-building process. And as noted in subsequent chapters, it appears that the international community, while eventually acknowledging the need to employ a mix of approaches, continued to disproportionately favor accommodation and as such weakened the foundations for a lasting peace.

Getting the Right Mix of Approaches

Furthermore, one must not expect too much from justice, for justice is merely one aspect of a many-faceted approach needed to secure enduring peace in a transitional society.

—Richard J. Goldstone,
first prosecutor of the Yugoslav Tribunal[57]

Individual peace-building approaches generally are not capable of building a lasting peace in isolation from other peace-building approaches. Moreover, when peace-building approaches operate, they generally do so in relation to other approaches. The task of foreign policy practitioners is to ascertain the proper role for each approach and to apply an appropriate mix. As noted by General Nash, "the reality is, that all the world is a compromise of many, many issues and as you try to go towards an objective state an objective goal, you've got to work things in stages and you have to balance things."[58]

Although some diplomats contend that the approach of accommodation may be sufficient in and of itself, most commentators would agree with the assessment that "the military and security components of peace-building are a critical part of the peacemaking process," and that "peacekeeping remains essential to international efforts to prevent the renewed outbreak of violence or military hostilities in a country." Furthermore, the prompt deployment of competent and capable peacekeepers may promote confidence in the peace-building process.[59]

In the case of Bosnia for instance, most observers would acknowledge that "the final factor smoothing the path to Dayton was the international community's new willingness to use force, especially air power, as a partner to diplomacy."[60] Observers would also readily acknowledge that the application of economic sanctions on the FRY were insufficient in and of themselves to deter Serbia's aggression against neighboring states. As will be discussed below, however, the employment of economic inducements against Croatia and later Serbia to turn over indicted war criminals to The Hague for trial, and thus neutralize their ability to inhibit the peace-building process, and the use of economic inducements to prompt the handover of Slobodan Milosevic, were highly effective.

Unfortunately, foreign policymakers frequently underestimate the need to adequately employ all relevant approaches, and thus in the Bosnia case, they were slow to utilize the approach of the use of force. According to Elizabeth Cousens, despite the fact that very clear legal justification existed for the use of force, "various explanations account for the under-use of armed force to respond to the Yugoslav wars, from the nationally parochial through the bureaucratically predisposed and militarily arcane, to the ontologically confused." [61] This failure to grasp the utility of the use of force is all the more difficult to understand as key foreign policymakers often set forth compelling rationales for the use of force to protect human rights. For instance, in a now declassified memorandum from Assistant Secretary of State John Shattuck to Secretary Christopher on 19 July 1995, Mr. Shattuck argues:

> We know from these recent and past events what will happen if the Bosnian Serbs' "ethnic cleansing" campaign is not stopped. And, we know that the ever growing refugee problem poses both a humanitarian catastrophe and a security problem as population flows disrupt the delicate balance in the Bosnian Federation and neighboring countries. On human rights and humanitarian grounds alone, the disaster of Srebrenica demands that the international community use the authority it has to protect the remaining safe areas, including through the use of military force.[62]

Regrettably, on frequent occasion, foreign policymakers may inartfully mix the employment of most or all of the approaches, resulting in the creation of a set of circumstances where the approaches work at cross-purposes and are inconducive to the establishment of peace. For instance, in the Bosnia conflict the UN deployed lightly armed peacekeepers which provided some protection to civilians, but did not act decisively when confronted with large-scale ethnic cleansing and genocide against Bosnian Muslims. During the same period, policymakers enacted, but initially failed to enforce a no-fly zone over Bosnia; established safe areas without protecting them; and authorized, but never employed, force to deliver humanitarian aid.

When EU policymakers sought to address the initial conditions of conflict in Bosnia, and the Serbs and Croats escalated their behavior, the prevailing guide to action for the EU lay in accommodation and tightly calibrated displays of force, rather than the meaningful use of force. The contradictory employment of the various approaches came to a head when in the summer of 1995 NATO forces were prohibited from using force to protect the UN designated safe areas of Srebrenica and Zepa because of the risk of Serb retaliation against lightly armed peacekeepers stationed in those safe areas.[63]

In large part because of the failure of the international peace builders to settle on a proper and effective mix of approaches, Yugoslavia slid into a decade of war marked by crimes against humanity and acts of genocide. The next chapter chronicles the origins of the conflict, identifies the primary parties and briefly describes the nature of the atrocities which characterized the conflict, and which led to calls for the increased utilization of the approach of accountability.

Part II

Precursors to Justice: Self-Identity, Political Will, and Moral Obligation in the Peace-Building Process

Chapter 4

The Road to War: War Crimes and the Crime of War in Yugoslavia

War has no mind, and it cannot tell what could or could not at any moment be of value to the opposing side; for this reason, the wisest course of action in war becomes the destruction of absolutely everything—houses and cultivated plots, bridges and museums, and naturally, first and foremost, human beings and their livelihood.

—Milovan Djilas[1]

After the death of Yugoslav leader Josip Tito in 1980, many experts expected an outbreak of conflict in Yugoslavia. And yet, eleven years later, the brutal war in the former Yugoslavia seemed to catch the international community by complete surprise. Upon the outbreak of violence in the spring and summer of 1991 the European states and the United States found themselves unprepared to comprehend and respond to the complex character of the conflict, the barbaric nature of the crimes committed against civilians, and the effective use of history and nationalism to incite civilian atrocities and to placate domestic opposition to crimes against humanity. In large part the widespread use of war crimes as a means for achieving policy objectives provided a clear basis for invoking the norm of justice and using accountability as a means for building peace. The complex nature of the conflict, and the slow comprehension of its many facets, however, undermined the ability of the European states and the United States to craft a coherent response, let alone employ the relatively intricate approach of accountability in the most effective manner.

To establish a sufficient understanding of the conflict necessary to evaluate the extent to which the norm of justice did, and could have, played a role in the peacebuilding process, this chapter begins with a short review of the history of conflict in the Balkan region often invoked by parties to the conflict to justify their contemporary acts. The chapter then surveys the factual background to the most recent conflict in the former Yugoslavia. Here the chapter describes the extent to which nationalism was invoked to stoke the flames of war and the extent to which war crimes were committed to achieve the population redistribution necessary for the creation of mono-ethnic states.

This chapter is not meant to constitute an exhaustive or comprehensive history of the Yugoslav conflict, but rather to serve as a brief primer on the historical and ethnic circumstances so often invoked by the nationalist leaders to incite violence.[2] Similarly, this chapter does not seek to comprehensively catalogue the nature and extent of atrocities committed in the former Yugoslavia but rather seeks to illustrate the systematic and brutal nature of the atrocities, and to make the point that the commission of atrocities was central to the accomplishment of Slobodan Milosevic's political objectives and was not merely a by-product of the conflict.

Historical Fodder for Nationalism and Incitement to War Crimes

Our aim remains the unification of all Serbian lands. Borders are drawn up with blood.

—Ratko Mladic,
Bosnian Serb military leader[3]

Like most geographic regions of Europe, the Balkan Peninsula has been the site of many years of violent conflict, interspersed with years of peace and occasional prosperity. As with the history of most regions, it provides political leaders ample material from which to draw in their efforts to invoke nationalism and ethnic identity as a means for motivating popular support for territorial conquest and ethnic cleansing.

In the case of Yugoslavia, the seeds for drawing ethnic and other distinctions go back nearly a thousand years. Although the people of the different regions of the former Yugoslavia share many common attributes, differences among their religious and historical experiences have led to the growth of strong separate ethnic identities. The primary ethnic and other identities in the former Yugoslavia are Albanians, Bosniacs (so-called Bosnian Muslims), Croats, Gypsies, Hungarians, Jews, Macedonians, Serbs, Slovenes, more recently self-identified Yugoslavs, as well as a small number of Turks and Circassians.[4] The region's strategic position at the southern crossroads of Europe and Asia also has been the source of historic turmoil. Since early history, the region has been invaded, contested, and ruled successively or concurrently by the Macedonian, Roman, Byzantine, Slav, Bulgar, Venetian, Austro-Hungarian, Ottoman, and the Nazi German empires.[5]

By the ninth century, Christianity had become the predominant faith throughout the region, with the western portion (what is now Croatia and Slovenia) largely Roman Catholic, and the eastern section (Serbia, Montenegro, and Macedonia) mostly Eastern Orthodox. A defining moment in the early history of the region occurred on St. Vitus Day (28 June) in 1389, when the Ottoman Turks defeated

Serbian forces at the battle of Kosovo Polje (Field of the Blackbirds) in what is today Kosovo. Thereafter, the eastern portion of the Balkans was brought under a period of Ottoman control from which they did not emerge until the early twentieth century. During the Ottoman reign, many of the people living in rural areas were able to preserve their culture, while many of those living in the major cities, particularly in Bosnia, converted to Islam to better their economic positions and avoid substantial taxes required of non-Muslims. While Serbia and Bosnia existed under five centuries of Ottoman control, the Catholic Slovenes and Croats were absorbed by the Hapsburg Empire and were influenced by centuries of close contact with Austria, Hungary, and Italy.

Two Balkan wars were fought in 1912 and 1913, which resulted in the retreat of the Ottoman Empire from the Balkan Peninsula. During these conflicts, Serbian nationalists resorted to ethnic violence on a massive scale. As the International Commission to Inquire into the Causes and Conduct of the Balkan Wars reported in 1914, "houses and whole villages [were] reduced to ashes, unarmed and innocent populations [were] massacred *en masse*, incredible acts of violence, pillage and brutality of every kind—such were the means which were employed by the Serbian soldiery, with a view to the entire transformation of the ethnic character of these regions."[6]

With the withdrawal of the Ottoman forces, Serb nationalists turned their attention to the Hapsburg Empire, which had annexed Bosnia-Herzegovina in 1908. One of the sparks igniting World War I occurred at this time in Sarajevo when Gavrilo Princip, a Bosnian Serbian nationalist, assassinated Austrian Archduke Ferdinand on 28 June 1914. Notably, the Archduke, who was heir to the Hapsburg throne, was killed on the anniversary of the Battle of Kosovo. The creation of an independent entity was first realized after World War I when King Alexander of Serbia proclaimed the Kingdom of Serbs, Croats, and Slovenes, which in 1929 became Yugoslavia, meaning "Land of the South Slavs."

The unity achieved under King Alexander was fragile, with the Croats pushing for ever greater self-government within a looser confederation. In 1929, with the support of Italian dictator Benito Mussolini, the Ustasha (meaning "uprising") movement was born, with the goal of Croatian independence—if necessary through violence. In 1934, a member of the Ustasha assassinated King Alexander, and a weak regency was appointed to rule in place of Alexander's ten-year-old son. This set the stage for the invasion of Yugoslavia by the Axis powers in 1941.

During World War II, the Axis powers occupied Yugoslavia and partitioned the country into German and Italian spheres of influence. Croatia became a puppet state (comprised of today's Croatia and Bosnia-Herzegovina) of Hitler's Nazi Germany, with the Ustasha leader Ante Pavelic placed in political control.[7] The Ustasha regime regarded Croatia's two million Serbs as a threat, which they set about to eliminate through mass extermination.[8] To that end, Pavelic stated "the Slavoserbs are the rubbish of a nation, the type of people who will sell themselves to anyone and at any price, and to every buyer."[9] Mile Budak, one of Pavelic's chief deputies, declared the Ustasha plan for the Croatian- and Bosnian-Serbs on 22 July 1941, "we shall slay one third of the Serbian population, drive away another third, and the rest we shall convert to the Roman Catholic faith and thus assimilate into

Croats. Thus we will destroy every trace of theirs and all that which will be left, will be an evil memory of them." Echoing this policy, the Ustasha governor of western Bosnia, Victor Gutisch, urged that the territory under his control be "thoroughly cleansed of Serbian dirt."[10] Hence, the term "ethnic cleansing" was first coined, not by the Serbs, but by the Croats during World War II.

To accomplish its goal, the Ustasha regime established an extermination camp at Jasenovac, which rivaled the infamous Nazi death camp at Auschwitz in its brutal efficiency. In all, a million and a half Serbs were "ethnically cleansed" by the Ustasha during World War II—over 500,000 were killed and a million were driven from the territory to seek refuge in other countries. According to German military reports, the passion with which the Ustasha pursued the genocide of the Serbs seemed excessive even in the eyes of the SS.[11]

Resistance to the Axis occupation of Yugoslavia came from the communist Partisan forces, led by the Croatian-born Josip Broz Tito and by Serb nationalist Cetnicks—who fought as much against each other as against the German occupiers.[12] On the heels of Allied victories in the south Balkans, Tito's Partisans eventually established control over the entire Yugoslav territory. In revenge for the Croat atrocities, Serb nationalists murdered over 100,000 Croatian prisoners when the Ustasha surrendered in May 1946.[13] Despite the large numbers of atrocities on both sides, only a handful of war crimes trials were held after the war, and most of these were perceived as attempts to silence those opposed to the new communist order.[14]

After the war, Tito established a federal system in Yugoslavia consisting of six republics: Bosnia-Herzegovina, Croatia, Macedonia, Montenegro, Serbia, and Slovenia, and two autonomous provinces, Kosovo and Vojvodina, within the Republic of Serbia. The internal boundaries were designed to dampen nationalist aspirations of the various ethnic groups by distributing their populations as much as possible among the republics.[15] Tito also liberally employed the Yugoslav secret police to quell ethno-nationalist aspirations.[16]

In 1948, the Soviet premier, Joseph Stalin, expelled Yugoslavia from the Cominform, an organization of Eastern Communist nations, for "pursuing an unfriendly policy towards the Soviet Union."[17] This action led to fears of a Soviet attack, which intensified after the Soviet invasion of Czechoslovakia in 1968. This fear of Soviet invasion, coupled with Tito's totalitarian rule and economic prosperity provided the glue which held Yugoslavia together. Tito's death on 4 May 1980, the collapse of the Soviet threat in the late 1980s, and, some would argue, the weakening economy that accompanied the reduction in international assistance, provided an opportunity for those interested in attaining political power to tap into suppressed feelings of ethnic identity and historical grievances in order to support their bids for power.[18]

The Burning of Yugoslavia

If the Republic of Bosnia votes for independence the Serb paramilitaries will "make the Muslim people disappear, because the Muslims cannot defend themselves if there is war."

—Radovan Karadzic, former President of Republika Srpska and indicted war criminal[19]

The utilization of ethno-nationalism, coupled with class distinction,[20] as a tool for attaining political power necessarily required the political elites to call for a rearrangement of the Yugoslav system of government, leading to the termination of its existence.[21] As Warren Zimmermann, then U.S. ambassador to Belgrade, observed, "the breakup of Yugoslavia was a classic example of nationalism from the top down."[22]

Whereas Croats and Slovene leaders sought to attain greater autonomy, and possibly independence for their republics, the Serbs sought to retain the state of Yugoslavia, but to reorganize the governing structures to enable Serbs to exercise increasing influence over state institutions. The primary ideological backdrop of the Serbian plan was a 1986 manifesto prepared by members of the Serbian Academy of Arts and Sciences and signed by 216 prominent intellectuals, which attacked the most fundamental aspects of the Yugoslavian constitution and argued for the promotion of Serbian interests by force if necessary. The document, known as the SAAS Memorandum, argued that Tito had consistently discriminated against the Serbs and that Serbia had been subject to economic domination by Croatia and Slovenia. It spoke of the "physical, political, legal and cultural genocide against the Serb population in Kosovo" as well as discrimination against Serbs who resided in other republics.[23]

Later that year, Slobodan Milosevic, riding a wave of Serbian nationalism, became Serbian Communist Party chief. Milosevic solidified his position by provoking and then using federal troops to ruthlessly crush a series of crises in the autonomous province of Kosovo, where Albanians outnumbered Serbs ten to one. Kosovo became Milosevic's launching pad in his quest to extend his power to the rest of Yugoslavia. If, as one commentator put it, "the hatred that astounded the world in Yugoslavia was engineered, not innate," [24] it was Milosevic who was the chief engineer.

Most observers believe that the Security Council could have put an early halt to the Balkan conflict, but that at the time the members of the council lacked the political will to take the necessary measures, such as instituting air strikes and committing troops to a combat situation.[25] Some commentators even argue that the war could have been avoided had the international community committed to recognizing the Yugoslav republics and the dissolution in the summer of 1991 and thereby sending a clear signal that the use of force to maintain Yugoslavia would be unacceptable.[26]

Despite the growing public pressure to respond to the Bosnian atrocities, the major powers were unwilling or unable to institute vigorous actions to halt the abuses.[27] Instead, they adopted a series of largely symbolic Security Council resolutions, which gave the appearance of engagement, but which did little to stem the atrocities, and in some cases may have even facilitated them.[28]

In the case of Kosovo, the Europeans, despite their experience in Bosnia, appeared to be caught off-guard by the violence. As observed in early January 1997 by United Nations human rights investigator Elisabeth Rehn, "unfortunately Europe has not been on its toes enough. The U.S. on the other hand has understood how sensitive the situation there really is."[29] The peace builders thus spent much of the first year of the conflict attempting to employ limited economic inducements and the approach of accommodation to persuade the parties to cease hostilities. And despite its success in Bosnia, the peace builders initially eschewed the use or the threat of force for Kosovo. These efforts proved futile, and over time the peace builders became involved in active mediation. These initiatives, however, were too late in coming and the peace builders eventually were compelled to use force in order to bring a halt to the ethnic cleansing, and, according to many commentators, to rescue the credibility of NATO.

War and War Crimes in Croatia and Bosnia

The ascent of a hard-line Serbian nationalist government in Serbia in the late 1980s fanned anti-Serb nationalism in the republics of Croatia and Slovenia. At the same time, Milosevic's efforts to create a more centralized Yugoslavia under Serbian dominance engendered strident resistance from the leaders of Croatia and Slovenia, Franjo Tudjman and Milan Kucan, respectively, who desired to convert Yugoslavia into a loose confederation that would dilute Serbian influence.[30] Flexing his political muscle, in the spring of 1991, Milosevic blocked Stipe Mesic, a Croat, from assuming the Federal presidency, despite the fact that the constitution provided that the presidency rotate annually among the republics and it was Mesic's turn to fill the office.

After a series of negotiations with Milosevic over a new Yugoslav constitution proved futile, Croatia and Slovenia declared their independence on 25 June 1991. Importantly, Croatia failed to offer concrete guarantees for the security of the 500,000 Serbs living within its borders, and in fact undertook a number of actions designed to threaten and intimidate Serbians living in Croatia, in particular by adopting the flag of the former Ustasha regime. A week earlier, U.S. secretary of state James Baker, visiting Belgrade, had warned of the "dangers of disintegration," urged that Yugoslavia maintain "territorial integrity," and he said the United States "would not recognize unilateral declarations of independence."[31] Milosevic took this as a green light to use force to halt secession and to protect the Serbs living in Croatia and Slovenia. "What they read between the lines of the Baker visit," writes Ambassador Zimmermann, "was that the United States had no intention of stopping them by force."[32] Milosevic began by sending the Serb-dominated Yugoslav National Army (JNA) into Slovenia to crush that republic's nascent militia. After the Slovenes withstood repeated attacks and actually defeated the JNA in several engagements, Milosevic agreed to a European Community-brokered cease fire, while he turned his attention to Croatia.

The JNA, aided by local Serbian insurgents, inflicted heavy casualties on the inexperienced and outgunned Croatian forces and quickly took control of one-third of Croatia's territory.[33] On 20 November 1991, following the Serbian siege and capture of the Croatian town of Vukovar, the JNA and Serbian paramilitaries committed the first major atrocity of the conflict. Upon entering the city, Serb forces massacred some 200 Croatian patients (mostly wounded soldiers) at the Vukovar hospital, and disposed of their bodies in a mass grave. The mass grave was later discovered by United Nations forensic investigators,[34] and led to the indictment of three JNA officers and the Serb mayor of Vukovar by the Yugoslav Tribunal.

During the course of the conflicts in Croatia and Bosnia-Herzegovina, the peace builders utilized a number of mechanisms in order to promote a peaceful resolution of the crisis. Initially, they employed a series of UN-sponsored mediations under the direction of Cyrus Vance, and a separate EU process under the chairmanship of Lord Peter Carrington.[35] When these efforts failed to produce results, the peace builders combined them in 1992 and adopted a joint UN/EU approach initially under Cyrus Vance and David Owen. The joint UN/EU mechanism created the International Conference for the Former Yugoslavia (ICFY) which was based in Geneva and was jointly chaired by the United Nations representative and the European Union representative. Other members included the United States, France, Russia, United Kingdom, China, a representative of the OSCE and Organization of Islamic Countries, and Yugoslavia's neighboring states.[36] In 1993 David Owen was replaced by Carl Bildt,[37] and Cyrus Vance by Thorvald Stoltenberg.[38] In 1994 the ICFY was replaced by the Contact Group consisting of the United States, Germany, France, Russia, and the United Kingdom. Italy subsequently joined the Contact Group.

Despite the plethora of organizations created to promote peace-building in the former Yugoslavia, until the negotiation of the Dayton Accords, the majority of the important decisions were made by the five permanent members of the UN Security Council. After fighting broke out in Slovenia and Croatia in 1991, Belgrade requested that the Security Council impose an arms embargo on Yugoslavia to prevent an escalation of the conflict.[39] Later, the Security Council reaffirmed that its arms embargo would continue to apply to all parts of the former Yugoslavia, "any decisions on the question of the recognition of the independence of certain republics notwithstanding."[40] The only state truly effected by the arms embargo was Bosnia, which was left with no means to defend itself, while Serbia had all it needed in terms of military equipment and supplies. President Clinton had campaigned on a pledge to lift the arms embargo on Bosnia, but backed down when the United Kingdom and Russia made clear that they would veto any efforts to lift the embargo.

For six months, repeated efforts by the European Community and the Conference on Security and Cooperation in Europe to broker a durable cease-fire in Croatia failed to yield tangible success. Finally, after thousands had been killed in the fighting, in January 1992, Croatia and Serbia agreed to the deployment of a United Nations peacekeeping force (known as UNPROFOR) to oversee the withdrawal of the JNA and the disarming of local forces in the areas of conflict inside Croatia.[41] Later that month, the European Community and the United States formally recognized the new independent states of Croatia and Slovenia.[42] During the next four years, despite the arms embargo, Croatia would rearm and make preparations for a successful military campaign to retake its lost territory.

In the meantime, the Bosnians were forced to choose between remaining in what was becoming a Serbian ethnic dictatorship or seeking a hazardous independence. As illustrated by the introductory quote to this section, the leader of the Bosnian Serb political party, Radovan Karadzic, clearly signaled the carnage that would follow any declaration of independence by Bosnia, and that the aim of this carnage would be to "make the Muslim people disappear."[43] Despite such threats, on 1 March 1992, the Bosniac and Croatian people of Bosnia-Herzegovina voted overwhelmingly for independence. At the time of the vote, Bosnia consisted of three main ethnic groups: Bosniacs (43 percent of the population), Serbs (31 percent), and Croats (17 percent).[44] While these groups are defined on the basis of religion, Bosnia was largely a secular society. For instance, a 1985 survey found that only 17 percent of its people considered themselves believers and interfaith marriage was extremely common.[45]

Although almost all Bosnian Serbs boycotted the poll, independence was the choice of 63 percent of the total electorate. On 6 April the European Community recognized the new independent nation of Bosnia-Herzegovina, with the United States following suit the next day.[46] Macedonia was subsequently recognized as well.[47] On the day of Bosnian recognition, the Bosnian Serbs, under the leadership of their self-styled president, Radovan Karadzic, proclaimed the formation of an independent "Republika Srpska" (Serbian Republic of Bosnia and Herzegovina), whose government was located in the resort village of Pale in southeast Bosnia just outside of Sarajevo. The Serbs immediately launched attacks against the Croatian and Bosniac populations in northeast and southern Bosnia with the goal of connecting Serb populated regions in north and west Bosnia to Serbia in the east.[48] Assisted by some 45,000 JNA troops, the Serb insurgent forces seized control of 70 percent of Bosnia's territory. By the middle of April, the Bosniacs were left with control over only a few islands of territory within Bosnia—Sarajevo, Mostar, Bihac, Tuzla, Srebrenica, and Gorazde—which were the target of continuous sniper fire and were shelled relentlessly by JNA and Serb insurgent forces.[49]

The Serbs had planned their attack well in advance. Belgrade began to arm and finance local Serb militias more than six months before Bosnia declared its independence.[50] Moreover, according to Borisav Jovic, who had been commander and chief of the JNA, in January 1992, Milosevic issued a secret order to start transferring all Serbian JNA officers who had been born in Bosnia back to their native republic.[51] On 19 May 1992, in an unsuccessful attempt to head off the threat of United Nations sanctions against Serbia for its involvement in the hostilities in Bosnia, Serbia announced the withdrawal of the JNA from Bosnia-Herzegovina. When the JNA pulled out, however, it demobilized 85 percent of the officers and men, and also left behind most of the army's equipment. The demobilized troops, under the command of former JNA 9th Army Corps chief of staff, Ratko Mladic, together with local insurgents and Serbia based-militias, became a new Bosnian Serb army, which continued to receive assistance and instructions from Serbia.[52] Not deceived by this tactic, on 30 May the Security Council adopted Resolution

757, which imposed a sweeping trade embargo on the FRY with the objective of applying pressure on the FRY to meet United Nations demands to cease outside aggression and interference in Bosnia.[53]

However, the initial draft of the sanctions resolution (Resolution 757) was substantially watered down to satisfy Russian objections. For example, an exception was inserted into the resolution allowing for the transshipment of goods across the territory of Serbia, which were readily diverted to destinations within Serbia itself. Another exception allowed for the shipment of humanitarian items to Serbia, including cigarettes, vodka, clothing, and heating oil, which were freely diverted to the Serb army and paramilitary forces.[54] The embargo, moreover, did not cover shipments to Serb-controlled territories in Bosnia. Nor did the resolution provide for enforcement such as maritime interdiction of vessels trading with the FRY or the placement of monitors at Serbia's borders. These loopholes and lack of enforcement were to enable Serbia to successfully circumvent the sanctions.[55] Even after the sanctions were incrementally strengthened through the adoption of Resolution 787 in November 1992 and Resolution 820 in April 1993, they had no perceptible impact on the willingness or ability of the Bosnian Serbs to continue to wage war and commit atrocities.

Another type of sanction pursued was the exclusion of Serbia from the United Nations and other international organizations.[56] When Yugoslavia broke apart in 1992, Croatia, Slovenia, Bosnia, and Macedonia each applied and was accepted as a new member of the United Nations. But Serbia knew that the Security Council was unlikely to approve its application any time soon. So instead, Serbia and Montenegro announced that they were the continuation of the old Yugoslavia and were thus entitled to continue its membership at the United Nations. This was, after all, what Russia had been allowed to do after the breakup of the Soviet Union in 1991. The United States, which was opposed to this action, circulated a draft Security Council resolution that would have denied the FRY's claim and confirm that Yugoslavia's membership in the United Nations had been extinguished with the dissolution of that country. In order to obtain Russian support, however, the resolution was substantially weakened,[57] and subsequently the UN Legal Counsel interpreted the text as precluding the FRY from participating in the General Assembly, but permitting it to continue to maintain its mission at New York and participate in other United Nations bodies.[58] What was intended to be a legal rejection of the FRY's claim to the Yugoslav seat at the United Nations, in effect, became a new kind of suspension which the International Court of Justice later said was "not free from legal difficulty."[59]

The main thrust of early Security Council action in Bosnia was to provide humanitarian aid. This led to a gradual expansion of the size and mandate of UNPROFOR, the UN Protection Force, which had originally been created to monitor the cease-fire between Serbia and Croatia.[60] In response to frequent Serb attacks on United Nations humanitarian aid convoys, on 13 August 1992, the Security Council adopted Resolution 770, which authorized governments to take "all measures necessary" to ensure the safe delivery of relief aid in Bosnia. This was the same formula contained in Resolution 678, authorizing the use of massive military force to expel Iraq from Kuwait. International expectations were high for a corresponding response in Bosnia. But, unlike Resolution 678, Resolution 770 led to no military intervention. There was no attempt to launch air strikes and no plan to send in coalition forces. As U.S. Secretary of State Lawrence Eagleburger explained two weeks after the adoption of the resolution, such action would "not be stomached on either side of the Atlantic."[61]

While waiting for the sanctions to take effect, the Security Council found itself faced with a new challenge when Bosnian Serb aircraft began to attack civilian targets from their air base in the Bosnian Serb-controlled city of Banja Luka.[62] The Bosniacs, who had no air force, were extremely vulnerable to such "ethnic cleansing by air" and the casualties quickly mounted. In response, on 9 October 1992, the Security Council adopted Resolution 781, imposing a "no-fly zone" over Bosnia. At the urging of the British and French, the clause providing for enforcement of the no-fly zone was omitted from the resolution. Instead, the resolution called only for monitors to report on violations. During the next six months there were over 465 documented violations of the no-fly zone.[63] Yet, it was not until 31 March 1993 that the Security Council adopted Resolution 816, authorizing NATO to enforce the no-fly zone, and it was not until 8 February 1994 that NATO would finally take action to shoot down Serb aircraft violating the ban.[64]

But by far the most controversial of all of the actions taken by the Security Council was the creation of so-called safe areas in response to the sustained Serb attacks on the Bosniac population centers at the beginning of 1993. The attacks on Srebrenica, in eastern Bosnia, were particularly ruthless in the spring of 1993 and the city was on the brink of collapse by the beginning of April.[65] On 16 April the Security Council adopted Resolution 819, which demanded that all parties treat the city as a "safe area" free from armed attack. A week later, the Council adopted Resolution 824, designating the predominantly Bosniac cities of Sarajevo, Tuzla, Zepa, Gorazde, and Bihac as additional safe areas. As a quid pro quo for the withdrawal of Serb forces, UNPROFOR was assigned the task of overseeing the demilitarization of the safe areas. Yet, the Security Council provided no real enforcement component to the safe area concept. While the UNPROFOR commander indicated that it would take 35,000 troops to protect the safe areas, the Security Council authorized only a 7,500 troop reinforcement to accomplish the mandate. When the Serbs attacked the safe areas, the UNPROFOR forces retreated, and tens of thousands of defenseless civilians were massacred and carted off to mass graves in the nearby countryside.[66] "Historians will show," wrote the editors of *The New Republic* shortly after the Srebrenica massacre, "that the most important allies of the Bosnian Serbs have been the peacekeeping forces of the United Nations."[67] In the winter of 2002 a Dutch-based organization published a report finding that the Dutch military and the Dutch government shared near-equal responsibility with the UN and the French UNPROFOR commanders for failing to prevent the Srebrenica massacre. In response to the report the Dutch government resigned.

Throughout the conflict, international observers, including information-gathering missions under the auspices of the United Nations Human Rights Commission, the European Community, the Conference on Security and Cooperation in Europe, the International Committee of the Red Cross, Amnesty International, and Helsinki Watch, began to document widespread abuses occurring in Bosnia.

Through these reports, the world learned of mass forced population transfers of Bosniacs, organized massacres and the physical destruction of whole towns, the systematic and repeated rape of thousands of Bosniac women and young girls, and the existence of over 400 Serb-run detention centers.[68] Based on the observations of his own special envoy, Secretary-General of the United Nations Boutros Boutros-Ghali, reported to the Security Council that the Serbs of Bosnia-Herzegovina, with support from the JNA, were "making a concerted effort to create ethnically pure regions" in the republic, and that the "techniques used are the seizure of territory by military force and intimidation of the non-Serb population."[69] These methods were as effective as they were brutal. Ultimately, the Serbs expelled, killed, or imprisoned 90 percent of the 1.7 million non-Serbs who once lived in Serbian-held areas of Bosnia.[70]

Roy Gutman of *Newsday*, the first journalist to visit the Bosnian Serb concentration camps, wrote on 2 August 1992, "the Serb conquerors of northern Bosnia have established two concentration camps in which more than a thousand civilians have been executed or starved and thousands more are being held until they die."[71] Four days later, on 6 August, Penny Marshall of International Television News (ITN) filmed conditions at the notorious Omarska concentration camp in Northern Bosnia.[72] She captured startling footage of "men at various stages of human decay and affliction; the bones of their elbows and wrists protrude like pieces of jagged stone from the pencil thin stalks to which their arms have been reduced."[73] The ITN footage resulted in an international outcry for something to be done to stop the atrocities.

These grievous abuses of human rights occurred throughout the duration of the conflict in the former Yugoslavia.[74] The policy of ethnic cleansing employed by Milosevic's forces came to include:

> laying siege to cities and indiscriminately shelling civilian inhabitants, "strangling" cities (i.e., withholding food deliveries and utilities so as to starve and freeze residents); executing noncombatants; establishing concentration camps where thousands of prisoners were summarily executed and tens of thousands subjected to torture and inhumane treatment; using prisoners as human shields; employing rape as a tool of war to terrorize and uproot populations; forcing large numbers of civilians to flee to other regions; razing villages to prevent the return of displaced persons; and interfering with international relief efforts, including attacks on relief personnel.[75]

Some of the most heinous human rights violations occurred in the Serb-run concentration camps in Bosnia including those established at Susica, Omarska, Keraterm, and Trnopolje. In these camps the prisoners were forced to witness and endure both mental and physical torture. The prisoners were forced to commit acts of sexual mutilation and other violence on one another. The United Nations Commission of Experts concluded that the victims were routinely beaten and often subsequently killed. Rape was also a common tool of Serbian ethnic cleansing. The rapes and sexual assaults on Bosnian Muslims and Croats occurred on a grand scale and as part of a coordinated policy of ethnic cleansing.[76] Many of the rapes, 600 out of the 1,100 documented cases, occurred in the detention facilities. Although the main targets of rape were Bosniac women, men were also subjected to sexual assault.[77]

Despite numerous resolutions demanding that Serbian forces halt aggressive military actions against "safe areas," the Serbian forces encircled the villages that they planned on taking over and prevented any non-Serbs from leaving.[78] They cut off the humanitarian relief, which created food shortages, sanitation problems, and electrical difficulties.[79] The Serbian forces then began a campaign of constant shelling and sniper fire. Upon entering the villages, the Serbs would destroy the Bosnian historical, religious, and cultural property. The paramilitary forces then terrorized non-Serb citizens with random killings, rapes, and looting.[80]

The Serbian government also made numerous claims that Serbian civilians were subjected to war crimes by Croatian and Bosnian government forces. While, as noted immediately below, the Croatian army engaged in systematic brutal acts of inhumanity against the Serb population when it recaptured the Krajina region,[81] little evidence was produced to verify a systematic campaign of atrocities against Serbian civilians by Bosnian government forces.[82] In fact, as reported in a now declassified State Department cable, in February 1993, when U.S. embassy officials in Serbia sought confirmation of mass graves of Serbian civilians near Kamenica in eastern Bosnia—which Radovan Karadzic had used as justification for holding up UN convoys to the Bosnian town of Zvornik— they found that of the bodies exhumed "all appeared to be adult male combatants," and concluded that "despite lurid allegations in the press of torture, burning and mutilation, the grave sites near Kamenica appear not yet to have yielded evidence of atrocities."[83]

In March 1993, the embassy officials were able to confirm atrocities committed against Serb civilians by Croatian forces and the death of Serbian civilians in areas of fighting with the Bosnian government army. The embassy, however, concluded that in the case of the Bosnian government forces, "it is not clear that civilians were targeted."[84] The embassy concluded that, while Serb civilians have been among the victims of war crimes, the Serbian government engaged in an energetic campaign of exaggerating the extent of those crimes and used these exaggerations to justify further ethnic cleansing and attempted genocide on their part.[85] This assessment is important given that the United States and Europeans frequently absorbed such Serbian propaganda and reiterated the view that "all sides" were responsible for atrocities. While technically correct, it was grossly misleading in its suggestion that the scale of atrocities by all sides was roughly equivalent.

In fact, Serbian forces frequently committed crimes against Serbian civilians who sought to remain within Bosnian government-controlled territory. According to the Office of the Prosecutor's staff, a significant portion of the testimony concerning Serb general Stanislav Galic, who had commanded the Sarajevo Romanija Corps, which laid siege to and shelled Sarajevo from 1992-1995, will relate to a number of atrocities committed against Serbians by forces under the general's command.[86]

In the midst of the war between the Bosnian government forces and the

Bosnian Serb forces, Cyrus Vance and David Owen presented their cantonization plan, which sparked a war between Bosnian Croat and Bosnian government forces. This conflict was characterized by brutal atrocities by both forces, and resulted in the indictment of twelve Croatian generals and civilian leaders, and six Bosnian government generals and camp commanders.[87] When in 1995 the Croatian army retook Krajina, it subjected the remaining Serb population to ethnic cleansing and war crimes, including expulsion, torture, and murder. In April 2001, the Tribunal's prosecutor Carla Del Ponte told CNN that she had been about to indict the Croatian president Franjo Tudjman for crimes against humanity and war crimes immediately before his death in 1999 for actions taken during the Croatian offensives against the Knin and Krajina in 1995, which killed and displaced hundreds of thousands of Serbs. [88]

The nature of the crimes are illustrated by a brief review of some of the most important indictments of the Tribunal, which include:

- Dragan Nikolic, the first person indicted by the Tribunal on 4 November 1994, was the commander at the camp Susica, where detained Muslims and non-Serbs were held after Serb forces took over the town of Vlasenica in April 1992. Between late May and October 1992, 8,000 people were detained in the hangar in Susica camp where they were subjected to terrible living conditions, beatings that often resulted in death, torture, and sexual assault. Nikolic is accused of grave breaches of the Geneva conventions, crimes against humanity, and violations of the laws or customs of war for his role as commander of the camp.[89]

- Zeljko Meakic, the chief of security and subsequently camp commander; Momcilo Gruban, a shift commander; and Dusan Knezevic, indicted on 13 February 1995, for crimes committed against Bosnian civilians at the Omarska Camp. Meakic and Gruban were indicted for their leadership roles in the Omarska Camp. Knezevic did not work exclusively at the camp, but entered the Omarska Camp to kill, beat, and physically abuse prisoners. At the camp, prisoners were routinely killed, raped, sexually assaulted, beaten, and otherwise mistreated. Living conditions at Omarska were also brutal. Prisoners were crowded together with little or no facilities for personal hygiene, and they were fed starvation rations once a day. The little water they received was ordinarily foul. Prisoners had no change of clothing and no bedding, and they received no medical care. All three men have been indicted for crimes against humanity, grave breaches of the Geneva conventions, and violations of the laws or customs of war. Meakic was also indicted for genocide.[90]

- Blagoje Simic, president of the Serbian Democratic Party and president of the municipal assembly; Milan Simic, president of the Executive Board; Miroslav Tadic, assistant commander for logistics, and Simo Zaric, chief of National Security Service, indicted on 21 July 1995 for the ethnic cleansing of Bosnian Croats and Muslims in Bosanski Samac. In April 1992 Serb military forces from the former Yugoslavia forcibly seized control of the town and subsequently took control of the whole municipality of Bosanski

Samac, announcing that the government of the municipality had been replaced by the "Serbian Municipality of Bosanski Samac." The town had 17,000 Croats and Muslims before Serb military forces took over in April 1992, but had fewer than 300 non-Serbs by May 1995.[91]

- Dusko Sikirica, commander of the Keraterm Concentration Camp; Dragan Fustar, shift commander; Nenad Banovic, guard and interrogator; Predrag Banovic, guard and interrogator; Dragan Kulundzija, shift commander; Damir Dosen, shift commander; and Dusan Knezevic, who entered the camp to physically abuse detainees, indicted on 21 July 1995, for crimes committed at the Keraterm Camp. According to the indictment, between 24 May 1992 and 30 August 1992 Bosnian Serb authorities in the Prijedor municipality unlawfully segregated, detained, and confined more than 7,000 Bosnian Muslims, Bosnian Croats, and other non-Serbs from the Prijedor area in the Omarska, Trnopolje, and Keraterm camps. At the Keraterm camp, the majority of the detainees were military-aged males. Detainees at the Keraterm camp were so crowded together that often they could not sit or lie down. There were few or no facilities for personal hygiene and the water supply was inadequate. They had no change of clothing, bedding, or medical care and were fed starvation rations once a day. Interrogations were allegedly conducted on a daily basis and regularly accompanied by beatings and torture. Killings, sexual assault, and other forms of physical and psychological abuse were also commonplace at the Keraterm camp. The camp guards and others who came to the camps used all types of weapons and instruments to beat and otherwise physically abuse the detainees. Bosnian Muslim and Bosnian Croat political and civic leaders, intellectuals, the wealthy, and non-Serbs who were considered as extremists or to have resisted the Bosnian Serbs were especially subjected to beatings, torture, and/or killing. At a minimum, hundreds of detainees, did not survive.[92]

- Radovan Karadzic, president of the Republika Srpska and head of the Serbian Democratic Party, and General Ratko Mladic, commander of the Bosnian Serb Army, indicted on 24 July 1995, for crimes committed against the people of Bosnia-Herzegovina, including genocide. Between April 1992 and July 1995, the people of Bosnia-Herzegovina were rounded up and detained in prison camps, victims of military action against civilians, taken as hostages, and subjected to other forms of physical and psychological abuse. Places of worship and businesses of non-Serbs were also destroyed. As the highest ranking officials during this time, Karadzic and Mladic are accused on the basis of individual criminal responsibility, as well as superior criminal responsibility. Karadzic and Mladic were also indicted as a result of their leadership positions on 16 November 1995 for the crime of genocide committed during the siege of Srebrenica. In early July 1995, the safe area of Srebrenica was attacked by the Bosnian Serb army. Some Bosnian Muslim civilians in Srebrenica sought protection at the UN compound in Potocari; others, including armed Bosnian military personnel, fled through the woods toward Tuzla. On the way to Tuzla, many Bosnian Muslims were attacked by Bosnian Serb military personnel. Those who were not able to reach Tuzla were trapped behind Bosnian Serb lines and subsequently captured by, or surrendered to, the VRS. Many Bosnian Muslims were summarily executed at the location of surrender or capture or at assembly points. Up to 7,000 of those who fled to Potocari were summarily executed in the compound or transported to other areas and massacred. As a result of the Bosnian Serb attack on the safe area and other actions, the Muslim population of Srebrenica was virtually eliminated.[93]

- Milan Martic indicted on 25 July 1995 for violations of the laws or customs of war as a result of his position as head of internal affairs and president of the self-proclaimed Republic of Serbian Krajina. According to the indictment, during the summer of 1991, the armed forces of the Republic of Croatia and the armed forces of the self-proclaimed Republic of Serbian Krajina were engaged in armed conflict. The local Serb forces, with help from the Yugoslav Peoples' Army, defeated the Croatian army in numerous battles, taking control of approximately one-third of the Republic of Croatia, including Western Slavonia. A cease-fire commenced in January of 1992 and the United Nations Protection Force was installed in areas held by the Serbian forces. On 1 May 1995, the Croatian army attacked Serb forces in Western Slavonia and drove them back into the Serbian part of Bosnia. Allegedly, in retaliation, the Serb forces were given orders by Martic to attack three Croatian cities, including Zagreb. On 2 and 3 May, the Serb forces fired long-range rockets into the center of Zagreb, injuring and killing civilians.[94]

- Tihomir Blaskic indicted on 10 November 1995 for crimes committed against Muslims in the Lasva Valley during the war between Croatia and Bosnia in 1992. He was the commander of the regional forces of the Croatian Defense Council which committed serious violations of international humanitarian law against Bosnian Muslims in Bosnia and Herzegovina, including murder, taking hostages, and inhumane treatment of civilians. Blaskic was found guilty of all counts on 3 March 2000 and sentenced to forty years in prison.[95]

- Mile Mrksic, Miroslav Radic, Veselin Sljivancanin, and Slavko Dokmanovic indicted on 7 November 1995 for crimes committed against non-Serbs during the siege of Vukovar. According to the indictment, on about 20 November 1991, the JNA and Serb paramilitary soldiers aided, and abetted by Dokmanovic, and under the command or supervision of Mrksic, Radic, and Sljivancanin, removed at least 200 non-Serb individuals from the Vukovar hospital and then transported them to a farm building in Ovcara, where they beat them for several hours. Afterward, soldiers transported their captives in groups of about ten to twenty to a site between the Ovcara farm and Grabovo, where they shot and otherwise killed at least 198 men and 2 women. After the killings, the victims were buried by bulldozer in a mass grave at the same location.[96]

- Gojko Jankovic, Janko Janjic, Dragan Zelenovic, and Radovan Stankovic indicted on 26 June 1999 for enslavement, rape, and torture committed at Foca. According to the indictment, from at least July 1992 to February

1993, Muslim women, children, and the elderly were detained in houses, apartments, and motels in the town of Foca or in surrounding villages, or at detention centers such as Buk Bijela, Foca High School, and Partizan Sports Hall. Many of the detained women were subjected to humiliating and degrading conditions of life, brutal beatings, and sexual assaults, including rapes. Jankovic, Janjic, and Zelenovic were all subcommanders of the military police and paramilitary leaders in Foca at the relevant time.[97]

- Momcilo Krajisnik, former president of the Assembly of Serbian People in Bosnia and Herzegovina, indicted on 21 March 2000 for crimes committed against the people of Bosnia and Herzegovina. Pursuing actions intended to secure control of various municipalities of Bosnia and Herzegovina that had been proclaimed part of the Serbian Republic of Bosnia and Herzegovina, the Bosnian Serb leaders, including Krajisnik, Biljana Plavsic, and Radovan Karadzic, are accused of persecution of non-Serbs on political, racial, and religious grounds, deportations, exterminations, and other acts. Because of his leadership role, Krajisnik is accused of individual and superior criminal responsibility for genocide, crimes against humanity, grave breaches of the Geneva conventions, and violations of the laws or customs of war.[98]

- Biljana Plavsic, former acting president of the Serbian Republic of Bosnia and Herzegovina, indicted on 7 April 2000 for pursuing a course of conduct that involved the creation of impossible conditions of life, persecution, and terror tactics in order to encourage non-Serbs to leave the area, deportation of those reluctant to leave, and the liquidation of others in Bosnia and Herzegovina. Her role as a leader of the Bosnian Serbs gives her individual criminal responsibility and superior criminal responsibility for acts of genocide, crimes against humanity, grave breaches of the Geneva Conventions, and violations of the laws or customs of war.[99]

Given the nature of the atrocities and the superior fire power of the Serbian forces, the possibility for a peace settlement remained remote until the military balance on the ground began to change in 1995. From May through October of that year, Serb forces suffered a series of defeats at the hands of the Croatian and Bosnian armies. Obstacles to the use of NATO air power had been removed with the repositioning of UNPROFOR troops, both forcibly in the case of Srebrenica and Zepa, and voluntarily in the case of Gorazde. A Bosnian Serb mortar attack on the Sarajevo marketplace on 28 August, which killed thirty-seven Bosniac civilians, prompted a reluctant NATO to finally approve the U.S. proposal for air strikes. Thus, in August 1995, the United States launched "Operation Deliberate Force," a massive bombing campaign against Serb targets the purpose of which was to silence the Serb artillery and produce a diplomatic breakthrough. As a result of the bombing campaign, and the advance of Croatian and Bosnian forces on the ground, the Serbian regime agreed to Contact Group-sponsored negotiations at the Wright-Patterson Air Base in Dayton, Ohio.

The Dayton negotiations, held over a period of three weeks in November 1995, produced the Dayton Accords. The accords provided for the de jure continuation of a Bosnian state divided into two entities, the Croat-Bosniac Federation and the Republika Srpska. The division of political responsibility was such that both entities possessed significant competencies and all decisions made by the central government were subject to a complicated process wherein each ethnic group could exercise one or more substantive or procedural vetoes. The Dayton accords also provided that a NATO-led Implementation Force would be deployed in Bosnia to separate the opposing armies and keep the peace. This force was later transformed to a Stabilization Force (SFOR). The accords further provided for elections to be conducted by the OSCE and for the creation of an Office of the High Representative, who would exercise significant plenipotentiary powers.

Despite the deployment of tens of thousands of NATO troops and thousands of international assistance and aid personnel, many Western government officials acknowledge the Dayton Accords failed to promote the reintegration of Bosnian society and served as the framework for a slow de facto partition.[100] This outcome was aided in large part by the continuing presence of indicted and unindicted individuals who were responsible for planning the campaign against a sovereign Bosnia and for orchestrating the commission of atrocities, and who persisted in their efforts to partition Bosnia despite the international presence.

War and War Crimes in Kosovo

On 1 December 1918, following the end of World War I, Kosovo became a part of the Kingdom of Serbs, Croats, and Slovenes, which as noted above subsequently became Yugoslavia, though never legally part of Serbia. In 1919, in response to a denial of their basic human rights, including the right to education in the Albanian language, an estimated 10,000 rebels took up arms against the central government of the kingdom. The suppression of this revolt involved the commission of widespread atrocities against Kosovo Albanians, the arming of Serbian civilians, and the relocation of Kosovo Albanian women and children to internment camps in central Serbia. Subsequent to this revolution, the central government accelerated a colonization program, promising sizable tracts of land and exemption from taxes for ethnic Serbians willing to relocate to Kosovo.[101]

In 1929, Yugoslavia was divided into nine governorships, with the territory of Kosovo being dispersed among three governorships. From that time until World War II, much of the land held by Kosovo Albanians was confiscated and transferred to the state. In 1933, the government of Yugoslavia also began negotiations with the government of Turkey regarding the prospects for expelling between 200,000 and 300,000 Kosovo Albanians to Turkey. In 1938 an agreement was reached with Turkey to forcibly relocate as many as 400,000 Kosovo Albanians. This agreement was frustrated by the outbreak of World War II.[102]

During World War II, when Yugoslavia was occupied by Axis forces, Kosovo was partitioned between Bulgaria, Albania (governed by Italy), and Germany. Following the end of the war, when the state of Yugoslavia was reconstituted, the 1946 Yugoslav constitution provided that Kosovo would be an autonomous region within the Republic of Serbia. Although the 1946 Yugoslav constitution did not address in detail the rights and obligations of the autonomous region of Kosovo, the Serb Republic constitution provided that Kosovo would direct its own economic and cultural development and that it would be responsible for protecting the rights of its citizens.[103] At this time, the Yugoslav government relaxed the restrictions on the use of the Albanian language and reduced the intensity of the colonization program, which had been halted by the world war—during which many of the Serbian colonists had been forced to return to Serbian territory.

In 1963, Yugoslavia adopted a new constitution, which promoted Kosovo to an autonomous province, but effectively decreased some of its federal rights. Yet, in 1968 the constitution was amended to provide autonomous provinces the status of "sociopolitical communities" which was the same term used to describe the other republics making up Yugoslavia. The autonomous provinces were also provided the right to engage in all activities associated with republic level status, except for those tasks which were of concern to the Republic of Serbia as a whole. In early 1969, the Kosovo Albanians were permitted to fly the Albanian flag as their "national emblem," and later that year the University of Prishtina was established. Throughout the 1970s the Kosovo Albanians increased their participation in the economic sector, political bureaucracy, and local police forces, with Kosovo Albanians holding two-thirds of the membership in the local League of Communists, and three-fourths of the membership in the local police and security forces.[104]

In 1974, Yugoslavia adopted yet another constitution, which provided that the Autonomous Province of Kosovo, as well as the Autonomous Province of Vojvodina, would be entitled to a status nearly equivalent to that of the other six republics of Yugoslavia. In particular, Kosovo was entitled to participate in the federal government, with its own representative on the rotating federal presidency and with elected parliamentarians in the federal parliament. Moreover, Kosovo adopted its own constitution, as authorized by the Yugoslav constitution of 1974.

In the early 1980s, after Tito's death, and in response to perceived and real discrimination by the Kosovar Albanians, the Kosovo Serbs began to agitate for a return to the earlier political system, in which the Kosovo Serbs held greater privilege and power. In 1985, the Serbian Academy of Sciences drafted a "Memorandum," which essentially called for a revocation of the rights accorded Kosovo under the 1974 constitution, and the creation of a greater Serbia.[105] In 1987, Slobodan Milosevic, then a deputy to the president of the Serbian Party, traveled to Kosovo to hear demands by Kosovo Serbs. In response to an orchestrated riot by Serbian nationalists, Milosevic delivered an extemporaneous speech calling for the "defense of the sacred rights of the Serbs."[106] In late 1987, Milosevic used the growing political unrest in Kosovo as a platform for assuming the presidency of the Serbian League of Communists.

In early 1988, the Serbian Assembly adopted amendments to the Serbian constitution which removed Kosovo's control over the Kosovar police force, criminal and civil courts, civil defense, and economic, social, and education policy. Moreover, the amendments effectively prohibited the use of Albanian as an official language in Kosovo. To force these amendments through the Kosovo parliament as required by the federal constitution, members of the Serbian security forces surrounded the Kosovo parliament building with tanks and armored personnel carriers, and inserted special police and Communist Party functionaries among the Kosovo delegates.[107] These actions were met by mass demonstrations of the Kosovo Albanian population and resulted in the declaration of a state of emergency in Kosovo by the Serbian regime.

In March and June of 1990, the Assembly of the Republic of Serbia issued a series of decrees meant to entice Serbs to return to Kosovo, while suppressing the rights of the Kosovo Albanians. The decrees for instance created new "Serb only" municipalities, forbade the sale of property to Albanians by departing Serbs, closed the Albanian language newspaper, closed the Kosovo Academy of Sciences, and dismissed several thousand Kosovo Albanian state employees. In response, on 2 July 1990, the Albanian members of the Kosovo Assembly declared Kosovo "an equal and independent entity within the framework of the Yugoslav federation."[108] The Serbian regime reacted by dissolving the Kosovo Assembly and the government. And finally, in late 1990 the Serbian regime expelled 80,000 Kosovo Albanians from state employment.

The members of the dissolved Albanian assembly responded by holding a secret meeting and creating a constitutional law for the Republic of Kosovo, and then holding a referendum on the question of whether Kosovo should be declared a sovereign and independent republic. According to Kosovo Albanian sources, 87 percent of eligible voters participated in the vote, with 99 percent voting in favor of independence. Subsequently, using the same procedure of underground voting, the Kosovo Albanians held an election on 24 May 1992, whereby they elected a new assembly and government.[109] In the spring of 1998, the Kosovo Albanians held a second round of parliamentary elections as required by their constitutional law.

From 1989, the Kosovo Albanians were denied not only the ability to participate in the federal government, but also the ability to participate in the local formal political structures responsible for determining the political fate of Kosovo. Moreover, the Kosovo Albanians were subjected to a systematic denial of their basic human rights, which included a policy of arbitrary arrests, police violence, detention incommunicado, torture, summary imprisonment and economic marginalization. As a result, in the mid 1990's some elements of the Kosovo Albanian population formed the Kosovo Liberation Army, which murdered members of the Serbian police and military forces and perceived Kosovo Albanian collaborators.

Commencing in the winter of 1998, Serbian forces engaged in a brutal crackdown in Kosovo ostensibly aimed at extinguishing the KLA and its popular support, but in reality aimed at ethnically cleansing large swaths of Kosovo. As part of their campaign, the Serbian forces terrorized local civilian populations, murdered vast numbers of noncombatants, and laid siege to numerous villages.[110] As a result of the new campaign of Serbian ethnic aggression, over 350,000 civilians were displaced and over 18,000 homes were deliberately destroyed, and almost half of the population centers were subject to siege. The intensity of the campaign of terror, ostensibly to drive the KLA from Kosovo, rapidly increased in the autumn of 1998.

In the face of these atrocities, the international peace builders responded with humanitarian assistance, mild economic sanctions,[111] and public declarations of the need to stop the atrocities. Although the peace builders had eventually been compelled to use force in Bosnia and had stationed over 30,000 troops to prevent renewed hostilities, they initially eschewed even the threat of the use of force in Kosovo.[112]

Added to these mild measures, the peace builders, led by Russia and the United States, declared that the KLA was a terrorist organization.[113] These declarations were taken as a green light for Mr. Milosevic to continue his aggressive actions against the Kosovo population. As the intensity of the conflict increased, the peace builders continued to identify the KLA as terrorists, but they sought to offset this with a call for an enhanced role for the Yugoslav Tribunal.[114] The Office of the Prosecutor, however, failed to adequately engage and did not launch serious investigations nor issue any indictments in response to these initial atrocities.

With the failure of these initial efforts, and under intense public criticism for their apparent failure to learn the lessons of Bosnia, the peace builders, in the form of the Contact Group, spent the summer of 1998 attempting to mediate a peace agreement between the parties, and to increasingly employ the threat of the use of force. Much of the summer was thus spent with U.S. diplomats shuttling between Prishtina and Belgrade attempting to craft a mutually acceptable agreement, and with U.S. and U.K. officials, under the direction of General Wesley Clark, seeking to build a NATO consensus to use force.

The draft agreements prepared by the United States generally sought to accommodate the Serbian interests in the territorial integrity and sovereignty of the FRY, while providing certain human rights protections for the people of Kosovo. Like the Dayton Accords, the draft agreements proposed a complicated system of government which was likely to lead to political gridlock. During this time, NATO made arrangements with Albania and Macedonia to assist them in securing their borders, and held ground and air exercises in Albania in August 1998.[115] The aim of these exercises was to demonstrate "NATO's capability to project power rapidly into the region."[116]

The mediation efforts and the shows of force, however, failed to quell the conflict or abate the atrocities. In fact, in the midst of the negotiation the Serbian regime began a policy of rounding up Kosovo Albanian men, and placing them in camps reminiscent of the Bosnian concentration camps.[117] In the face of increasing atrocities, the peace builders embarked on two contradictory efforts. First, they marshaled sufficient political and public support for the use of air strikes against Serbian forces, [118] and second they sent Ambassador Richard Holbrooke on a mission to the FRY to negotiate an arrangement for monitoring (similar to the early arrangements in Bosnia—which were widely regarded as failures). The resulting Holbrooke/Milosevic deal provided for the stationing of unarmed monitors—a walk back from the Bosnia situation where UNPROFOR forces were lightly armed,[119] and the provision for unarmed NATO over flight—

another walk back from the Bosnia situation, where armed NATO forces enforced a no-fly zone.[120] The weakness of the deal aside, the primary effect was to temporarily diffuse international support for the use of force.

In light of the unarmed nature of the monitors and the perceived retrenchment of the threat to use force, the Serbian regime continued its attacks on the civilian population. Public criticism and demand for action reached a peak shortly after 15 January 1999, when Serbian military and paramilitary forces massacred over forty civilians in the Kosovo town of Racak. The massacre was met by a series of public denunciations by President Clinton,[121] Secretary of State Albright,[122] the chairman of the OSCE,[123] the European Union, and UN Secretary-General Kofi Annan.[124] Most of the declarations called for an investigation by the Yugoslav Tribunal, and for the perpetrators to "be brought to justice."[125]

As a result of the Racak massacre, the collapse of the Holbrooke/Milosevic deal, the apparent failure of earlier mediation efforts, and political pressure (especially from the U. S. Congress), the peace builders, led by the United States, modified their approach to one of "diplomacy backed by force," which include increased reliance on the threat of the use of force,[126] invocations of the norm of justice,[127] and the introduction of direct mediation in the form of proximity peace talks similar to those held at Dayton.[128]

The Rambouillet/Paris peace talks, which were held in early February and again in mid-March 1999, addressed a wide range of issues similar to those addressed at Dayton. The primary provisions provided for the withdrawal of most Serbian military, police, and paramilitary forces, the transformation/disarmament of the KLA, the creation of new municipal and regional structures of government, and the creation of a process for determining Kosovo's final status after the expiry of a three-year interim period. The negotiations also covered the nature and extent of an international peacekeeping force, the means for reconstituting the police force, the protection of minority rights, the protection of cultural property, and the creation of a process for the return of property nationalized by the Serbian regime.

At the end of the talks, the Kosovo delegation signed the agreement, while the Serbian delegation refused to sign, and increased the intensity of its military campaign in Kosovo. In response, NATO launched a strategic air campaign, striking targets in Kosovo and Serbia proper. During the course of the air campaign, the Yugoslav Tribunal indicted Mr. Milosevic and a number of other top officials for orchestrating crimes against humanity in Kosovo. After 78 days of NATO bombing and an apparently increasing willingness of the NATO member states to authorize the deployment of ground troops, Mr. Milosevic agreed to remove Serbian military forces from Kosovo and to allow the deployment of NATO forces and the creation of an interim administration operated by the United Nations. The NATO victory came, however, after Serbian forces had expelled 1.5 million Kosovo Albanians, killed tens of thousands more, and destroyed most of their homes.

To formalize the arrangement, the UN Security Council adopted resolution 1244 which established the mandate for the NATO deployment and set forth a framework for United Nations administration of Kosovo for an interim period. In early July, NATO deployed its forces and within the next week the UN appointed Bernard Kouchner to head the United Nations Mission in Kosovo (UNMIK).

As in Bosnia, torture and abuse were an integral part of the Serbian military campaign in Kosovo. "Retaliatory and armed action, torture and ill-treatment, arbitrary detention, forced disappearances, harassment and discriminatory treatment [were] widely reported."[129] The Office of the United Nations High Commissioner for Refugees (UNCHR) received many reports that Kosovars were "being arbitrarily arrested for questioning and kept in pre-trial detention for periods well beyond the legal time limit." In addition, UNHCR stated that many of those detained complained that they were tortured and abused.[130]

The United Nations' concern over human rights violations began early in the conflict as a response to stories of attacks and massacres in Gornje Obrinje, Klecka, Golubovac, Volujak, Malisevo, Rausic, Glogovac, and Gremik. The most well-publicized massacre in the region occurred in Racak on 15 January 1999. According to a report of the UN Secretary-General, Serb forces brutally murdered "45 unarmed civilians, including 3 women, at least 1 child and several elderly men, 11 in houses, 23 on a rise behind the village and others in various locations in the immediate vicinity of the village. Many of the dead appeared to have been summarily executed, shot at close range in the head and neck."[131]

NATO Secretary-General Javier Solana commented that, "Sadly, the massacre and events surrounding it appear indicative of the pattern of disproportionate use of force by the authorities of the Federal Republic of Yugoslavia in retaliation for provocation by Kosovo Albanian paramilitaries." Autopsies were performed in Prishtina in the presence of the Kosovo Verification Mission monitors, but the FRY refused to delay the autopsies until the Finnish experts arrived in Prishtina.[132]

The nature of the campaign is illustrated by a brief review of the primary indictment issued for the war in Kosovo, that of Slobodan Milosevic and others in the highest level of the Yugoslavian government. On 24 May 1999, the former president of the Federal Republic of Yugoslavia, Slobodan Milosevic, was indicted for crimes committed against ethnic Albanians in Kosovo. Also indicted were Milan Milutinovic, Nikola Sainovic, Dragoljub Ojdanic, Vlajko Stojilkovic, and former Serbian president Milan Miltinovic. In the indictment, the International Criminal Tribunal charged Milosevic and the others with "Crimes against Humanity" and "Violations of the Laws and Customs of War."[133]

According to the indictment, between January 1999 and continuing through June 1999, police forces of the FRY along with Serbian police and paramilitary units undertook operations to force approximately 740,000 ethnic Albanians from their villages and into the neighboring countries of the FYR of Macedonia and the Republic of Albania, thus creating a monumental refugee crises. The indictment charges FRY and Serbian forces, under the auspices of the indicted officials, of waging a widespread campaign of looting and burning the homes and villages of Kosovo Albanians. Further charges include multiple counts of robbery, verbal and physical abuse, and the seizure of identification papers to prevent Albanians from returning to their homes by effectively erasing all traces of their presence. By far the most serious charges cited in the indictment as "Crimes Against Humanity" are the multiple counts of murder. These charges refer to the incidents of mass killings of ethnic Albanian men, women, and children. Hundreds of ethnic Albanians died from shelling, grenade attacks, beatings, and direct gunfire at the hands of FRY and Serbian forces during the six-month period stated in the indictment. Many ethnic Albanians, particularly men and young boys, were executed as they tried to escape or hide from the police forces charged with the task of their complete expulsion from the region.[134]

Faced with a dissolving country in a state of ethnic conflict characterized by crimes against humanity on the front step of Europe,[135] the European states and the United States sought to craft a response suitable to end, or at least contain, the conflict. In crafting their approach, the powerful European states and the United States considered not only the necessity of ending the conflict and protecting human rights but also the need to calculate their own strategic interests and domestic concerns. Moreover, the ability of the states to craft an effective response was influenced by the relative power of various nonstate and substate actors. As a result of the complicated nature of the conflict and the number of states and institutions involved in peace-building, all four of the primary approaches to peace-building were relied upon. Unfortunately, the mix of approaches was crafted in an ad hoc fashion absent any overall plan, and, as a result, the actions of the peace builders generally failed to accomplish the objectives of containing the conflict or protecting human rights. To develop the understanding of how and why the international community reacted to the conflict, the next chapter will discuss the interests of the primary peace builders and track their efforts to promote a resolution of the Yugoslav conflict.

Chapter 5

The International Response: Self-Interest Wrongly Understood

[Lt. Gen. Rose has] done everything to water down the decisiveness of the free world in punishing crime and fascism. . . . We will be asking for an impartial, objective commander, one who will implement UN resolutions on the ground . . . and not a general who protects the interests of his government.

—Bosnian parliament statement demanding the UNPROFOR Bosnia commander's removal[1]

The surprise of the international community at the outbreak of the war in the former Yugoslavia was matched only by its surprise at being unable to prevent the spiraling escalation of the conflict and its inability to craft a coherent and consistent diplomatic and military response. The failure of the international community, particularly the European powers and the United States, to adequately respond to the conflict was largely the result of their often divergent and occasionally contradictory strategic interests, and their tendency to use the Yugoslav peace-building process as a means for promoting their ancillary interests and objectives or for responding to domestic issues.[2]

To develop an understanding of the actions taken by those states and institutions that played the role of peace builders and the various interests influencing the peace process as well as to thoroughly answer the first and second questions set forth in the first chapter, this chapter identifies the primary international stakeholders who acted at one time or another as peace builders and examines their interests and objectives.

State Interest: Who Had What at Stake in the
Former Yugoslavia

The Serbs repeatedly exaggerated the extent of the [BiH army] "raids" out of
Srebrenica as a pretext for the prosecution of a central war aim: to create a
geographically, contiguous and ethnically pure territory along the Drina. . . .
The extent to which this pretext was accepted at face value by international
actors and observers reflected the prism of "moral equivalency" through which
the conflict in Bosnia was viewed by too many for too long.

—UN report on the Srebrenica massacre

The primary international stakeholders possessing an interest and capacity to assist in resolving the Yugoslav conflict were the United States, Russia, the United Kingdom, France, and Germany. Other stakeholders included the states of Albania, Austria,[3] Bulgaria, Greece, Hungary, Italy, the Netherlands, and Romania. This section will deal with the first group, and throughout the remainder of the study the authors will indicate the interests of the second group where relevant. In particular, this section will note the very divergent goals of the interested stakeholders, their apparently inherent biases concerning the parties and notions of justice, and the influence their lack of understanding of the region had on their development of a suitable approach to peace-building and their willingness to incorporate the norm of justice into the process.

United States

After the collapse of the Soviet Union in December 1991, Yugoslavia lost its strategic importance to the United States. Preoccupied with the Persian Gulf War and the future of the disintegrating Soviet Union, the United States was satisfied to leave the handling of the Yugoslav conflict to the member states of the European Union.[4] In 1989, when Mr. Milosevic was consolidating power, an interagency review by the Bush administration concluded that Yugoslavia held no strategic interests for the United States.[5] When the fighting began in 1991, Secretary of State James Baker bluntly explained his government's lack of interest by saying, "We don't have a dog in that fight."[6] From that point on the Bush administration's policy revolved around the notion that the United States had no strategic interest in the Balkan conflict, European institutions should bear the responsibility for resolving the conflict, and U.S. efforts were best directed at managing the dissolution of the Soviet Union.

By the time President Clinton assumed office it had become clear that a resolution of the Balkan crisis was in U.S. strategic interests, and it was not going to be accomplished by the Europeans. But rather than seeking a leadership role for the United States, the Clinton administration initially sought to exclude the norm of justice and erode the moral imperative to become involved in the crisis because it did not possess the political will to do so. With the appointment of Secretary of

State Albright in 1996, the Clinton policy began to shift and eventually came around to supporting the actual indictment of Milosevic and the use of force to end his reign of terror in the Balkans.[7]

Even after receiving reports of Serb-run death camps in Bosnia in August 1991, the United States was hesitant to act. According to the then Bosnian desk officer at the State Department, the Bush administration's policy at the time amounted to "let's pretend this is not happening."[8] The day after the ITN footage of Omarska aired worldwide, President Bush told a news conference, "we know there is horror in these detention camps. But in all honesty, I can't confirm to you some of the claims that there is indeed a genocidal process going on there."[9] Thereafter, U.S. officials were instructed to avoid using the "genocide" label with respect to Bosnia, so as not to trigger moral and legal obligations under the Genocide convention, which obligates parties to prevent and punish acts of genocide.[10] Despite a number of public statements condemning the atrocities in the former Yugoslavia, the State Department devoted almost no resources to the actual investigation of crimes and no resources to determining whether the atrocities were part of an attempted genocide. According to the former Yugoslav desk officer, Richard Johnson, the team responsible for compiling evidence for the UN War Crimes Commission consisted of a foreign service officer with no experience in the Balkans, and a volunteer intern.[11] In response, for the first time since the Vietnam war, a State Department official, George Kenney, resigned in protest of U.S. policy.

Despite Bill Clinton's campaign pronouncements calling for the use of force to protect civilians in Bosnia, and a then classified Department of State cable indicating that by January 1993 there were reports of at least sixteen rape camps in Bosnia,[12] the U.S. policy did not immediately change when the Clinton team took over in 1993. The Clinton administration feared that if it identified the Serbian atrocities as attempted genocide then it would create a moral imperative to use force and would limit the ability of the United States to negotiate with Milosevic and Karadzic.[13] Given that the United States was at this time not ready to take the lead from the European Union, the State Department embarked on a campaign to actively erode the moral imperative to use force to create a just peace.

An illustration of this approach can be found in Secretary of State Warren Christopher's 18 May 1993 testimony before the House Foreign Affairs Committee. In response to pressing questions from Congressman McCloskey, Christopher refused to acknowledge that the Serbian forces were committing genocide in Bosnia, asserting instead that "all sides" were responsible for the atrocities there—thus removing the imperative for action.[14] In fact, according to Richard Johnson the evening before his testimony, Secretary Christopher's office "sought urgent information from the [State Department's] Human Rights Bureau on Bosnian *Muslim* atrocities only" (emphasis in original), and during the testimony "insinuat[ed] that Bosnian Muslims [were] suspected of genocide themselves."[15] Presumably, in the mind of Christopher, if all parties were equally culpable, then the Clinton administration would not be morally at fault for failing to take adequate action to stop the atrocities.[16]

Secretary Christopher's testimony was remarkable in that five months earlier, on 11 January 1993, a classified memorandum was prepared by the State Department's Bureau of Intelligence and Research, the first sentence of which read, "Over the past year Bosnian Serbs have engaged in a range of deliberate actions contributing to the attempted genocide of Bosnian Muslims."[17] The memorandum, since declassified, went on to state that the Bureau of Intelligence and Research "believes there is substantial evidence indicating that Bosnian Serb efforts to eliminate Bosnian Muslim communities have been widespread, systematically planned, and ruthlessly implemented," and that "the results of well-organized genocidal activities are evident throughout Bosnia."[18] The memorandum also directly implicated the political leadership of Serbia in the planning and conducting of the campaign of attempted genocide.[19] Interestingly, Secretary Christopher subsequently undertook similar efforts to downplay the genocidal nature of crimes being committed in Rwanda despite assessments from the Office of the Legal Adviser and the Bureau of Intelligence and Research finding that genocide was in fact occurring in Rwanda.[20]

Secretary Christopher's testimony was all the more detrimental to the peace process as in March 1993, two months before his testimony, a then classified Department of State cable from Belgrade argued unconfirmed accounts of atrocities against Serbs "have been widely publicized and embellished as part of a propaganda campaign in support of Serbian war aims in Eastern Bosnia,"[21] which were characterized as crimes of genocide. The cable then pointed out that Radovan Karadzic himself was using the "all sides are responsible" argument to justify the Serbian offensive against Srebrenica. Secretary Christopher's testimony lended important credibility to the war rhetoric of Radovan Karadzic.

Notwithstanding the INR memo and mounting evidence of Serbian culpability, the Clinton administration would continue to assert a line of moral equivalence among the parties for the next two years. In fact, when Congressman Frank McCloskey (D-Ind.) sent a letter in April 1993 to Secretary Christopher, asking whether genocide was occurring in Bosnia and who was responsible, the State Department spent six months attempting to craft a response. Secretary Christopher never replied to Congressman McCloskey, and failed to ever publicly address the question of the Serbian forces' culpability for genocide despite strong pressure from career officers and legal experts from within the State Department to identify the Serbian forces as responsible for attempted genocide. This pressure took the form of a State Department Legal Office memo urging use of the term genocide; a memorandum from the Yugoslav desk, cleared by all the relevant bureaus, finding that the atrocities committed by the Bosnian Serbs "constituted actions that met the international definition of genocide;" a dissent channel memorandum signed by 12 foreign service officers calling for a drastic change in U.S. policy and identifying the Bosnian Serbs as responsible for genocide; and the resignation of three more State Department officials—Marshall Harris, Steve Walker, and John Western.[22]

Secretary Christopher's commitment to avoiding the introduction of the norm of justice into the process by acknowledging the Serbian forces' attempt to commit genocide significantly handicapped the ability of the United States to play an active and constructive role in the peace-building process. In fact, the United States even found itself in the position of preparing to vote against a UN Human Rights Commission resolution condemning Serbian atrocities in Bosnia that it had initially drafted because a number of Islamic countries had successfully amended the resolution to include a condemnation of genocide. The vote against was averted when a watered down reference to genocide was moved to the resolution's preamble.

The Clinton administration's hesitance reflected its desire to avoid the fate of the last Democratic domestic reform-oriented White House, under President Lyndon Baines Johnson. Johnson's ambitious domestic agenda had been derailed by Vietnam, and the Clinton team feared that American casualties in Bosnia could similarly sink its plans for health care reform, crime prevention, and education.[23] As one political analyst concluded at the time, "risk avoidance appears to have acquired the force of doctrine at the Pentagon. In the Clinton administration, the concern borders on an obsession with both military and civilian leaders whose view on the use of force was molded by the war in Vietnam."[24]

As recounted by Richard Johnson, when Eli Wiesel argued to Undersecretary of State Peter Tarnoff and Tim Wirth that the Bosnian concentration camps and mass murder required intervention, Tarnoff asserted that "failure in Bosnia would destroy the Clinton presidency." Wirth then elaborated that although he "agreed with Weisel that the moral stakes in Bosnia were high . . . there were even higher moral stakes at play: 'the survival of the fragile liberal coalition represented by this Presidency.'"[25]

The active effort to minimize the impact of the norm of justice and to erode the moral imperative to intervene with the use of force would remain the official U.S. government position until March 1995, when it was fatally undermined by a leaked CIA study, which found that 90 percent of ethnic cleansing had been carried out by Serbs pursuant to a policy designed to destroy and expel the non-Serb population from Serb-controlled areas.[26]

Throughout its first four years, the Clinton administration's Balkan policy suffered from the absorption into the political decision-making process of a number of propaganda points initiated by the Milosevic regime, or by simply superficial historical and political commentary. [27] For instance, the notions of ancient ethnic hatreds, a conflict between warring factions, and the equal responsibility of all sides for atrocities permeated the political discourse and public statements of key policymakers such as Secretary of State Warren Christopher and even President Clinton himself.

Compared to its European allies, the United States was less worried about the establishment of a "Muslim state" in the South Balkans and was generally more sympathetic to the victim status of the Bosniacs. Like the British, however, many U.S. policymakers operated from a flawed assumption about the nature of the conflict, and thus they too readily accepted the view that some partition along religious or ethnic lines was the most appropriate means of settling the conflict. Secretary of State Warren Christopher, for example, declared in 1993 that "the hatred between all three groups, the Bosnians and the Serbs and the Croats, is almost unbelievable. It's almost terrifying, and it's centuries old. . . . The United States simply doesn't have the means to make people in that region of the world like each other."[28] Some commentators contend, however, that the ethnic hatred argument was cynically adopted by the political leadership in the United States and other Western governments as a means for deflecting public criticism of their "mistakes and indecisiveness," which enabled the continued commission of atrocities.[29]

As a result of these preoccupations, the first important Clinton administration foray into the peace-building effort, that of advocating a plan pushed by the U.S. Congress to lift the arms embargo on Bosnia and engage in NATO air strikes against Serbian targets, met with dismal failure. President Clinton had sent Secretary of State Warren Christopher to Europe to rally support for the idea, but by the time Christopher had returned, he had himself become convinced of the European view that the peace builders should not "choose sides," and his relatively incoherent presentation and willingness to back down in the face of moderate criticism by some European states reinforced the European perspective that the United States was neither interested in nor capable of leading a coalition of peace builders to resolve the crisis.[30]

The Clinton administration's understanding of the conflict was further limited by the Pentagon's apparent refusal to conduct a comprehensive analysis of the nature of the conflict and the utility of the use of force. The Pentagon presumably feared that if it were to conduct such an analysis it would find that the use of force, and possibly the approach of accountability, were in fact the preferred means to resolving the conflict and would find itself pushed into taking a more active role in the Balkans. As a result, the Pentagon, like the State Department, tended to rely upon myths propagated by the Serbian regime, in particular the mythological tenacity of Serbian fighters and the difficulty of fighting in Yugoslav terrain.[31]

As the crisis in the former Yugoslavia dragged on and as Secretary Christopher was replaced by Secretary Albright, the United States began to more clearly understand its strategic interest in resolving the Yugoslav conflict, in particular the risk that the conflict could spread to Macedonia and Albania, and from there to Greece and Turkey, could undermine U.S. leadership in the post-Cold War era, and that acquiescence in ethnic cleansing and genocide on the European continent could set a permissive and dangerous precedent.[32] At this time the United States also increasingly sought to involve NATO as the security element of the peace-building efforts as opposed to United Nations peacekeeping forces.

Initially the United States preferred that the European Union take the lead on peace-building in the former Yugoslavia as it desired to strengthen European Union peace-building competencies and it hoped to rely upon decisions of the European Union for political cover. The United States was also open to a role for the OSCE, as the United States and Germany exercised considerable political clout within the organization. With an increasing understanding of the strategic interests of the United States associated with the Yugoslav conflict, the United States sought to move the peace-building efforts from the European Union to the United Nations Security Council, and then from there into the Contact Group, where it believed it could most effectively exercise leadership.[33] As a result, the United States took the leading role in the negotiation of the Dayton Accords, and later in the Rambouillet/Paris Accords (despite the location of the negotiations in France).[34]

The United States was also particularly sensitive with respect to whether its actions concerning the Yugoslav crisis might negatively impact political developments in Russia. Thus, for instance, in the winter of 1993 the United States delayed the announcement of its plan to lift the arms embargo on Bosnia and engage in NATO air strikes against Serbian targets until after completion of a scheduled referendum on the Russian presidency for fear that its announcement might undermine President Yeltsin's success in the referendum.[35] The United States policy of "Russia First," adopted by the Clinton administration was criticized by many career foreign service officers as it seriously—and in their view unnecessarily—undermined efforts to adopt a coherent and effective Yugoslav policy. The Russia First policy also unduly encouraged the Russian government to play a substantial role in the Yugoslav crisis at a time when its attention was distracted by a succession of internal economic crises and the war in Chechnya.

Russia

The Russian Federation was strongly opposed to any aggressive international action against the Serbs. Russia is linked to Serbia by religion, alphabet, and history.[36] "It's not so much that they love the Serbs," wrote London-based journalist Gwynne Dyer, but that "they simply cannot believe that in a conflict between Christians and Muslims, Slavic Orthodox Christians can be the villains and Muslims the victims." [37] Russian hard-liners exploited these sentiments and pressured the Yeltsin government at various times to exercise a de facto veto at the Security Council whenever forceful measures against the Serbs were being considered.[38]

According to a now declassified State Department cable, the pressure to side with the Serbian regime was significantly augmented by a Russian media which "maintaining its purported 'balance' continued to present a pro-Serbian view of the Bosnian conflict," and which was highly susceptible to Serbian propaganda—in particular, notions that the Bosnian forces staged massacres of their civilians to prompt NATO intervention.[39] According to the cable:

> Despite overwhelming evidence (at least in Western eyes) of continued Serb butchery, the Russian body politic remains decisively pro-Serbian. Although some within the [Ministry of Foreign Affairs] freely admit that the Russian press is biased, the story Russians are getting—both from the media and from most Russian politicians—is remarkably one-sided.

As such, Russian policy essentially consisted of opposition to NATO air strikes to compel Serbian compliance with UN resolutions or humanitarian law—unless UNPROFOR forces were directly attacked; objections to the authority of the Secretary-General to cooperate with NATO; support for the demilitarization of Sarajevo; and the characterization of the conflict as a civil war.[40]

Moreover, Yeltsin's advisers were quick to draw parallels between the position of the Serbs and the Russians, and Serbia and Russia in their respective crumbling federations.[41] Thus, in addition to political survival, the Yeltsin government had a compelling interest in precluding the setting of an interventionist precedent by the international community, which could be used against Moscow in its dealings with its own minorities.[42] The possibility of creating such a precedent became all the more poignant when Russia launched its military offensive against separatist rebels in Chechnya, wherein it committed numerous crimes against humanity, and engaged in indiscriminate attacks on civilian targets.

In the early stages of the Yugoslav crisis, however, Western peace builders could have acted with a relative free hand in Yugoslavia as Russian political elites were preoccupied with the survival of the Soviet Union. After the dissolution of the former Soviet Union, Russia aggressively sought to retain the great power status of the Soviet Union and actively engaged on the Yugoslav issue. As such, Russia was particularly interested in having the conflict resolved through the UN Security Council, and subsequently through the ad hoc Contact Group. According to Mark Almond, "Russia eagerly grasped this chance to return to the world stage, but more for strategic reasons and much less due to an often stated sense of Orthodox brotherhood linking it with the Serbs." [43]

Russia also possessed important financial interests as it was the primary arms supplier to Serbia. Although the Soviet Union voted in favor of an arms embargo on the entire territory of the former Yugoslavia, Russia consistently violated the embargo, and subsequently vetoed resolutions which sought to tighten the embargo by banning the flow of military supplies from Serbia to the Croatian and the Bosnian Serbs. Some commentators have also alleged the Russian peacekeeping forces "were doing maneuvers with the Serbs, helping them in their 'ethnic cleansing' of Croats and even flying helicopters (forbidden by the UN no-fly zone) for the Serbs, and training the Serb militias." [44]

By so strongly allying itself with the Serbian regime, Russia was able to secure for itself a renewed foothold in Europe. As explained by British analyst Jonathan Eyal, "in a neat move and at little cost, the Russians have established their stake for a sphere of influence in the Balkans. The have also made sure that, even if Mr. Milosevic is replaced by a more pro-Western ruler in Belgrade, no Yugoslav President will be able to ignore Moscow, for it will only be Russian troops which will guarantee an enduring Yugoslav presence in Kosovo." [45] And having once secured a foothold, it became in the Russian interest to seek to undermine effective Western action in the Balkans. According to former national security adviser Zbigniew Brzezinski, "it's quite clear the Russians don't want NATO to succeed. . . . They viewed this essentially as an exercise of what they call American hegemony. I don't believe that as of today all of a sudden they have an interest in this being a success for NATO and the United States they're going to do everything they can during the implementation phase to complicate it." [46]

United Kingdom

At all times the United Kingdom played a central role in the formulation and execution of international policy with respect to the Balkan conflict, and in particular with respect to the role of justice. Under the stewardship of John Major, this policy was exclusively directed at an approach of accommodation and coercive appeasement centered around a desire to resolve the conflict through the quick partition of Croatia and Bosnia and the deployment of peacekeepers to quell the conflict.

As noted by British historian Mark Almond, Britain's "influence within the UN Security Council, NATO, the UN/EU peace process and the peacekeeping mission on the ground has been pivotal. In many ways, the war provided a valuable opportunity for Britain to consolidate its privileged, but increasingly threatened, position in the diplomatic arena. In Bosnia as elsewhere, Britain has been "punching above her weight." According to Almond, unfortunately, "far from contributing to a resolution of the conflict and a diminution of its ferocity. British policy has effectively colluded at prolonging the fighting while protecting aggressors from effective counter-attacks by the victims. Under the guise of impartiality, Britain—along with France—has been on the side of the Serbian forces." [47] As a result, according to one British historian, Britain's early Yugoslavia policy, with the support of Greece and the Netherlands, was one "of appeasement and indifference," [48] with little room for the notions of justice or use of force.[49] This may have been the case given that Britain's political institutions, in particular policymakers in within the House of Commons and Foreign Office, were heavily influenced by Serbian propaganda.[50]

The particularly appeasement-oriented nature of Britain's policy was in part the result of the perceived significant parallels between Yugoslavia and Northern Ireland "as irremediable inter-ethnic conflicts." [51] As noted by James Gow, the experience with Northern Ireland led British policymakers to conclude that "an external act in favor of one belligerent against the interest of the other could only antagonize the latter and incite further bloodshed." [52] As a result, the United Kingdom under the leadership of Prime Minister John Major initially objected even to the deployment of peacekeepers.[53] After the deployment of peacekeepers, the British sought to constrain the mandate of the peacekeepers to that of humanitarian aid. The British government then argued that the presence of its troops in UNPROFOR made assertive military action, such as air strikes against the Serbs, unacceptable because the Serbs would retaliate against the United Nations forces.[54]

As the United Kingdom was uninterested in the meaningful threat of the use of force, it saw no real role for NATO in the peace-building process. In addition, because of strained British and American ties in the early years of the Clinton administration, the British were not particularly keen on involving America too deeply in efforts designed to resolve the conflict, and they preferred instead to rely on the European Union institutions as proposed by France and Germany. The United Kingdom, moreover, was quite reluctant to use the OSCE mechanism because of the fairly prevalent influence of America within that organization, as well as the influence of Germany.[55]

As the British held the rotating chair of the European Union for a six-month period during a particularly crucial time of the crisis in the summer of 1992, they became deeply involved in the process elements of the mediation efforts, and in August 1992 sought to relaunch the stalled peace effort by hosting the International Conference on the Former Yugoslavia in London. As noted above, the conference participants, with the subsequent endorsement of the Security Council, decided to unify European and United Nations mediation efforts under the co-chairmanship of United Nations envoy Cyrus Vance and David Owen of Britain.[56]

Notably, when the Vance-Owen venture came under intense criticism for de-linking Serbian abuses from the peace negotiations—in direct violation of the London principles adopted at the August meeting—and when they sought to legitimize the ethnic division of Bosnia and allow the Serbs to buy time while continuing to push ahead with ethnic cleansing,[57] the British government supported their efforts as the most viable "process" for resolving the dispute. In Britain's view, the best way to stop the atrocities was to stop the war. Britain was, therefore, reluctant to embrace any actions against the Bosnian Serbs that could potentially disrupt the peace negotiations, which as a result limped on without a major breakthrough during four years of fighting. As for the Bosnian government, the British position closely reflected that of David Owen's, which was "to demoralise the Bosnian side." In fact, he told the "U.S. media that his strategy was to 'shatter the Muslims' illusion' that they might get outside aid."[58]

Because of their complete commitment to a negotiated settlement, the British were willing to embrace the partition of Bosnia as the optimal "solution" to Mr. Milosevic's strategy of creating a greater Serbia.[59] In fact, in May 1994, Foreign Office minister Douglass Hogg told London audiences that "[The Bosnians] have to recognise military defeat when it stares them in the face. . . . Land has been seized by force and there is going to have to be acquiescence in that."[60] According to Mark Almond, "British elder statesman, Sir Edward Heath, shared the official line and put the purpose of the arms embargo quite clearly when he argued the only way to bring about an end to the war was to defeat or intimidate, not the Serb forces, but the Bosnian government . . . [declaring] '[s]o long as you hold out any hopes to the Bosnians . . . then you abolish any hopes of peace." [61]

The British willingness to support the partition of Bosnia also stemmed from a general lack of sympathy for Muslim victims, the perception of the Serbs as the traditional allies of the United Kingdom, the influence of Serbian lobbyists close to the Tory Party, and a general misconception and oversimplification of the nature of the conflict.[62] On this last point, for example, European Union mediator David Owen often sought to explain the conflict as the result of the fact that "these characters are locked in history." [63] The British government also expressed concern about any efforts that might lead to the creation of a "Muslim state" in the so-called backyard of Europe, and London generally rejected the idea that the Bosniacs were the victims of Serbian aggression.

As a result of its fear that an active tribunal would require the British government to "choose sides," the United Kingdom actively sought to undermine the effective operation of the Tribunal, as will be discussed below, while publicly supporting the notion of a role for justice in the peace process. The British government under John Major's leadership sought to use the Tribunal to characterize all parties as equally responsible for atrocities and thus, like the early Clinton years, sought to erode the moral imperative to take sides in the conflict.

Ironically, while the British political leaders were the most committed to the approach of accommodation, on the ground in Bosnia some of the military units which most aggressively defended humanitarian convoys and civilian centers were British.[64] Similarly, the British aid organization and British intellectuals took the lead in providing assistance and arguing for a more cogent European policy in Bosnia.[65] The commanding officers though, in particular General Michael Rose, remained committed to the line of moral equivalence and the approach of accommodation.[66] As noted above, one British commander was even quoted by Reuters news service as describing indicted war criminal Ratko Mladic as having a "presence," and that when he "had power he wielded it ruthlessly," which "brought him some grudging respect, if not admiration." [67] This is the same General Mladic who was indicted by the Yugoslav Tribunal for genocide for his role in the massacre of over 7,000 unarmed men at Srebrenica.

During the early stages of the Yugoslav crisis, the British government, under the advice of Foreign Secretary Hurd, had adopted a policy of embracing Russia as a counterweight to its weakened and tense relationship with the United States.[68] According to Mark Almond: "A leaked Foreign Office memorandum was explicit in its argument that Russia could be relied on to block U.S. moves which Whitehall opposed but felt unable to veto in the UN Security Council. One diplomat wrote in the summer of 1993: 'the U.K. has consistently opposed this lunatic idea [the lifting of the arms embargo], but our style has been cramped by the need to tend this 'special relationship' . . . It has been reassuring, however, to know that when the crunch came . . . the Russian veto would definitely be forthcoming if necessary." [69] As such, the United Kingdom sought to include Russia within the mediation process as much as possible, and to ensure that the actions of the European Union did not infringe upon the perceived prerogatives of Russia. Ultimately, however, the United Kingdom abandoned this approach as Russia became more and more recalcitrant and non-responsive to Western attempts to resolve the crisis.

With the change in government from Tory to Labour in 1996, the British policy underwent a fundamental transformation. The new U.K. leaders recognized the need to prevent continued ethnic cleansing and genocide on the European continent, rejected the approach of accommodation pursued by the Tory government, took seriously the role and value of the Yugoslav Tribunal, and exhibited an increased willingness to use force. The new government also significantly increased the resources it made available to the Tribunal, enabling it to enhance its ability to both investigate additional cases, as well as try those in detention. The SAS and other British forces operating in Bosnia were also directed to aggressively seek the apprehension of war criminals present within their sector, and they launched some of the first operations to arrest indictees.

Importantly, with the change in government, the United Kingdom began to challenge the United States for leadership on the issue, particularly during the subsequent NATO air campaign against the FRY in the spring of 1999. In fact, most commentators believe it was Prime Minister Tony Blair who pressured President Clinton into publicly acknowledging the need to prepare for a ground offensive in Kosovo. An act which demonstrated the commitment of NATO and prompted Milosevic to agree to NATO demands.

France

Like the United Kingdom, France deemed it to be in its strategic interests to take a leading role in the formulation of the international response to the crisis in the former Yugoslavia. The French perspective was more complicated than that of the United Kingdom in that, although it was highly sympathetic to the Serbian position, it was also responsible for initiating the humanitarian airlift into Sarajevo (which had the intended side-effect of curtailing the potential for Western use of force),[70] and Paris placed its soldiers in the most at-risk areas, which resulted in over seventy five casualties.

As characterized by Oliver Lepik, "Given the helpless international context as regards the tragic situation in the former Yugoslavia, France has taken a singular stand. Paris will not be accused of inactivity or indifference, as the French *Casques Bleus* are on the front line. . . . Paris was the active instigator of humanitarian aid: and President Francois Mitterrand made a foray into Sarajevo in June 1992 and opened the way to this aid in the besieged Bosnian capital. His active policy enabled him to draw attention to other less committed, European partners. Nevertheless, France's attitude is not without ambiguity and ambivalence."[71]

As further explained by John Laughland, "it is only by understanding France's other foreign policy priorities, especially her preoccupation with the European Union and Germany, that one can make sense of her apparent blindness and lack of judgment. . . . In other words, French policy towards the former Yugoslavia, overtly under President Mitterrand and less obviously under President Chirac, has been all about France, and very little about Yugoslavia."

Central to an understanding of France's position is a recognition that France was highly concerned with the dissolution of the Soviet Union and the fall of the iron curtain. Where other governments welcomed the freeing of Central and Eastern Europe, France "regarded the liberation of peoples from communism as a geopolitical threat." This was compounded by the view of President Mitterrand that "in general, nations should group themselves together in larger regional entities ('les grands ensembles'), like the Soviet Union, and that preservation of these entities was a self-evidently good thing." This perspective limited the role for the application of justice because in a conflict exclusively characterized as one resulting from the "destruction of state order through the forces of nationalism," there was little room for individual culpability or the assignment of blame.[72]

As such, France initially focused on managing the conflict through the European Union. This had the added advantage for France of demonstrating the capacity of the European Union to function as a cohesive entity capable of resolving threats to political and economic stability on the European continent.[73] France also sought to begin the process of augmenting the NATO security structure with a Western European Union (WEU) security structure, which was the precursor to the European Security and Defense Policy.[74] France then sought to further anchor Germany in the political and security elements of the European Union and WEU and deepen the Franco/German core of the union.[75] In a memorable presentation at The American University in Washington, D.C., during the early stages of the Yugoslav conflict, the French ambassador proudly proclaimed that as the United States was taking the lead on formulating a political response to the dissolution of the former Soviet Union, the European Union would be formulating the response to the Yugoslav conflict.[76]

However, as their German allies began to make clear their preference for recognition of Croatia and Slovenia and their belief that it was necessary to use force to resolve the Yugoslav conflict, the French became uneasy with their policy of promoting the European Union as the most proper forum for responding to the conflict. Moreover, as the Germans made clear their view of the Serbs as the primary aggressors, the French took private umbrage at the German propensity to "chose sides," especially as the Germans were not choosing the Serbian side, whom the French considered their traditional allies in the Balkans[77] and, they believed, it was the Serbians who should be the most appropriate allies of the European Union in this conflict.[78] The French were also unsettled by the frank German acknowledgment that in order to make the threat of the use of force credible, it would have to involve U.S. forces and that NATO was the proper institution to invoke and, if necessary, carry through on such threats.[79]

In reevaluating its strategy, France considered an enhanced role for the OSCE, but Paris declined to strongly support its involvement because of the unwieldy nature of the body and because France played no special role in that forum. Rather, France decided it would best serve its interests if it were to arrange for the matter to be shifted to the Security Council.[80] Although this would necessitate the involvement of the Americans, it was a forum where the French could constrain the actions of the Americans if necessary through exercise of the French veto, and where the Germans were not present. The French also placed great confidence in UN Secretary-General Boutros Boutros-Ghali.

In the end, France's policy could be characterized as one of coercive appeasement, which supported the extensive accommodation of Milosevic's demands coupled with the deployment of lightly armed peacekeepers and the provision of humanitarian assistance to minimize the level of human suffering associated with the accommodation of Milosevic's plan for a greater Serbia. To further this approach, France consistently resisted the application of economic sanctions. According to former secretary of state James Baker, French foreign minister "Roland Dumas, in fact, suggested that we take another look at the modest sanctions then in force against Serbia, saying, 'We do not want to penalize a major player.'"[81] This approach was followed consistently through the crises, and even in 2001, when the international community prepared to successfully apply conditionality on assistance to Serbia in order to induce the surrender of Milosevic to the Hague, France objected.

With respect to the use of force, France initially supported the deployment of peacekeepers in an effort to recapture the policy initiative from Germany. If France had forces on the ground it could dictate European and thus international policy. Once its peacekeepers were on the ground, President Mitterrand was able to effectively assert that "military escalation was a dead end."[82] However, internal French opposition to the "pro-Serb policy" and the continued publicity about

Serb atrocities eventually forced the government to support UN Security Council Resolution 776 authorizing the peacekeeping troops to use force if attacked.[83]

Mounting domestic criticism and the refusal of the Bosnian Serbs to accept the Vance-Owen peace plan—supported by France—ended Frances's pro-Serb policy. According to Oliver Lepik, "in France this was understood as a bitter failure, and the French immediately took the tough U.S. line towards the Bosnian Serbs, [voting] on 31 March 1993 in favour of Resolution 816 mandating the enforcement of the 'no fly zone.' Recognizing that NATO was the only viable organization to enforce the Zone." [84]

As noted immediately above, the French considered themselves to be traditional allies of the Serbs, and were initially unconvinced of the nature of the atrocities being committed by the Serbian regime.[85] Even after these atrocities became widely publicized, French military officers spied for the Serbian forces, and, according to one report, scuttled NATO's attempts to arrest Radovan Karadzic by providing him with detailed information on a planned NATO operation to secure his arrest and extradition to The Hague to stand trial for genocide.[86]

According to journalist Chuck Sudetic, the French ambassador to the United States conveyed to him "that the lesser war criminals were best left to themselves. 'We have to help them become democratic,' he said. 'Look at Germany. After the war we had a lot of criminals who became nice guys with families.'" France's defense minister, Alain Richard, even mocked the credibility of the Tribunal, calling it a "spectacle," with the prosecutor for the Tribunal responding that NATO's French sector in eastern Bosnia is a "safe haven" for Serb war criminals.[87]

The French record on arresting war criminals in its sector in Bosnia has been so weak that former UN War Crimes Tribunal prosecutor Louise Arbour publicly lashed out at France for its "deliberate policy" of avoiding arrest of indicted war criminals in its zone of operations. According to Arbour, in 1998, "most of the indicted war criminals are living in the French sector." Judge Arbour also criticized French defense minister Alain Richard, who had called the Tribunal's work "show justice," pointedly declaring "that is an expression of contempt for the more than 200 witnesses who have testified. . . . To suggest that they took part in a show is contemptible and shocking." In response to this pressure, French forces acted on a sealed indictment and staged a high-profile raid in April 2000 at the home of Momcilo Krajisnik—arresting him while he was in his pajamas. Mr. Krajisnik had served as representative of the Republika Srpska on the Bosnian rotating presidency from 1995 to 1997.[88]

When the crisis in Kosovo erupted, the French took a similar approach to the one they had pursued in Bosnia, seeking to blame the Kosovo Albanians and not the Serbs for the atrocities. On one notable occasion, French defense minister Alain Richard proclaimed that "the KLA, not the Serbs" were the "main destabilizing factor" in Kosovo, and that in order to quell the conflict the West would have to "station tens of thousands of soldiers on the spot if we wanted to prevent the KLA from establishing territorial control, and the allies are opposed to this. . . . So we have to adopt other solutions such as cutting off KLA financing abroad and going back to threats of air attacks."[89] When asked about these remarks, William Walker, the head of the Kosovo Verification Mission stationed in Kosovo for the purpose of monitoring human rights abuses stated, "I don't know why he said that. . . . It's ridiculous," and went on to explain that the Serbs were responsible for most of the noncompliance and recounted a number of Serbian examples of obstructionism of the operation of the Kosovo Verification Mission.

Finally, although France recognized the need to work within institutions such as the European Union and the United Nations, it perpetually harbored the notion that it was a great European and world power and that any action it took should be designed to confirm and enhance its status in this regard. As a direct result of these efforts, the Dayton Accords were signed in Paris, and the Kosovo peace negotiations were held in Rambouillet and Paris. Despite the appearance of importance, however, the French were ultimately unable to exercise significant influence over either set of negotiations as they were perceived as too biased by first the Bosnians and then the Kosovars, and they were also not entirely trusted by their American and British allies.

In a continuing effort to evaluate France's role in the failed international efforts to prevent the attempted genocide in Bosnia, and to seek to establish an accurate historical record, the French parliament opened an investigation in December 2000 into France's role in the fall of Srebrenica. At the hearing two Dutch officers (one was in Srebrenica during the Serb attack and the other was the chief of staff of the peacekeepers at the time) testified that in refusing to order air strikes against Bosnian Serb troops, French general Janvier allowed the 1995 Srebrenica massacre to be carried out unchallenged.[90] According to a *New York Times* report shortly after the massacre, a Dutch officer reported that he had told General Janvier, "We need F16's swooping down now." The general replied that he would sleep on it.[91] In fact, one source reports that General Janvier never had any intention of employing air strikes, and he had even prepared an explanation for the decision not to use air strikes the day before the fall of Srebrenica.[92] Developing an understanding of France's role in the Balkan conflict is particularly important for France, as it was a French General, general Morillon, who in 1993 had promised the residents of Srebrenica that he would keep them safe.[93]

Germany

The initial German response to the conflict was based on its semi-special relationship with Yugoslavia formed through extensive economic ties and Germany's desire to promote stability in Central and Eastern Europe. Germany was also initially keenly interested in promoting the success of a common European approach to resolving the conflict. Importantly, however, according to Michael Libal, "once the Yugoslav state began to disintegrate, Germany's indirect interests in the region spoke strongly in favor of a peacefully managed dissolution."[94] In particular, Germany sought a peaceful dissolution of Yugoslavia as it feared that a serious outbreak of hostilities would threaten German interests throughout Central and Eastern Europe, and would result in a tide of refugees flowing into Germany.[95] Given that Germany had no significant geographical buffer between it and the Balkans, it feared it would suffer these consequences to a greater degree than other West European states, in particular France and the United Kingdom.[96]

In the end, Germany's concerns proved valid as Europe's' engagement in Central and Eastern Europe was significantly delayed, and Germany became host to over 400,000 refugees. The expenditures on refugees assistance coupled with its humanitarian aid to the region amounted to approximately $10 billion. According to Michael Libal, Germany thus came to perceive Serbia as presenting a triple threat to European interests, encompassing "a war against the principles, the security interests, and the pocketbooks of the European states, not least Germany."[97]

Moreover, given Germany's role in the atrocities and genocide committed during World War II, Germany found itself responsive to the Yugoslav crisis and in particular the need to prevent the further commission of crimes against humanity on the European continent.[98] Germany was thus quick to support international efforts to mediate the conflict, with the preferred mediator being the European Union, and to resort to the threat of the use of force, with the preferred entity being NATO.[99] With Germany's economic and emerging political involvement in Central and Eastern Europe, Germany possessed a somewhat unique sense of the significance of the Yugoslav conflict for the European continent and reacted in a more serious and concerned manner than many of its European allies until well after the widespread scale of the atrocities became known. Germany also held a number of high hopes for the European Union and feared that the Yugoslav crisis, if handled poorly, would consume much of the political energy that would otherwise be devoted to the further development of the European Union—as was in fact the case.

In addition to the European Union, Germany was supportive of attempts to use the OSCE, which it chaired during the early stages of the conflict, as a means for mediating the dispute given that a number of the Central and East European states followed Germany's lead on certain foreign policy matters and thus its political weight would be enhanced.[100] Germany, however, generally disliked the idea of invoking the United Nations, as it exercised little control over United Nations mechanisms, and policymakers generally considered the United Nations bureaucracy to be significantly less competent than the European Union bureaucracy.

When Germany sensed the unwillingness and inability of the European Union to craft a coherent and aggressive approach to stopping the conflict, and when it came under intense domestic pressure,[101] Germany chose to engage in unilateral action in an attempt to move the European policy from one of coercive appeasement to constructive engagement.[102] The most prominent example of this was Germany's declaration in December 1991 that, by January 1992, it would recognize Croatian independence with or without the support/consent of the European Union. Germany, was however, slow to recognize the seriousness of the war rhetoric emanating from Belgrade, and it underestimated the extent of atrocities that would accompany the armed conflict.[103] Prime Minister Kohl was also "the first in European Community circles to speak of Serb aggression as the cause of the conflict, shifting the interpretation from that of a civil war to that of a war between sovereign states,"[104] and thus the first to interject the norm of justice into the process. Unfortunately, as noted by Alex Danchev, "the credibility of the German approach depended ultimately on the ability and willingness of the international community to use military force. Yet none of them, least of all Germany, was prepared to protect the new independent states by military means."[105]

The unilateralism of Germany resulted in significant criticism by Germany's European partners.[106] As explained by John Laughland,

> It was common knowledge that the French government was seething at having been forced into a corner by Germany, and policy-makers were adopting an anti-German stance with astonishing alacrity. The short-lived German stand in favour of Slovenia and Croatia only confirmed Mitterrand's suspicion that the Germans needed to be brought to heel by a unified European policy largely inspired and controlled by France.[107]

Accordingly, "from this point onwards, it is no exaggeration to say that a desire to contain Germany was a significant element in the elaboration of both French and British policy in Yugoslavia."[108] In fact, according to Alex Danchev, "[the EC mediators], the U.S. Secretary of State Warren Christopher and the French Foreign Minister Roland Dumas all held Genscher responsible for the widening warfare in the Balkans."[109]

As a result, German diplomatic efforts were sidelined and its European allies sought to increasingly rely upon mechanisms such as the Security Council wherein Germany was not represented.[110] Germany's allies also embarked on a propaganda campaign of sorts designed to erode any support in the United States or elsewhere for its interventionist policy. In particular they sought to promote the notion that German foreign policy was guided by a resurgence of its historical alliances and its desire to extend its hegemonic interests over Central and Eastern Europe as well as southeastern Europe.[111] As a result of the effective sidelining of Germany's diplomatic initiative, Germany played little role in the application of the norm of justice, and in fact the country provided only minimal support to the Tribunal throughout its existence.

Self-Identity and Self-Interest: The Institutional Response

The futures of both NATO and the United Nations depend on the outcome in Bosnia and Kosovo. Failure in either is unthinkable, since it would only pull us back into another protracted and costly mess.

—Richard Holbrooke, U.S. Ambassador
to the United Nations[112]

In addition to the states mentioned above, a number of international institutions played a key role in the development of a response to the Balkan conflict. The most important institutions were the European Union and the United Nations.

The European Union

The approach of the European Union was characterized by its desire to further cement cohesion within the union by demonstrating its ability to adeptly deal with foreign policy crises on the European continent.[113] The approach of the EU was also characterized by deep internal rivalries, a general lack of competence necessary to handle the Yugoslav crisis, and a pull toward moral equivalence.[114] On the whole, the policy that emerged from this set of circumstances was a policy of supporting a unified Yugoslavian state.

At the time of the Yugoslav crisis, the European Union was in the process of deepening the political and economic commitments of its members and expanding the authority of the European Commission. In particular, the European Union had recently adopted an initiative to establish a common foreign and security policy, and the Yugoslav conflict was seen as the first test of that initiative.[115] With the now infamous words of Luxembourg foreign minister Jacques Poos on 28 June 1991, "this is the hour of Europe. It is not the hour of the Americans,"[116] the European Union signaled its desire to replace the United States as the primary agent of political stability on the European continent. The EU was also seized with a touch of Euro-nationalism, which expressed itself in the following declaration by Jacques Delors, president of the European Community in 1991, "we do not interfere in American affairs, we trust America will not interfere in European affairs." The United States easily embraced this Euro-nationalism, with Secretary of State James Baker noting in his memoir, "It was time to make the Europeans step up to the plate and show that they could act as a unified power. Yugoslavia was as good a first test as any."[117]

As further explained by Mark Almond, in 1991 the European Union member states were preparing to sign the Maastricht Treaty, which set the foundation for a fully integrated Europe. The prospect of the dissolution of a state occurring while the Europeans were on the brink of the further integration of independent states caused serious cognitive dissonance and prevented them from adequately grasping the nature of the Yugoslav conflict.[118] Moreover, the member states of the EU feared that a crisis in Yugoslavia could derail their own efforts toward further integration. As a result, the president of the EC Council of Ministers, Jacques Santer, declared "we have to try all means to save the Yugoslav Federation at this moment," with John Major adding that "the great prize is to hold the federation together."[119]

After the outbreak of hostilities, the European Union generally supported plans for partition of Croatia and Bosnia, while rejecting calls for the use of force beyond traditional peacekeeping. The European Union representatives also sought to draw on the European Union's prestige and relative financial wealth to offer the parties to the conflict closer political relations with the European Union and economic incentives for parties willing to cooperate, such as access to the European Union market and financial assistance. [120]

The approach of the EU was thus heavily characterized by accommodation and economic inducement. For example, in 1991 the EU extended the hope of EU "association and possible membership to a *united* Yugoslavia, hoping that this 'carrot' would induce the presidents of the six Yugoslav republics to reach a peaceful agreement."[121] At the time, the EU also offered an aid package of nearly $1 billion.[122] When these efforts failed, the EU adopted economic sanctions.

The ability of the European Union to cope with the Yugoslav crisis and to adequately embrace the norm of justice was handicapped by the fact, that despite the goals and hopes of a common foreign and security policy, Europe was rife with national divisions. As explained by European historian Mark Almond, "The European Community remain[ed] bedeviled by national rivalries despite all the talk of common policies and a new united identity," and by a reliance on outdated political and historical perspectives. As a result, "the breakdown of Yugoslavia brought out deep-seated Anglo-French suspicions of Germany which were partly shared and partly played on by the Serbian regime. Just as British and French politicians revealed that in their heart of hearts they could not see Germany as anything other than in essence a domineering and aggressive nation, so they remained trapped with an inherited vision of 'plucky little Serbia,' the ancient ally against the *Boche*."[123]

As observed by former Secretary of State James Baker the ability of the EU to grapple with the crisis was hampered by the approach of unanimity, which required "rigid adherence to acting only when every EC member state was in agreement," and resulted in an approach that "caused both delays (as all members had to be polled for even the smallest decision) and lowest-common-denominator policies." The EU approach was further hampered by their "tendency to become prisoners of their own history, falling back on alliances that had been developed decades or even centuries before," and as such, "the parties in the region quickly learned to play the Europeans off against one another, effectively neutralizing the EC."[124]

The efforts of the European Union were further undermined by the unilateral behavior of some of its members, in particular Greece. For instance, on 9 February 1994, in response to the Sarajevo marketplace massacre, NATO indicated it was prepared to use air strikes if the civilian massacres did not cease. On 15 February, Greek foreign minister Carlos Papoulias traveled to Serbia to meet with Slobodan Milosevic, where he expressed Greece's significant reservations regarding any NATO action. At this time, Greece held the rotating presidency of the EU. According to a now declassified State Department cable, the Greek foreign minister and Milosevic publicly agreed that threats of air strikes were "damaging to the negotiating process because they encouraged the forces that dvocate the military option."[125]

The United Nations

Given the failure of the EU to adequately address the Yugoslav crisis, and France and the United Kingdom's desire to minimize Germany's influence, the United Nations became the international institution most involved in seeking a resolution of the conflict.[126] While the Security Council created the Tribunal, and voted for the deployment of UN peacekeepers, and the eventual use of force in Bosnia, the overall approach of the Security Council was one of accommodation and economic inducement,[127] with the approach of the Secretary-General and his designates being one of appeasement—as determined by a subsequent UN report, and one of anti-justice characterized by moral equivalence.[128]

While the United Nations is generally presumed to represent the views of its constituent members, in the case of the Yugoslav conflict, the UN Secretariat, under the leadership of Secretary-General Boutros Boutros-Ghali, possessed its own agenda, which differed from those of many of its members, and in particular from the Security Council.[129] This situation was augmented by the fact that Secretary-General Boutros Boutros-Ghali maintained a particularly acrimonious relationship with the U.S. Ambassador to the United Nations, and he held the U.S. role in the United Nations in low esteem.

The Secretariat of the United Nations perceived itself to be the custodians of the New World Order, which was not to be dominated by the only remaining superpower, as the United States believed, and balanced by the European Union, as the Western European states believed, but rather was to be guided and shaped by the United Nations. The Secretariat also eschewed the use of force, preferring a continuation of the United Nations's traditional peacekeeping mandate, with no extension into peace making or peace-enforcing.[130] Finally, it generally resented the focus on crises in Europe over Africa. Notably, while visiting besieged Sarajevo, the Secretary-General proclaimed that he could name at least ten places in Africa where the conditions were worse.[131]

The Secretary-General's approach was also deeply influenced by his preference for accommodation over all other approaches to peace-building.[132] In June 1995, one month prior to the Srebrenica massacre, he confided to *Washington Times* columnist Georgie Anne Geyer, "the result of the negotiations may not be equity, but it may be peace. Then you have a problem: what is more important, peace or peace at the expense of certain principles of equity? My theory is that what happens in a war is so terrible that peace is better, even if it is not a just peace."[133] He also predicted, "in six months, nobody would talk about Yugoslavia and they would continue killing themselves for years."[134] Thus, even when the Security Council adopted the statute for the Yugoslav Tribunal, the Secretariat supported its creation, but threw up unnecessary administrative obstacles to its quick establishment and its effective operation,[135] so that it would not interfere with the conduct of negotiations.

As a result of these perceptions, the Secretary-General persistently sought to limit the mandate of the UNPROFOR units serving in Bosnia and Croatia to use force, even after the Security Council had explicitly authorized the use of force.[136] The Secretary-General also sought to prevent states from using force outside of the

UNPROFOR framework after such force was approved by the Security Council.[137] In close cooperation with Boutros-Ghali, the Secretary-General's representative for Bosnia, Yasushi Akashi, consistently denied permission for NATO to use air strikes in response to gross violations of the UN protected safe areas, and Akashi sought to undermine the ability of NATO to effectively deter acts of violence by limiting which targets could be struck when NATO air strikes were employed.[138] As recounted by Georgie Anne Geyer "the UN representative in Bosnia, Yasushi Akashi, was stoically intent on not using force even in the face of European genocide." According to Akashi, use of force was not possible, because "we would be perceived as the enemy and that would endanger our carefully constructed relations with the parties. We are impartial; we are in a war, but we are not at war. Once we became a party to the war, we would have to liquidate our efforts—withdraw or cut down."[139]

The result of this approach was, according to Geyer, that the UN acted "with a rigid moral neutralism, a non-use of force, and a utopian idea that fanatics like the Serbs can be won over by rationality. With this mentality, the approach soon became devoid of any sense of justice or any element of truth." According to former Japanese UN ambassador Yoshio Hatano, as recounted by Geyer, "as a Japanese, Akashi may still retain some of the Japanese character, which places peace above justice." The ambassador noted that "in Japan, peace tends to equal justice. Because of Japan's experience in the last war, justice tends to be sacrificed." Mr. Akashi may also have been influenced by his desire to engage Japanese forces in UN peacekeeping operations and the recognition that this hope would be dashed if UN forces became involved in the direct use of force in Bosnia.[140]

As a consequence, when NATO did finally employ air strikes, in the spring of 1995, the UN did not redeploy its peacekeepers. In fact a number of UNPROFOR troops remained in Serb headquarters during the air campaign, as according to Akashi, "they had to be there," as "they were [the] liaison with the Serbs, . . . " and "for reassurance to the Serbs and for keeping channels of communication."[141] They, of course, became hostages. In the end, according to Michael Sells, "by focusing the UN mission on the supply of humanitarian aid while refusing to stop the campaign of genocide, the UN Security Council created a system that put UN peacekeepers as suppliers of humanitarian aid to Bosnia—as hostages." In his view, "whether or not they were actually detained by radical Serb militias was not important. They could be detained at will and thus served as hostages whether or not they were confined." Serbian forces were thus able to "violate with impunity dozens of UN resolutions demanding free flow of humanitarian aid, liberation of concentration camps, access to camps by war crimes investigators, and protection of civilians."[142]

The meaningful use of force was further undermined by the efforts of the UN and EU negotiators as well as the early UNPROFOR commanders to create and maintain a perception of moral equivalence between the victims and the aggressors.[143] As recounted by Peter Maass, in his memoir, the first Canadian commander of UNPROFOR, General MacKenzie told French president Francois Mitterrand, 'there is strong but circumstantial evidence that some really horrifying acts of cruelty attributed to the Serbs were actually orchestrated by the

Muslims against their own people, for the benefit of an international audience."
According to Maass, MacKenzie has since softened this assertion, but he continues to claim "there is more than enough blame to go around for all sides, with some left over."[144] After the conflict, General MacKenzie is reported to have been retained by SerbNet, a Serbian lobby, and paid $10,000 per public speech.[145]

As a consequence of this approach, as noted by one Scandinavian UNPROFOR soldier, "this is a ridiculous war, none of us can figure out why in God's name we're here. In our area, we hear shooting all the time, but we are forbidden—get that, forbidden!—to know who is shooting. UN rules!"[146] The coercive appeasement employed by UNPROFOR led to deadly consequences. As recounted by Michael Sells, on 8 January 1993, "a French contingent of UN peacekeepers was escorting the Bosnian Deputy Prime Minister, Dr. Hakija Turajlic, into Sarajevo. They were stopped at a Serb army checkpoint. When the Serb soldiers asked the French peacekeepers to open up the armored car—against their orders and with the certain knowledge of what would follow—they complied, then stood aside and watched as a Serb soldier shot the unarmed Dr. Turajlic dead. When the same French peacekeepers came home to France, they were decorated for heroism."[147]

Such action led to convoluted attempts of UNPROFOR forces to justify their action. For instance when the UN commander General Rose refused to protect the UN safe area of Gorazde in the spring of 1994 from Serbian attacks, he declared that he had not been authorized to "protect" the safe area, only to "deter" attacks on it. Yet it was Rose who had refused to use a credible threat of NATO air strikes to deter the Serb army from violating the enclave in the first place.[148] Earlier, in the autumn of 1993 General Rose and French General Bertrand de Lapresle responded to the Serbian aerial bombardment of the Bihac safe zone by limiting NATO air strikes to the runway from which the planes were being launched, despite the presence of planes in nearby hangars. Moreover, it has been reported that, during the same period of time, the SAS forces "were supposed to give NATO coordinates for the air strikes against Serb artillery and anti-aircraft batteries, but they deliberately held back the coordinates or gave false coordinates to thwart the effectiveness of any NATO strikes."[149]

It is important to note that not all UNPROFOR commanders fit this mold, and that in particular, British lieutenant general Rupert Smith "and many UN officials in besieged Sarajevo believed that the Bosnian Serbs needed to be confronted by force. As long as they were allowed to block UN supply convoys, shell UN safe areas and storm UN observation posts, the Bosnian Serbs would only be emboldened and their behavior worsen." Unfortunately, such officers were often perceived as tainted in their views by more senior UN officials and were referred to as "in 'le milieux Bosnjak' or in the Bosnian Muslim world in Sarajevo and therefore couldn't see the war from the proper perspective." According to David Rohde, "the difference was that Smith saw the Serbs as abusing their advantage in firepower and had to be challenged. Janvier, on the other hand, viewed the Muslims as abusing the safe areas to draw the UN into fighting the war for them."[150]

The approach of the UN eventually culminated in a passive UNPROFOR response in the face of the Srebrenica massacre. In fact, according to David Rohde, "later that day [12 July 1995, the commencement of the fall of Srebrenica], Akashi would send a cable and a sample letter to the UN in New York criticizing the French Security Council resolution calling for the UN to use force to retake the safe area [Srebrenica]. Akashi said the resolution raised 'unrealistic expectations' and it 'blurs the lines between neutral 'peacekeeping' and taking sides or 'peace enforcement.'"[151] As a result, the UN was replaced by NATO and the United States as the primary institutions responsible for bringing an end to the conflict.[152]

Journalistic and Scholarly Commentary: Mere Punditry or Disproportionate Influence?

While not traditionally imbued with the power and authority of states and international organizations, in the context of the Yugoslavian crisis journalists and scholarly commentators contributed significantly to the political decision-making process concerning applicable approaches. As noted above, the role of Roy Gutman and Penny Marshall in discovering and reporting on Serbian-run concentration camps was pivotal in creating public pressure on the American and European policymakers to reconsider their early approach of accommodation. In the age of CNN twenty-four-hour global news, the public often had access to as much real-time information as states and international organizations.[153] Given the highly complex nature of the crisis, there was significant opportunity for a diverse collection of journalists and scholars to influence the process, including radio, television and print journalists, historians, social scientists, legal scholars, and foreign policy analysts.

A number of key journalists were instrumental in overcoming the artificial constraints of "balance" and "self-censorship" to promote an awareness of the extent of the atrocities and the genocidal nature of the conflict—and were often relied upon by states and international organizations as primary sources of information.[154] While some criticized the "biased" nature of the press when reporting on atrocities, many journalists adopted the view of David Reiff, who noted, "it is said that the press corps became too involved with what was going on in Bosnia, that it should have remained more dispassionate. There is some truth in this. It is hard to be dispassionate about ethnic cleansing and mass murder."[155] Among the key journalists covering the crisis for the major media were Christiane Amanpour of CNN, Tom Gjelten of NPR,[156] Roy Gutman of *Newsday*, Ed Vulliamy of the *Guardian*, Elizabeth Neuffer of the *Boston Globe*, Janine di Giovanni of the *Sunday Times*,[157] Jonathan Landay of the *Christian Science Monitor*, Barbara Demick of the *Philadelphia Inquirer*,[158] and Yves Heller of *Le Monde*.[159] The reporting of local journalists, such as Kemal Kurspahić, was also important in this regard.[160] After the signature of the Dayton Accords and at the crucial time when the efforts to apply the norm of justice were hampered by claims by SFOR and others that it was impossible to locate any of the indicted war criminals, it was fashionable for journalists to personally interview indicted war criminals living near SFOR bases.[161]

Several historians and political scientists such as Norman Cigar,[162] Noel Malcolm,[163] Robert Donia, and John Fine Jr.[164] played a crucial role in accurately explaining the historical circumstances relevant to the conflict and accurately identifying the objectives of the Croatian and Serbian regimes. Other historians and political scientists, by design or inadequate research, perpetuated many of the superficial assessments concerning "ancient ethnic hatreds" and "tribalism" that supported an approach of moral equivalence, accommodation and the minimization of justice,[165] which were absorbed into the foreign policy decision-making process.

A number of legal scholars contributed to the development and application of the norm of justice by arguing for its incorporation into the peace process and by providing direct assistance to the mechanisms created during the peace process to promote justice. Most notable of these scholar-practitioners were Cherif Bassiouni[166] and Ted Meron.[167]

Unfortunately, a significant amount of commentary regarding the Yugoslav conflict was produced in the journalistic and scholarly tradition of "objective indifference" which frequently incorporated Serbian initiated propaganda,[168] inadvertently legitimized the campaigns of ethnic cleansing,[169] often clouded the perspective of policymakers relying on those works, and contributed to what could be called an epidemic of moral equivalence.[170] Other writings, which earnestly reflected social science analysis, sometimes were arguably technically accurate, but were relied upon by proponents of inaction or supporters of the Serbian and Croatian campaigns to undermine effective Western action.[171] Less rigorous social science,[172] military,[173] and journalistic commentary[174] wittingly and unwittingly republished propaganda produced in Belgrade.[175] Finally, a number of works were published which intentionally sought to justify the actions of the Serbian[176] and Croatian[177] governing regimes and consequently legitimize their campaigns of ethnic cleansing.

A typical example of the progress of Serbian propaganda through the scholarly and academic community can be found with the two Sarajevo marketplace massacres on 5 February 1994 and 28 August 1995. According to now declassified State Department cables, in response to these massacres, which were deemed by UN experts to have been carried out by the Serbian forces laying siege to Sarajevo, Belgrade undertook an aggressive campaign of propaganda to persuade the Serbian people and the international community that the Bosnian government had in fact shelled its own people or set off mines in the marketplace.[178] The American Serb lobby then began to issue press releases repeating this propaganda and making the more general claim that the Bosnians themselves had undertaken a propaganda campaign to convince the international community that they were the victims of genocide—complete with staged massacres.[179] These claims then found their way into a full-length commentary in *The Nation*.[180]

Although the initial and primary approach of the peace builders was accommodation, the nature of the atrocities committed, the accompanying public outcry, and the interests of some of the primary peace builders to promote a new world order based on justice compelled the peace builders to employ the approach of accountability. Reluctant to fully embrace accountability, the peace builders only gradually developed the institutions necessary for its full application to the peace-building process. Similarly, as many of the influential peace builders were uncertain of the effect of the norm of justice on the peace process, or were outrightly hostile to its application, they sought to quietly undermine the effective development and operation of the institutions necessary to incorporate the norm of justice into the peace-building process. The next chapter will detail the events surrounding the creation of the Yugoslav War Crimes Commission and the Yugoslav Tribunal and will examine the perceived value of these institutions for the peace-building process as well as the efforts of various states to support or undermine this justice-based venture.

Part III

Creating and Employing Justice-Based Institutions during the Initial Phase of the Peace-Building Process

Chapter 6

Establishing the Yugoslav War Crimes Commission and Yugoslav Tribunal: A Judicial Placebo

The Tribunal represents a chance not only for Bosnia but for the world. We can presume to forget what only God and the victims have standing to forgive, or we can heed the most searing lesson of this century, which is that evil—when unopposed—will spawn more evil.

—Madeleine Albright, U.S. Secretary of State[1]

Justice was held out, in reality, as an alternative to real immediate measures to confront the crime or the criminals.

—Mohamed Sacirbey, Ambassador of Bosnia-Herzegovina to the United Nations[2]

The decision to apply the norm of justice and an approach of accountability during the Yugoslav crisis was in large part a response to the initial failure of other approaches, notably appeasement (the doomed Vance/Owen peace process), economic and diplomatic inducements (in the form of watered-down Security Council-imposed sanctions), and use of force (the deployment of too few UN peacekeepers with too weak a mandate, and the reluctance to institute a policy of air strikes or commit combat troops). With daily reports of Balkan brutalities and massacres in the news, there was growing public pressure on the governments of the permanent members of the Security Council to be seen as doing something to respond to the unfolding humanitarian catastrophe.

The story of the establishment of the Yugoslav War Crimes Commission in October 1992, and the Yugoslav War Crimes Tribunal seven months later, suggests that the members of the Security Council embraced the norm of justice mainly as a public relations device, while giving breathing room for the other approaches of peace-building to succeed.³ There was little expectation that the approach of accountability would succeed where the other approaches had failed. Indeed, some of the members of the Security Council saw the various approaches as fundamentally incompatible, and they would work behind the scenes to undermine the institutions of justice. Other members saw the institutions of justice as useful, not in accomplishing justice, but in achieving other goals, such as isolating offending leaders and marshaling support for more aggressive responses.

Despite low expectations for the norm of justice, as this chapter illustrates, once established, institutions of justice may take on a life of their own—in ways their founders might not have fully anticipated. Once the War Crimes Commission reported that grave breaches of the Geneva convention and the crime of genocide had been committed, there was intense momentum for prosecution of offenders; once the Yugoslav Tribunal was created, there was pressure to adequately staff and finance it; and once indictments were issued by the Office of the Prosecutor, there was pressure for governments to employ force or further economic inducements to ensure that such persons could be brought to trial.

In telling the political story of the creation of the War Crimes Commission and the Yugoslav Tribunal this chapter seeks to answer the third, fourth, fifth, and sixth questions set out in chapter 1, in particular the extent to which the competing interests of peace builders influenced the selection of approaches, the effect of existing institutions and regimes on the ability of the peace builders to employ various approaches, the desire and ability of peace builders to create additional regimes, and the extent to which preexisting rules and norms facilitated the creation of mechanisms of justice.

To structure this discussion, this chapter examines the circumstances giving rise to the creation of the War Crimes Commission, the events leading to the decision to create the Yugoslav Tribunal, the extent to which existing international law facilitated the institutionalization of the Tribunal, the political interests influencing the selection of the first prosecutor, and the dynamics of arranging a stable source of funding for the Tribunal.

Preliminary Efforts to Institutionalize the Norm of Justice through the Establishment of the Yugoslav War Crimes Commission

The only crime that has not been committed in the case of Bosnia and Herzegovina is that which in another place and another time Bertrand Russell called the crime of silence.

—Representative of Spain to the UN Security Council⁴

There were those who believed that the top priority of the Security Council is to achieve a political settlement [to the Yugoslav conflict], and that everything that impedes this goal should be really checked. They were fearful of the Commission.

—Cherif Bassiouni, chairman of the Yugoslav
War Crimes Commission[5]

For the first full year of the conflict, the efforts of the peace builders were dominated by the approach of accommodation. This approach was so predominate that, in order to perpetuate the circumstances of moral equivalence, the British, upon the recommendation of Mr. Milosevic's diplomats, persuaded the UN Security Council to impose an arms embargo on all the parties to the conflict. From 1991 to 1992 as the accounts of atrocities began to emerge from the former Yugoslavia, and as the culpability of Serbian forces became more clear, the peace builders came under increasing pressure to augment their approach of accommodation with other approaches.

In light of the perceived failure of the European powers to end the conflict through accommodation, and coming under mounting public criticism for its inactivity and its own failed approach of deferring to its European allies, the United States sought to invoke the norm of justice and called for the UN Security Council to declare that those responsible for war crimes would be punished. As a result of American and French efforts to add the norm of justice to the tools of the peace builders, on 13 July 1992, the Security Council adopted Resolution 764 in which it stated that persons who commit violations of "international humanitarian law" in the former Yugoslavia will be held individually responsible.

Given the nonimpact of this resolution, and the apparent failure of its other actions to yield any result, the United States came under increasing public pressure to have the Security Council authorize the use of force. In light of the United States unwillingness to participate in military action, and strong criticism of the point person for U.S. policy—Deputy Secretary of State Lawrence Eagleburger—for his close ties to Serbia and to Mr. Milosevic and his apparent over-accommodation of Serbian ethnic aggression, the United States found itself in a position in which it needed to be seen as taking action, but action short of military force.[6] The United States thus settled on the further application of the norm of justice in the form of an investigative commission. The idea of a commission, and/or a tribunal, originated with a number of human rights organizations, in particular Human Rights Watch, and was intended to establish an historic record of the atrocities and lay the foundation for holding those who did not heed the Security Council's warning accountable for their misdeeds. The Department of State was particularly attracted to the idea of a commission as it harbored a deep distrust of international tribunals and opposed the creation of a permanent international criminal court. Moreover, the State Department viewed a commission as an entity whose existence could be terminated in the event there appeared to be a peace settlement emerging, whereas a Yugoslav tribunal would likely become an entity capable of taking independent actions.[7]

Under United States pressure, on 13 August 1992, the Security Council adopted Resolution 771, which called upon states and international humanitarian organizations to submit to the Council "substantiated information" in their possession concerning war crimes in the former Yugoslavia. Two months later, the Security Council unanimously adopted Resolution 780, which established an impartial commission of experts to assess the information submitted pursuant to Resolution 771, as well as information obtained as a result of its own field investigations.

During the negotiation of Resolution 780, the United Kingdom, believing that the pursuit of war criminals might damage prospects for a peace settlement under the Vance/Owen framework, made no secret of its preference that the commission be limited to a passive group that would merely analyze and collate information that was passed to them.[8] The British government reluctantly agreed to the commission's investigative authority only after high-level interventions by U.S. officials. However, the United Kingdom managed to undermine this authority by insisting that the commission be funded from existing UN resources rather than include in the resolution a specific budget for the commission. The United States found it hard to object, having insisted for years on a "zero-growth" UN budget. As a consequence, it took over a year for the commission to obtain sufficient funding to conduct investigations in the field. All the while, evidence was being destroyed, witnesses were dispersing, and memories were fading.

Handicapped by its scant budget, the War Crimes Commission devoted its first months to producing an analysis of the law applicable to the atrocities occurring in the former Yugoslavia, which it presented in the form of an interim report to the Secretary-General in February 1993. The War Crimes Commission's interim report defined the relatively new term of "ethnic cleansing" in the context of the Yugoslav conflict as "rendering an area wholly homogeneous by using force or intimidation to remove persons of given groups from the area." Based on the submissions of governments and international organizations, the commission determined that ethnic cleansing had been carried out in the former Yugoslavia "by means of murder, torture, arbitrary arrest and detention, extrajudicial executions, rape and sexual assault, confinement of civilians in ghetto areas, forcible removal, displacement and deportation of civilians, deliberate military attacks or threats of attacks on civilians and civilian areas, and wanton destruction of property."[9] The commission concluded that the policy and practices of ethnic cleansing constituted crimes against humanity, grave breaches of the Geneva conventions, and the crime of genocide. On the basis of these conclusions, the commission recommended that the United Nations set up a war crimes tribunal to prosecute the perpetrators of these international crimes.

In September 1993, the chairman of the War Crimes Commission, Fritz Kalshoven, resigned his post to protest the failure of the United Nations and individual governments to provide the commission with the resources necessary to fulfill its mandate. Kalshoven's resignation was taken as confirmation that the commission would amount to nothing more than a "toothless study," in the words of the *New York Times*.[10] Two weeks later, the vice chairman of the commission, Torkel Opsahl, died of a heart attack in his Geneva office, prompting an international headline that read, "UN War Crimes Body in Disarray on Anniversary."[11] To the surprise of many, the resulting personnel changes transformed the commission into a more vigorous entity under the leadership of its new chairman, the energetic and resourceful Cherif Bassiouni, an Egyptian born professor of law at DePaul University in Chicago.

With a voluntary staff of fifty attorneys and law students and $800,000 in grants obtained from the Soros Foundation, the Open Society Fund, and the John D. and Catherine T. MacArthur Foundation, Bassiouni set about creating the commission's documentation center and database at DePaul University's International Human Rights Law Institute.[12] By April 1994, the documentation center had systematically catalogued and analyzed over 64,000 documents and had created a computerized archive of over 300 hours of videotapes containing testimonies of individuals as well as footage capturing the carnage of the Yugoslav conflict.[13]

Subsequently, thirteen governments contributed a total of $1,320,631 to the commission's voluntary trust fund, enabling the commission to undertake thirty-four field investigations in Bosnia and Croatia under the direction of Commissioner William Fenrick of Canada. Commissioner Christine Cleiren of the Netherlands took on the task of organizing an investigation into rape and sexual assault. Under her direction, a forty member all-female team of attorneys, mental health specialists, and interpreters interviewed 223 women in seven cities in Bosnia and Croatia who had been victims of or witnesses to rape.[14] Commissioner Hanne Sophie Greve of Norway conducted an in-depth investigation into the ethnic cleansing of the Prijedor region of Bosnia. From some 400 interviews of witnesses to the destruction there, Greve was able to document how the Serbs in Prijedor had carefully prepared their campaign before Bosnia declared independence on 6 April 1992. At the end of April 1994, the commission submitted its final report, totaling eighty-four pages, along with twenty-two annexes containing 3,300 pages of detailed information and analysis.[15]

As detailed below, the commission's interim report generated significant momentum toward the establishment of an international war crimes tribunal for the former Yugoslavia. In addition, its final report was especially important in that it "revealed the large picture—the connection between Belgrade and the Bosnian Serb policy and tactics of ethnic cleansing in Bosnia."[16] Commissioner Fenrick ended up becoming the legal adviser to the international prosecutor, and Commissioner Greve was called on as an expert witness in the Tribunal's first trial in 1996.

Much of the commission's documentation, however, ended up unopened and unused in a Tribunal storage closet. Staff of the Office of the Prosecutor have put forward a number of possible explanations for this apparent lack of diligence—none of which are entirely convincing. First, it is alleged that the commission did not approach its mission in a prosecutorial fashion and therefore little attention was paid to issues of chain of custody or reliability of sources. The staff of the Prosecutor's Office thus believed that they should independently develop their own evidence for use at trial. Second, once the Office of the Prosecutor was established, its staff of professional investigators felt that they had to prove themselves and were disinclined to rely on the work of other bodies. Finally, because of persistent funding difficulties, the Office of the Prosecutor lacked the personnel to carefully sift through the materials collected by the commission and other international bodies.[17] Regardless of the reason, the failure to make use of the material provided by the Bassiouni Commission likely contributed to the Office of the Prosecutor's inability to link Slobodan Milosevic to the atrocities committed by the Bosnian Serb forces, and as such the Yugoslav leader remained unindicted for his role in the Bosnian atrocities until 22 November 2001.

Taking the Next Step: Creating the Yugoslav Tribunal

Some assert outright that the creation of the Tribunal reflects the incapacity of the international community to deal with the tragic conflict raging in the former Yugoslavia. [For them] the judicial solution has been adopted for want of a better one, as an "ersatz" for the political solution; the establishment of the Tribunal is thus viewed as no more than a sign of weakness, if not hypocrisy, on the part of the United Nations.

—Antonio Cassese,
Chief Judge of the Yugoslav Tribunal[18]

The published work of the War Crimes Commission created the distinct impression that, in their pursuit of accommodation, the peace builders had minimized the nature of the atrocities being committed and had marginalized notions of justice in order to reach some sort of peace agreement. The work of the War Crimes Commission, and the failure to reach any agreement, highlighted the inadequacy of the approach of accommodation in a conflict marked by acts of genocide. As a result, the commission members, and to an increasing degree the international media, began to call for the creation of an international criminal tribunal. These efforts were obstructed to the extent possible by those peace builders, in particular the British government, at the behest of David Owen and Cyrus Vance, who were interested in pursuing an undiluted approach of accommodation.

Because Resolution 780 contained no reference to the creation of an international criminal tribunal, but rather a provision requesting the Secretary-General to take account of the commission's conclusions and "make recommendations for further appropriate steps," the creation of the Tribunal was not as straightforward or automatic as those arguing for an enhanced role for justice might have desired.

Some of the members of the Security Council hoped the War Crimes Commission's work would eventually lead to domestic trials in the former Yugoslavia. For instance, in the case of Ethiopia, the international community provided funding, attorneys, and judges to facilitate the prosecution of some 3,000 officials of the fallen Mengistu regime.[19] But in the absence of radical changes in the governing regimes of Serbia, Bosnia, and Croatia, there was little likelihood that the Balkan states would diligently prosecute their own citizens or fairly prosecute the citizens of the other Balkan states for war crimes. While states which were not party to the conflict could potentially prosecute Balkan war crimes under what is known as "universal jurisdiction," it would be difficult for them to obtain custody over offenders or access to evidence. Thus, national prosecutions did not present an answer to the Balkan conundrum.

Other members of the Security Council favored less invasive accountability mechanisms such as monetary compensation for the victims and their families, the establishment of a truth commission to identify perpetrators by name, and implementation of employment bans and purges (referred to as "lustration") that would keep such perpetrators from positions of public trust.[20] The main argument for noncriminal measures was that they could achieve much of what prosecution seeks to accomplish, such as reparation, documentation, and punishment, without jeopardizing the peace process. Since none of the members of the Council supported a major military intervention in Yugoslavia as in Iraq, the cooperation of the leaders of the various parties to the conflict would be needed to put an end to the fighting and the violations of international humanitarian law. In their view it would not be realistic to expect the Yugoslav leaders to agree to a peace settlement if they knew that following the agreement they would find themselves or their close associates facing potential life imprisonment.

As noted above, historically, amnesty or de facto immunity from prosecution has often been the price for peace. While an amnesty deal may have hastened an end to the Yugoslav conflict, there were several countervailing interests that favored prosecution. First, the members of the Security Council, as parties to the Geneva conventions[21] and the Genocide Convention,[22] may have been under a legal obligation to prosecute. Despite U.S. efforts to characterize the conflict as a civil war and to avoid the genocide label, this obligation was arguably triggered when the War Crimes Commission issued its preliminary report, concluding that the atrocities in Yugoslavia could be characterized as grave breaches of the Geneva conventions and genocide.[23]

Each of the Geneva conventions of 1949 contains a specific enumeration of "grave breaches," which are war crimes committed in international armed conflicts for which there is individual criminal liability and for which states have a corresponding duty to prosecute.[24] Parties to the Geneva conventions have an obligation to search for, prosecute, and punish perpetrators of grave breaches of the Geneva conventions unless they choose to hand over such persons for trial by another state party.[25] The commentary to the Geneva conventions, which is the official history of the negotiations leading to the adoption of these treaties, confirms that the obligation to prosecute is "absolute," meaning that states parties can under no circumstances grant perpetrators immunity or amnesty from prosecution for grave breaches of the conventions.[26]

Like the Geneva conventions, the Genocide Convention provides an absolute obligation to prosecute persons responsible for genocide.[27] Moreover, the Genocide Convention grants each of its parties the right to bring an International Court of Justice case against any other party where there is a dispute as to the interpretation or application of the convention.[28] Thus, had an amnesty for peace deal been pursued, the members of the Security Council could have found themselves in the awkward position of defending their actions before the World Court.

In addition to this potential legal problem, there are several practical reasons why an amnesty for peace deal would not have made sense under the circumstances. Failure to prosecute genocidal crimes in the Balkans would have served as a virtual license to repeat the crimes.[29] At the same time, Bosniacs who had suffered at the hands of the Serbs might seek personal revenge if no effort was made to bring those responsible for their suffering to justice. Moreover, where the United Nations gives its imprimatur to an amnesty for crimes of this magnitude there is a risk that regimes in other parts of the world will be further encouraged to engage in systematic brutalities to achieve nationalist objectives.

Thus, in the conclusion of its preliminary report submitted in February 1993, the War Crimes Commission joined a growing international chorus publicly calling for the creation of a Nuremberg-like tribunal to try persons believed to be responsible for atrocities in the former Yugoslavia.[30] U.S. bureaucrats, who had long been opposing the UN effort to establish a permanent international criminal court,[31] were initially reluctant to support the idea of an ad hoc war crimes tribunal for the Balkans. But in his last days in office in December of 1992, Secretary of State Lawrence Eagleburger announced that the United States had identified ten suspected war criminals, including Slobodan Milosevic, who should be brought to trial before a modern day Nuremberg Tribunal.[32] This became known in government circles as the "naming names speech." Eagleburger told the press the speech had been prompted by his recent meeting with Eli Wiesel, the noted author who survived the Nazi death camps. "He persuaded me that these people needed to be named and that this conduct could not go on," Eagleburger said. "It was my last opportunity to do it and I did it on my own."[33] Eagleburger was also apparently motivated by the fact that President Bush, who was due to leave office in January 1993, had already taken the extraordinary step of committing ground troops to Somalia, and it was nearly impossible that troops would also then be sent to Bosnia, and he desired to be seen as "doing something" about the atrocities.[34]

Sensing momentum toward the creation of a tribunal and wanting to be perceived as leading the charge, two months later, France circulated a draft Security Council resolution in New York calling for the creation of a Yugoslavia war crimes tribunal, together with a report prepared by a committee of French jurists containing a detailed analysis of the legal issues involved in the endeavor.[35] The French draft Security Council resolution proposed an innovative two-step approach to the establishment of a Yugoslavia war crimes tribunal, under which the Security Council would initially commit itself to the establishment of such a tribunal, and later approve the statute for the Tribunal.

On 22 February 1993, the Security Council adopted Resolution 808 in which it decided in principle to establish an international tribunal "for the prosecution of persons responsible for serious violations of international humanitarian law committed in the territory of the former Yugoslavia since 1991."[36] At the time of the vote on the resolution, four of the permanent members of the Security Council delivered stirring remarks endorsing the concept of an international judicial solution to the Balkan crisis. The fifth permanent member, China, merely reserved its position on the matter. The delegate of France, the primary sponsor of the resolution, stated:

> Prosecuting the guilty is necessary if we are to do justice to the victims and to the international community. Prosecuting the guilty will also send a clear message to those who continue to commit these crimes that they will be held responsible for their acts. And finally, prosecuting the guilty is, for the United Nations and particularly for the Security Council, a matter of doing their duty to maintain and restore peace.

The U.K. representative remarked:

> There has been an outburst of anger at these shocking developments. All parties share responsibility for these breaches. We believe that the Serbs have been most culpable in these hideous practices, but we also believe that all such actions must be condemned; they must be investigated; and the perpetrators must be called to account, whoever is responsible, throughout the territory of the former Yugoslavia.

According to the U.S. representative:

> This will be no victor's tribunal. The only victor that will prevail in this endeavor is the truth. . . . The events in the former Yugoslavia raise the questions of whether a State may address the rights of its minorities by eradicating those minorities to achieve ethnic purity. Bold tyrants and fearful minorities are watching to see whether ethnic cleansing is a policy the world will tolerate. If we hope to promote the spread of freedom, or if we hope to encourage the emergence of peaceful, multiethnic democracies, our answers must be a resounding "no."

The Russian representative expressed similar sentiments:

> [Today's] Resolution should serve the purpose of bringing to their senses those who are ready to sacrifice for the sake of their political ambitions the lives and dignity of hundreds and thousands of totally innocent people. Nor should we forget that violations of international humanitarian law are also taking place in the course of other armed conflicts. We believe the Council's adoption of today's resolution will also serve as a serious warning to those guilty of mass crimes and flagrant violations of human rights in other parts of the world.

As indicated through their public remarks, the permanent members of the Security Council invoked the traditional roles of justice, including justice for the victims, establishing accountability for individual perpetrators, deterrence of further atrocities in the former Yugoslavia, restoration of peace, the establishment of an accurate historic record for a conflict in which distortion of the truth has been an essential ingredient of the ethnic violence, and deterrence of atrocities elsewhere. In light of these and other remarks, Payam Akhvan of the staff of the International Tribunal contends that "the deliberations of the Security Council indicate that the complementarity of peace and justice was considered and accepted by virtually all member states."[37]

Other commentators, however, have maintained that "nothing could be further from the truth than to say that there was a consensus on the compatibility between peace and legal justice."[38] There was widespread belief that questionable motives lurked behind the Security Council's articulated rationales for the Tribunal. Several commentators argued the Council's justifications were merely a pretense, calculated to mask the reluctance of the Western powers to take resolute action to repress the policy of ethnic cleansing.[39] Others believed the Tribunal would be used as a "bargaining chip," to be bartered away at the negotiating table.[40]

Professor David Forsyth of the University of Nebraska wrote that, for the United States, the creation of the Tribunal was an instrument for pacifying critics that would generate "the appearance of action against gross violations of human rights, but without great sacrifice of outsiders' blood or treasure." [41] In fact, Richard Holbrooke expressly acknowledged that when it was created, the Tribunal was widely perceived in the U.S. government as little more than a public relations device.[42] In addition to the public relations benefit, the United States recognized that even without bringing a single perpetrator to trial, an international indictment and arrest warrant could serve to isolate offending leaders diplomatically, strengthen the hand of domestic rivals, and fortify the international political will to expand economic sanctions or approve air strikes.[43]

At the time the Security Council adopted the statute for the Yugoslav Tribunal, the peace builders had undertaken extensive efforts to accommodate/appease the aggressor parties through the UN/EU mediation process, had employed economic inducements through the strongest package of economic sanctions adopted against any state, and had declined to authorize the use of force or even to lift the arms embargo against the Bosnian government. With the failure of these approaches readily apparent and the subject of extensive media attention and withering criticism, the peace builders found themselves in a situation where they were required to take some action, any action, to demonstrate that they were engaged in seeking a solution to the crisis. The creation of a tribunal readily served that purpose.[44]

Despite the need to be seen as taking action, some members of the Security Council continued to harbor doubts as to the utility of the Tribunal. According to Forsyth, the United Kingdom considered the Tribunal an impediment to a negotiated peace, but "knew that opposing criminal prosecution could be politically awkward" and therefore played a "double diplomatic game of public endorsement but private opposition." [45] China and Russia, he suggests, were opposed to the creation of the Tribunal but "for reasons of deference to a hegemonic U.S., or to deflect criticism from their own human rights record chose not to vigorously contest an ad hoc court" of limited jurisdiction.[46]

In the end, some commentators have concluded that, "however landmark in [its] breadth, not only was the promulgation of the Yugoslav Tribunal Statute painfully slow, but [it] effectively served as little more than [a] topical antiseptic in the treatment of the malignancy of genocide." [47] The test of whether in fact the international community genuinely intended to actively rely upon the norm of justice to combat genocide and build peace in the former Yugoslavia would be in how aggressively the Security Council and other member states of the United Nations sought to build the institution provided for in Security Council Resolution 808. Would the Tribunal be designed to be nothing more than a paper tiger—a so-called Potemkin Court? Or would the Security Council build in teeth and provide the necessary support for an effective judicial institution? The next three sections address these questions in terms of the Tribunal's institutional framework. Specifically, they examine whether the Tribunal was given the authority, structure, qualified personnel, and financial resources necessary to effectively accomplish its mission.

The Keystone for the Foundation of the Yugoslav Tribunal: The Regime of International Humanitarian Law

The United Nations, which over the years has accumulated an impressive corpus of international standards enjoining States and Individuals to conduct themselves humanely, has now set up an institution to put those standards to the test, to transform them into living reality. A whole body of lofty, if remote, United Nations ideals will be brought to bear upon human beings. Through the Tribunal, those imperatives will be turned from abstract tenets into inescapable commands.

—First Annual Report of the Yugoslav Tribunal[48]

The first step in establishing the Yugoslavia War Crimes Tribunal was drafting its statute. Preexisting international law concerning the commission of war crimes and acts of genocide played a crucial role in promoting the application of the norm of justice in the peace-building process in enabling the relatively quick creation of a statute and by properly limiting the jurisdiction of the Tribunal. Importantly, the regime of international law is not self-executing, but rather is given effect through the actions of states or institutions. The entity charged with drawing upon international law to create the Tribunal's statute would thus exercise determinative control over how effectively it was utilized to promote the functionality of the norm of justice within the peace-building process.

In accordance with Security Council Resolution 808, the responsibility for drafting the statute was given to the United Nations Office of Legal Affairs. The decision to delegate the responsibility for drafting the Tribunal's statute to the Legal Office had the advantage of expediting the process, but in another instance of process influencing outcomes, it also diminished the ability of individual governments to shape the statute to their liking.

The UN Legal Office decided that the Tribunal would be established by a Chapter VII decision of the Security Council approving the Tribunal's statute, rather than ratification of a charter by states. This would ensure the Tribunal's swift creation and require all states to comply with its orders. Modeled loosely on the Nuremberg Charter, the UN Legal Office's proposed statute provided for criminal liability of persons who planned, instigated, ordered, committed, or otherwise aided and abetted in violations of international humanitarian law in the territory of the former Yugoslavia. It expressly incorporated the theory of command responsibility and banned the obedience to orders defense.

The Legal Office decided to pursue a more conservative approach to the enumeration of the Tribunal's subject matter jurisdiction than would likely have resulted from a negotiated text, confining the Tribunal's jurisdiction to crimes that were beyond doubt recognized as customary international law. In this way, the Legal Office sought to ensure that the Yugoslav Tribunal would not be subject to the kinds of criticisms leveled at the Nuremberg Charter for its alleged imposition of ex post facto law. In the years since Nuremberg, international humanitarian law had been codified in several widely ratified treaties, notably the Geneva conventions of 1949, the additional protocols of 1977, and the Genocide convention, creating a deep consensus as to what constituted an impermissible act during the time of war.

Thus, the Legal Office's statute provided for jurisdiction over four different international crimes committed in the territory of the former Yugoslavia after 1 January 1991:

Grave Breaches of the Geneva Conventions of 12 August 1949, which include the willful killing, torture or inhumane treatment, causing great suffering or serious injury to people protected by the conventions, and the extensive destruction and appropriation of property, not justified by military necessity and carried out unlawfully and wantonly. Grave breaches of the Geneva Convention further include compelling prisoners of war or civilians to serve in the forces of a hostile power, willfully depriving a prisoner of war or a civilian of the rights to a fair and regular trial, the unlawful deportation or transfer or unlawful confinement of civilians, and the taking of civilian hostages.

Violations of the laws or customs of war, which include the employment of weapons calculated to cause unnecessary suffering, the wanton destruction of population centers not justified by military necessity, the attack of undefended population centers, the seizure of, destruction or willful damage done to institutions of religion, charity, education, and the arts and science, the willful destruction or damage of historic monuments and works of art and science, and the plunder of public or private property.

Genocide, which is defined as the intentional attempt to destroy, in whole or in part, a national, ethnic, racial or religious group by killing members of the group, causing serious bodily or mental harm to members of the group, deliberately inflicting on its members conditions of life calculated to bring about the group's physical destruction in whole or in part, imposing measures to prevent births within the group, or forcibly transferring children of the group to another group. Punishable crimes of genocide also include conspiracy to commit genocide, direct and public incitement to commit genocide, attempts to commit genocide, and complicity in genocide.

Crimes against humanity, which include the following acts committed against any civilian population in times of international or internal armed conflict: murder, extermination, enslavement, deportation, imprisonment, torture, rape, persecution on political, racial and religious grounds, and other inhumane acts.

While these crimes form a wide net of accountability, the Legal Office's cautious standard self-consciously omitted from the Tribunal's jurisdiction the two 1977 additional protocols to the 1949 Geneva conventions, which apply the laws of war to "internal conflicts." In particular, the Legal Office feared that including the Additional Protocols, which had not been ratified by the United States, would trigger U.S. objections to the draft Statute and lead to a potential frenzy of amendments. This was a miscalculation; for the U.S. opposition to the additional protocols rested on the narrow ground that they would give members of the Palestine Liberation Organization and other armed groups who committed terrorist acts a right to prisoner-of-war status. The United States had since declared that the other provisions of the protocols represented customary international law, and had required its troops to comply with the provisions of the protocols during the recent Persian Gulf conflict. In fact, the United States felt that the application of the additional protocols to the Yugoslavia situation might prove critical, especially if the Tribunal were to find that the conflict in Bosnia was a civil war rather than an international armed conflict covered by the grave breaches provisions of the 1949 Geneva Convention.

The UN Legal Office also took a conservative approach to the penalties available to the Tribunal, ruling out capital punishment in light of the United Nations human rights bodies' efforts to outlaw the death penalty. However, this decision was a matter of significant controversy because at the time, 132 out of 181 states still provided for the death penalty for war crimes and genocide under their relevant national laws.[49] Furthermore, the Nuremberg Tribunal provided a precedent for imposing capital punishment for crimes under international law. Moreover, there was no question of unfairness to the defendants since capital punishment was provided for in the criminal code of Yugoslavia.[50] Finally, by prohibiting the Tribunal from imposing capital punishment, the statute would result in a significant disparity in sentencing: the most culpable individuals who would be tried by the international tribunal would escape capital punishment whereas those who simply carried out their plans and orders would be subject to the harshness of this sentence in domestic courts.

While the members of the Security Council each had their own set of problems with the statute that the Legal Office had devised, they were concerned that any attempt to revise it would result in lengthy negotiations and undesirable political compromises. In the weeks since the adoption of Resolution 808, the war in Bosnia had greatly intensified. Fighting had begun between the Bosnian Muslims and Croats, who had been allies against the Serbs in the first year of the war. The same week the Secretary-General submitted the Legal Office's proposed statute, Croatian defense forces had rounded up thousands of Muslim men in raids on the city of Mostar and had deported them to detention centers, which were little better than the Serb-run concentration camps. Meanwhile, the Bosnian Serbs were conducting a fierce assault on the Muslim towns of Zepa and Srebrenica, which had swollen with thousands of refugees from surrounding villages.

With these events as a backdrop, the five permanent members of the Security Council decided during informal meetings that there should be no amendments and no further discussion on the Legal Office's draft statute for the Tribunal. Thus, on 25 May 1993, the Security Council, acting under Chapter VII of the United Nations Charter, unanimously adopted the Statute of the Yugoslav Tribunal as proposed by the UN Legal Office.[51] In an attempt to put their own gloss on the statute's provisions, several of the members of the Council offered "clarifications" during their explanations of vote on Resolution 827.

In spite of the cynical intentions of at least some of the members of the Security Council, the creation of the Yugoslav Tribunal has had a powerful impact on the development of international law. At the time of this writing, the Tribunal had already produced more case law interpreting war crimes and international criminal procedure than the Nuremberg and Tokyo trials combined. Because of the Tribunal's special expertise, domestic courts have begun to cite its jurisprudence in cases involving international humanitarian law. The Tribunal's rules of procedure (discussed below) have become a model for a number of domestic legal systems, and the development of the Statute and Rules of the Yugoslav Tribunal fueled momentum toward the establishment of an international criminal court.

Politics at Play: Selecting the Personnel Charged with Carrying out the Work of the Yugoslav Tribunal

If you want an institution to fail, give it weak leadership. But strong leadership alone does not guarantee success.

—staff member of the Yugoslav Tribunal[52]

The first step in transforming the Yugoslavia War Crimes Tribunal from a paper court into an operational judicial institution was to appoint its principal officers: the eleven judges and the prosecutor. While the system for the selection of judges was based upon the process for selecting judges for the International Court of Justice—and thus relatively impervious to significant political manipulation, the process for selecting the prosecutor was placed entirely in the hands of the Security Council—and became the scene of an intense dispute which reflected the peace builders' varying perspectives concerning the appropriate role of the norm of justice.

Five months after the Security Council's decision to establish the Yugoslav Tribunal, the General Assembly elected an impressive group of jurists from a list of forty-one candidates from thirty-eight countries to serve as its judges:

Gabrielle Kirk McDonald, a former federal court judge of the United States; Antonio Cassese, a noted Italian international humanitarian law scholar; Georges Michel Abi-Saab, a distinguished Egyptian law professor; Li Haopei, the legal adviser of the Chinese Foreign Ministry; Germain le Foyer de Costil, presiding judge of the French Court of Major Jurisdiction of Nanterre; Lal Chand Vohrah, a senior Malaysian high court judge; Sir Ninian Stephen, former governor-general of Australia and judge of the Australian High Court; Adolphus Godwin Karibi-Whyte, former Nigerian Supreme Court judge; Elizabeth Odio Benito of Costa Rica; and Rustam Sidhwa of Pakistan.[53] The quality of those nominated (and disposed to serve) suggested that at least some of the members of the international community were taking the Tribunal seriously and willing to give it a chance to carry out its mandate.

The nine men and two women elected to the Tribunal's bench were from both civil and common law countries; three from Asia, two from Europe, two from Africa, two from North America, and one each from Latin America and Australia. There are several striking characteristics about the composition of the panel selected. The first of these is the absence of a practicing Muslim on the bench, especially since Muslims constituted by far the largest portion of the victims of atrocities in the former Yugoslavia.[54]

Four of the eleven judges, however, did come from countries with a predominantly Muslim population—Malaysia, Nigeria, Egypt, and Pakistan—and might therefore be uniquely sympathetic to the Muslim victims. Indeed, an opposite argument could be made—that there was a far greater number of Muslim countries represented on the bench than would be warranted by the percentage of Muslims to the total world population or the percentage of Muslim countries to the total number of countries in the world. In contrast, the nominee for the Tribunal's bench from Russia (the one state with the closest historic ties to Serbia), Mr. Valentin G. Kisilez, a member of the Presidium of the Kaliningrad Regional Administration, was defeated ostensibly to avoid a pro-Serbians bias.[55] This drew Russia's ire in light of the unwritten rule that all permanent members of the Security Council are represented on an important UN institution.[56]

Also notable was the absence of a British judge. The official British explanation was that they did not put forward a candidate in order not to prejudice the possible selection of Scottish attorney general John Duncan Lowe, who was then among the leading candidates for the position of the Tribunal's prosecutor. However, it has been suggested by other UN diplomats that the real reason was that Britain was afraid that, like Russia, its candidate might suffer an embarrassing defeat because of Britain's prominent and controversial role in the Bosnian crisis. [57] Indeed, at the time of these elections, Bosnia was preparing a submission for the International Court of Justice, which would charge Britain with complicity in genocide for having opposed the lifting of the arms embargo on Bosnia and the U.S. proposal for air strikes against Serb bases.[58]

When the judges met for the first time at The Hague on 17 November 1993, there were no premises for the Tribunal and no permanent staff. The General Assembly had not yet taken a formal decision on the Tribunal's budget, and it would be nearly a year before a prosecutor would take office. The judges decided to begin work immediately on the rules of procedure, so that they would be ready by the time the Office of the Prosecution was up and running.[59]

Judge Cassese, who had been elected by the ten other judges to serve as the president of the Tribunal, set an ambitious two-month deadline for the promulgation of the Tribunal's rules. By way of comparison, it took a committee of American judges and law professors four years to draft the federal Rules of Criminal Procedure in the early 1940s.The task facing the judges was particularly difficult because, in contrast to the substantive provisions of international humanitarian law, there had been little development of international criminal procedure in the years since the Nuremberg Tribunal (which itself had but eleven rules covering four pages of text). The United States quickly prepared a lengthy draft set of rules for the judges' consideration, along with a detailed commentary explaining the purpose and application of each proposed rule. With the short timeframe, and no other detailed proposals to draw from, the judges agreed to use the U.S. draft as their starting point. On 11 February 1994, the Yugoslav Tribunal adopted 125 rules, covering some seventy pages.[60]

As a result of the drafting process, the judges ended up embracing a largely adversarial approach to their Rules of Procedure, rather than the inquisitorial system prevailing in continental Europe.[61] Yet, there were a few significant deviations from the adversarial system, which have been the subject of criticism from some quarters. First, as at Nuremberg, there is no rule against hearsay evidence. Second, under certain circumstances, witnesses against the accused can testify anonymously (using voice and image-altering technology). Third, the practice of plea bargaining and granting of immunity were not included. Fourth, the Prosecutor was given the right to appeal an acquittal. And finally, a form of mini-trial in absentia was established under Rule 61 in cases in which the prosecutor has been unable to secure the presence of the accused.

In contrast to the successful and timely selection of judges, the selection of the Tribunal's prosecutor was marred by difficulties. Without a prosecutor, the Tribunal could not begin investigations or issue indictments or international arrest warrants. Consequently, the delay in the selection of the prosecutor undermined the norm of justice, in particular any deterrent value the Tribunal might have had while the fighting in Bosnia raged on.

The statute of the Yugoslav Tribunal provides that the prosecutor would be selected by the Security Council. At the time the statute was adopted in May of 1993, not even the most cynical of observers would have guessed that it would take the Council fourteen months to agree on a candidate for the position. The problem began when the Islamic and nonaligned members of the Security Council proposed Cherif Bassiouni, the Egyptian-born DePaul University professor and chairman of the War Crimes Commission, for the post. As the author of two dozen books and over a hundred articles on international criminal law, Bassiouni was arguably the world's leading authority in the field. It did not hurt that he was also a long-time friend of Secretary-General Boutros Boutros-Ghali, that he had years of courtroom experience arguing extradition cases, and that he had proven himself to be a creative and effective administrator in establishing the War Crimes Commission's Documentation Center at DePaul. On the surface, he seemed to be the ideal person for the job.

Despite these credentials, the United Kingdom decided to wage a campaign against the selection of Bassiouni. A senior UN official was quoted as saying that "Britain had been vociferous in opposing Bassiouni [on the grounds] that his lack of experience and administrative skills would get in the way of doing the job successfully."[62] But the real reason for the British opposition, wrote the UN correspondent to the *London Times*, was that Britain was afraid Bassiouni would "quickly bring charges against Serb leaders," which would disrupt the Vance-Owen peace negotiations.[63] This view was confirmed by Diego Arria, Venezuela's representative to the Security Council, who said, "Bassiouni was seen as a threat to the peace process. He was seen as a fanatic who had too much information. In fact, he is a cautious and careful man. They made a great mistake [in opposing him], and made a mockery out of the Tribunal."[64] Thus, the British government was willing to minimize, some would say even sacrifice, the norm and institution of justice in order to create "space" for continued efforts at accommodation.

The British campaign against Bassiouni rankled the UN Secretary-General, who told Britain to "put up or shut up."[65] The statute of the Tribunal called for the prosecutor to have "the highest level of competence and experience in the conduct of investigations and prosecutions of criminal cases." Partly to highlight Bassiouni's lack of prosecutorial experience, the British responded by proposing Scottish attorney general John Duncan Lowe for the post. The Islamic and non-aligned members of the Council, who had openly accused Britain of being the main force behind the European refusal to intervene to stop Serbian aggression, lobbied hard to block the appointment of Lowe. In informal polling, each candidate received seven votes in favor, seven votes against, with one country, Brazil, abstaining. The United States voted for Bassiouni, but the other four permanent members of the Security Council—France, Britain, Russia, and China—all opposed him. Part of Bassiouni's problem was that the United States had not aggressively lobbied for him, reportedly because Secretary of State Warren Christopher did not want the Tribunal to be seen "as an American show,"[66] and because he feared that "it would indicate the United States had 'taken sides.'"[67] Hungary, which had voted against Bassiouni, later let it be known that it would have taken just one letter from the United States to change its vote in his favor, and Brazil, which had abstained, stated that it would have been influenced by a strong U.S. campaign.[68]

When told of the deadlock, Secretary-General Boutros-Ghali tried to force the issue by formally nominating Bassiouni and trying to force a vote. While substantive decisions of the Security Council are subject to the permanent member veto, elections can be by simple majority vote. However, the fate of Bassiouni's candidacy was sealed when the United Kingdom proposed that the selection of the prosecutor should be by consensus. The other members of the Council accepted the British proposal ostensibly because it would ensure that the prosecutor would enjoy the international respect and standing necessary to ensure the effective performance of his responsibilities vis-à-vis the members of the international community and the undivided support of the Security Council.[69] But this informal decision, which would allow any Security Council member to veto a candidate for the post, was more responsible than anything else for the subsequent delays in appointing the prosecutor. This was in fact just what Britain had planned in proposing the consensus requirement, since it gave the Vance-Owen peace process additional breathing room before the commencement of prosecutions.

After Britain and France vetoed Bassiouni, the Secretary-General nominated former Indian attorney-general Soli Henhangir Soreabjee, who was then vetoed by Pakistan.[70] By now, said one Western diplomat, "frustration was giving way to desperation."[71] Finally, on 21 October 1993, the Secretary-General nominated Ramon Escovar Salam, a former Venezuelan attorney general, who drew no objection from any of the fifteen weary Security Council members. Escovar had impressive credentials. As attorney-general of Venezuela, he ran an office of 3,000 lawyers, and he had demonstrated his independence by spearheading corruption charges against his own country's president, Carlos Andres Perez, who was dismissed from office.[72] However, he was also a man with political ambitions, and just days before he was to have taken up the post in February of 1994, Escovar abandoned the job to become interior minister of the new Venezuelan government with the possibility of later assuming the newly created office of prime minister.[73]

A week after Escovar's withdrawal, one of the worst atrocities in the Balkan conflict occurred, when the Serbs fired a mortar bomb into the open-air market in the center of Sarajevo, killing forty-nine civilians and seriously wounding over 200 others.[74] Yet, for the next five months, the Security Council proved unable to agree on a replacement for Escovar, with Russia blocking a Canadian candidate, Christopher Amerasinghe, and an American candidate, Charles Ruff, each of whom had the support of the other fourteen members of the Council.[75] Russia made it clear that it would not vote for anyone put forward by a NATO member country on the ground that a Tribunal headed by a Westerner would be biased against the Serbs.[76] As one Security Council member remarked, the search for a prosecutor had turned into "a ghastly nightmare."[77]

On 7 July 1994, the Security Council finally selected Justice Richard J. Goldstone of the Appellate Division of the Supreme Court of South Africa to serve as the prosecutor.[78] Justice Goldstone had achieved international acclaim as the chairman of the Standing Commission of Inquiry regarding Public Violence and Intimidation ("Goldstone Commission"), which investigated the causes of the violence and the political intimidation that occurred in South Africa during the apartheid regime.[79] After successfully getting the Tribunal up and running and establishing sufficient political support necessary to begin the process of imbedding the norm of justice in the peace-building process, Justice Goldstone resigned to resume his position as a member of the Constitutional Court of South Africa in late 1996. On 28 February 1996, the Security Council appointed Louise Arbour, a member of the Court of Appeals for Ontario, Canada, as the new prosecutor as of 1 October 1996. While a competent judge, Arbour had never before served as a prosecutor or head of a prosecutor's office or agency.[80] After three years, Arbour resigned to assume a seat on the Canadian

Supreme Court, which more suited her expertise and skills. In September 1999, the Security Council appointed Carla Del Ponte, a career prosecutor and former attorney-general of Switzerland to be the Tribunal's third prosecutor. Del Ponte had made a name for herself prosecuting South American drug traffickers and members of the Italian and Russian Mafias, and she was strongly backed by the United States because of her close cooperation with the Drug Enforcement Administration in pursuing money laundering operations in Switzerland.[81]

Financing the Tribunal: Who Pays the Price for Justice?

All these undertakings are costly—of that there is no doubt; but if the United Nations wants to hear the voice of justice speak loudly and clearly, then the Member States must be willing to pay the price.

—Judge Antonio Cassese, President of
the Yugoslav Tribunal[82]

If done right, international justice is not cheap. Erecting courtrooms, offices, and jails; paying the salaries of judges, prosecutors, defense counsel, investigators, translators, secretaries, and security guards; and conducting trials in three official languages can cost hundreds of millions of dollars. The requirement for substantial funding both placed the Tribunal within a matrix of unrelated interests and procedures, which, although not concerned with the nature or role of justice, had the effect of limiting and delaying funding for the Tribunal and thus contributed to its lack of initial effectiveness and provided an opportunity for those peace builders interested in limiting the role of justice, to further obstruct the Tribunal's development.

While the expenses of international justice might seem perfectly reasonable when compared to that of domestic justice, as a creature of the Security Council the Yugoslav Tribunal was funded out of the budget of the United Nations. In seeking funding, the Tribunal encountered problems of competing institutional interests within the UN system, and interference from entirely unrelated issues, especially the nonpayment of U.S. dues and a history of bureaucratic mismanagement which pushed the UN to the verge of bankruptcy.

As a result, it took eight years, from 1993 to 2001, for the Yugoslav Tribunal to grow from a homeless organization with eleven judges and an approved budget of just $500,000 to an institution with a staff of 2,100 drawn from seventy-four countries, several facilities, and an annual budget of over $100 million.[83] During its first several years, the Tribunal was remarkably underfunded. The primary source of the Tribunal's early funding difficulties was a clause in its statute that provided, "the expenses of the International Tribunal shall be borne by the regular budget of the United Nations in accordance with Article 17 of the Charter of the United Nations."[84] This meant that the General Assembly, rather than the Security Council, would control the Tribunal's funding. The argument in favor of this approach was that if the international community was really serious about prosecuting war criminals, then the entire community should be prepared to ensure the necessary funding for the effective functioning of the International Tribunal. But the drawback to this source of funding was that the budget of the International Tribunal would be at the mercy of a little known UN body called the "ACABQ"—the Advisory Committee on Administrative and Budgetary Questions.

The sixteen-member ACABQ meets behind closed doors and issues no summary records. Yet its power within the UN is second only to that of the Security Council itself. This is because a decade ago, at the insistence of the United States, the UN adopted a procedure that requires the members of the ACABQ to reach consensus on the budget of the organization before it can be adopted by the General Assembly.[85] This was intended to impose greater discipline on UN spending and allow the United States more control over the organization's spending priorities. Unfortunately, in the context of the Tribunal, it had the unintended consequence of allowing a small group of ideologically motivated states to starve a worthwhile institution of funding.[86]

The mode of funding stipulated in the Tribunal's statute provoked an acrimonious debate among the members of the ACABQ and General Assembly. At the center of the controversy was the constitutional question of competence and authority for the budget and the relationship between the General Assembly and the Security Council concerning the financing of operations approved by the Security Council. Article 17 of the United Nations Charter makes clear that the General Assembly has exclusive competence over appropriations of funds. During the ACABQ's consideration of the Tribunal's budget, several members argued the Security Council had usurped the authority of the General Assembly by requiring it to appropriate funds for the Tribunal out of the general budget.[87] As a consequence, instead of the $32.6 million the Secretary-General requested to fund the International Tribunal for its first year of operation,[88] the ACABQ and General Assembly granted a provisional budget of one-third that amount in a resolution that "expressed concern that advice given to the Security Council by the Secretariat on the nature of the financing of the International Tribunal did not respect the role of the General Assembly as set out in Article 17 of the Charter."[89]

By the time Richard Goldstone took office a year later, things had improved only slightly. The General Assembly had approved a bare-bones $32 million budget that would cover only the cost of renting office space, rental and contracting of equipment and services, and salaries and expenses for a staff of 108 (11 judges, 19 prosecutors, 22 investigators, 10 defense counsel, 10 members of the Registry, 12 clerical staff, 12 security guards, and 28 interpreters).[90] In all, 75 percent of the funds budgeted were allocated for the judges, administration, and overhead.[91] Less than two percent of the total was budgeted for the critical work of tracking down witnesses, obtaining and translating their accounts, exhuming mass graves and conducting postmortems, and providing medical and forensic expertise.[92] And no funds at all were budgeted for witness protection, counseling, and security.

This first budget betrayed an extraordinary lack of understanding of the task facing the prosecution. For the next several months, Goldstone shuttled back and forth between The Hague and New York, "ingratiating himself with the various UN policy wonks who control funding, working the maze of power and pettiness."[93] With Goldstone's help, the Secretary-General submitted a revised budget of $39 million for 1994-1995, which was approved by the General Assembly. Meanwhile, Goldstone's efforts resulted in the receipt of voluntary contributions of $8.3 million from thirteen countries,[94] and the loan of fifty-three personnel, mostly from the United States, at no cost to the UN.[95]

The Tribunal initially used offices provided by the International Court of Justice in The Hague to conduct its work. In 1994, the Tribunal moved into its own offices in a wing of the Aegon Insurance Company Building in The Hague. Its first courtroom and a twenty-four-cell detention facility were completed later that year.[96] Four years later, two additional courtrooms were erected in the Aegon Building, funded by voluntary donations from the United States, the United Kingdom, and the Netherlands.

In 1995, the United Nations faced a funding crisis that pushed it to the brink of insolvency, with significant consequences for the Tribunal. UN members owed the organization $3.1 billion.[97] The Secretary-General seized upon this opportunity to slow the supply of funds to the Tribunal to a trickle. The efforts of the Secretary-General to limit the effectiveness of the Tribunal comprised part of his more comprehensive efforts to support David Owen and Cyrus Vance's approach of accommodation, and his personal belief that too much attention and too many resources were being devoted to the Yugoslav conflict at the expense of more compelling conflicts.

As a consequence of the Secretary-General's actions, the Office of the Prosecutor was prevented from spending money to send investigators into the field to investigate the massacre of 8,000 civilians at the UN "safe area" of Srebrenica. A subsequent UN report sponsored by the new Secretary-General found that the massacre at Srebrenica was the result of an overreliance on the approach of accommodation which had become one of appeasement and was in effect a thinly veiled indictment of Secretary-General Boutros Boutros-Ghali's approach.[98]

As a result of the financial constraints, the Office of the Prosecutor was also precluded from recruiting lawyers, or renewing contracts of then current personnel. Evidence already gathered from refugee interviews began to pile up unsifted and untranslated.[99] And the Tribunal's first trial involving a Serb prison camp guard captured in Germany, which was scheduled to begin in November 1995, was postponed until 7 May 1996, for want of $78,000 for expenses for defense counsel and investigators.[100] Sensing the consequences of the Secretary-General's efforts to limit the effectiveness of the Tribunal, Richard Goldstone, normally the consummate team player, decided the time had come to take his case to the international press. "If these restrictions continue, they will render unconscious the Yugoslav Tribunal," Goldstone told Ray Bonner of the *New York Times*.[101] "The criminal justice system cannot conduct itself if resources are turned on and off," he added.[102]

The General Assembly eventually circumvented the efforts of the ACABQ and the Secretary-General on 7 August 1995, by approving a resolution deciding that in the future, half of the Tribunal's financing would come from the UN peacekeeping budget,[103] with member countries assessed at the weighted scale used for UN peacekeeping activities. Under this procedure, the Security Council would have a greater degree of influence in determining the budget as compared to the regular budget process.[104] Thereafter, the Tribunal's financial situation improved steadily. The United Nations approved a $41 million budget for the Tribunal in 1996, a $48 million budget in 1997, and a $70 million budget in 1998.[105] These figures have been augmented by in-kind contributions of equipment and loaned personnel (approximately fifty a year), and voluntary cash contributions from twenty-eight countries and organizations, which by the end of 2001 have totaled over $14 million.[106]

To put the amounts allocated by the General Assembly for the operation of the Tribunal in perspective, the 1992 trial of New York mob boss John Gotti cost the U.S. government $75 million[107] and the 1997 trial of Oklahoma City bomber Timothy McVeigh cost the U.S. government $50 million.[108] The Nuremberg Tribunal, with its staff of 2,000, including more than 100 prosecutors, would cost hundreds of millions of dollars today.[109]

In 1998, the U.S. Government Accounting Office (GAO) conducted a study of the Yugoslav Tribunal which concluded that with available resources the Tribunal "does not have the capacity to handle its current workload [with over 30 indictees in custody], and the problem is likely to get worse." The GAO noted that the Tribunal receives new information at the rate of 20,000 pages of documents a month, which it has been unable to process. Altogether, the backlog of evidence potentially "vital to ongoing or planned investigations" includes "over 800,000 pages of documents, about 9,000 photographs, and so much unviewed videotape we estimate it would take one person over two years to watch." The GAO added that the Tribunal could not provide investigators to conduct work in Kosovo without seriously hampering ongoing investigations and trial preparations. The GAO also pointed out that the Tribunal's trial backlog of cases raised fair trial concerns, as indictees have to wait for up to three years before their trials can begin.[110]

The formation of the War Crimes Commission and the creation of the Yugoslav Tribunal created an unprecedented opportunity to involve the norm of justice and the approach of accountability in the peace-building process. Given the unfamiliarity of the peace builders with the requirements of creating such mechanisms, and the desire of some peace builders to stall for as long as possible their development or effective operation in order to maintain space for the approach of accommodation, both the commission and Tribunal experienced a period of development characterized by near fatal challenge and uncertainty. As will be discussed in the next chapter, the operation of the Tribunal was no less troubled or controversial.

Chapter 7

The Operation of the Yugoslav Tribunal: A Record of Self-Imposed Limits

The [UN] Security Council established the Tribunal. It's our parent, and parents have responsibilities. You don't give birth to a child and then leave the child to fend for itself.

—Gabrielle Kirk McDonald, President of
the Yugoslav Tribunal[1]

Like all institutions of justice, the Tribunal was designed so that once it was established it could operate free of political influence or concerns. Unlike other institutions of justice, however, the Tribunal was established to play a role in the peace-building process and thus at a minimum had to be functionally aware of its mandate and purpose and seek to act in a manner that involved justice in the peace-building process while strictly adhering to the requirements of impartiality and fairness. Unfortunately, the quasi-political nature of the Tribunal was not lost on certain peace builders who sought to undermine its effectiveness in order to preserve the approach of accommodation and forestall the use of force. Moreover, the Tribunal itself, more specifically the Office of the Prosecutor, at important times failed to acknowledge or comprehend its important role in the peace-building process. While subsequent chapters of this book examine the influence of external forces on the performance of the Tribunal, the focus of this chapter is on the internal matters over which the Tribunal exercised exclusive control. On the whole, the Office of the Prosecutor often acted in a timid and tardy manner and this was exploited by those who sought to minimize its influence on the peace-building process.

In critically reviewing the operation of the Yugoslav Tribunal this chapter seeks to further answer questions three, five, six, and seven as set out in chapter 1, in particular the extent to which the competing interests of the peace builders, as well as nonstate actors influenced the activity and effectiveness of the Tribunal, the influence of the Tribunal on the actual ability of the peace builders to infuse the norm of justice into the peace-building process, the effectiveness of the Tribunal as a mechanism of justice, and the extent to which the norm of justice, as exercised through the Tribunal was compatible with other approaches employed during the peace-building process.

To structure this discussion, this chapter explains and critiques the prosecutor's initial indictment strategy, examines the effect of the Rules of the Road agreement on the ability of the domestic justice system in Bosnia to effectively function and the motives behind the agreement, explores the consequences of the Office of the Prosecutor's narrow construction of its mandate and inability to fully comprehend its role in the peace-building process, and describes how the relative passivity of the Office of the Prosecutor led to its failure to contribute to a deterrence of the war in Kosovo.

Indictment Strategy: From the Bottom-up (to the Middle)

The reputation of the [UN War Crimes Tribunal] has been badly tarnished by its refusal to indict [Serbian President Slobodan] Milosevic [for Bosnian War Crimes]. There is no other figure in the former Yugoslavia as responsible for this bloodshed.

—anonymous European ambassador[2]

In order to meet the objectives of justice, as detailed in chapter 2, and in order to effectively influence the peace-building process, it is necessary for a tribunal to focus its efforts on the most senior individuals believed to be culpable. At Nuremberg and Tokyo, the international tribunals prosecuted the highest surviving members of the Nazi and Japanese military and civilian leadership, leaving lower-level perpetrators to be prosecuted before domestic courts and military commissions. According to the Yugoslav Tribunal's first prosecutor, Richard Goldstone, the Tribunal would follow a similar strategy for issuing indictments, which would be governed by two important factors: first, indictments would focus on the persons in senior positions of authority who are most responsible for the crimes; and second, decisions with regard to indictments would be taken "without regard to political considerations or consequences."[3]

Notwithstanding Goldstone's pledge and protestations, the chief investigators embarked on a program of investigation of low-level perpetrators. As one of the Office of the Prosecutor's senior prosecutors, Minna Schrag, recounts, "as we began to work, it was apparent that we could not start as they did at Nuremberg and Tokyo, with cases against the military and political leaders." [4]

The first person to be tried by the Tribunal, Dusko Tadic,[5] was a Bosnian Serb traffic cop, who was described in one newspaper account as "no more than a monstrous tadpole in a pool of sharks."[6] At the time of his trial, Tadic, who had been arrested in Germany, was the only person in the Tribunal's custody. In justifying the decision to proceed against Tadic, Minna Schrag wrote:

Mr. Tadic is not a senior official comparable to the members of the German High Command who were the first persons tried at Nuremberg. But to the victims of Mr. Tadic and his colleagues, to those who suffered as a result of the actions of ordinary prison guards and police officials, it is very important that some of their torturers be brought to justice. Only by prosecuting particular individuals at all levels of responsibility, can we hope to persuade the victims that justice has been done. . . . We can not possibly prosecute every prison guard who caused great suffering in Yugoslavia, and our primary focus is on the leaders who were responsible for instigating and directing the crimes. At the same time, we think prosecutions of prison guards and others like them have significant symbolic value and that it is our obligation to pursue some of them.[7]

Tadic's trial took over a year to complete, at a cost of some $20 million. In the end, he was convicted of only two murders, and given a sentence of twenty years imprisonment.[8]

Even some of the Tribunal's most staunch supporters have criticized the decision to prosecute Tadic before the Yugoslav Tribunal, when Germany had indicated that it was ready and willing to prosecute him domestically. Thus, Hanne Sophie Greve, the Norwegian judge who served on the War Crimes Commission, proclaimed Tadic "is not the level of person I would like to see at the Hague. I think they should have aimed higher up."[9] Even Richard Goldstone acknowledged that Tadic was far from the ideal first defendant before the Yugoslav Tribunal. "It is highly unsatisfactory that someone at the level of Dusko Tadic should face trial and that those who incited and facilitated his conduct should escape justice and remain unaccountable. But it's really an academic question because we had no choice; Tadic was the only accused available to bring before the Tribunal at a time when the judges, the media, and the international community were clamoring for us to begin prosecutions."[10]

Due to such pressure, a one-time departure from Goldstone's policy of focusing on leaders might have appeared to be justified—though it violated his pledge to take prosecutorial decisions "without regard to political considerations or consequences." However, it was not to be just a one-time exception. In the first five years of the Tribunal's operation, most of the defendants tried before the Tribunal were of a similarly low level. They included foot soldiers like Drazen Erdemovic,[11] prison camp guards like Hazim Delic and Esad Landzo,[12] and members of paramilitary units like Anto Furundzija.[13] The highest-ranking defendants to date have been Slavko Dokmanovic,[14] the Croatian Serb mayor of Vukovar; Zdravko Mucic, a Bosnian Croat prison camp commander,[15] and Tihomir Blaskic, a Bosnian Croat colonel (subsequently promoted to general).[16]

As a result, the Office of the Prosecutor came under criticism for tying up its scant resources on such low-level cases, especially as higher level defendants are beginning to surrender themselves or be apprehended. In a February 1997 audit of the Rwanda Tribunal prepared by Karl Pashke, the United Nations inspector general, Pashke criticized the failure of the Office of the Prosecutor to comply with Richard Goldstone's directive that the prosecution strategy should focus on "national figures."[17] Pashke's report concluded, "The absence of a revitalized prosecution strategy and leadership will not allow the Office of the Prosecutor to achieve its objectives. This is the single most significant failing. Unless that is corrected, the Tribunal will have been created to little effect."[18] These words could have just as easily been written about the Yugoslav Tribunal. In response to these criticisms, in July 1998, the Office of the Prosecutor announced that it was dismissing indictments against fourteen Serbs accused of atrocities at the Omarska and Keratem prison camps. According to Deputy Prosecutor Graham Blewitt, "the decision takes into account an investigative strategy that focuses on the people in more senior positions of authority. We decided to cut loose those people who are, in effect, the minor offenders, leaving them for domestic courts to prosecute."[19] Subsequently, the Office of the Prosecutor embarked on a policy of indicting only those responsible for "major" war crimes, or those in positions of important civil or military command responsibility.

Even more troubling than the Office of the Prosecutor's initial failure to focus on senior-level defendants were the indications that the ability of the prosecutor to obtain incriminating information from the United States and its European allies was affected by political considerations, in particular with respect to Slobodan Milosevic. During the Dayton negotiations, chief U.S. negotiator Richard Holbrooke refused to address the issue of Mr. Milosevic's responsibility for the atrocities in Bosnia, saying it is "not my role here to make a judgment," and adding, "you can't make peace without President Milosevic."[20] Although Mr. Milosevic was indicted by the International Tribunal for the role he played in atrocities in Kosovo in 1999 during the actual conflict,[21] it was not until 22 November 2001 that he was charged for his crimes in Bosnia. Importantly, he was not charged with the Bosnian crimes until he was already in custody in The Hague. This led at least one commentator to conclude, "it appears likely that Slobodan Milosevic was at least implicitly promised some type of immunity from prosecution in return for his reducing support to the Bosnian Serbs and agreeing to the Dayton Accords."[22]

Despite possessing sufficient evidence for Secretary of State Lawrence Eagleburger to declare in December 1992 that Mr. Milosevic was responsible for war crimes in Bosnia, for years, the United States failed to provide this evidence to the Tribunal, and as such the Office of the Prosecutor was unable to indict Mr. Milosevic.[23] The Office of the Prosecutor sought to highlight the necessity of greater cooperation by bringing the world's attention to the evidence of Serbia's involvement in Bosnian atrocities (including in particular the Srebrenica massacre) via the Rule 61 hearing held to review the indictments of Karadzic and Mladic.[24] Upon the conclusion of the hearing, presiding judge Claude Jorda ruled that based on conclusive evidence "a plan existed, designed at the highest Serbian political and military level," and the judge all but ordered the prosecution to bring charges against Mr. Milosevic.[25]

In addition to a lack of cooperation by the United States and other governments, the staff of the Prosecutor's Office charged with reviewing the case against Mr. Milosevic failed to adequately consider their legal options. In particular, they failed to adequately assess the fact that, as the civilian commander of the Serb military and police forces, Mr. Milosevic could be prosecuted under the theory of command responsibility for failing to prevent his forces from committing war crimes in Bosnia. Unfortunately the staff of the Prosecutor's Office was constrained by Prosecutor Arbour's proclamation that she would not indict Mr. Milosevic for crimes in Bosnia until she had an airtight case against him.[26]

Given the United States and the EU's reliance on Mr. Milosevic's cooperation as the key to the success of the Dayton Accords, it is not surprising that the United States and the United Kingdom would withhold evidence from the Office of the Prosecutor, such as wire taps, electronic surveillance, and satellite photography that would have facilitated Mr. Milosevic's indictment for war crimes in Bosnia. The two governments justified dragging their feet by blaming their complex domestic laws and procedures for delays in declassifying intelligence information.[27] At the height of the Kosovo crisis in the spring of 1999, however, the U.S. and British governments belatedly came to the conclusion that Mr. Milosevic was not the solution to peace in the former Yugoslavia—he was the problem. In several speeches in April and May, Madeleine Albright signaled that the United States was not opposed to an indictment of Mr. Milosevic.[28] Simultaneously, U.S. and British officials began to turn over long-awaited sensitive intelligence material to the Office of the Prosecutor.[29]

Almost immediately thereafter, on 27 May 1999, the Office of the Prosecutor issued an indictment charging Mr. Milosevic and four other top FRY officials with responsibility for deporting 740,000 Kosovo Albanians and for the murder of 340 others.[30] The charges were based on two theories of liability. The first is command responsibility: the responsibility of a superior for actions committed by his subordinates. The second is personal responsibility for committing, planning, instigating, ordering, or aiding and abetting war crimes and crimes against humanity.

Full application of the norm of justice would have dictated the indictment of Mr. Milosevic in 1995, if not earlier. But Mr. Milosevic remained unindicted until 1999 as a result of the prevalence of the approach of accommodation, the institutional inadequacies of the Tribunal, and the failure of the United States and Britain to realize until 1999 the value of such an indictment to peacebuilding. While staff of the Office of the Prosecutor have frequently claimed there was insufficient evidence to indict Milosevic for the crimes in Bosnia until 2001, much of the material supporting the indictment was readily accessible many years earlier.[31]

On the positive side, although focused on relatively low-level perpetrators, the Tribunal's early cases set several judicial milestones. Particularly important were its holdings that there could be individual criminal responsibility for war crimes in internal armed conflict, that rape constituted a war crime and a crime against humanity, and that military and civilian leaders could be criminally liable for the acts of their subordinates over whom they exercise effective control. Moreover, the development of the Tribunal's extensive Rules of Procedure and Evidence and the conduct of its trials demonstrated that international justice could function fairly and effectively, and thus its operation served as a model for subsequent ad hoc tribunals.

Rules of the Road Agreement: Detouring Justice

The Rules of the Road are a source of unanimous resentment by the local judiciary and prosecutorial services.

—Fionnualla Ni Aolain, Special Representative of
the Prosecutor of the Yugoslav Tribunal[32]

Although the Yugoslav Tribunal was never intended to be the exclusive forum for the prosecution of Yugoslav war criminals, it became so as a result of political compromises made with Mr. Milosevic referred to as the Rules of the Road Agreement. The Rules of the Road Agreement signed in the aftermath of the Dayton Accords was designed by Ambassador Holbrooke and Mr. Milosevic to limit the role of justice by hampering domestic prosecutions, and thereby limiting the parties' use of justice and centralizing the use of justice in the hands of the Tribunal—which had a more limited capacity to prosecute large numbers of war criminals. The Rules of the Road Agreement also directly undercut the strategy of prosecuting the major war criminals and letting the domestic courts prosecute the lower-level criminals.

The "Rules of the Road Agreement," concluded on 18 February 1996 by the parties to the Dayton Accords, provided that the parties would arrest persons in their territories for domestic prosecution for war crimes and crimes against humanity only pursuant to an indictment deemed consistent with international legal standards by the Office of the Prosecutor of the Yugoslav Tribunal.[33] The Rules of the Road Agreement was entered into in the aftermath of the arrest by the Bosnian government of two Bosnian Serb military officers who had mistakenly driven into Sarajevo. Upon this arrest, the Bosnian Serbs threatened to suspend implementation of the Dayton Accords and the Rules of the Road Agreement was negotiated as a means of accommodating their objection.

In practice, the agreement required local police forces to send all information and evidence they had available to them concerning suspicions that an individual had committed war crimes to the Office of the Prosecutor for review. Arrest of an individual could occur only when the Office of the Prosecutor indicated in writing to the local authorities that there existed sufficient evidence to provide a basis for proceeding further.[34] In the spring of 1996, the governments of the Republic of Bosnia and Croatia sent over 1,600 cases to be reviewed by the Office of the Prosecutor.[35] "The short-term result was a paper logjam at the Tribunal, which did not have the resources to spend on a flood of domestic case briefs."[36]

The Tribunal's deputy prosecutor, Graham Blewitt, told the authors that his office was willing to participate in the Rules of the Road Agreement only on the naïve assumption that the Office of the Prosecutor would be given sufficient resources to process the cases.[37] He said it soon became clear the resources would not be provided and he suspected this suited those who would seek to prevent the arrest of any war crimes suspects other than those indicted by the Tribunal. In response, the Office of the Prosecutor "issued a deadline that if we don't get the resources to commence this series by December of 1998 then we are pulling out of the process. Which means that the parties can go back and start arresting people again."[38] Prior to the deadline, personnel were provided to the Office of the Prosecutor to conduct Rules of the Road review by Canada, the American Bar Association's Central and Eastern European Law Initiative, and the Coalition for International Justice.[39] It was not until five years later that the Office of the Prosecutor, with the assistance of these organizations, eventually processed the information.

Unfortunately the Rules of the Road compromise severely limited the role of justice in the peace-building process as with its limited facilities, resources, and personnel, the Tribunal could prosecute only a handful of cases per year. While the Tribunal can achieve representative justice through the prosecution of a few exemplary cases, for there to be meaningful deterrence, victim catharsis, and the creation of an accurate historical record, prosecutions must be more widespread. As such, domestic war crimes prosecutions in Serbia, Bosnia, and Croatia are crucial to achieving justice and peace in the former Yugoslavia. Moreover, domestic war crimes prosecutions have the advantage of being able to "demonstrate the willingness to be active rather than passive in the face of massive violations of human rights, fair and open trials can allow for confidence in building the idea of the rule of law itself, and they are the first step in meaningful institutional building within the legal system." [40]

The effect of the Rules of the Road Agreement was to entirely override the domestic legal structure in the area of war crimes. Local authorities "felt that they were being by-passed by external agreement, and that no consideration had been given to the integrity of their own legal culture in the process." As a result, many of those under investigation were able to flee or to remain in positions of authority as the papers for their arrest awaited action by the Office of the Prosecutor in The Hague.[41]

Achieving Its Objectives: Suffering from a Myopic Mandate

The [UN war crimes] tribunal was established to get to the very heart of evil, not only to punish but to eradicate and purify, to rip out the root and ensure those responsible are brought to justice and it does not happen again.

—Judge Claude Jorda, President of the Yugoslav Tribunal[42]

To effectively contribute to the peace-building process, it was necessary for the Tribunal to seek to accomplish to the fullest extent possible the traditional objectives of the norm of justice, which include denying collective guilt by establishing individual responsibility, enabling the dismantlement of institutions responsible for perpetuating the commission of atrocities, establishing an accurate historical record, providing a cathartic process for victims, and deterring further instances of violence in the current conflict as well as deterring atrocities in similar conflicts. This section will examine how the Office of the Prosecutor's primary focus on individual responsibility limited its ability to achieve these other objectives. Because of the inability of the Tribunal to deter future crimes, the next section will examine the impact of the Tribunal's actions on the Kosovo crisis.

In the end, it may appear that the Office of the Prosecutor suffered from a fear of mission creep beyond its overly narrow interpretation of its mandate to establish individual responsibility. As such, the Office of the Prosecutor generally failed to fulfill the other four important functions of justice, and thereby minimized its meaningful impact on the peace-building process.

Establishing Individual Responsibility

Many of the Serbs, Croats, and even Bosniacs may have been "willing executioners," to borrow a phrase from Daniel Goldhagen's recent best-seller.[43] But, contrary to the myth perpetrated by some scholars, the people of the former Yugoslavia were not in any way uniquely predisposed to commit genocide. Like the former Yugoslavia, the populations of numerous countries around the globe have experienced a long history of tension marked by periods of hatred and conflict between ethnic, racial, and national groups; but most of these countries are not likely to experience the mass atrocities that characterized the conflict in the former Yugoslavia. The distinguishing factor in the former Yugoslavia was that the Serbian and Bosnian Serb leaders, in particular, used provocation, incitement, propaganda, official sanction, coercion, and opportunities for personal gain to transform ordinary citizens into mass murderers.[44]

One of the most important functions of the Yugoslav Tribunal, therefore, was to disclose the way the Yugoslav people were manipulated by their leaders into committing acts of savagery on a mass scale. While this would not completely absolve the underlings for their acts, it would make it easier for victims to eventually forgive, or at least, reconcile with former neighbors who had been caught up in the institutionalized violence.

To achieve this function, the Office of the Prosecutor should have quickly issued indictments for the responsible leaders, charging them with genocide. The 24 July 1995 indictments of Bosnian Serb political leader Dr. Radovan Karadzic, and Bosnian Serb military commander General Ratko Mladic, which included the charge of genocide, and the subsequent Rule 61 hearing in which the evidence supporting this charge was publicly aired, was a bold step in this direction. Moreover, the indictments of Karadzic and Mladic, which came on the eve of the Dayton peace talks, had the positive effect of barring them from the negotiations.

Yet, by failing to simultaneously indict the most responsible leaders in 1995—Slobodan Milosevic of Serbia and Franjo Tudjman of Croatia—as well as the other leading members of the Bosnian Serb power circle, this was to constitute a step forward accompanied by two steps back. Franjo Tudjman was never indicted for his crimes, and it was not until 22 November 2001, after he was in custody in The Hague on the Kosovo charges, that Milosevic was indicted for the role he played in the genocide in Bosnia. Similarly, it was not until the spring of 2000 that Momcilo Krajisnik, who after Dayton, had served as the Serbian member of the Bosnian presidency, and Biljana Plavsic, who had been Karadzic's chief deputy and after Dayton served as president of the Republic Srpska, were indicted for genocide.[45]

Unfortunately, the Office of the Prosecutor concentrated its resources in its early years on investigating, indicting, and (in a handful of cases) trying low-level and mid-level perpetrators, including foot soldiers, traffic cops, and prison camp guards. Since obedience to orders is not a defense that may be raised before the Yugoslav Tribunal, these cases suggested that ordinary citizens, rather than the leaders, were most to blame for the atrocities. In this way, the Office of the Prosecutor missed an opportunity to play an important role in the peace process by establishing individual responsibility of leaders rather than suggesting the collective guilt of the masses.

Creating an Accurate Historical Record

As noted by Supreme Court Justice Robert Jackson, the chief prosecutor at Nuremberg, one of the most important legacies of the international war crimes trials following World War II was that they documented the Nazi atrocities "with such authenticity and in such detail that there can be no responsible denial of these crimes in the future and no tradition of martyrdom of the Nazi leaders can arise among informed people." [46] As such, creating a credible account of international crimes "prevents history from being lost or re-written, and allows a society to learn from its past in order to prevent a repetition of such violence in the future." [47]

To accomplish the objective of establishing the truth and creating an accurate and comprehensive historical record, it is incumbent upon institutions of justice to ensure that they investigate and make public at the appropriate time all relevant information concerning the nature of the conflict and the atrocities or war crimes committed during the conflict. It is also incumbent upon the institutions of justice to ensure that their proceedings enjoy the maximum coverage both within the region of the conflict and on the international level.

To attain these objectives the Office of the Prosecutor was endowed with a number of unique powers and responsibilities in the form of the Rule 61 hearing, which allowed the Tribunal to publicly review and confirm the indictment of any accused.[48] The Tribunal unfortunately held only one major Rule 61 hearing—that of Radovan Karadzic and Ratko Mladic. In fact, when requested by the press to discuss some of the information relating to the indictment of Mr. Milosevic for crimes against humanity in Kosovo, Prosecutor Arbour refused to disclose the "voluminous" information that her office had compiled indicating

Mr. Milosevic's responsibility for war crimes in Kosovo until "the prosecutors office [was] required to disclose it to the defense in the event of a trial."[49]

Moreover, the Office of the Prosecutor failed to adequately comprehend the nature of its mission and to undertake serious and systematic efforts to establish the truth. In an odd twist, when the U.S. Department of State pressured the Office of the Prosecutor to publicly disclose some of the evidence against Mr. Milosevic in order to help make the case against war crimes before world opinion, "the Tribunal itself urged that much of the U.S. material it receives be kept secret for fear of alerting Serb authorities to 'crime scenes' that they can then try to clean up." [50] Although this may be a proper approach for the purpose of preserving crime scenes, it does not exhibit an understanding of the complex mandate or objectives of the Tribunal and in particular the necessity of establishing the truth and deterring future war crimes.

Most conspicuous of the Office of the Prosecutor's other failings was its neglect of the educational and deterrent role played by the Tribunal. For example, when the George Soros Foundation arranged to have the Tribunal's first trial broadcast into Serbia and Republika Srpska, the prosecution began its presentation with several weeks of dry testimony by a British historian. Viewers soon lost interest in the unenthralling proceedings. Reflecting this development, *Court TV* coverage waned from six hours of daily gavel-to-gavel coverage during the first days of the proceedings to a brief nightly highlight after the first month. During this period, the number of print journalists covering the trial dwindled from over a hundred to less then a handful. According to lead trial prosecutor Grant Niemann, "the popular appeal and educational aspect of the trial was not part of our consideration at all. Our prosecution strategy, including the order of our witnesses, was designed to secure a conviction, not boost the ratings of *Court TV*." But, as Fred Graham, the chief anchor and managing editor of *Court TV*, pointed out, "the prosecutors should have realized that if they presented their case in such a way as to bore the world into tuning them out, they had failed to accomplish an important part of their mission."[51]

The Tribunal further inhibited the assessment of the truth and creation of an accurate historical record by adopting a policy of dismissing cases when the defendant died prior to the issuance of the judgment. Consider the case of Slavko Dokmanovic, a Croatian Serb, charged with responsibility for the greatest single massacre of the 1991 war in Croatia, that of the execution of 261 people forcibly taken out of a hospital in Vukovar, eastern Croatia.[52] The Dokmanovic case was the most important of all the Tribunal's early cases because, at the time of the Vukovar massacre, the Yugoslav army answered solely to Serb leaders, with Slobodan Milosevic at the top of the chain of command. "It could be that when all the evidence is in, we will go straight up to Mr. Milosevic," the Tribunal's deputy prosecutor Graham Blewitt was quoted as stating on the eve of the Dokmanovic trial.[53]

After the completion of the trial, and just a few days before the Tribunal was scheduled to issue its judgment, Dokmanovic was found dead in his cell. The judges presiding over the Dokmanovic trial decided to dismiss the case because there was no longer a living defendant over whom to pass judgment and sentence.[54] Since Dokmanovic was present during his entire trial, the Tribunal's decision was not compelled by interests of fairness. While an appropriate course of action for a national court, in light of its unique role in establishing the historic record of atrocities during the conflict in the former Yugoslavia, the Tribunal should have rendered its judgment notwithstanding Dokmanovic's death or converted it into some form of an official report. By committing suicide, Dokmanovic literally prevented history from being written about Mr. Milosevic's and the Serbian government's responsibility for the Vukovar massacre.

In cases where indictees have been killed before being brought to trial the Tribunal appropriately dismissed the indictment. The Office of the Prosecutor, however, refused to release for public review the information upon which the indictment was based. Moreover, since Judge Goldstone left the Office of the Prosecutor, there have been no additional Rule 61 hearings. The Office of the Prosecutor thus closed an avenue for making available to the public information about certain indictees likely to commit suicide, be assassinated, or die of natural causes before they could be brought to trial. The consequences of this approach are significant as many of the most notorious indictees and suspects have been killed—either by SFOR troops attempting their arrest, or in some instances possibly by individuals higher in the chain of command, who they might implicate. Deceased indictees include: Dragan Gagovic, the former chief of police in Foca, the location of notorious rape camps (killed by French SFOR after crashing a roadblock);[55] Slavko Dokmanovic,[56] former JNA officer (committed suicide in custody on 29 June 1998 days before a verdict that might have established the culpability of the Yugoslav army and implicated Mr. Milosevic); Zeliko Raznatovic, a.k.a. Arkan,[57] head of the paramilitary Serbian Volunteer Guard, a.k.a. Tigers, who acted in close cooperation with Serbian authorities (murdered in a Belgrade hotel on 15 January 2000); Slobodan Miljkovic, former Bosnian Serb paramilitary leader, known as Lugar (shot by a policeman in the Serbian city of Kragujevac for insulting the policeman's girlfriend); Srdjan Knezevic,[58] the former leader of the Bosnian Serb paramilitary unit known as the "White Wolves," and deputy police chief in Pale and a close ally of Karadzic (shot by a masked assailant outside of his home in Pale); and Milan Kovacevic,[59] responsible for the operation of the Omarska, Keraterm, and Trnopolje concentration camps (died of a heart attack while in custody at The Hague).

As noted above, Prosecutor Carla Del Ponte declared she was close to issuing an indictment of Franjo Tudjman just before his death. With his passing there will never be an opportunity for the Tribunal to fully explore the culpability of the Croatian regime all the way to its highest office. Moreover, without a trial of Tudjman it is unlikely that the full extent of the Croatian plan for ethnic cleansing of non-Croats from Croatian-held territory will be realized.[60] The Office of the Prosecutor could have appropriately issued a report detailing the evidence which led it to the brink of an indictment, without issuing any formal findings of culpability. Alternatively, the Office of the Prosecutor could have provided its information to an independent Truth Commission—had it not so successfully lobbied against the creation of such a commission as will be discussed below.

The consequences of the Tribunals' failure to adequately establish an accurate historical record, or to permit other institutions to do so, can be illustrated by the following statement by Zoran, a twenty-seven-year-old mechanic in the Republika Srpska in response to the Tribunal's guilty verdict on charges of genocide against General Krstic[61] for his role in the Srebrenica massacre, "if I had some power I would not put Krstic on trial, I would give him an award compared to what they (Muslims) did to us (Serbs) in the past I do not think that we are even with Srebrenica."[62] Similarly, in response to a call by a British SAS officer for the arrest of individuals who "organised the concentration camps, the torture, the rape camps; the ones who forced women and children to walk through minefields," the current mayor of Stolac, Zdravko Guzman, proclaimed, "the victims are exaggerating. . . . It's time to forget about the past, and turn instead to the future."[63]

More striking was a poll of the Serb people taken in 2001 by the Belgrade advertising agency Strategic Marketing, which found that when asked to name their heroes, the top four responses were Ratko Mladic, Radovan Karadzic, Zeljko Raznatovic "Arkan," and Slobodan Milosevic—all of whom had been indicted by the Tribunal for genocide and/or crimes against humanity.[64] When asked to name "Who was to blame for the wars in the former Yugoslavia?" the most often cited answers were: former Croatian president Franjo Tudjman and former Bosnian president Alija Izetbegovic followed then by Slobodan Milosevic. The primary causes of the war were identified as Croatian nationalism, U.S. strategic interests, disintegration of the USSR, and President Izetbegovic's Islamists. According to a report on the poll by War & Peace Reporting, apparently none of the respondents identified "ideologue novelist Dobrica Cosic, the Serbian Academy of Arts and Sciences, the Serbian Orthodox Church, Yugoslav People's Army generals nor Vojislav Seselj. Not even massacres or genocide." In the end, according to the report, "just 10 percent of Serbs know anything about war crimes which their people may or may not have committed. Yet 85 percent were fully aware that crimes had been committed against them."[65]

Dismantling Institutions and Discrediting Leaders Responsible for Atrocities

Recognizing the importance of excluding war criminals from institutions of public governance and power in a postwar society, the Dayton Accords provided that persons indicted by the Tribunal are barred from holding public office or military positions.[66] Had the Office of the Prosecutor focused sufficient energy and resources on its objective of dismantling and discrediting institutions responsible for the commission of atrocities during the early stages of its operation it could have utilized this provision to substantially promote peace-building in Bosnia. Although the Office of the Prosecutor indicted Karadzic and Mladic in an attempt to exclude them from the peace-building process and thereby ensure its integrity, it failed to follow through by publicly indicting other high-level

Bosnians who were to assume positions of power. In fact, the Office of the Prosecutor failed to indict Momcilo Krajisnik, one of "the individuals who ran illegal operations that resulted in the deaths of thousands of Bosnians,"[67] until April 2000.[68] After signing the Dayton Accords Mr. Krajisnik ran for and was elected as the Serbian member of the Bosnian presidency on the platform of ethnic separation of Bosnia. During his time in office he effectively stalled any development of a unified or reintegrated Bosnia. The five-year delay in Mr. Krajisnik's indictment is difficult to explain as he is indicted for crimes stemming from many of the same activities as Karadzic, and the fact that Krajisnik and Karadzic operated in tandem throughout the war was no secret to any interested observer.[69]

Similarly, the Office of the Prosecutor indicted Biljina Plavsic for genocide only after she had served as the president of the Republika Srpska during a crucial phase of the Dayton implementation process.[70] Again, most of her acts were carried out in tandem with Radovan Karadzic and thus there was little additional evidence required to form an indictment for her. Moreover, as reported by the International Crisis Group, there are over seventy-five indictable major war criminals who currently hold positions of power and influence in the Republika Srpska and who continue to work to further the agenda of ethnic partition that led to the war.[71]

Providing a Cathartic Process for Victims

The Tribunal also generally failed to aid the victim catharsis process. First, whereas the parties to the conflict estimate that between eight and twelve thousand individuals are responsible for war crimes, the Tribunal has indicted less than a hundred. And as discussed above, due to the Rules of the Road Agreement very few perpetrators have been prosecuted by domestic courts. As such many of the perpetrators are still at large in the communities in which they committed the crimes, and this naturally prevents the catharsis process from even beginning. Also, given the paucity of indictments, the Office of the Prosecutor failed to interview a substantial number of the victims and thus denied them an opportunity to "tell their story," an essential part of some healing processes. Not only, however, have the Office of the Prosecutor's investigators failed to interview many of the victims, they have actively discouraged other international organizations from interviewing victims as prior interviews of "potential witnesses" may skew subsequent interviews and thus inhibit the efforts of the Office of the Prosecutor to secure a conviction.

The Tribunal also failed to pay adequate attention to the role of victim compensation. Although the Statute of the Tribunal does not provide the Tribunal with the authority to award victim compensation, it does provide the Tribunal with the power to order the return of stolen property or the proceeds resulting from the sale of such property.[72] Moreover, the Security Council resolution establishing the Tribunal (Resolution 827) includes a clause declaring that the creation of the Tribunal was without prejudice to the future establishment of a victim compensation program. What the drafters of the resolution had in mind was a procedure similar to that devised for the victims of the Iraqi invasion of Kuwait, in which frozen Iraqi assets and proceeds from Iraqi oil sales would be dispersed to victims through a UN Compensation Commission.[73] To date, such an institution for Bosnia or Kosovo has not been set up by the Security Council, and with the permanent lifting of sanctions in 1996, frozen government assets no longer exist to fund such a program. Although the Tribunal has a limited ability to influence the process of victim compensation, it made no meaningful efforts to articulate the need for such compensation, and oddly enough is occasionally being perceived as "using" the victims of atrocities to prove their various cases and to establish successful professional records of conviction—while paying little regard for the interests of the victims the Tribunal was ostensibly designed to protect.[74]

Although the Tribunal has been unable to achieve many of these objectives because of the Office of the Prosecutor's myopic focus on securing convictions, even if it were to adopt a more expansive view of its mandate it would unlikely possess the resources or capacity to fully accomplish these objectives. The Office of the Prosecutor, however, bears much of the blame, for the failure to pursue these ends as it actively opposed the creation of additional justice-based mechanisms that might be able to accomplish these objectives. Specifically, Prosecutor Arbour fervently opposed the creation of a nonamnesty Bosnian Truth Commission notwithstanding the fact it was supported by all three parties to the conflict. If a truth commission is ever created it may significantly advance the victim catharsis process and facilitate the creation of an adequate historical record—in particular with respect to those individuals who played a central role in the commission of atrocities, but who are now deceased. A truth commission may even be capable of generating leads and information of use to the Office of the Prosecutor in its prosecutions, and it could possibly be linked to an internationally funded victim compensation program, as in South Africa.

The Kosovo Crisis: A Failure to Deter

There can be no lasting peace without justice.

—NATO's 17-point statement on Kosovo [75]

You can't make peace without President Milosevic.

—Richard Holbrooke[76]

The failure of the Office of the Prosecutor to actively undertake to achieve the various objectives relevant for institutions of justice due to its myopic approach on building a safe prosecutorial record led the Tribunal to fail in its most important task—deterring future crimes. The Tribunal failed to contribute to the deterrence of war crimes in Kosovo by (1) declining to indict Slobodan

Milosevic and other top Serbian government leaders in a timely manner for their orchestration of war crimes in Croatia and Bosnia; (2) refusing to publicly declare and exercise its jurisdiction over the conflict; (3) exercising undue delay in forming and deploying investigative teams; and (4) failing to make clear and authoritative statements early in the conflict that individuals in specific positions of authority could and would be held accountable for atrocities committed in Kosovo. The lack of effort on the part of the Office of the Prosecutor was mirrored by a lack of support—and at times active interference—by the European Union and UN Security Council.

The Nonindictment of Slobodan Milosevic: Setting the Precedent

As noted above, prior to the Kosovo crisis, the Office of the Prosecutor failed to indict Mr. Milosevic for the crimes committed in Bosnia, and the NATO forces operating in Bosnia failed to arrest Karadzic and Mladic who had been indicted for crimes of genocide. Had Mr. Milosevic been indicted, he would have been aware of the consequences of his actions, and, more important, the international community would not have had the flexibility of seeking to accommodate his interests in Kosovo, which as in Bosnia, led to appeasement. Had Mr. Milosevic been identified by the Office of the Prosecutor as responsible for the genocide in Bosnia, the United States and its NATO allies would likely have been compelled to use force earlier, as discussed below, and they might have been able to prevent many of the crimes committed against the people of Kosovo.

Moreover, had the NATO forces actually arrested Karadzic and Mladic, this, combined with an indictment of Mr. Milosevic, might have deterred further aggression by Mr. Milosevic. According to former prosecutor Goldstone, "if Karadzic and Mladic had been arrested five years ago, when the indictments were issued, the crimes in Kosovo may well have been prevented. It would have shown a will to act, and it would have chilled the spine of Milosevic."[77] Similarly, as noted by Secretary of State Albright, "[t]he strongest deterrent message that could be sent into Kosovo would be the immediate apprehension, not only of the remaining indictees [of the Tribunal], but of the persons who are the subject of sealed indictments."[78] On the contrary, the fact that Mr. Milosevic was not indicted and that Karadzic and Mladic had not been apprehended despite NATO being fully aware of their whereabouts,[79] likely emboldened Mr. Milosevic.

As noted above, many commentators assume the reason Mr. Milosevic remained unindicted was that at this point in the peace-building process the approach of accommodation overrode the approach of justice and Mr. Milosevic was deemed to be "too valuable as an interlocutor to Western powers and a guarantor of the U.S.–brokered Dayton accords that ended the war in 1995," to be indicted.[80]

Failing to Exercise Proper Jurisdiction

The crisis in Kosovo emerged at a time when the Tribunal had begun to make meaningful progress in the apprehension and prosecution of low- and mid-level indictees. Fearing a drain on its resources, the Office of the Prosecutor eschewed meaningful involvement in the Kosovo crisis. When pushed by public commentators and those interested in the success of the Tribunal to become more involved and to assert jurisdiction, the Office of the Prosecutor responded with a number of surprising assertions about lack of jurisdiction. First, the Office of the Prosecutor claimed that it was unsure whether it exercised jurisdiction over the conflict because it might not be an international conflict. Second, the Office of the Prosecutor reasoned that the Kosovo crisis might not be an armed conflict, thus rendering the office incapable of pursing any prosecution.

Both of these arguments were widely perceived as straw man arguments as (1) the Statute of the Tribunal clearly provided that "the International Tribunal shall have the power to prosecute persons responsible for Serious Violations of International Humanitarian Law Committed in *the Territory of the Former Yugoslavia since 1991,*"[81] and (2) crimes against humanity and violations of the laws and customs of war—which are applicable to internal as well as international conflicts—were within the jurisdiction of the Tribunal. Similarly, the express purpose of the Serbian government in committing the acts was to destroy the Kosovo Liberation Army, which was engaged in an armed struggle for independence. Prosecutor Arbour, however, maintained the lack of jurisdiction up until the moment NATO began its air strikes, declaring in April 1999, "from the minute the first bomb hit in Kosovo, it became an international conflict."[82]

Surprisingly, even when the prosecutor was confronted in October 1998 with the fact that the jurisdiction of the Tribunal had become a subject of negotiation between Ambassador Holbrooke and Mr. Milosevic, the prosecutor objected to the negotiations, but she did not use the opportunity to assert the jurisdiction of the Tribunal. Rather, she inferred that the Security Council might need to modify or expand the mandate of the Tribunal in order to provide adequate jurisdiction. In the prosecutor's words,

> Following reports that the U.S. envoy Mr. Richard Holbrooke was not able to obtain any concessions from President Milosevic . . . regarding the jurisdiction of this Tribunal over events in Kosovo, I wish to make a strong and unequivocal statement regarding this Tribunal's jurisdiction. . . . The jurisdiction of this Tribunal is not conditional upon President Milosevic's consent, nor is it dependent on the outcome of any negotiations between him and anyone else. It is for the Judges of this Tribunal to interpret such jurisdiction and for the Security Council to modify or expand.[83]

Importantly, when faced with atrocities committed against the Serb population by Kosovar Albanians at the end of the NATO air campaign, the prosecutor again asserted a possible lack of jurisdiction. Particularly in response to the massacre of fourteen Serb civilians, she issued a statement condemning the acts and proclaiming that her office will "investigate all serious crimes falling within the jurisdiction of [the Tribunal]." She then qualified this by stating, "to the extent that some charges must be linked to the existence of an armed conflict, this is a question of fact and a question of law, informed by the jurisprudence of the Tribunal," and merely promised "further inquiry."[84]

This unfortunate trend continued into the Macedonian conflict. In response to credible reports in August 2001 of the murder of at least ten civilians and the torture of another forty to fifty in the presence and likely under the direction of Ljube Boskovski, the Macedonian minister of interior, the Office of the Prosecutor responded with a timid assertion of general jurisdiction over Macedonia, but it did not publicly declare that such acts, if true, were punishable as war crimes and that the Office of the Prosecutor would undertake an active and aggressive investigation.[85] As a result of the involvement of the highest Macedonian police official in the torture of civilians and the failure of the Office of the Prosecutor to aggressively assert jurisdiction, Betsy Anderson of Human Rights Watch reported in August 2001 that "Persistent police abuse in Macedonia is simply shocking. . . . Ethnic Albanians are being severely abused, and in some cases beaten to death, without the slightest prospect of accountability."

Investigative Delay

While the Tribunal cannot assert jurisdiction where none exists or launch investigations where there is no evidence of a crime, Prosecutor Arbour adopted an overly narrow interpretation of her mandate, which led to significant delays in the investigation of crimes. In the spring of 1998 when atrocities were first committed on a large scale in Kosovo, former prosecutor Richard Goldstone declared that the current prosecutor "should work day and night investigating the circumstances in which innocent civilians and particularly innocent women and children were slaughtered in those opening days of the violence in Kosovo."[86] Goldstone warned that the quick investigation of war crimes allegations was necessary to prevent further atrocities.[87] Despite this and other calls for active investigation of atrocities in Kosovo, Prosecutor Arbour refused to undertake an aggressive program of investigations, opting instead for a restrained and cautious approach—consistent with her restrained approach to asserting jurisdiction.

In October 1998, a full six months after the first atrocities had been reported and after NATO had threatened air strikes to prevent further atrocities, the prosecutor sought permission from the Yugoslav government for her and ten aides to begin investigations of war crimes in Kosovo. Predictably, the Serbian government denied this request,[88] and invoked the Office of the Prosecutor's own uncertainty concerning its jurisdiction, declaring, "the official position of [the FRY] regarding the Tribunal and Kosovo is that the Tribunal has no jurisdiction to conduct investigations in Kosovo and the Tribunal will not be allowed to do so." [89] Mr. Milosevic also threatened to close the Prosecutor's Liaison Office in Belgrade, which had been cooperating on matters concerning Serb victims in the Croatian and Bosnian conflicts.[90]

Rather than simply asserting her jurisdiction and making arrangements to travel to Kosovo via Macedonia, Prosecutor Arbour sent a letter to the Security Council protesting Mr. Milosevic's denial of visas.[91] She also sent a letter to the FRY government stating that "the prosecutor does not accept the refusal by the FRY to allow Kosovo investigations."[92] As could be expected, these letters did not result in the granting of visas.

The prosecutor then abandoned her efforts to enter Kosovo for four months until after the massacre of forty-five civilians at Racak in January 1999. Again, she applied for visas for her and her team to travel to Kosovo, and again they were denied. Despite the fact that the OSCE had deployed a 2,000 strong KVM mission, she was still unable to gain access—although under substantial pressure from the United States and the United Kingdom, she did travel to the Macedonian side of the border of Kosovo, with press corps in tow, and she made an attempt to enter. This gesture, however, was perceived widely as too little too late to constitute a meaningful assertion of her authority. As will be discussed below, the prosecutor's voice was noticeably absent from the negotiations occurring in Rambouillet and Paris, and, but for the intervention of the Tribunal's president, Judge Gabrielle McDonald, the Tribunal's authority might have been seriously eroded during the negotiations.

It was not until after NATO had conducted a strategic air campaign against Serbian forces and compelled their complete withdrawal from Kosovo that the prosecutor eventually was able to enter Kosovo and conduct investigations.

Individual Responsibility

Well into the bombing campaign, on 23 May 1999 the Office of the Prosecutor tardily announced the indictment of Mr. Milosevic.[93] The indictment included Serbian president Milan Milutinovic, Serbian federal deputy prime minister Nikola Sainovic, Serbian federal chief of staff General Dragoljub Ojdanic, and Serbian interior minister Vlajko Stojilkovic. Although the indictment was publicly acclaimed as a bold step by the Office of the Prosecutor, most experts and many members of the U.S. and U.K. governments believed that the indictment was long overdue, and that its ultimate impact had been undermined by a series of previous statements by the Prosecutor's Office which had signaled to Mr. Milosevic and other high government officials that the Office of the Prosecutor was unlikely to indict them, and thus may have emboldened their commission of crimes prior to the indictment. Had the Office of the Prosecutor indicted Mr. Milosevic for crimes in Bosnia, or signaled early in the Kosovo conflict that Mr. Milosevic and other high government officials would bear responsibility for any crimes committed, this may have had a deterrent effect.

Unfortunately, until the day of the indictment, the Office of the Prosecutor had not made firm statements regarding the FRY government's role in the war crimes committed in Kosovo. As late as February 1999, Deputy Prosecutor for the Yugoslav Tribunal Graham Blewitt commented on the rumors that, if the

Office of the Prosecutor were given full and complete access to investigate mass killings in Kosovo, blame could climb to the top of the highly centralized Yugoslav government, including Mr. Milosevic. He responded vaguely that "any person who has some ability to control what happens would be looked at closely."[94]

In March 1999, Arbour undertook to send a series of letters to the Yugoslav embassy at The Hague, reminding FRY leaders of their potential criminal liability under international humanitarian law, but the embassy refused to accept the letters. Arbour made the same announcement publicly.[95] She explained that the letters informed the FRY officials of their failure to comply with the orders of the Tribunal, and explained that Arbour was deeply disturbed that humanitarian law violations continued to occur in Kosovo. Arbour said her investigations into war crimes was progressing "through means that I am not prepared to make public."[96] The letters did not, however, indicate that those officials would be held responsible for crimes committed in Kosovo by their subordinates under the principle of command responsibility.

In fact, the Office of the Prosecutor's vague statements about the prospect of indicting those who ordered human rights abuses continued right up until the Milosevic indictment. In April 1999, Arbour mentioned that her investigators were compiling information that "could lead" to an indictment of Mr. Milosevic and his aides.[97] In another interview in April, Arbour merely "hinted that she might soon indict [Milosevic]." When asked about the prospect, she reiterated the Office of the Prosecutor's policy of not discussing investigations in progress. But, she continued, "it should be pretty apparent where things are going."[98] It was only after the European Union's Council of Foreign Ministers issued a joint statement "saying they wanted Mr. Milosevic and his top aides brought to the Hague" that Arbour proclaimed ""Now our strategy is only to charge the top."[99]

When questioned about her reluctance to authoritatively assert the jurisdiction of the Tribunal and to comment on the potential responsibility of high-level Serbian officials, Prosecutor Arbour confided that her caution was a deliberate policy of the Office of the Prosecutor designed to ensure that "this tribunal can't be a lynch mob, pursuing politically correct indictments. . . . We have to guard against being used as part of any demonization campaign that NATO governments might wage against Milosevic." This comment suggests that the prosecutor was more concerned with public perception of her work than with deterring or preventing the commission of crimes against humanity in Kosovo. Moreover, she insisted that "any case the Tribunal might bring against Milosevic and his senior lieutenants must be as close to ironclad as circumstances permit."[100] Importantly, the statute of the Tribunal permits the prosecutor to seek an indictment upon the reasonable belief that an individual committed war crimes, and it does not require an "ironclad" level of proof to bring a case, or even to obtain a conviction.

Nonetheless, the Office of the Prosecutor's indictment of Mr. Milosevic, however tardy, had the effect of preventing the international community from negotiating a Dayton-style peace agreement which would have allowed him to achieve many of his objectives. The indictment did not, however, prevent Russia and Finland from negotiating an end to the armed conflict with Mr. Milosevic.

The details of American, Russian, and European negotiations with Mr. Milosevic and the role of justice will be discussed in greater detail in chapter 11.

The Role of "Interested" Parties

The failure of the Office of the Prosecutor to actively assert its jurisdiction and aggressively pursue investigations may have resulted from the tepid support it received from the Security Council, the United States, and the European Union despite their public proclamations of support for the Tribunal. In fact, in at least one instance the EU undertook activities which actively undermined the authority of the Tribunal.

On 31 March 1998, the Security Council passed Resolution 1160 concerning the crisis in Kosovo. Although the original draft of the resolution explicitly stated that the Yugoslav Tribunal had jurisdiction in Kosovo, the final version of the resolution omitted this language.[101] Rather, the final draft "[urged] the Prosecutor to begin gathering information related to crimes that may fall within the jurisdiction of the International Tribunal."

On 23 September 1998, after the Drenica and Decani massacres, the Security Council passed Resolution 1203, which "called for prompt and complete investigation, including international supervision and participation, of all atrocities committed against civilians and full co-operation with the International Tribunal for the Former Yugoslavia, including compliance with its orders, requests for information and investigations." And after the Racak massacre, the Security Council again reiterated its demands that the FRY cooperate fully with the Yugoslav Tribunal.[102] At no time, however, did the Security Council threaten economic or other sanctions on the FRY for its failure to cooperate with the Tribunal or to cease the commission of atrocities.

Throughout the Kosovo crisis the Security Council remained passive, even in the face of stern letters from the Tribunal's president Judge McDonald, which extensively documented the FRY's failure to comply with the demands of the Security Council.[103] In September 1998, for instance, Judge McDonald sent the Security Council a three-page letter documenting the FRY's continued noncompliance with the mandate of the Yugoslav Tribunal and asking the Security Council to "impress upon [the FRY] the need to honor its pledges under the Dayton Agreement and its obligations under Security Council Resolutions and under international law." McDonald noted that the Yugoslav Tribunal had previously reported to the Security Council that the FRY had refused to surrender several indicted war criminals and "failed to adopt legislation to facilitate cooperation with the International Tribunal." Judge McDonald also complained that "no action was taken by the Security Council beyond . . . the issuance of a presidential statement."[104]

In November 1998, Judge McDonald complained that the Yugoslav Tribunal's prosecutor was denied entrance into Kosovo to perform investigations. Judge McDonald stated that "I shall once again report this non-compliance to the Security Council . . . I will urge the Council to vindicate its authority and respond forcefully to the action of [the FRY]."[105] The Security Council, however, took no meaningful action.

While the Security Council shrank from seeking to compel compliance with its resolution, the United States and its NATO allies demurred with respect to providing the Office of the Prosecutor with the necessary information to support an indictment of top Serbian officials. From the beginning of the conflict in Kosovo, most of the NATO governments established teams within their intelligence agencies to gather secret evidence from satellite imagery, electronic eavesdropping, and cross-checking refugee accounts on war crimes. It was not until the day before the indictment was released, however, that the United States government "handed over 'long-sought' classified information that implicated [Milosevic] personally in the chain of command responsible for crimes against the ethnic Albanian population of Kosovo."[106] The last-minute release of the documents was labeled as part of a "persistent tug-of-war over classified evidence that [had] frequently put the United States at odds with the Tribunal."[107] According to press reports, the Western governments also "reportedly pressured the Tribunal to refrain from indicting Milosevic," as, until the air campaign started, they were set on an approach of accommodation and Mr. Milosevic was perceived of as "the guarantor of peace in the region."[108]

Whereas the Security Council and the United States failed to support the limited efforts of the Tribunal with respect to Kosovo, the EU at times actively undermined those efforts. For example, in November 1998, a month after Mr. Milosevic had refused to allow Prosecutor Arbour into Kosovo to investigate the Racak massacre, the FRY issued visas to Finnish forensic experts sent from the European Union to investigate various war crimes sites. The European Union experts did not consult with the Yugoslav Tribunal and accepted significant restrictions on their investigations. Specifically, the FRY allowed the EU experts to examine only certain sites and required that the EC findings be turned over to local authorities in Serbia and not to the Yugoslav Tribunal or any other international organization.[109] By agreeing to conduct their work under such limitations, the effective results of the investigations were significantly limited, while allowing Mr. Milosevic to claim that he was permitting international review of the situation, and he was thus not obligated to permit the Tribunal to conduct additional investigations.

The Kosovo Crisis Epilogue: Investigating NATO

Shortly after the conclusion of the NATO air campaign, Amnesty International and Human Rights Watch submitted reports to the Office of the Prosecutor of the Yugoslav Tribunal alleging that NATO had committed war crimes within the Tribunal's jurisdiction. Similar complaints were received from a committee of the Russian parliament and from a group of law professors based at Osgoode Hall Law School in Toronto, where the prosecutor, Louise Arbour, had taught for several years.

According to these reports, over half of the casualties of the NATO intervention were civilians. The reports criticized the strategy of high-altitude bombing, the use of cluster bombs and depleted uranium shells, as well as the intentional destruction of nonmilitary targets, including television stations, power generating plants, and water and sewage processing facilities. In one alleged case, the pilots attacking the Grdelica bridge realized too late that they had hit a civilian train, but, since the bridge had not been destroyed in the first wave, the attack was renewed, and the train was hit a second time, killing a large number of civilians.[110]

In a public effort to demonstrate independence and even-handedness, in her last month in office, the Tribunal's prosecutor, Louise Arbour, ordered a preliminary review of the evidence and the applicable law by an internal committee led by her chief legal adviser, William Fenrick, a seasoned former Canadian military lawyer who had served on the War Crimes Commission. Among the other members of the committee were Russian, American, and British lawyers and investigators. While the inquiry was conducted in a professional and comprehensive manner and was perceived by the prosecutor as an effort to fairly apply the norm of justice, the mere fact of holding an inquiry met with a swift condemnation by officials in Washington and other NATO capitals. The White House denounced as "completely unjustified" the idea of an inquiry into possible war crimes by NATO commanders during the bombing campaign. White House spokesman Jim Fallin said NATO "fully followed the laws of armed conflict in training, targeting and operations" and "undertook extraordinary efforts to minimize collateral damage." The primary objection to the pseudo investigation was its perceived creation of moral equivalence between Slobodan Milosevic's actions in Kosovo and NATO's humanitarian intervention.

As such, the Tribunal's new prosecutor, Carla Del Ponte, tried to downplay the examination shortly after she assumed her new office, saying "at this point, it is just an inquiry, not a proper investigation." But she added, "the prosecutor cannot just receive the complaints and say, 'Oh no, it's nothing,' and throw it away."[111] Subsequently, Del Ponte widened the probe by sending a list of questions related to the conduct of the bombing campaign to Washington and other NATO capitals. At the same time, Del Ponte reportedly assured NATO officials that "she would not carry this exercise far and that she was embarrassed by having to deal with a tendentious process inherited from her predecessor."[112]

In an unprecedented move, on 8 June 2000, Del Ponte made the 100-page report on the NATO bombing campaign available to the public. The report concluded that NATO was not in fact responsible for war crimes, although it did criticize as excessive some of the air strikes.[113] In transmitting the report to the Security Council, Del Ponte said although "some mistakes were made by NATO," she was "very satisfied that there was no deliberate targeting of civilians or unlawful military targets."[114]

The report had a resoundingly negative impact within the U.S. Department of Defense and within the NATO military establishment. Many inside commentators note that the investigation significantly cooled the interest of NATO in risking its troops to apprehend Karadzic and Mladic, and drastically reduced the possibility for future humanitarian interventions—particularly when the Permanent International Criminal Court comes into being. A prevailing view was that "why should NATO forces risk casualties in arresting these individuals if the NATO forces then might be subject to investigation themselves by the Office of the Prosecutor if their efforts were found to be unsuitable in the view of the Prosecutor's academic colleagues?" NATO was also keenly aware that although the prosecutor justified her actions on the basis that she could not simply dismiss arguments brought to her attention by academics and the Russian Duma, in fact for over four years the Office of the Prosecutor had expressly avoided making any comment on an academic report filed with the prosecutor in 1996 laying out a detailed and credible case for the indictment of Slobodan Milosevic for his crimes in Bosnia.[115] Interestingly, once the new prosecutor determined she would like to pursue a case against Milosevic for these crimes, the Office of the Prosecutor reportedly used the report as a template and retained one of its authors as a consultant.

While NATO clearly is not immune from the laws of war or the jurisdiction of the Tribunal, more careful and sophisticated consideration should have been given to the matter before so publicly launching a pseudo investigation in direct contradiction to numerous statements that the prosecutor would not discuss potential cases or ongoing investigations.

Although announced as a major step forward in the utilization of justice as a tool for building peace, the Yugoslav Tribunal's record is one of mixed achievements. The relatively limited initial impact on the peace process is the result of a lack of genuine commitment to the norm of justice by some of the most important peace builders, and a reluctance to allow the approach of accountability to augment the approach of accommodation. The limited impact is also the direct result of the Tribunal's at times intentional ignorance of the political context in which it was created and forced to operate. For a period of time the Office of the Prosecutor sought to conduct itself like a domestic prosecutor before a national court and failed to grasp the unique nature of its role and mandate. When the Prosecutor's Office did act consistent with its broader mission, it was often timid and tardy. Moreover, as will be discussed below, many of the major peace builders were unwilling to compliment the approach of accountability with sufficient use of force to ensure the apprehension of indicted war criminals.

While the Tribunal did play an important role in the Kosovo crisis through its indictment of Milosevic, given the slowness in the development of the Tribunal and its relatively limited initial impact, the Bosnian government sought to employ an additional mechanism of justice—that of the World Court. The FRY also sought to invoke the forum of the World Court as a means for constraining NATO action against Serbia in response to its war in Kosovo. As will be discussed in the next chapter, the Bosnian genocide case ultimately proved to be of little value in the peace process, and in the NATO intervention case the Court—by its very nature—was unable to act in time to limit the NATO action, and the United States and some of its European allies missed an opportunity to publicly make their case for humanitarian intervention.

Chapter 8

The International Court of Justice: A Misled Opportunity

There can be no peace without justice, no justice without law and no meaningful law without a Court to decide what is just and lawful under any given circumstance.

—Benjamin B. Ferencz, a former Nuremberg prosecutor

On 20 March 1993, during the height of the Yugoslav conflict, the government of Bosnia and Herzegovina filed suit against the government of the FRY in the International Court of Justice.[1] In its pleadings, the Bosnian government asked the Court to find and declare that between April 1992 (the beginning of the Bosnian war) and December 1995 (the conclusion of the Dayton Accords) Serbian forces engaged in a campaign of genocide against the non-Serb population of Bosnia and Herzegovina, and that the FRY bore responsibility for these and related violations of the Genocide Convention. The FRY unsuccessfully sought to have the case dismissed for lack of jurisdiction and then filed counter claims of genocide on behalf of the Serbian population of Bosnia. In 1999, Croatia filed a similar case against the FRY alleging the commission of crimes against humanity and genocide.[2]

On 11 May 1999, the FRY filed a case against the United States and nine other NATO members in the International Court of Justice alleging that their bombing campaign against the FRY violated its right to territorial integrity and political independence as enshrined in the UN Charter, and further that the air strikes violated the Geneva conventions and the Genocide Convention.[3]

The focus of this chapter will be to answer questions three, four, five, seven, and nine set forth in chapter 1, in particular to what extent the interests of the parties themselves guided them toward institutions of justice, to what extent the parties and peace builders felt bound by preexisting rules and norms, to what degree the parties and peace builders were able to invoke existing institutions of justice and were these institutions capable of giving the necessary effect to the norm of justice, to what extent did the various approaches compete for primacy—specifically, in the Bosnian case, in terms of accountability versus accommodation and in the Kosovo case in terms of use of force versus accountability, and to what degree did the states learn about their ability to use justice as a tool and did they adjust their behavior accordingly.

To further the understanding of these questions, this chapter briefly examines the merits of the Bosnian case and explores the extent to which the United States and its European allies failed to embrace the case as a means for peacebuilding. This chapter also examines the extent to which the American and European governments failed to support the efforts of the Bosnian government, and in some instances exerted pressure on the Bosnian government to drop the case in furtherance of their approach of accommodation. The chapter then examines how the FRY sought to employ the norm of justice and to use the institution of the International Court of Justice to further the pursuit of its interests in the Kosovo conflict, and the reluctance of the United States and its allies to utilize the Court as a means for making their case against Serbian aggression and defending the notion of humanitarian intervention. The chapter then discusses how this reluctance stemmed from their assessment of the relative lack of utility in utilizing an international judicial institution to make their case for intervention.

The Court Will Now Hear the Case of Bosnian Genocide

This is a clear attempt to change the biological structure of the city. We will defend our frontiers biologically.

—anonymous Bosnian Serb official in Brcko, on attempts by
Muslim refugees to return to their homes in the region[4]

At a time when all of Bosnia's major cities were under seige, international peacekeeping efforts had proven futile, and the international negotiation process was stalled, the Bosnian ambassador to the United Nations, Mohamed Sacirbey, working with a team of legal experts, including Francis Boyle, Thomas Franck, Khawar Qureshi, Phon van den Biesen, Alain Pellet, and Brigitte Stern, sought to involve the World Court in the peace-building process by filing a case against Yugoslavia for genocide.[5]

The primary motivation for filing the case was to bring renewed attention to the conflict and its consequences for the people of Bosnia, to characterize the conflict as one based on a policy of genocide, and to guard against the increasing tendency of Western policymakers to portray all sides as equally responsible for the conflict and the ensuing atrocities as a means toward facilitating their efforts at accommodation.

The Bosnian government also sought to achieve the objective of creating an accurate historical record of the responsibility of the FRY for the genocide in Bosnia to counter the efforts of Western policymakers and some "historians" to portray the conflict as growing out of ancient ethnic hatreds, which facilitated the policymakers efforts to create moral equivalency among the parties. The Bosnian government also deemed that such a record would be indispensable in the reconciliation process, and would be relevant for decisions relating to the implimentation of any subsequent peace agreements. Importantly, by clearly establishing the responsibility of state institutions, as opposed to the collective responsibility of the Serbian people, the Court could also enable the process of reconcilation to move beyond broad recriminations and lay the foundation for the rebuilding of mutual relations among the ethnic groups in Bosnia.

The adjudication also sought to serve the necessary purpose of operating as a cathartic process for the victims of genocide by providing them an opportunity to publicly recount the atrocities committed against them and their families through the supporting documents submitted by Bosnia and to have this evidence assessed by an independent judicial body. The case could also have had the effect of aiding in deterring of future acts of genocide by the Serbian state institutions in areas such as Kosovo and Vojvodina by publicly disclosing details of the Serbian plans for an ethnically pure greater Serbia, and by identifying and aiding in the delegitimization of those institutions primarily responsible for crimes of genocide necessary to implement these plans.

Given the limits of the Yugoslav Tribunal discussed in the preceeding chapter, these functions of the genocide case took on even greater importance to the Bosnian government, and they might have been given greater relevance by the Western governments had they properly perceived the role of justice in the peace-building process.

Overview of the Substance of the Case

In an effort to shape the nature of the peace process and to establish what they considered a just basis for the resolution of the conflict, the Bosnian government sought to prove three main points. First, that Serbia had developed detailed plans to pursue an armed conflict in order to create an ethnically pure greater Serbia. According to the Bosnian government, genocide against non-Serb populations formed a key element of this plan. The preparations for the greater Serbia project included the drafting of the so-called FRAME memorandum which envisioned the arming of paramilitaries and civilian organizations and the incitement to genocide, the actual distribution of weapons to paramilitary operations such as Arkan's Tigers by the Yugoslav Ministry of the Interior, and the purging of the Yugoslav National Army (JNA) of non-Serb officers. The FRAME memorandum also detailed plans for the disarmament of non-Serb Bosnian Territorial Defense forces, the restructuring of the chain of command of Bosnian-Serb Territorial Defense forces to report directly to the General Staff of the JNA in Belgrade, and the direct involvement of JNA forces in early acts of genocide against the people of Bosnia and Herzegovina.

The second element of Bosnia's case was the presentation of a detailed catalogue of crimes of genocide, which include the widespread and systematic killing of civilians and noncombatants; the specific targeting of political, commercial, and medical elites; widespread and systematic torture and infliction of mental anquish; the organization of an intricate network of concentration camps; the systematic destruction of cultural property; the utilization of mass rape as a tool of terror; the forced expulsion of entire communities; the encirclement, shelling, and starvation of other communities such as Sarajevo; and the entire extermination of still other communities such as Srebrenica.

The third element of Bosnia's case related to the meticulous detailing of the role of the FRY government in carrying out its plan to use genocide to create an ethnically pure greater Serbia by actively aiding, supervising, and directing the crimes of genocide against non-Serbs. Specifically, these acts allegedly included: active and direct JNA military involvement in crimes of genocide before May 1992, the wholesale transformation of the JNA into the Bosnian Serb army, the reintroduction of regular JNA army units and special forces into Bosnia to aid in the commission of acts of genocide—in particular the Srebrenica massacre, the continued supply of weapons, ammunition, and logistical support, the financial and logistical support of paramilitaries operating out of Serbia proper, the detailing of JNA officers to Bosnian Serb units, and eventually the exercise of direct command and control over the Bosnian Serb army.

The FRY government denied these claims and asserted that it was in fact the Bosnian government forces that were undertaking a campaign of genocide against Serbians living in Bosnia.

Activities of the United States Related to the Case

In contrast to the strong public support of the United States for the work of the Yugoslav Tribunal, the United States and its European allies exhibited a serious lack of enthusiasm for the World Court case. In particular, the United States never publicly declared its support for the case, nor provided the Bosnian government with unclassified or declassified information in its possession that could have been useful in Bosnia's case. Moreover, on more than one occasion, a high ranking U.S. diplomat, at the behest of Slobodan Milosevic, encouraged the Bosnian government to drop the case.

The rationale for the lack of public support and the pressure to drop the case were related to ongoing attempts by the United States and European governments to accommodate the Serbian regime. According to this view, had the Court declared that the Serbian regime was responsible for genocide, then it would have been nearly impossible to continue efforts to mediate the Vance/Owen Peace Plan or to negotiate the Dayton Accords. Similarly, in the early stages of the implementation of the Dayton Accords, a ruling from the World Court would have undermined the efforts to treat all sides equally and to apply pressure on the Bosnian government to secure necessary compromises.

Moreover, the reluctance to support the case was part of the larger U.S. and European policy to avoid publicly stating that the atrocities in Bosnia amounted to genocide, and to avoid publicly identifying Slobodan Milosevic as legally responsible for the war crimes committed in Bosnia or Kosovo.

The reluctance of the United States to support the case also rested on the fact that some government officials were uncomfortable with the state of Bosnia engaging in any independent actions that could not be managed or controlled by the peace builders and which complicated their efforts at accommodation. For instance, when the president and prime minister of Bosnia declared Bosnia's support for the NATO action in Kosovo in order to prevent another genocide, the Office of the High Representative publicly rebuked them for this declaration of support, contending it was not proper for them to be making such remarks.

Importantly, some U.S. and European government officials may have been sensitive to the fact that if the ICJ were to find that genocide had in fact been committed against the people of Bosnia from early 1992, this would serve to recriminate those individuals who assiduously denied the occurrence of genocide and who argued against the necessity of military intervention on the grounds that it would have interfered with their ability to pursue the approach of accommodation.

Had the United States embraced, or at least publicly supported, the Bosnian case, it could have utilized the case to bolster its public justifications for its subsequent use of force against Serbian forces in Bosnia, and its humanitarian intervention in Kosovo. In the case of Kosovo, the United States could have argued that the compelling justification for NATO action was based on the fact that, given the crimes of genocide committed against the people of Bosnia, the international community could reasonably conclude that Mr. Milosevic's forces were intent on and capable of committing genocide against the people of Kosovo as well.

Implications of the Case for the Crisis in Kosovo

Had the U.S. and European governments assisted the Bosnian government in their case or undertaken a more active assessment of its merits, they might have been in a better position to assess the nature of the Kosovo conflict. In particular, the Western states might have better understood that the ethnic cleansing occurring in Kosovo was a repetition of the acts carried out against the people of Bosnia and that it was part of a larger plan for an ethnically pure Serbia that might involve future acts of ethnic cleansing and genocide against the non-Serb populations in Vojvodina, Sandzak, and possibly Montenegro and Macedonia if it were not stopped in Kosovo. Although the peace builders eventually came to this conclusion, they did so only after nearly eighteen months of atrocities and the displacement of 1.5 million refugees.

Similarly, a better understanding of the Bosnian case would have served to blunt initial policy considerations for the partitioning of Kosovo as part of a peace settlement, as this would further perpetuate the interests of the Serbian nationalist regime, and not only build upon, but actually ratify, the use of geno-cide as a means of creating an ethnically pure greater Serbia.

Institutional Impediments

In addition to the lack of support from the peace builders, the impact of the Bosnian case on the peace process was minimized by the nature of such interna-tional adjudication. Although filed in 1993, as of the time of publication of this book, there have been no oral arguments on the merits of the case and thus it has not been possible for the Bosnians to publicly make their case, let alone for the World Court to make a ruling on the case—which usually occurs from six to twelve months after the oral hearings.[6] While the Court did issue a provisional order on 8 April 1993 directing all parties to cease acts of genocide and comply with the obligations of the convention, there is no evidence this order had any impact whatsoever on the level of atrocities committed in the conflict.

Moreover, as is customary with proceedings before the World Court, the parties agreed that the pleadings and accompanying evidence would be kept confidential until the oral hearings. Bosnia has thus not been able to rely upon the detailed compilation of information to present its case in a coherent fashion outside of the World Court—although much of the information nonetheless found its way into the public domain in an ad hoc fashion.

As a result of these political and institutional limitations, the ultimate effect of the case will be to accomplish little more than establishing an accurate his-torical record, and to some degree providing a vehicle for victim catharsis—both of which will occur years too late to have a significant effect on peace-building.

The Court Will Now Hear the Case of NATO Aggression

We will remember 1999 as the year in which sovereignty gave way in places where crimes against humanity were being committed.

—Kenneth Roth, Executive Director of
Human Rights Watch

As the NATO member states prepared to launch air strikes against the FRY in October 1998, and again in February/March 1999, they articulated very clear moral grounds—to stop atrocities—and security grounds—to prevent the con-flict from spilling over to neighboring European countries. NATO, however, declined to articulate a legal justification for the intervention. Reportedly, even the Department of State's legal adviser explicitly declined to provide the secre-tary of state with a legal justification for the humanitarian intervention.[7]

Sensing the reluctance of the NATO member states to articulate a clear jus-tice-based case for their intervention, the FRY saw an opportunity to invoke the norms and institutions of justice to limit NATO's ability to use force. The

NATO states responded, not by invoking the norm of justice on their behalf, which they clearly could have done, but rather with short descriptions of the atrocities committed by the Serbian forces, and narrow and technical jurisdictional arguments in an effort to get the Serb case dismissed. In so doing, the NATO member states missed a significant opportunity to meld their decision to invoke the use of force with the norm of justice in order to create a solid justification for their actions in Kosovo and to further the precedent for legitimate humanitarian intervention.[8] In fact, they missed an opportunity to craft this justification and to form precedent before an institution of justice.

Although the reluctance to "make their case" before the World Court can be ascribed to a general mistrust of the Court by some states and the fear of the inherent uncertainty associated with judicial determinations, the prevalent reason is likely the embryonic nature of the justifications for humanitarian intervention and the concern that each possible legal underpinning carried with it the specter of a practical consequence that the NATO member states hoped to avoid. Unfortunately the policy of silence is a blunt and weak tool for navigating these concerns and in the long term may have exacerbated and legitimized the objections to the legitimate use of force for humanitarian intervention.

To explore further the nature of the case for humanitarian intervention, the remainder of this chapter will examine the case made by the FRY before the Court and set forth the arguments which the NATO members states could have made had they engaged on the merits, and the likely responses of the Serbian regime.

Humanitarian Intervention—Was There a Case to Be Made?

Prior to the initiation of the case before the World Court, the nearest the NATO member states had come to articulating a legal rationale for their intervention in Kosovo was to cite various resolutions of the Security Council, in which the Council had determined that the actions of the FRY in Kosovo constituted a threat to peace and security in the region and, pursuant to Chapter VII of the UN Charter, demanded a halt to such actions. The NATO member states never dwelled on these Security Council resolutions, however, since they did not employ the talismanic phrase "states may take all necessary means," which would have constituted an express Security Council authorization for the use of force.

To make its case before the World Court, the FRY retained the distinguished British international law expert Ian Brownlie—who also represented them before the Court in the case brought against the FRY for its acts of genocide in Bosnia. Professor Brownlie argued to the Court that (1) the NATO intervention was an unlawful use of force because it violated Article 2(4) of the UN Charter, which provides that each state is entitled to territorial integrity and political independence; (2) the members of NATO breached the 1949 Geneva conventions by targeting civilians and using depleted uranium weapons; and (3) the attack against the FRY constituted a form of genocide in violation of the Genocide Convention.[9] As noted above, the United States and its NATO allies generally declined to rebut these arguments; rather they challenged the Court's jurisdiction on technical grounds.

While the technical arguments were successful for some of the respondents, what the NATO member states failed to grasp was that the FRY was using the norms and institutions of justice to seek a victory not primarily in the courtroom in The Hague, but in the court of public opinion. By making his case before the World Court (and the world media), Mr. Milosevic took another step in his quest to level the moral playing field between the FRY and NATO—and to employ the principle of moral equivalism which served him well in the Bosnian conflict. Coming amidst reports that NATO bombs had gone astray or were mistargeted—destroying hospitals, civilian convoys, and even the Chinese embassy in Belgrade, the case before the World Court further eroded public support in several NATO countries for the policy of continuing air strikes and decreased the general support for the potential deployment of a NATO ground force.

The Politics of Genocide

While the legality of the NATO humanitarian intervention was certainly debatable, the NATO member states may have more successfully blunted Mr. Milosevic's strategy if they had fully outlined the legal case for the air strikes early in the campaign, or at least during the preliminary stages of the case before the World Court, while simultaneously making their technical arguments challenging the Court's jurisdiction. The NATO member states could have, for example, argued the 1948 Convention on the Prevention and Punishment of the Crime of Genocide authorizes those countries that have ratified it, which would include all the NATO member states, to "undertake to prevent and to punish" genocide.[10] Moreover, it could reasonably be argued the duty to cooperate in the prevention of genocide had attained the level of a preemptory norm of international law (*jus cogens*).[11] Such norms supersede other treaty rights and obligations—including the UN Charter. Further, the NATO member states could have argued that, as a party to the Genocide Convention, the FRY had impliedly waived its right to invoke territorial integrity to shield it from international action to halt attempted genocide.

This argument would have been particularly compelling if at the time of the World Court case the NATO member states had publicly declared that genocide or attempted genocide was occurring in Kosovo and that Slobodan Milosevic and the Serbian nationalist regime were responsible for this genocide. Although the British government made such a declaration, the United States and other nations remained reluctant to make such proclamations as they feared this would inhibit their ability to subsequently accommodate Mr. Milosevic, which they believed might be necessary in order to bring an end to the conflict. In particular, when asked during his confirmation hearings why he had not publicly referred to Mr. Milosevic as a war criminal, Ambassador Holbrooke indicated that he might at any time during the Kosovo conflict have been called upon to travel to Belgrade to negotiate with Mr. Milosevic and this would have limited his ability to do so.[12]

The argument would have carried even more weight if the Office of the Prosecutor had issued an indictment against Slobodan Milosevic charging him with attempted genocide prior to or early on in the NATO air campaign. Yet, given the Western governments' internal debate as to whether an indictment of Mr. Milosevic would frustrate the possibility of attaining a negotiated peace settlement and prevent them from employing the approach of accommodation, and their consequent delay in providing the necessary information to the Office of the Prosecutor to support an indictment, it was not until June that the Tribunal issued its indictment. Importantly, the Office of the Prosecutor failed to indict Mr. Milosevic on charges of genocide, it limited the charges to war crimes and crimes against humanity.

Had the NATO member states sought to avail themselves of the opportunity to justify their humanitarian intervention on legal grounds they could have asserted a second rationale—that intervention designed to prevent grave human rights abuses is not prohibited by Article 2(4) of the UN Charter. As that article is designed to prohibit the use of force aimed against the territorial integrity or political independence of a state (unless such force is authorized by the Security Council or is taken in self-defense), the NATO member states could have persuasively argued that as they explicitly rejected claims of independence for Kosovo and publicly reaffirmed the territorial integrity and political independence of the FRY, the purpose of the air strikes could not be construed to either impair territorial integrity or challenge political independence.

NATO's reluctance to rely on this legal rationale reflected fears that the precedent would encourage other countries to intervene in less altruistic circumstances. It was for this reason some Western countries condemned the Indian invasion of Bangladesh in 1971 and the Tanzanian invasion of Uganda in 1979. While these invasions put an end to mass slaughters, in each case the self-interest of the invading state was clearly involved.[13] NATO apparently feared that it might be perceived as building on this precedent as its strategy at times appeared calculated more to punish and de-claw the Milosevic regime for its past atrocities than to halt the human rights abuses currently being committed. Yet, fears of abusive invocation of the doctrine of humanitarian intervention must be balanced against compelling need for a contemporary and realistic interpretation of article 2(4) in light of the reemergence of Security Council paralysis in the face of mass atrocities. With NATO's movement toward the introduction of ground troops and increasing attacks directed at those military units responsible for the continued atrocities in Kosovo, NATO cleared the presumption of political self-interest which tainted the Indian and Tanzanian actions.

NATO could have simultaneously argued that, based on the facts pertaining to the dissolution of the former Yugoslavia and the failure of the FRY to be recognized as a state under international law, NATO's actions did not contravene article 2(4). When Croatia, Slovenia, Bosnia, and Macedonia achieved their independence, the Security Council declared in Resolution 777 of 1992 that the FRY did not constitute the heir to the international legal personality of the former Yugoslavia and thus was not entitled to continue the UN membership of the former Yugoslavia, a position that was confirmed by the General Assembly in Resolution 47/1.[14] Given Kosovo's claim for independence and Montenegro's indication that it might seek to secede as well, the legal process of dissolution may legitimately be considered to be continuing at that time. The FRY's status remained in question until the new Kostunica government applied for and was given membership in the UN as "a new state" in October 2000. Thus, an argument could be made that the FRY did not in 1999 possess full rights of sovereignty and territorial integrity as protected by Article 2(4) of the UN Charter.

Notably, several of the NATO member states referenced Security Council Resolution 777 and General Assembly Resolution 47/1 in their statements to the Court, but they argued only that the FRY does not have a right to bring a case since it is not a party to the UN Charter and the Statute of the World Court. In their eyes the problem with taking the argument to the next level was that if the FRY was not deemed a sovereign state, it could not be held responsible for failing to abide by the treaties of the former Yugoslavia, including the Geneva conventions and the Genocide Convention. This concern was overstated, however, since nonstate actors could still be held personally responsible for war crimes, crimes against humanity, and genocide under customary international law and principles of *jus cogens.*

A final argument that NATO could have made to justify its humanitarian intervention was that the people of Kosovo were entitled to self-determination and thus to exercise their right of collective self-defense. Even Ian Brownlie, the counsel for the FRY, recognized that self-determination has become a peremptory norm of international law.[15] As the Kosovo Albanians represented a clearly defined group of people with a distinct identity who had been systematically denied fundamental human rights and the opportunity to engage in collective democratic self-governance, they were entitled to self-determination. In the very unique circumstances facing the people of Kosovo, the internationally recognized right of self-determination includes the right to resort to force (other than by terrorism) and to seek independence.[16]

The question is slightly more complicated when it relates to whether the right of self-determination includes the right to call upon other states to engage in collective self-defense against the aggression of a totalitarian regime. The International Court of Justice rejected the Reagan administration's attempt to assert such a rationale for intervening in Nicaragua in 1985, stating "[t]he Court cannot contemplate the creation of a new rule opening up a right of intervention by one State against another on the ground that the latter has opted for some particular ideology or political system."[17] But the situation in Kosovo was different in that NATO was not intervening to impose democratic government in the FRY, but to protect the Kosovo Albanians from ethnic cleansing and genocide. Of course, making this argument would have required the United States to indicate its willingness to recognize Kosovo's independence—a step which may have complicated relations with certain European states unwilling to contemplate an independent Kosovo.

Given their potential downsides, NATO's reluctance to embrace one or more of these legal justifications is perhaps understandable, though misconceived. While these relatively novel arguments may not have ultimately carried the day in the World Court, there would likely have been a sympathetic reception to them in the United Nations General Assembly, as well as in the court of public opinion. Although NATO successfully concluded its air campaign, the lack of an articulated legal stance weakened international and domestic support for the intervention, undermined the authority of the Security Council, and diminished international respect for the rule of law.

Like the Yugoslav Tribunal, the World Court proved to be a limited forum for infusing the norm of justice into the peace-building process. While the World Court suffered from well-known institutional limitations, the major peace builders were both reluctant to use the Court as a tool for peace-building and very intent on discouraging the parties to the conflict from employing a mechanism over which the peace builders did not exercise control. In large part the peace builders hoped to promote a negotiated resolution of the conflict and were reluctant to encourage or permit any action that might constrain the compromises that might be necessary at the negotiating table. The next three chapters detail the negotiation process in Bosnia and Kosovo, with a focus on the competition between the approaches of accountability and accommodation and the role of the use of force.

Part IV

The Role of Justice in the Negotiation Phase of Peace Building

Chapter 9

The Dayton Negotiations: Getting to Yes with War Criminals

We have an obligation to carry forward the lessons of Nuremberg. Those ac-
cused of war crimes, crimes against humanity and genocide must be brought to
justice. There must be peace for justice to prevail, but there must be justice
when peace prevails.

—William Jefferson Clinton, U.S. President

The convening of the Dayton negotiations in November 1995 offered a unique opportunity to implement President Clinton's maxim that there must be justice when peace prevails in order to establish a truly lasting peace. Unfortunately, the integration of the norm of justice into the negotiation phase of the peace-building process is more complicated than it might appear. To find its way into the Dayton negotiation process, the norm of justice would first have to over-come the heavy disposition toward accommodation in earlier Yugoslav peace negotiations. In fact, during the earlier negotiations sponsored by the UN/EU justice played almost no role, and much diplomatic energy was expended simply trying to bring the use of force approach into play.

Once the accommodation norm was contained to a more appropriate status and the use of force approach was allowed to create a space for more meaningful negotiations, there was an opening for the norm of justice. Justice, however, still had to overcome a general lack of seriousness and understanding among many of the key third-party mediators concerning the role and functions that justice could serve with respect to peace-building. The norm of justice also found itself in competition with the other approaches influencing the negotiation phase of the peace-building process—mainly, the accommodation approach. Even the structure of the negotiations themselves played a part in minimizing the em-ployment of the norm of justice.

Most important, however, in order to accomplish the primary objective of the Dayton negotiations, which was to compel Mr. Milosevic to sign a peace agreement, it was necessary to intentionally minimize the norm of justice, and to rely upon elements of antijustice, such as moral equivalence, legitimization of war criminals, and possible de facto immunity. As noted by one Western diplomat during the negotiation, "there comes a time, when you have to choose between some absolute justice and moving forward in peace."[1] While the Europeans sought to exclude the norm of justice and the Bosnian delegation sought to maximize its application, the Americans sought to accept some limited role for justice, while pursuing a primary approach of accommodation.

As observed by one commentator in favor of the predominance of the norm of justice, the fact of a negotiated settlement with Milosevic was inherently contradictory to the essence of the norm of justice. As noted by Helen Fein, "whereas intervention is required against acts already deemed criminal in international law, conflict-resolution or mediation model[s] may only be appropriate before the commission of crimes against humanity and sends the wrong message when invoked during genocide, overlooking or rewarding crime and aggression." According to Fein, "if we view genocide as state crime rather than 'ethnic conflict,' we are constrained to prevent, deter and stop it, rather than to negotiate in the middle with its perpetrators."[2]

Given the intense competition between justice and accommodation, and between accommodation and the use of force, this chapter will primarily focus on question eight as set forth in chapter 1 which relates to the extent to which the competition between the various approaches influenced the development of peace-building regimes. This chapter will also shed light on questions one, two, three, six, seven, nine, and ten, in particular, how the interests of various peace builders influenced their view of the utility of the various approaches, the extent to which various approaches evolved during the peace-building process, the manner in which the evolving interests of the parties influenced the change or modification of approaches, which regimes did the peace builders create in order to promote their efforts and to what extent did these regimes permit the incorporation of various approaches, to what extent the approaches competed for primacy, whether the peace builders learned through the peace-building process how better to apply the various approaches, and whether the eventual combination of approaches incorporated in the peace-building process created an effective foundation/framework for postsettlement implementation of the agreement.[3]

To structure this discussion, this chapter will review the initial debate over the use of force versus accommodation during the early stages of the conflict, examine the efforts to promote the role of justice immediately before the commencement of the Dayton negotiations, and detail the dynamics and compromises of the Dayton negotiations.

Prelude to Dayton: Accommodation versus Use of Force

The search for a juster peace than was obtainable at the negotiating table has inflicted hardship and havoc on innocent civilians within the former Yugoslavia and exacted a heavy price from the already weak economies of the neighboring states.

—David Owen, co-chair of the International
Conference for the Former Yugoslavia[4]

Prior to the Dayton negotiations, the conflict in the former Yugoslavia can be divided into two predominant phases. The first phase from 1991 until the spring of 1995 was dominated by efforts by the United Nations and the European Union to mediate a peace based almost exclusively on the approach of accommodation. As noted by Ed Vulliamy, "the relegation of justice to the subconscious or even to oblivion did not start at Dayton. Dayton can be seen as the culmination of a series of events in which negotiations with the aggressors in the genocide were concerned mostly with keeping Western forces from intervening in the war than on the concerns of stopping the genocide."[5] The primary institution for conducting the negotiations was the joint UN/EU International Conference on the Former Yugoslavia. Although the UN deployed peacekeepers to the region, they were essentially prohibited from using force except for their own self-defense. In his book, *Endgame Srebrenica*, David Rohde chronicled how this approach culminated in the Srebrenica massacre.[6]

The second phase was marked by the increasing legitimate use of force both by NATO air assets and by a joint Croatian/Bosnian military campaign against Serb forces in northwestern Bosnia from the spring through the autumn of 1995. Most commentators agree that these actions created circumstances necessary for the negotiation of the Dayton Accords.

The UN/EU Peace Conference (1991-1995): The Embodiment of Accommodation

From 1991 to 1995 the primary rationale for a preference for accommodation over the use of force was that, if the international community employed air strikes against the Bosnian Serb forces, the Yugoslav army would enter the war in support of the Bosnian Serb army. Although this view was publicly stated by the primary peace negotiators, a then classified Department of State cable unequivocally reports on 17 February 1994 that in light of the 9 February 1994 NATO ultimatum threatening air strikes "there is, so far, no indication that the Yugoslav Army is planning to initiate a general mobilization in Serbia either in anticipation of or reaction to NATO air strikes."[7] In fact, the cable reported that in light of the perceived seriousness of the threat and the perception of Western resolve, the Bosnian Serbs would comply with the NATO demand after a period of brinkmanship.[8]

Despite this and other assessments, from 1991 to 1995 the UN/EU peace conference proposed a series of peace plans for the de facto and de jure partition of Bosnia. Although occasionally a party would tentatively accept a plan as a tactical move to curry favor with the international community or to forestall international sanction, on the whole the plans were systematically rejected by all the parties.

The representatives of the Croatian government rejected the plans in large part because they did not adequately deal with Croatia's long-term security concerns, did not encompass a resolution of the Serb-controlled areas of Kosovo, did not provide Croatia with as significant a portion of Bosnian territory as it believed it was entitled, and, most important, because the Croatian government believed, correctly, that over time it would be able to recapture the Serbian-controlled areas of its territory.

The Serbian regime rejected the plans ostensibly because, although they generally ratified Serb territorial conquest, they did not provide Serbs with a viable political and economic entity. In reality, the Serbian regime was aware that the longer it continued the peace process, the longer it could continue its territorial conquest, the more it could solidify its territorial gains already achieved, and it could complete its policy of ethnic cleansing.

The representatives of the Bosnian government rejected the plans as they objected to being granted one-third of the territory of Bosnia despite the fact Bosnians constituted a majority of the population, because they believed the plans ratified and encouraged ethnic cleansing, and because they disapproved of the entire appeasement nature of the peace process. The Bosnian government also objected to a number of the specifics of the plans, including provisions to place Sarajevo under UN administration and to grant the Serbian regime the power to establish an independent state after the initial phase of the settlement. Given the Bosnian government's antipathy toward the appeasement nature of the peace process, together with the positive rhetoric emanating from the United States, the Bosnians also hoped that the United States would soon take over the process and put forward terms more conducive to a just peace and more limiting to Serbian regime's designs for a greater Serbia.

Concerning the role of justice, the UN/EU co-chairmen adhered to the traditional view of a conflict between peace and justice, and they squarely adopted the approach of accommodation, which quickly became one of appeasement. According to Ed Vulliamy:

> The history of appeasement of the Serbs is the history of the entire war. There were countless moments when the Serbs were told not to cross a line, and that they faced dire consequences if they did; and every time the bluff was called, the West climbed down, and the handshakes resumed. Some of the Serbs' more infamous "last chances" may be briefly recalled: the fall of Jajce in 1992; the revelations of systematic mass rape in December; successive water- and bread-queue massacres in Sarajevo; the shelling of orphanages and hospitals; the first debacle at Srebrenica and the farcical establishment of the "safe havens" that came out of it; the Serbs' pretense of accepting the Vance-Owen plan; two bloody crises in Bihac and two even bloodier ones in Gorazde.[9]

In an attempt to limit what might be perceived as overzealous application of the accommodation norm, the EU Council of Foreign Ministers adopted the principle during the London Conference that it would not propose peace plans which ratified the gains of ethnic cleansing. The United States endorsed the same view, with Assistant Secretary of State John R. Bolten declaring before the UN Human Rights Commission that "unquestionably, such political gains and violent territorial changes will never be recognized or sanctified by civilized persons."[10] Despite numerous similar public commitments, the co-chairmen of the peace process admittedly put forward proposals which legitimized territorial conquest involving ethnic cleansing and genocide. In fact one of the co-chairmen, David Owen, expressly notes in his memoirs how he was irritated by the Dutch foreign minister's objection to a peace plan because it rewarded ethnic cleansing, but chose not to make an issue of it because it could be dismissed as purely moralistic and because he "personally liked" the Dutch representative.[11]

Despite the heavy utilization of the approach of accommodation and the exclusion of the norm of justice and the use of force, the efforts of the UN/EU peace process did not produce peace, and in fact actually encouraged the parties to commit ethnic cleansing and continue the conflict.[12] The most notable example of this was when the UN/EU proposed the Vance-Owen Peace Plan, which divided Bosnia into ethnic cantons, the Serb and Croat parties began to ethnically cleanse those cantons to which they had been assigned authority.[13] In fact, the UN/EU accommodation approach permissively led to the commission of so many atrocities that even UN special rapporteur for Human Rights Abuses in the Former Yugoslavia Tadeusz Mazowiecke felt obliged to resign in July 1995, charging that the failure of the UN and the international community to make any serious effort to stop atrocities in Bosnia made it impossible for him to continue.[14]

During the early stages of the UN/EU peace process, the United States supported the efforts of the process, and Washington eschewed the use of force. Notably, during the 1992 presidential campaign then governor Clinton "proclaimed that a Clinton administration would act to end the killing." America he intoned, "would not be party to an agreement that rewarded ethnic cleansing by supporting any partition plan that seemed to ratify Serb gains."[15] As noted above, after entering office, however, President Clinton acquiesced to the UN/EU approach and permitted his secretary of state to embark on a public campaign of moral equivalence by declaring that all sides were responsible for the atrocities and to undertake a campaign to erode the moral imperative to take effective action by intentionally avoiding a reference to the acts of the Serbian forces as constituting attempted genocide against the people of Bosnia.[16]

Incrementalizing the Use of Force

With the failure of the UN/EU peace process, the continuing atrocities and civilian massacres in Bosnia, and the continued occupation of large parts of Croatia, the Bosnian and Croatian governments launched a counteroffensive in

August 1995 to try to push back Serbian forces. Although only Croatian and Bosnian troops took part in the counteroffensive, much of their equipment was American and German made, and their training was provided mainly by an American military consulting firm comprised primarily of retired American military officers.

The combined Croatian/Bosnian military action met with significant success in that it cleared Serbian forces from the Krajina region and threatened the remaining Serbian forces in Eastern Slavonia. The Croatian capture of Krajina, was, however, marked by atrocities committed against Croatian-Serb civilians. The advance also cleared Serbian forces from much of western Bosnia, rolling them back to Banja Luka. It was believed if the offensive continued, the Croatians and Bosnians may well have been able to defeat the Serbian forces and thereby reunify Bosnia. The international community, however, had not abandoned its commitment to accommodation and was concerned about the use of force by a military entity it could not control, which might result in further atrocities and tens of thousands of refugees.

Using diplomatic pressure, deceit, and the threat of air strikes, the United States forced the Croatians and Bosnians to bring their offensive to a halt on 12 October 1995. Many of the U.S. officials engaged in forcing a halt to the offensive would later acknowledge that had the offensive been allowed to continue, and a way found to prevent the displacement of civilians, it would likely have led to the reunification of Bosnia and a significantly more sustainable peace than the one achieved at Dayton.

During roughly the same time frame as the Croatian/Bosnian offensive, the United States concluded that relying almost completely on the approach of accommodation had failed and, in light of the continuing atrocities and the intense public criticism of a failed policy, it was necessary to use force—controlled by NATO. In particular, two important failures of the approach of accommodation led to the decision to advocate the use of force.

First, in mid-August 1995, Serbian forces overran the UN safe haven of Srebrenica, murdering as many as 7,000 men and raping and otherwise torturing the women and children. During the massacre, Dutch UN soldiers stood by passively, many in their underwear after being forced to turn over their uniforms to the Serbian soldiers who then, disguised as UN soldiers and in UN vehicles, pursued survivors fleeing the city.[17] Second, on 28 August 1995, the Bosnian Serb army shelled the Sarajevo marketplace for a second time, killing thirty-eight civilians, and wounding eighty-five more—mostly women and children.

On 30 August 1995, NATO launched limited air strikes against Serbian forces in Bosnia and continued these air strikes until the Serbian regime in Belgrade agreed to a number of conditions, which they had failed to agree to in the four years of UN/EU diplomacy. These included removing their heavy weapons from the "weapons exclusion zone" around Sarajevo, refraining from attacking UN-declared safe areas, and granting full freedom of movement to UN personnel, including free use of Sarajevo's airport.

Until the autumn of 1995 most of the international mediators and policymakers discounted the role of the use of force. One key player, however, was keenly aware of the ability of NATO military power to bring an end to the conflict—Slobodan Milosevic. As recounted by General Wesley Clark, shortly after the initialing of the Dayton Accords and prior to their signature, Milosevic confided to him that with the limited air strikes "NATO won the war." When Clark expressed doubt as to whether this limited action had in fact brought about an end to the war, Milosevic declared, "it was your NATO, your bombs and missiles, your high technology that defeated us . . . we Serbs never had a chance against you."[18]

At the time, however, unsure of exactly how to build peace by using force—or to what extent the use of force approach strengthened their negotiating position,[19] and the extent to which they desired to minimize the approach of accommodation, the United States and the EU powers decided to halt the bombing. In conjunction with the 12 October 1995 cease-fire, they arranged for Contact Group-sponsored negotiations in the United States.[20]

Setting the Stage for Justice?

Gandhi said that there were two kinds of peace, the peace that silences the guns and the peace that makes the guns irrelevant. It is the first kind of peace that Holbrooke brought to Bosnia.

—David Reiff[21]

As the international community prepared for the Dayton negotiations and raised expectations for the chance to craft a lasting peace, those involved in the process made a number of public and private declarations concerning the need to incorporate the norm of justice into the process—statements which had been missing from earlier attempts to negotiate a peace in the former Yugoslavia. While on their face supportive of the norm of justice, these statements comprised part of a conscious or unconscious effort to set the stage where justice would be largely (and possibly unnecessarily) sacrificed in order to reach a political settlement with Milosevic. By loudly and publicly proclaiming their support for the norm of justice in the negotiations, the negotiators satisfied public calls for justice, while creating negotiating space for the norm of accommodation and the deployment of a number of antijustice acts.

Sensing the erosion of the influence of the norm of justice, and recognizing its potential sacrifice in a negotiated settlement, Justice Goldstone indicted the two primary Serb culprits, Radovan Karadzic and Ratko Mladic, respectively, for genocide on 24 July 1995, and again on 16 November 1995, in the midst of the Dayton negotiations, for the Srebrenica massacre. The prosecutor also held a Rule 61 hearing concerning atrocities committed by Dragan Nikolic at the Susica concentration camp, which involved numerous acts of torture and murder.[22]

Proclaiming the Necessity of Justice

By his own account, as the lead U.S. negotiator, Ambassador Holbrooke took the initiative in proclaiming the need for the role of justice in the Bosnian peace process.[23] According to David Reiff, "with every gesture, Holbrooke seemed to be ramming home the point that what was going on in Bosnia was disgusting and unacceptable; and that the forthright assertion of a moral standpoint on this great crime was not a travesty of diplomacy, but the only standpoint from which diplomacy could be effectively pursued."[24]

Moreover, Ambassador Holbrooke recounts expressly stating to President Clinton immediately prior to and after the negotiations that it was necessary to arrest Karadzic and Mladic in order to not only serve justice but also to bring lasting peace to Bosnia.[25] He also committed to the Bosnian government that he would ensure that no compromises were made on bringing war criminals to justice.[26] Holbrooke was supported in this endeavor by Secretary Christopher, who, on the opening day of the negotiations shortly before shaking Slobodan Milosevic's hand, identified the need to respect human rights and hold accountable those responsible for atrocities as one of the four essential conditions for a peaceful settlement of the conflict.[27] Interestingly, there is no record of any senior U.S. government officials signaling that it would be necessary to employ the approaches of accommodation or positive economic inducement to create the basis for a lasting peace.

Underlying these public statements, however, was a calculated approach to accommodate the interests of Slobodan Milosevic in order to accomplish the objective of a negotiated settlement. This strategy was foreshadowed by the fact that Ambassador Holbrooke had earlier made a calculated determination, in September 1995, that it was proper to negotiate with indicted war criminals Ratko Mladic and Radovan Karadzic in Belgrade in order to establish a ceasefire for the Sarajevo region. Ambassador Holbrooke rationalized this contact with indicted war criminals on the basis that they did not constitute a separate negotiating team, that he did not shake their hand, and that Raoul Wallenberg and Folke Bernadotte had similarly negotiated with Adolf Eichmann and Heinrich Himmler to "save lives during the second world war."[28] Notably, this rationale was similar to that invoked by the UN/EU negotiators during their many attempts to accommodate/appease those responsible for the atrocities in order to bring an end to the conflict, and which had failed to do so. As noted above, the "saving lives" rational, while encapsulated in only two words, is a powerful tool used by the negotiators to undermine the influence of the norm of justice.

The Institutions of Justice: Putting Justice to Work for Peace

Concerned that the role of justice might be minimized in the new American-led negotiation effort, the prosecutor and the president of the Tribunal, as well as various human rights organizations, set out to ensure that justice was adequately incorporated into the process.

During the summer of 1995, the UNHCR released reports that Serbian forces had reopened concentration camps in the Banja Luka area and purged at least 7,000 Muslims from the region and that 2,000 men were reported missing. The president of the Tribunal, Judge Antonio Cassese, fearing that the weak approach to the norm of justice might undermine efforts to bring a lasting peace to the former Yugoslavia, declared on the day the Dayton Peace Agreement was signed that "justice is an indispensable ingredient of the process of national reconciliation. It is essential to the restoration of peaceful and normal relations especially for people who have had to live under a reign of terror. It breaks the cycle of violence, hatred, and extra judicial retribution. Thus, peace and justice go hand-in-hand."[29]

On 9 October 1995, Judge Goldstone also conducted a Rule 61 hearing on the indictment of Dragan Nikolic, who was the commander at the Susica camp, where detained Muslims and non-Serbs were held after Serb forces took over the town of Vlasenica in April 1992. At the camp, detainees were subjected to terrible living conditions, beatings that often resulted in death, and sexual assault. At the Rule 61 hearing to confirm the indictment, extensive evidence was presented regarding the nature and extent of these atrocities and their role in the larger Serbian campaign of ethnic aggression.[30]

The most crucial act, however, was Richard Goldstone's indictment of Radovan Karadzic and Ratko Mladic for crimes of genocide. By virtue of their indictment, and the obligation of all states to apprehend them, Goldstone made it impossible for the United States and its European allies to invite Karadzic and Mladic to Dayton for the negotiations. Had they not been indicted, they in all likelihood would have been invited, and the Bosnian government would have reacted by objecting to their participation and threatening to boycott the talks. The Bosnian government then would have been accused of "sacrificing lives" in order to stand on the principle of justice. In the end, the participation of Karadzic and Mladic in the Dayton negotiations would have made it impossible to reach an agreement.

Importantly, however, the indictment of Karadzic and Mladic coupled with the nonindictment of Milosevic, suited the short-term interests of the negotiators as they could exclude the two individuals most likely to have a destabilizing impact on their efforts to achieve a negotiated settlement, while opening the opportunity to work with Milosevic as a legitimate partner in peace. The negotiators could thus maintain an appearance of embracing both the norm of justice and the norm of accommodation. Unfortunately, as will be discussed in chapter 10, the accommodation of Milosevic at Dayton, who was in fact the architect of the attempted genocide in Bosnia, emboldened him in his efforts to create a Greater Serbia and encouraged his attempt to ethnically cleanse Kosovo.

Negotiating the Dayton Accords

The Dayton Accords barely addresses the war criminal issue. And I think the only real provision is that all signatories are charged to cooperate with the international tribunal.

—Major General William Nash[31]

In November 1995, the parties to the Yugoslav conflict and representatives of the Contact Group gathered in Dayton, Ohio, to negotiate a series of accords designed to bring about the end to the war and the peaceful reintegration of Bosnia. Given the calculated effort to legitimize Milosevic as a reliable partner in peace, David Reiff observed that the only question for Dayton negotiators was just how unjust the agreement between those who instigated the genocide and those who were its intended victims would turn out to be.[32] Despite the primary emphasis on accommodation and the employment of a number of anti-justice acts, the efforts of the Tribunal, the Bosnian delegation, and many public commentators to infuse the negotiation with the norm of justice ensured that at a minimum the role of justice would be debated during the negotiations, and would in some small ways be reflected in the peace agreement.

It should be noted that the dispute over provisions relating to the norm of justice were not the only primary disputes during the negotiations. The Bosnian Serb delegation demanded the right to secede from Bosnia with the territory they had taken by force, that they be given the right to conduct their own foreign affairs, that territory recently liberated by the Bosnian army should be returned to Serbian occupation, that their supply corridor across northern Bosnia be widened, and that they be given access to the Adriatic Sea. The Bosnian government rejected all of these demands and itself sought to include within the accords the preservation of a unitary Bosnian state, termination of the arms embargo, and termination of Croatian and Serbian support for separatist forces within Bosnia.[33]

Resetting the Stage for Accommodation

Whereas the norm of justice would require the presence of truthful declarations concerning Mr. Milosevic's culpability, and his prosecution for war crimes, the perceived necessity of Mr. Milosevic's participation at Dayton required that he be legitimized as a partner in peace and that his culpability be obfuscated.[34] To accomplish this objective Secretary Christopher arranged for the now famous "handshake" among the three presidents, which reinforced the perception of their moral equivalence, and rehabilitated Mr. Milosevic. If President Izetbegovic was willing to shake the Serbian president's hand, then there would be no bar to full American and European engagement with Mr. Milosevic as a legitimate partner.

Christopher, however, characterized the handshake in these terms:

Before my opening statement, I walked around the table to these three, encouraged them to shake hands. Although they had done so before, I believed that such an act—like the Rabin-Arafat handshake on the White House's South Lawn—would provide an important boost symbolically, not only for the delegates in Dayton, but for the millions watching around the world.[35]

The rehabilitation and legitimization of Milosevic was particularly important because, despite the significantly weakened position of Mr. Milosevic, much of the American and European efforts were directed at persuading Mr. Milosevic to accept a plan favorable to his interests, while maintaining a minimum threshold of provisions that would allow them to declare they had brought peace to Yugoslavia and had maintained Bosnia's status as an independent state.[36] Similar efforts were directed at Mr. Tudjman, whose sole goal seemed to be a fixed timetable for the reestablishment of Croatian government control over all Croatian territory, and the creation of an opportunity for the future erosion of Bosnian sovereignty. Most of the diplomatic squeeze was saved for the Bosnian delegation, which was on numerous occasions threatened with closure of the talks and the withdrawal of international support. In order to pressure the victim it was necessary to minimize both Milosevic's role as the aggressor and Bosnia's role as the aggrieved.

The Nature of the Dayton Peace Accords

To secure a just peace, it would have been necessary to reverse much of the gains of ethnic cleansing and attempted genocide, and to weave throughout the agreement the operation of various mechanisms of justice in order to delegitimize and remove from power those responsible for the war and the atrocities and those most likely to inhibit the return to a multiethnic society and the creation of a democratic state. The main negotiators, however, feared that an attempt to craft a peace agreement based on these principles would not be accepted by Milosevic and they were unwilling to further threaten the use of force to accomplish these objectives. Importantly, many U.S. officials now believe that it would have been possible to pressure Milosevic at Dayton into accepting a more just peace than that which was drafted at Dayton.

Because of their belief in the limited nature of the Dayton peace process, there was a significant amount of tension during the negotiations between those participants who desired a peace deal—that is, a piece of paper with three signatures (most notably the American and French delegations), those who sought to appease various parties (most notably the British and European Union delegations), and those who sought a peace package—that is a structured set of commitments which, if fulfilled, could promote the peaceful reintegration of Bosnia (the Bosnian delegation and in some instances the German delegation).

Similarly, during the Dayton negotiations, there were differing degrees of recognition that the various commitments contained within the accords would function interdependently. The United States and German delegations, together with the Bosnian delegation, recognized that without the implementation of all the Dayton provisions, the accords would likely create a divided Bosnia, as the institutions intended to serve as the foundation for the reintegration of Bosnia were constructed on the conviction that those coming to power would be selected by the silent majority who wished for a unified state, and would not be controlled by the powerful nationalist minority intent on dividing or destroying Bosnia. Since the adoption of the Dayton Accords, most member states of the international community have come to accept that the success of the accords rests on the implementation of the right of return for refugees, the wide exercise of freedom of movement, and the arrest of war criminals in order to provide the basis for free, fair, and secure elections. Together, these factors formed the democratic foundation for the reintegration of Bosnian civil society.[37]

Because of the prevalence of the peace deal objective and the lack of an understanding of the integrated nature of a peace agreement, a situation existed in which there was little ability for the norm of justice to operate. Much of the time spent during the Dayton negotiations revolved around preventing the emergence of any "deal-breakers" from undermining the chance of getting a signed agreement—no matter how essential those deal-breakers were to a meaningful or lasting peace. As will be discussed below, and as indicated by General Nash's comment above, Milosevic's identification of any meaningful language on war crimes as a deal-breaker led to an essentially symbolic reference to the obligation to cooperate with the Yugoslav Tribunal, and the exclusion of indicted war criminals from holding public or military office. While these provisions were championed by Secretary Christopher as major accomplishments,[38] they are basic obligations of international law and they constituted the barest minimum that could be included given the level of atrocities committed in Bosnia.

Moreover, the emphasis on a peace deal required the active undermining of the application of the norm of justice during the negotiations. Whereas justice would require rectitude and retribution, and, for instance, would dictate that the ethnically cleansed towns of Srebrenica and Zepa be returned to the Bosnian government, the international community found itself in a position in which it enabled the Serbian regime to retain control over these towns as that appeared essential in order to create a "defensible" peace. In fact, the Bosnian government was required during Dayton to expend considerable capital negotiating for the return of refugees from Zepa who had fled into Serbia and who were being held in camps. The refugees were then exchanged for concessions on other issues that were on the negotiating table.

The influence of moral equivalence and the continuing need to treat all sides equally created a situation in which the Serbian regime was promised 49 percent of the territory, and thus the Bosnian government was required to hand over to the Serbian regime territory which had been liberated during the October offensive.

War Crimes Provisions Proposed by the Bosnian Government

While justice would require that a variety of mechanisms be created to cull war criminals from civil society, the need to accommodate the interests of the aggressors and the legitimate security concerns of third-party states who were providing military forces to secure the agreement dictated that no more than minimal or symbolic provisions concerning war criminals be incorporated into the agreement. This tension was rife at Dayton. In fact, as noted by Kenneth Doubt, "at Dayton, the more the Bosnian delegation insists on justice, the less the Bosnian delegation is viewed as being interested in peace."[39]

Despite this factor, during the Dayton negotiations, the Bosnian delegation made significant efforts to push for connecting justice with peace, which was a direct reflection of the fact that the Bosniacs were the group most victimized by war crimes.[40] Out of its desire to ensure that the accords sufficiently obliged the parties and the international community to arrest, extradite, and prosecute war criminals, the Bosnian delegation proposed a number of specific provisions:

- To clearly establish the baseline that each party was responsible for the removal of war criminals from Bosnian society, the Bosnian delegation proposed that the General Framework Agreement include an obligation for each party to "arrest, detain, and transfer to the custody of the [International Tribunal] any and all indicted war criminals who reside in or transit through or are otherwise present on their territory."[41] To promote compliance with this provision, the Bosnian delegation further proposed that the General Framework Agreement include a clause providing for economic and other sanctions to be applied against parties not complying with the obligation to cooperate with the International Tribunal. These provisions were supported by the prosecutor for the War Crimes Tribunal, Richard Goldstone, who immediately prior to the convening of the Dayton negotiations met with U.S. government officials and requested that the surrender of indicted war criminals be made a condition of any accord reached in Dayton, and that sanctions be maintained against Serbia until it surrendered indicted war criminals in territory under its control.[42]

- To ensure not only that Croatia and Serbia, as parties to the General Framework Agreement, should be obligated to arrest and extradite individuals indicted for war crimes but also that the Federation and Republika Srpska substate entities should be similarly obligated, the Bosnian delegation proposed that the constitution contain a provision requiring the substate entities to "assist the Government of Bosnia and Herzegovina to discharge its obligations towards the [International Tribunal]." [43]

- To assist the Bosnian central government in removing war criminals from positions of influence, the Bosnian delegation further proposed that a joint EU/NATO/International Tribunal "Mechanism" be created to vet and remove from the formal and informal military and police structures of the entities and central government forces "individuals reasonably suspected of responsibility for war crimes." [44] This proposal was complimented by a requested provision indicating the responsibility of the IFOR commander to "provide all necessary assistance to the Mechanism for the purposes of screening all individuals in the army of the Republika Srpska, and to facilitate the Mechanism's discharge of any such individual reasonably suspected of responsibility for war crimes."[45]

- Finally, the Bosnian delegation sought a general provision excluding those suspected of committing war crimes from holding elected office or other public positions, and a more specific provision to the effect that the Republika Srpska would within ninety days of the signing of the accords exclude from its parliamentary assembly any individual convicted or indicted for war crimes by the International Tribunal.[46]

Proposals of the Serbian Delegation

During the Dayton negotiations, Slobodan Milosevic again expressly contested the authority and jurisdiction of the Yugoslav Tribunal and identified any obligation to arrest indictees as a deal-breaker, while denying that any Serbian forces had committed atrocities or violations of international humanitarian law.[47] The Serbian delegation thus objected to the inclusion of any references to the Tribunal or to its mandate. In particular, the Serbian delegation objected to any provisions which would require the parties to cooperate with the Tribunal or to exclude from military service or public office any indicted war criminals.

Response of the International Community

Driven by the need to secure a peace deal, the members of the Contact Group generally objected to the inclusion of such specific obligations as proposed by the Bosnian delegation on the basis that they were unnecessary. At one point during the negotiations, the representative of the Contact Group for the negotiations on the Bosnian constitution declared that a letter had been received from the Office of the Prosecutor of the International Tribunal explaining that a general reference to an obligation to cooperate with the International Tribunal would be sufficient.[48] Subsequently it emerged that the prosecutor had not in fact sent such a letter and had not been consulted during the course of the negotiations.

More specifically, the Contact Group, led by the British and French, rejected any attempt to require the reimposition of sanctions on parties not cooperating with the International Tribunal, and indicated to the Bosnian delegation that they had personal assurances from Slobodan Milosevic that he would ensure cooperation with the Tribunal—including compelling the surrender of Ratko Mladic and Radovan Karadzic. In fact, as recounted by General Clark, Milosevic expressly avoided making any commitment to ensure the arrest and extradition of Karadzic and Mladic.[49] The failure to create a mechanism for the automatic reimposition of sanctions proved a crucial strategic mistake as, subsequent to Dayton, Slobodan Milosevic expressly refused a personal request by Ambassador Holbrooke to fulfill his "promise" to have Karadzic and Mladic removed to The Hague.[50] Without the meaningful ability to reimpose sanctions, there was simply no incentive for Mr. Milosevic to cooperate with the Tribunal. And, as discussed below, the International Crisis Group has concluded that the single most important factor relating to the nonimplementation of the Dayton Accords and the persisting de facto partition of Bosnia was the continued presence of Karadzic in Bosnia.[51]

Concerning the creation of a vetting mechanism, the Contract Group feared this would involve EU and International Police Task Force (IPTF) personnel too deeply in the operation of the military and police structures of the substate entities and that they might be perceived as biased in the event that they removed a disproportionate number of officials from one of the parties.

With respect to the participation of IFOR in the vetting mechanism, the Contact Group military representatives at Dayton steadfastly refused to commit to any involvement in activities associated with the apprehension of war criminals, including the assignment of staff to assist in the identification of those likely responsible for war crimes. The military officers at Dayton also indicated they would avoid contact with those actually indicted by the International Tribunal. According to Ambassador Holbrooke, he and other government officials supported the creation of such a vetting mechanism, and they raised the issue before senior Pentagon officials who rejected the proposal on the basis that it represented a significant step toward mission creep.[52]

The NATO military representatives at Dayton further rejected the Bosnian proposals on the basis that they interpreted Article IV paragraph 6 of Annex 1 of the accord to provide IFOR unlimited authority to compel the removal or withdrawal of specific forces whenever IFOR determined that those forces constituted a threat or potential threat to either IFOR or its mission and that this provision included the right to remove indictees from the area of IFOR operation.[53] As will be discussed in chapter 12, NATO commanders would subsequently argue they had no mandate to arrest war criminals.

The one concession the Contact Group did make to the Bosnian delegation was to accept the premise that those indicted for war crimes could not stand for elected office or hold other public office after the Dayton Accords were signed. Thus, the Bosnian delegation's proposals were essentially reduced to two war crimes-related provisions.[54] The first appeared in the General Framework Agreement and provided that the parties were obligated "to cooperate in the investigation and prosecution of war crimes and other violations of international humanitarian law."[55] The second appeared in the constitution and provided that "no person who is serving a sentence imposed by the [International Tribunal], and no person who is under indictment by the [International Tribunal] may stand as a candidate or hold any appointive, elective, or other public office in the territory of Bosnia and Herzegovina."[56] Ambassador Holbrooke would subsequently claim that this second provision was a major success in limiting the ability of war criminals to influence the implementation of the Dayton Accords and to poison the development of civil society in Bosnia. Yet this provision did little to inhibit publicly indicted war criminals from exercising significant influence over the electoral process, or from blocking meaningful implementation of the Dayton Accords.

Here, too, the Yugoslav Tribunal missed an opportunity to enhance its impact on the post-Dayton peace-building process. Although the implementation of the provision was weak, the Tribunal could have used the opportunity to shift its focus from low-level war criminals to culpable high-level officials and prevent their negative influence on the peace process by publicly indicting them for their crimes. Rather, the Office of the Prosecutor continued its focus on relatively low- and mid-level criminals, and it embarked on a new policy of sealed indictments, which, although calculated to increase the likelihood of apprehending persons by surprise, essentially nullified the practical value of this provision of the Dayton Accords.

Despite the reticence of the Contact Group negotiators to adequately address the norm of justice, the Bosnian delegation did extract an implicit promise from the NATO representatives that IFOR would neither interact with indicted war criminals nor tolerate their presence in their area of operation. This was taken by some to mean that NATO forces would actively participate in the apprehension of indicted war criminals. But it was more likely intended to indicate that IFOR would take actions with respect to indicted war criminals that promoted its own interests rather than those of justice. In the end, as will be noted below, this commitment amounted to nothing more than a policy of avoidance.[57]

Somewhat ironically, the formal remarks of Secretary Christopher at the initialing ceremony at Dayton were titled, "The Dayton Peace Agreement: Building Peace with Justice," and in his first paragraph, he proclaimed, "the time has come to build peace with justice," arguing that the agreement represented "a victory for all those in the world who believed that with determination, a principled peace is possible."[58]

Action of the Security Council Relating to the Role of the Tribunal and the Dayton Accords

Following the conclusion of the Dayton Accords, the UN Security Council passed three important resolutions. On 22 November 1995, the Security Council enacted Resolution 1022, which provided for the suspension, and eventual termination, of economic sanctions against the FRY and the Republika Srpska. On 15 December 1995 the Security Council passed Resolution 1031 endorsing the establishment of IFOR, and on 21 December 1995 it adopted Resolution 1034, which dealt with a number of matters relating to the Yugoslav Tribunal.

In resolution 1022, the Security Council acknowledged that compliance with the orders of the Tribunal "constitutes an essential aspect of implementing the Peace Agreement," and in order to promote such compliance declared that if either the high representative or the IFOR commander informed the Security Council through the Secretary-General that the FRY or the Republika Srpska regimes failed to "meet their obligations under the Peace Agreement," the sanctions would automatically be reimposed unless the Security Council determined otherwise. Presumably the Security Council intended to include noncompliance with the orders of the Tribunal as well as other important elements of the peace accords. As noted by Paul Szas, however, in placing the trigger mechanism solely in the hands of the high representative and IFOR commander, the Security Council missed an opportunity to link the automatic reimposition of sanctions with a report of noncompliance which may be filed by the Tribunal under its rules of procedure.[59]

In Resolution 1031, the Security Council reaffirmed the obligation of all states to cooperate with the Yugoslav Tribunal and "recognized" that IFOR was permitted to use all necessary force to ensure compliance with the military annex, but it did not explicitly authorize IFOR to use force to ensure cooperation with the Tribunal or to apprehend indicted war criminals. Similarly, Resolution 1034 dealt with a number of important Tribunal-related issues, but with respect to the Dayton Accords, simply noted the reference to the Tribunal in the accords and did not elaborate upon the role of the Tribunal in promoting peace. According to Paul Szas, "it conspicuously failed to specify any additional powers or tasks to assist the Tribunal for the organs established or foreseen by the Agreement."[60]

The Consequences of Dayton

Rather than building upon the successful use of force, creating peace through justice and rolling back the gains of ethnic cleansing, the international community returned to its preference for accommodation and at Dayton formally ratified these gains. As a result the norm and institutions of justice were only minimally present in the agreement, and as a consequence indictable war criminals have maintained positions of power and influence and have exercised their ability to stall any meaningful implementation of the Dayton Accords.

In November 2000, the International Crisis Group documented the case of over seventy-five individuals indictable for major war crimes who held important positions of power and influence in nearly all the municipalities and political party structures across the Republika Srpska as well as the Srpska central government. These individuals held positions such as the president of the Supreme Court, the minister of defense, and the second highest ranking police officer. According to the International Crisis Group, at least seventeen indictable individuals hold positions in the Republika Srpska police force, and eleven hold seats on municipal councils—which they acquired in OSCE-supervised and certified elections. Almost all of these individuals are reported to meet regularly with key members of the international community operating in Bosnia despite the international community's awareness of their culpability for serious crimes committed during the conflict.[61]

According to the Crisis Group, some well-known indictable war criminals have been allowed and encouraged by the international community to assume positions of power because they were perceived as important to the implementation of the Dayton Accords. These included paramilitary leader Ljubisa Savic whose forces were responsible for numerous acts of ethnic cleansing was supported in his assumption of the position of deputy minister of the interior; Biljana Plavsic, later indicted for genocide,[62] was supported in her position as the prime minister [president] of Srpska and at one time received the protection of British SFOR troops; Petar Cancar, responsible for the ethnic cleansing of Foca and the establishment of rape camps, served with international support for a time as the Srpska minister of justice; and Momcilo Krajisnik, who, with international backing, was elected as the Serbian representative on the Bosnian presidency. Krajisnik was subsequently indicted for genocide against the people of Bosnia.[63]

The widespread presence of indictable war criminals in the institutions of power in the Republika Srpska and the failure of the international community to secure the arrest of those who were indicted emboldened the forces interested in continuing the campaign for ethnic partition during the post-conflict phase of the Yugoslav crisis. In particular, "[t]he failure to arrest Karadzic has sent a message to his wartime colleagues and political successors that they can obstruct return, actively work against Dayton implementation, exploit nationalist sentiments, and remain untouchable."[64]

The importance of securing the arrest of Mladic and Karadzic early in the implementation phase of the peace process was essential, as according to a Serbian judge interviewed by the International Crisis Group, "Karadzic and Mladic represent the single knot holding together a twisted thread of collective and individual guilt that must be untied for Bosnia to begin the reconciliation process."[65] According to the judge, "for the 'small-time' ethnic cleansers of Bosnia, Karadzic demonstrates that ethnic cleansing worked and that they can continue to rule over their fiefdoms, waiting for the weak resolve of the international community to dissipate entirely."[66]

Those interested in securing the ethnic separation of Bosnia have actively used their power and influence to undermine the conditions necessary for the fulfillment of the Dayton Accords by obstructing the return of refugees, inhibiting freedom of movement, and denying basic human rights to non-Serb minorities. In many instances, the public institutions themselves have actively prevented the fulfillment of these obligations,[67] as "often, those individuals who are meant to be protecting and supporting returning minorities are exactly the same individuals who expelled them in 1992-95."[68]

Individuals who were culpable for the atrocities committed during the war are able to continue the de facto partition of Bosnia and the denial of basic human rights to non-Serbs because they are allowed to control essential political and economic institutions. According to the ICG, "they function as pillars of their respective communities, dispensing political and economic patronage. Many control the local economies, both legal and illegal, while others continue to control illegal paramilitary groups." In fact, the ICG asserts, "in all [Republika Srpska] communities, indicted and suspected war criminals appear to enjoy respected status," and many receive protection from the Republika Srpska police force.[69]

In May 2001, a British SAS officer made public a report prepared under his command, which called upon the international authorities in Bosnia to arrest twenty-two Bosnian-Croatian individuals who had committed crimes during the war and were engaged in "the violent intimidation of refugees trying to return to Stolac, in south-eastern Bosnia, in 1998 and 1999." [70] According to the officer, while some war-crimes suspects were in hiding, most of those identified as torturers at the Dretelj, Heliodrome, and Gabela concentration camps still held power and were often sited in public by their former victims who had begun to return in small numbers and who were still subject to gross violations of human rights. Despite the report, none of the individuals identified were ever indicted or arrested.

The extensive presence of indicted and indictable war criminals significantly stifled the necessary public debate concerning the acts of Serbian forces during the conflict and truncated efforts to promote reconciliation. For instance, when a newspaper editor, Zeljko Kopanja, ran a series of editorials in Nezavisne Novine asking why individuals responsible for war crimes in Koricani and Teslic had not been arrested and put on trial by the Srpska government, he became the victim of a car bomb which destroyed both his legs. [71]

Had there been greater reliance on the norm of justice during the Dayton negotiations, and had the mechanisms proposed by the Bosnian government been incorporated into the agreement, many of these indictable war criminals would not have continued to exercise power and influence over the implementation of the accords. In all likelihood Bosnia now would be on a path toward ethnic reintegration as opposed to the path of de facto ethnic partition.

While many peace builders believed that justice and force could play a complimentary role with limited accommodation during the peace-building process, the negotiators responsible for the Vance/Owen plan and the Dayton negotiations believed that accommodation must be employed essentially free of the norm of justice and only limited force would be an appropriate compliment. As such the Dayton Accords reflect a peace deal built primarily upon accommodation, with only token recognition of the norm of justice and the existing mechanisms of accountability. Given that the Dayton negotiations stopped the war, but did not create a foundation for the successful reintegration of Bosnia, and as some commentators may argue encouraged Mr. Milosevic to take action against the Kosovo Albanians, the next two chapters examine whether the peace builders learned from their experience in Bosnia and more effectively integrated the various approaches in their response to the Kosovo crisis.

Chapter 10

Seeking Peace in Kosovo: The Relegation of Justice

As the most powerful nation committed to the rule of law, we have a responsibility to confront these assaults on humankind. One response mechanism is accountability, namely to help bring the perpetrators of genocide, crimes against humanity, and war crimes to justice. If we allow them to act with impunity, then we will only be inviting a perpetuation of these crimes far into the next millennium. Our legacy must demonstrate an unyielding commitment to the pursuit of justice.

—David Scheffer,
U.S. Ambassador for War Crimes[1]

Throughout the crisis in Kosovo, the international community was actively involved in attempting to bring an end to the ethnic violence. With the creation of the Yugoslav Tribunal, and the proliferation of public statements by high government officials (such as the one by David Scheffer immediately above) concerning the need to employ the norm of justice in order to promote a real and lasting peace, there was an expectation among many observers that the peace builders might heavily rely upon the norm of justice in the Kosovo peace process, and that there might even be some long term progress in efforts to reconcile the traditional tension between accommodation and justice in the peace-building process. There was also some expectation that given the halting effectiveness of the institutions of justice, the peace builders might use the process of peace-building to enhance the efforts of the Tribunal to give effect to the norm of justice by including specific obligations vis-à-vis the parties and the Tribunal within the text of an agreement.

Like the peace-building process in Bosnia, the use of force and accommodation approaches played central roles in the context of Kosovo. The debate as to which norm should take precedence, and when it should be utilized or relied upon was the subject of much public discourse and consumed a significant amount of political energy from the key peace builders, a dynamic which had its own influence on the peace-building process. And as in Bosnia, the Kosovo peace builders found it exceptionally difficult to meld the application of both the use of force and accommodation approaches, let alone incorporate the justice norm. A review of the events leading up to and through the negotiation of the Rambouillet/Paris Accords thus provides an opportunity to further elaborate on the questions addressed in the preceding chapter on the Dayton negotiations.

As with the last chapter, this chapter and the next primarily examine question eight as set forth in chapter 1, which relates to the extent to which the competition between the various approaches influenced the development of peace-building regimes. The chapter will also shed light on questions one, two, three, six, seven, nine, and ten.

The focus of this chapter and the next is therefore threefold, with this chapter detailing the efforts of peace builders prior to the Rambouillet/Paris peace conference, and the next examining the efforts during and after the Rambouillet/Paris conference. First, they tell the story of the peace-building process in Kosovo, with particular detail paid to the role of accommodation and the use of force in the process, the perceived inherent competition between these approaches, and the efforts to meld their application. This story is important to tell, because without an understanding of this dynamic, one might tend to overestimate the role of justice, or unduly focus on its role without understanding the primary role played by these other approaches. It is also important in order to understand how the norms and institutions of justice may further the effective application, or in some instances inhibit the effective operation, of other approaches.

Second, this chapter and the next examine the manner in which the norms and institutions of justice interacted with the other approaches to influence the use of mediation and negotiation as a means to build peace. For instance, did they limit or constrain the approach of accommodation by requiring that certain provisions be included in, or others excluded from joint declarations, Security Council resolutions and subsequent peace agreements; did they enhance the likelihood of the use of force by providing a legal justification for force; and did they constrain those with whom the peace builders could negotiate? Similarly, how did the efforts of stakeholders, such as the Yugoslav Tribunal, influential individuals, the media, and important NGOs compel the peace builders to rely upon the norm of justice to influence the peace-building process?

Third, this chapter and the next explore the extent to which the peace builders sought to weave the norms and institutions of justice into the agreements at hand, and thereby to promote the implementation of those agreements and a lasting peace. In this regard, the first question to explore is whether the peace builders actually considered the norm and/or institutions of justice to play an important role in implementation, and, if so whether they thought it was worth the hindrance to the negotiation process likely to be caused by pressing for its incorporation. And for those who have made strong public statements in favor of the norm of justice, the question is whether, in light of their public declarations, peace builders are committed to the incorporation of the norm of justice or whether they are merely more frequently incorporating the norm into the rhetoric of diplomacy while continuing to marginalize the norm in the negotiation process.

The Kosovo negotiations process may be usefully contrasted with the Bosnian peace process in order to verify some of the conclusions drawn in the preceding chapter and to further the development of additional conclusions concerning the role of justice. Importantly, the Kosovo negotiation process occurred approximately three and a half years after the Bosnian negotiation process, and thus it provides an opportunity to assess whether the peace builders had come to modify their views on the role of justice and the Yugoslav Tribunal in promoting a lasting peace, and whether they had learned how to better apply the norms and institutions of justice when they deemed them relevant. In particular, during these three years the international community had time to assess the nature of the Dayton Accords, evaluate the success of their implementation, evaluate the efficacy of the Tribunal, and further develop an understanding of the motivations and potential responses of the Serbian regime.

Crafting an Initial Policy (Were the Lessons of Bosnia Really Learned?)

All the signs are that the Serbs are going on with ethnic cleansing in the Kosovo area. It's the way [the Serbs] solve their problems in Croatia, in Bosnia and now in Kosovo.

—Brig. Gen. Wilhelm Figl,
Austrian Defense Attaché in Albania[2]

[Madeleine Albright] sent Mr. Milosevic "a very forceful message," her spokesman said, "in which the Secretary expressed her shock and dismay over the effects of the ongoing Serb military offensive in Kosovo." Shock and dismay? Please. The time is long past for sending messages and for feigning surprise at Mr. Milosevic's long established villainy. If President Clinton and the West are not prepared to act, they should at least have the decency to retreat into shamed silence.

—Editorial
The Washington Post[3]

Bosnia Redux

As noted in chapter 4, from the winter through the autumn of 1998, the Serbian forces engaged in a brutal crackdown in Kosovo aimed at extinguishing the KLA and its popular support. As with other attempts to "restore public order" in the former Yugoslavia, the Serbian forces murdered a large number of noncombatants and orchestrated a humanitarian disaster. As noted by Medecins du

Monde medical co-coordinator Olivier Brochu in October 1998, "our people saw [a] village in flames . . . destroyed. There were a lot of deaths. . . . [Displaced persons] have nowhere to go. All their houses have been destroyed, their animals killed. What are they expected to do? Between 70 and 80 percent of villages southwest of Prishtina have been destroyed. . . . We are talking about a humanitarian disaster."[4]

And like previous campaigns by Serbian forces, the civilian casualties were not mere incidental killings, but they were premeditated atrocities designed to terrorize the civilian population. According to one poignant report by the Kosovo Diplomatic Observer Mission concerning the massacre of thirty-four Kosovo Albanians by Serb forces, the monitors "found an elderly couple 'heavily mutilated. . . . The man was decapitated, his brain removed and left displayed beside his wife's corpse. ... The woman's throat had been slit and her left foot mutilated in an apparent attempt to cut it off."[5]

Moreover, Serbian officials were clear about their ultimate objectives. According to Serbian government official David Gajic who spoke on plans to repeat the "ethnic cleansing" of Decani in other regions of Kosovo, "we will do it, if not limited by the outside world."[6] Another paramilitary police officer put it as bluntly after describing the death of a suspected KLA leader, "Two million to go."[7] Importantly, unlike the peace builders, the Serbian forces did not mistake the conflict for one of sovereignty and nationalism, but saw it as a campaign of terror and profit. As described by a paramilitary officer named "Tony" who served with Arkan's White Tigers, "It was strictly business, not like a holy war, a sacred war. We were war profiteers, not soldiers. . . . We knew Kosovo was lost."[8]

As a result of the atrocities and the efforts to destroy the political institutions which served as the formal and informal linkages between the Kosovars and the Serbian regime, and that might have served as the institutional framework for negotiations,[9] the Kosovar civilian population grew increasingly hostile to continued territorial unification with Serbia and the FRY. The Kosovar population also began to identify with and increasingly support the aims of the KLA for armed resistance and the eventual creation of an independent and free Kosovo. As noted by a local KLA commander in the Drenica region, "to talk to anyone in a Drenica village from schoolteachers to elderly peasant women these days is to be told 'We are all KLA.'"[10]

The atrocities occurring in Kosovo did not take place in a historical vacuum. In fact, the primary peace builders were keenly aware of the nature of ethnic conflict in the region and of the difficulties in fostering a lasting peace in Bosnia. Thus, in the winter of 1998 when the peace builders were faced with increasing atrocities in Kosovo, Secretary Albright proclaimed at a London Contact Group meeting, "we are not going to stand by and watch the Serbian authorities do in Kosovo what they can no longer get away with doing in Bosnia." She added that "the only effective way to stop violence in that region is to act with firmness, unity, and speed."[11]

Accommodation as an Interim/Default Policy

In the face of familiar atrocities and the increasing radicalization of the Kosovar community, the peace builders initially responded with humanitarian assistance. While this approach served as a policy Band-Aid, it did not provide a means for achieving a meaningful end to the conflict.[12] The peace builders, led by the U.S. Department of State and working through the Contact Group, embarked on a two-pronged approach of limited economic inducement and accommodation from the autumn of 1997 to the early winter of 1998. The peace builders avoided any meaningful threat of the use of force, as according to Ambassador Holbrooke, the British, French, and Germans believed it necessary to obtain UN Security Council authorization prior to using force.[13] Ambassador Holbrooke also opined that the creation of a common strategy was hampered by the fact that "democracies take a while to get their act together"[14]

The prong of economic inducement was applied quite lightly, and entailed signaling to Mr. Milosevic that the limited existing economic sanctions would not be lifted against Serbia until he reversed his policy of economic aggression in Kosovo. In particular, the EU and the United States threatened to maintain the "outer wall" of sanctions, which entailed excluding the FRY from the IMF and World Bank, as well as the United Nations. The EU further committed to removing trade preferences which would affect approximately $250 million in exports. In addition, the United States noted it had never provided formal diplomatic recognition of the FRY, had no formal diplomatic relations with the FRY, and would continue to maintain that position until the situation in Kosovo (and Montenegro) improved.[15] Notably, at this time the peace builders did not threaten to impose additional economic sanctions despite the essentially meaningless and ineffective nature of the existing sanctions.

The prong of accommodation entailed three elements: (1) a commitment of political noninvolvement in the negotiation process, (2) a reaffirmation of the FRY's sovereignty and territorial integrity, and (3) an implicit green light for Mr. Milosevic to continue to use overwhelming force against the KLA by labeling it a "terrorist organization."

To make clear to the parties that the Contact Group would not become politically involved in the negotiation process beyond facilitating dialogue, the Contact Group declared on three separate occasions from September 1997 to February 1998 that it encouraged the parties to "join in a peaceful dialogue,"[16] challenged the parties to "assume their responsibility to promote stability and a solution," indicated it would "support a mutually agreed solution that respected democratic standards," and offered its support in implementing the Education Agreement.[17]

Concerning the reaffirmation of the FRY's sovereignty and territorial integrity, each Contact Group statement from 24 September 1997 to 25 February 1998 declared support for an enhanced status for Kosovo within the FRY.[18] The Contact Group members also ensured that each UN Security Council resolution dealing with the Kosovo crisis contained a reference to the sovereignty and territorial integrity of the FRY, as well as other states in the region.[19] On one instance, however, at the height of violence in Kosovo in May 1999, the Security Council reaffirmed "the territorial integrity and sovereignty of all States in the region," but it did not specifically mention the FRY as it had in all other relevant resolutions.[20] Official recollections of the reason for this omission vary. It remains unclear whether this language was the result of a drafting error, or intended to signal to the Serbian regime that the Security Council would contemplate some degree of independence for Kosovo.

Importantly, even after the escalation of violence against the people of Kosovo, and the removal of the condition from subsequent Contact Group statements, Ambassador Gelbard proclaimed in Prishtina on 26 March 1998 that a final settlement would necessarily result in "some form of enhanced status for Kosovo, within the borders of [the FRY],"[21] and again in July 1998 he testified before the House International Relations Committee that any solution to the conflict in Kosovo "can and must be found within existing international borders."[22] The support for the FRY's sovereignty and territorial integrity, while designed to accommodate the interests of the Serbian regime, was also based on the real-politik concerns of Contact Group members like Russia and the United Kingdom, which must contend with their own secessionists movements. Furthermore the principles of sovereignty and territorial integrity are well founded in the normative structure of public international law—although they do not justify nor permit the type of actions undertaken by the Serbian regime against the people of Kosovo.

With respect to the implicit green light to continue to use force against the KLA, at the request of the Russian member of the Contact Group, the 8 January 1998 Contact Group statement declared that it condemned "both violent repression of non-violent expressions of political views and terrorist actions to achieve political goals."[23] And then again at the behest of the Russian Foreign Ministry, which hosted the 25 February 1998 Contact Group meeting, the members of the Contact Group condemned "as terrorist actions, including those of the so-called Kosovo Liberation Army."[24] The Russian government also successfully persuaded the UN Security Council to include a condemnation of Albanian terrorist action in each Kosovo-related resolution adopted by the Council,[25] thus creating moral equivalence among the parties.

Although the effort to identify the Kosovar armed resistance as terrorists was led by the Russian Foreign Ministry, the U.S. Department of State also adopted an aggressive policy of identifying the KLA as a terrorist organization. Thus, on 15 January 1998, Ambassador Gelbard declared in Belgrade, "we strongly believe that violence is not the answer from either side, and we strongly oppose any kind of terrorist activity from Kosovo Albanians or anybody else, as well as violence fomented by government security forces."[26] Subsequently on 22 February 1998 he again declared in Prishtina, "As I have said before, I consider these to be terrorists actions, and it is the strong and firm policy of the United States to fully oppose all terrorists actions and all terrorists organizations."[27] In subsequent public statements, Mr. Gelbard threatened to take action to interrupt the ability of the KLA to sustain themselves through the full chain of supply."[28]

The invocation of the designation "terrorists" and the threat to impose sanctions on the organization was particularly important as "terrorists" was the term used by Mr. Milosevic to describe the KLA and served as the bedrock of his justification for the use of force. Moreover, the threat to impose sanctions eroded the moral imperative to become more involved because all sides were equally responsible—a situation Mr. Milosevic had successfully manipulated to his advantage in the Bosnian crisis. The U.S. government subsequently found that there was no basis for the KLA to be designated a terrorist organization. Moreover, despite the availability of his statements on the State Department website, the authors learned that Ambassador Gelbard privately complained to CNN that he had never identified the KLA as a terrorist organization and that the network ought to stop reporting that the United States provided the green light for the Serbian military offensive.

Settling on Accommodation, Feigned Economic Inducement, and Contrived Diplomatic Engagement

The approach of accommodation and moral equivalence did not prevent, and may have encouraged, the undertaking of an aggressive campaign of ethnic violence designed to destroy the KLA and to terrorize the ethnic Albanian population of Kosovo.

In response, the peace builders, working through the Contact Group, modified their approach in late February and early March 1998 to incorporate the approaches of economic inducement and enhanced diplomatic engagement while retaining the approach of accommodation at the core—in particular the reference to terrorism and to the sovereignty and territorial integrity of the FRY. The Contact Group also began to invoke the norm of justice and called for an enhanced role for the Yugoslav Tribunal. Backing away from its tactic of moral equivalism, it began to identify the Serbian regime as primarily responsible for the atrocities.[29]

To implement the sanction aspect of the approach of economic inducement, the Contact Group agreed only to impose a moratorium on government-financed export credit support for trade and investment, including those used for privatization, and it threatened to "pursue a freeze on the funds held abroad by [the FRY] and Serbian governments" and to continue the outer wall of sanctions if Serbia did not cooperate in bringing an end to the conflict. To apply the incentive aspect, the Contact Group promised to restore export credit support, and work to "improve the international position of [the FRY] and prospects for normalization of its international relationships and full rehabilitation in international institutions."[30] The Security Council added its weight to this particular element of inducement by affirming that "concrete progress to resolve the serious political and human rights issues in Kosovo will improve the international position of the [the FRY]" and enhance prospects for a normalization of relations, including full participation in international institutions.[31]

Secretary Albright also publicly proposed that the Contact Group establish a working group to study how best to "implement an assets freeze and a ban on foreign direct investment, should that prove necessary."[32] The Contact Group also pledged to support the imposition of a renewed UN arms embargo[33] (which was subsequently adopted by the UN on 31 March 1998),[34] and it committed not to provide equipment to the FRY that might be used for internal repression, and to deny visas to senior Serbian representatives responsible for repressive action by Serbian security forces in Kosovo.

Compared to the comprehensive economic sanctions imposed on the FRY during the Bosnia conflict, the mere discontinuation of government-sponsored export credits and the possibility of an assets freeze constituted pin-prick financial inducement—all the more so since the warning of an assets freeze provided the FRY time to move its assets from accounts held in those states which were members of the Contact Group. Similarly the offer of a possible lifting of the outer wall of sanctions did not appear credible as their imposition was also linked to Serbian behavior in Bosnia and the treatment of the democratic opposition within Serbia. Noticeably, even the Serbian regime was surprised by the limited nature of the economic inducements. As proclaimed by Vojislav Seselj, ultra nationalist leader of the Serbian Radical Party, "the decisions by the Contact Group are somewhat milder than first signaled and . . . the government of national unity has substantially stabilized the position of Serbia and Yugoslavia."[35]

The limited scope of the economic inducements was in large part a result of the unwillingness of Germany, France, and Italy to continue to employ economic sanctions as a tool to modify the behavior of Serbia given the economic cost to their domestic industry,[36] and the objection to increased sanctions by the other southeastern European states who had suffered significant economic hardship as a result of earlier sanctions.[37]

To promote enhanced diplomatic engagement, the Contact Group: (1) requested that the United Nations High Commissioner for Human Rights send a mission to Kosovo, (2) supported the return of the OSCE long-term mission and the establishment of a Kosovo specific OSCE mission, (3) encouraged OSCE member states to intensify visits to Kosovo by their diplomatic representatives in Belgrade, (4) committed to supporting Sant'Egidio's efforts to secure implementation of the Education Agreement, (5) proposed the creation of an international consortium including NGOs that would promote civil-society building in Kosovo and the distribution of humanitarian assistance, and (6) proposed enhancing the OSCE and UNPREDEP presence in Macedonia.[38] On 30 March 1998 the UN Security Council adopted Resolution 1160 calling for nearly identical measures.[39]

Like the economic inducements proposed by the Contact Group, these diplomatic measures were seen as "diplomacy light," and they had the effect of signaling that the Contact Group was not entirely serious about involving itself in the mediation of the Kosovo conflict, contrary to the recommendations of Romania, Bulgaria, Greece, and Albania.[40] By calling upon enhanced roles for the UNHCR, the OSCE, and even NGOs, the Contact Group signaled that it was unwilling to take a leading role in resolving the conflict, and it set the stage for the same type of institutional competition and disarray that had hampered efforts to achieve peace in Bosnia.

Given its aversion to the use of force, and its recognition that a pure reliance on accommodation would likely be insufficient, the Contact Group, for the first time in the conflict also invoked the norm of justice. They first called upon the Serbian regime to "invite independent forensic experts to investigate the very serious allegations of extra judicial killings," and they indicated that if the accusations were true they expected Serbian authorities to prosecute and punish those responsible. The Contact Group also asserted that its growing involvement in the issue was based on the members' "commitment to human rights values."[41] British foreign secretary Robin Cook, speaking on behalf of the United Kingdom and the EU, explained that "serious violations of human rights, of civil liberties, of the freedom of political expression, are matters of concern to every member of the international community and cannot be regarded simply as an internal matter" for Serbia.[42]

The Contact Group further sought to motivate the Yugoslav Tribunal's prosecutor by urging her to begin gathering information related to the violence in Kosovo, and members reaffirmed that FRY authorities had an obligation to cooperate with the Tribunal. The Contact Group members also pledged to make available to the Tribunal "substantiated relevant information in their possession."[43] Robin Cook further elaborated that the Contact Group had agreed that the prosecutor "should consider the prosecution of anyone who may have committed a violation of humanitarian law in Kosovo. We are clear and she is clear that she has the legal authority to do that. We invite her to consider whether indictments might be appropriate in the light of the evidence of the past week." Cook further declared "there must be no impunity for those who break international law."[44]

To compliment the efforts of the Contact Group, the UN Security Council also urged the prosecutor to "begin gathering information related to the violence in Kosovo that may fall within its jurisdiction."[45] The UN Security Council also created a committee to monitor the work of the Contact Group and to provide regular updates to the Council. Although widely perceived as a bureaucratic move, the creation of the committee subsequently furthered the role of justice as it provided a constant flow of information to the Council concerning violations of international humanitarian law by the Serbian regime in Kosovo.[46]

In addition to the actions of the Contact Group, the United States took a number of steps to more fully integrate the norm of justice. First, the United States distanced itself more firmly from the policy of moral equivalence when Secretary Albright declared, "we must avoid being paralyzed by the kind of artificial even-handedness that equates aggressors with their victims. We need to say clearly what is so clearly true: that responsibility for the violence lies squarely with Belgrade."[47] Secretary Albright also more aggressively urged the Office of the Prosecutor to immediately begin investigations and for Serbia to allow the ICRC and UNHCR to undertake their own investigations.[48] Finally, in order to prod the prosecutor, the United States announced a contribution of $1 million to support the Tribunal's investigations in Kosovo.[49] Disappointingly, though, the secretary of state expressly acknowledged in her announcement that the Office of the Prosecutor's investigators were required to obtain visas from Serbia in order to investigate the alleged crimes, and thus she provided Slobodan Milosevic with an effective veto over the ability of the Tribunal to have any meaningful role in stemming the atrocities.

The emergence of the norm of justice was in large part a result of the belief that the approach of accommodation was failing, an implicit recognition that the approaches of economic inducement and the policy of diplomatic engagement were not yet serious, and a reluctance to commit to the use of force. More specifically, its invocation was based on the realization that there was no identified role yet for the use of force, and that greater involvement of justice-based institutions (or their intentional exclusion by Mr. Milosevic) might provide a moral basis for the invocation of the use of force approach. The emergence of the norm of justice was also based on British foreign secretary Robin Cook's, and others, perception that the massive violation of human rights constituted a basis for involving oneself in what might otherwise be considered the internal matters of another state—something antithetical to a realist's perspective.

With respect to the implementation of the norm of justice, Secretary Albright's peculiar reference to independent experts and the responsibility of the FRY to undertake domestic prosecutions (in light of the existence of the Tribunal and the failure of the FRY government to prosecute a single individual for war crimes committed during the Bosnian conflict), can be seen as a direct criticism of the Tribunal's timidity in injecting itself into the crisis in Kosovo. This approach of creating competition among institutions of justice seriously undermined the Tribunal in that Mr. Milosevic subsequently granted access to independent investigators—who had no authority to issue indictments or hold trials, while denying access to Tribunal investigators, and then claiming he was in substantial compliance with the demands of the Contact Group. Mr. Milosevic was also able to claim that the Contact Group recognized the right of the FRY to prosecute those responsible for war crimes in Kosovo, and thus the Tribunal did not possess jurisdiction over the Kosovo matter.

Finally, the actual actions taken by the Contact Group and the United States, while signaling a role for justice, were not particularly significant. By acknowledging that the Office of the Prosecutor was required to obtain visas in order to conduct investigations, the United States undermined the Tribunal's efforts to gain visa-free access, and therefore Washington gave Mr. Milosevic the power to control whether and when, if ever, the Tribunal could conduct investigations. And by appropriating only $1 million—of which only $400,000 could be used for actual investigations, the United States appeared to actually diminish the perceived importance of war crimes prosecutions and the norm of justice.

The Contact Group's approach of minimal economic inducements, tepid diplomatic engagement, and calls for the greater application of justice during the winter of 1998 did little to dampen the conflict in Kosovo.[50] As acknowledged in June 1998 by Paddy Ashdown, leader of Britain's Liberal Democrats, "all the blandishments of the international community, all the sanctions, all the veiled threats have achieved absolutely nothing. There is no visible sign that any actions we have so far taken have encouraged Mr. Milosevic to be in the slightest more restrained. He is now using tanks, heavy artillery the maximum weapons of war."[51]

As a result of the failure of the weak policy response and the apparent replay of the accommodation approach which led to the prolonged Bosnia conflict, a number of prominent public officials called for a change in tactics. Czech president Vaclav Havel declared, "the earlier evil is confronted, the less we have to pay in human lives and suffering. Why for 11 years can one man expose the international community to ridicule? Why, when it was clear to any sensible person that Kosovo was bound to explode, do we have to wait for that explosion to happen?"[52] Similarly, U.S. ambassador Morton Abramowitz declared, "the United States and its allies have waited four months while Milosevic cleaned the clock of the Kosovo Liberation Army and [have] taken three weeks to discuss military action, with the result that 500 Albanian villages were destroyed."[53]

More specifically, important voices began to call for the use of force. In an open letter to Secretary of State Madeleine Albright, Senator Mitch McConnell (R-Ky.) declared, "it is well past the time for threats and NATO flyovers. . . . I urge you to work with Secretary Cohen to obtain the necessary European support for immediate air strikes against Serbian targets in order to secure a cease fire, full withdrawal of all Serb forces and the protection of refugees and displaced people."[54] Similarly, the *London Times* argued, "a 'limited' and 'phased' campaign will achieve no more than similar adventures did in the earlier stages of the Bosnian conflict. . . . An intense military assault is all that will make a compelling impression on Mr. Milosevic. The unappealing alternative is complicity in a human and political catastrophe on NATO's doorstep."[55] Not all important actors, however, supported the use of force. Italian prime minister Romano Prodi, for instance, declared, "whenever you send troops, you send hostages—potential hostages—to the situation."[56]

Prominent Kosovars committed to a peaceful resolution of the crisis warned that the approach of accommodation was failing and might lead to catastrophic results. For instance, Veton Surroi, editor of *Koha Ditore*, stated, "the dynamic of violence is a step ahead of what the international community has decided. There is a need for much greater force and pace from the international community if there is to be a peaceful solution to the situation in Kosovo."[57]

As a consequence of both the delay in active and meaningful engagement and the perception that the Serbian regime was accomplishing its objectives at the expense of the people of Kosovo, the political leadership in Kosovo who supported a peaceful resolution began to lose significant ground to those who supported armed resistance.[58] As noted by Shkelzen Maliqi, member of the Kosovo Albanian negotiating team, "The people arguing for peace are losing their arguments."[59] And as proclaimed by a villager after his village had been burned by Serbian troops, "we are all KLA now. . . . The Germans were here during the [second world] war, but nothing like this ever happened."[60]

The Clark Doctrine: Mediation under the Threat of Force

As in Bosnia, instead of firing up the engines, NATO is firing up excuses.

— Bob Dole, former U.S. Senator[61]

In light of the failure of previous approaches to promote a peaceful resolution of the dispute, and the increasing public pressure to use force, the peace builders decided to undertake active mediation of the conflict, and to increasingly employ the threat of the use of force. The United States, with the support of the United Kingdom, headed up the efforts to organize a Kosovo Albanian negotiating delegation in the summer of 1998 and undertook to persuade the parties to accept a peace agreement under the draftsmanship of the U.S. Department of State. Much of the summer was spent with U.S. diplomats shuttling between Prishtina and Belgrade seeking to work out an acceptable agreement, and with U.S. and U.K. officials, led by General Wesley Clark, seeking to build consensus within NATO for the use of force.

At one point the shuttle diplomacy efforts of the United States were superceded by those of the Russian government, which on 16 June 1998, issued a joint declaration with the FRY wherein the FRY committed to seeking to resolve the crisis by political means, ensuring freedom of movement and the return of refugees, and providing full access for humanitarian organizations. Not surprisingly, the Russian-FRY joint declaration made no mention of the norm or institutions of justice.

After it became apparent that the Russian-FRY arrangement was not being implemented, the United States resumed its active shuttle diplomacy. The draft agreements prepared by the United States generally sought to accommodate the Serbian interests in the territorial integrity and sovereignty of the FRY, while providing certain human rights protections for the people of Kosovo. The initial drafts were highly favorable to Serbian interests and provided for a system of institutional political gridlock similar to that written into the Dayton Accords. Subsequent drafts increasingly focused on the interests of the Kosovo Albanians more than those of Serbia. The penultimate agreement, which formed the basis for the Rambouillet talks, was in fact highly favorable on a number of issues for the Kosovo Albanians, although it did not present a workable form of provincial government.

While a complete textual analysis of the various agreements is beyond the scope of this chapter, it is useful to examine the extent to which the drafters incorporated the norms and institutions of justice within the several versions of the Rambouillet agreements. The first series of agreements produced over the summer of 1998 and the draft agreement of 7 October 1998 did not contain any mention of the norm of justice, the Yugoslav Tribunal, or other institutions of justice such as victim compensation commissions or truth commissions.

As a result of the persistent inclusion of the norm of justice in UN Security Council Resolutions,[62] and criticism by the president of the Yugoslav Tribunal, the Kosovo delegation, and a number of NGOs, in particular the Coalition for

International Justice, the draft agreement produced on 29 October 1998 included a clause providing that a human rights ombudsman be established under the agreement with the obligation to report to the Yugoslav Tribunal any information concerning the commission of war crimes which the ombudsman might come across during the regular conduct of the individual's duties.[63] The draft agreement also provided that all government authorities would be obligated to cooperate with the Tribunal, among other human rights organizations, and provide unrestricted access for investigative purposes.[64] Finally, the agreement provided under the heading of confidence building measures that each party was obligated to cooperate in the Tribunal's investigation of war crimes and that any amnesties for crimes committed during the conflict would not include war crimes.[65]

In the November draft agreement, the Department of State added a provision similar to a clause in the Dayton Accords providing that no person serving a sentence or indicted by the Tribunal may hold any office.[66] The November draft agreement maintained the provisions calling on all parties to cooperate in the investigation of war crimes and to allow complete access to international experts and Tribunal investigators, to exclude from an amnesty any individual responsible for war crimes, and to require that the human rights ombudsman provide relevant information to the Tribunal.[67] The draft also incorporated by reference UN Security Council Resolution 827 and subsequent resolutions, thereby incorporating the jurisdictional basis and Chapter VII requirements articulated by the Security Council.

Concerning the timing and context of the inclusion of the norm of justice into the Kosovo negotiation process, one might surmise that the U.S. Department of State and other peace builders did not view of the norm as having a particularly important role to play. The norm was entirely absent during the first rounds of drafting, which were entirely confidential, and it was not until after the drafts became public and were subjected to scrutiny by NGOs and important actors within the Department of State that they began to include references to justice. In fact, the authors have been told that the Department of State's Office of Human Rights and Democracy had to lobby hard with the primary drafters and the secretary of state for the inclusion of the norm of justice.

When the drafters did choose to incorporate the norm, they did so only to the extent that the norm had been incorporated within the Dayton Accords. They made no effort to expand the substance of the norm, or to include provisions that might have enhanced the effectiveness of the Tribunal, such as providing for visa-free access to Tribunal investigators or providing for the imposition of select sanctions for failure to comply with the Tribunal's orders. This lack of effort was particularly noticeable in that many government officials had subsequently concluded that the Dayton Accords provisions were inadequate, and it was well understood that the efforts of the Office of the Prosecutor to investigate the crisis in Kosovo were being stymied by the Serbian regime.

While the United States engaged in the exchange of draft peace agreements, Washington and the United Kingdom also continued to work with their NATO allies to build support for the use of force and to publicly issue increasingly strident remarks concerning the likelihood of the use of force in the event the Serbian regime did not cease the commission of atrocities and agree to a peaceful resolution of the crisis. On 28 May, the North Atlantic Council (NAC) announced that under Partnership for Peace arrangements it would assist Albania and Macedonia in securing their borders, hold ground and air exercises in Albania in August as well as ground exercises in Macedonia in September, and schedule a visit of NATO's Standing Force Mediterranean to the Albanian port of Durrës in early July. The aim of these exercises was to demonstrate "NATO's capability to project power rapidly into the region." NATO also signaled its readiness to take further deterrent and other measures as necessary, including taking action to halt or disrupt "a systematic campaign of violent repression and expulsion in Kosovo," and to provide "assistance" in the event of a humanitarian catastrophe.[68] At this time, none of the NAC declarations mentioned the norm or institutions of justice.

The new approach of active mediation with hints of justice and economic inducement, and an increasing suggestion of the willingness and ability to use force, did not serve to quell the conflict or abate the atrocities.[69] In fact, in the midst of the negotiations, the Serbian regime began a policy of rounding up Kosovo Albanian men, and placing them in camps reminiscent of the Bosnian concentration camps.[70] This action led a senior NATO diplomat to conclude: "there's a feeling that we dropped the ball over the summer. We allowed Milosevic to hoodwink us into thinking he would scale back the violence [in Kosovo], but it has only gotten worse."[71] The continuing atrocities, destruction of whole villages, and the murder of aid workers also undermined the ability of the Kosovar delegation to constructively participate in the peace talks.[72]

The failure of this new approach, according to General Clark, was in large part due to German and French reservations concerning the use of force without Security Council authorization. Additional factors included likely Russian assurances to Milosevic that no such authorization would be granted, European indecision as to their willingness to use force, a European propensity to announce progress in the negotiations when none existed, and, above all, the reliance on Milosevic as a "legitimate negotiating partner," when "for months it had been clear that a fundamental problem in Kosovo was Milosevic himself."[73]

As a result, there were again increasing public calls for a more aggressive incorporation of the use of force into the peace-building process. One of the most insightful and potentially influential calls for force came from *The Washington Post*'s editorial board, whose members which wrote:

> This humanitarian disaster [in Kosovo] cannot be ended without a political solution, and a political solution is impossible without a U.S. resolve to use force, if necessary, against Mr. Milosevic's marauding soldiers. President Clinton and his team have promised again and again to show such resolve, but their threats have proved empty. . . . What is unfolding is genocide at one remove. "A massacre is not necessarily committed only with knives," one displaced woman said. . . . The longer Mr. Clinton dithers, the greater the cost will be.[74]

The American and European members of the Contact Group became so desperate that they even considered a Serbian proposal that they fund "humanitarian centers" to which the Serbs would relocate the refugees fleeing from the destroyed villages. This plan was dropped after widespread public criticism served to remind those considering the idea that similar safe havens, such as Srebrenica, Zepa, and Bihac in Bosnia, became de facto concentration camps, which provided the Serbian regime with both domestic and international hostages, and, in the case of Srebrenica and Zepa, eventually became killing fields.[75]

The Milosevic/Holbrooke Deal: Coercive Appeasement

I love NATO . . . But let them know that people are dying.

—Xhavit Rudi, thirty-year-old refugee from Drenica[76]

As the atrocities in Kosovo continued to increase and as more refugees fled to neighboring Macedonia and Albania, the peace builders began to solidify international support for the use of force. Responding to intense lobbying efforts by the United States and the United Kingdom, on 13 October 1998 the NAC issued activation orders for both limited air strikes and a phased air campaign in Yugoslavia. Execution of the air strikes was to begin within ninety-six hours.[77]

With the threat of force finally credible, the United States sent Ambassador Holbrooke as a special envoy to negotiate a peace agreement. As a result of intermittent negotiations throughout October, and a ban by Secretary of Defense Cohen on the deployment of NATO peacekeepers,[78] two agreements were reached on 15 and 16 October 1998 which provided for the deployment of 2,000 unarmed monitors in Kosovo, the withdrawal of a limited number of Yugoslav army and Interior Ministry forces from the province, a number of provisions relating to the creation of a joint police force and local elections,[79] and the creation of a regime for unarmed NATO overflight.[80] These provisions were endorsed by the UN Security Council in Resolution 1203 on 24 October 1998. In light of this agreement, on 16 October 1998, the NAC reaffirmed its readiness to launch air strikes and set 27 October 1998, as a deadline for compliance by the FRY.[81]

The agreement was hailed as a success by the U.S. government and by Ambassador Holbrooke as it "internationalized the conflict," and provided for 2,000 OSCE observers who would serve to deter further atrocities and verify the provisions of the agreement relating to withdrawal of armed forces.[82] However, as observed by General Clark, while an important source of information, the vulnerable force which could readily be taken hostage "vitiated the implicit NATO threat against Milosevic or his forces."[83]

Outside the U.S. government the negotiators were widely criticized for squandering the credible threat of the use of force to achieve an agreement that would allow the Serbian regime to maintain a sufficient number of forces in the region to carry out its campaign of ethnic aggression. In addition, critics complained that the agreement provided for the deployment of a force similar to, but even weaker than, the failed UNPROFOR mission in Bosnia, contained no meaningful enforcement provisions, did not establish a meaningful level of self-government for the people of Kosovo,[84] and had the effect of dissipating the resolve of NATO members to use force. As Ambassador William Walker, head of the verification mission, would later comment:

> If we had landed a half million unarmed men on the beaches of Normandy in 1944, World War Two might still be going on. When you're in a situation where an awful lot of people have guns and are unwilling to obey the orders of people who don't, you have to think maybe we need someone here with some power to enforce. That's what a NATO force would do: create conditions of stability and security here. There's a role here for armed and unarmed people and right now we're trying to do everything with unarmed people and it's not going to work.[85]

The Milosevic/Holbrooke deal was also significantly criticized because it failed to include the interests of either the KLA or the Kosovo civilian leadership. Because the KLA was not a party to the agreement, its members felt as if they had been excluded from the negotiation process, and because there were no restrictions applicable to the KLA, the Serbian regime could almost immediately refuse to comply with the agreement on the basis that, if it withdrew any of its forces, the KLA would fill the vacuum.[86] According to Kosovar prime minister Bujar Bukoshi, the civilian leadership rejected the deal on the basis that "the Kosovo Albanian people have not endured ten years of martial law, the displacement of one-quarter of their population, the murder of thousands of citizens, and the destruction of 500 villages only to accept an agreement that amounts to surrender and capitulation to Serbian aggression."[87]

As a result of the nonutilization of the threat of the use of force, and the return to the prevalence of accommodation, the Serbian regime permitted a moderate number of observers to enter Kosovo, at which point the NAC suspended (but did not terminate) the NATO Activation Order.[88] The Serbian regime, however, significantly limited the effective operation of the international observers, refused to comply with the provisions of the agreement providing for troop withdrawal, and in fact may have actually increased the number of deployed troops[89] and continued its campaign of terror.[90] As noted by former secretary of defense Casper Weinberger, "by making . . . all kinds of strong statements [that] grave consequences will be faced by Mr. Milosevic, and then nothing ever happens, is the worst way to go about dealing with aggression and terrorism. The more you encourage it, the more you let the people involved know it is not going to be punished, the more you are going to have of it."[91]

Although much of the public commentary on the Holbrooke/Milosevic deal centered around the return to a failed policy of accommodation and the perceived squandering of the threat of the use of force, the deal was also subject to criticism for failing to make any mention whatsoever of the norm of justice or the need to cooperate with the Yugoslav Tribunal.[92] The deal was also subject to the criticism that it enhanced the stature of the individual most criminally responsible for the crimes in Kosovo. According to Peter Bouckaert of Human Rights Watch, with the deal, "Milosevic got everything he wanted [in Kosovo]. He finished his offensive. He created a humanitarian disaster that will force Albanians to focus on survival. . . . He created this mess, and now the West will clean it up. And he's still the guy to deal with."[93]

Given the increasing reference to the norm of justice and strong public commitments by U.S. government officials, the exclusion of the norm from the agreement may have been in large part the result of the perspective of the particular peace builder sent to negotiate the agreement. When asked by a reporter in Belgrade how he could trust Mr. Milosevic given his apparent culpability, Ambassador Holbrooke responded that the matter of culpability was an issue for the press to be concerned with, and that his priority was to "deal with the realities and do the best we can."[94]

Similarly, when questioned as to whether Mr. Milosevic could be taken as a guarantor of peace given his actions, and how the deal could be reconciled with Department of State declarations condemning him for the atrocities in Kosovo, Ambassador Holbrooke seemed to indicate that culpability for atrocities was a personal matter and one that ought not to be brought within the ambit of peace deal-making:

> I don't believe any purpose is served by characterizations of a personal nature in the middle of extraordinarily sensitive and difficult negotiations. We've made our views clear repeatedly. I have made my own views clear, and I don't see any reason to get into that. We are here to address the specific problems of the region and we look forward to discussing them with President Milosevic. I'll let others address that question other times and other ways.[95]

Ambassador Holbrooke further indicated that he considered matters of justice and peace to be separate, and that the norm of justice should not interfere with the goals of peace deal-making:

> I think the U.S. position has been consistent for a long time on this issue [war crimes]—for several years. Our interests are in compliance, verification, stability, the full implementation of the Dayton Agreement, and getting this extraordinarily turbulent part of the world more stable. . . . People say different things at different times, but the policy is very clear and consistent and it hasn't changed in any fundamental way—I stress the word fundamental, because you move around a little bit from time to time—but there's been no fundamental change in the policy since Dayton and before.[96]

And finally, when Ambassador Holbrooke, and Ambassador Hill were asked in December 1998 whether they would comment on the fact that Mr. Milosevic and other Serbian officials had declared "that they don't have any intention to deliver suspected war criminals to The Hague," Ambassador Holbrooke declined to take the question, while Ambassador Hill merely stated that "The Hague Tribunal is the appropriate place for people who are accused of war crimes—that it is the appropriate place, that it should be judged in The

Hague."[97] Importantly, this language mirrored that of Secretary Christopher's earlier answers to the similar questions when he sought to evade an identification of Milosevic's culpability.

Whereas Ambassador Holbrooke was reluctant to incorporate any mention of the Yugoslav Tribunal in the Milosevic/Holbrooke deal, during the same time period the president of the Tribunal, Judge McDonald, sent a number of formal reports to the Security Council detailing the noncompliance of the FRY with the orders of the Tribunal and calling upon the Security Council to take measures to compel the FRY's compliance.[98] After three such reports, and continuing public criticism of the peace builders for ineffectual action, on 17 November 1998, the UN Security Council adopted Resolution 1207, which recalled the resolution creating the Tribunal and noted the numerous letters provided to the Security Council by the president of the Yugoslav Tribunal charging that the FRY had failed to cooperate with the Tribunal. Resolution 1207 then provided in paragraph 4 that, acting under Chapter VII of the UN Charter, the Security Council reiterated its decision that all states must fully cooperate with the Tribunal and called upon the authorities of the FRY and the leaders of the Kosovo Albanian community to cooperate fully with the prosecutor.[99] But the Council took no further action to enforce the resolution in the face of continuing Serb noncooperation.

The Albright Doctrine: Diplomacy Backed by Force

Only the credible threat of military action will force Mr. Milosevic to listen.

—Veton Surroi, editor of *Koha Ditore* an
Albanian language daily in Prishtina[100]

On 15 January 1999, Serbian military and paramilitary forces massacred over forty civilians in Racak, Kosovo. Subsequent intelligence intercepts, reported in *The Washington Post*, established a clear link between the frontline forces responsible for the massacre and the subsequent attempt to cover it up, and high-level officials in the Serbian government. The massacre was met by a rapid series of denunciations by President Clinton,[101] Secretary of State Albright,[102] Ambassador Eide as chairman of the OSCE[103] on behalf of the presidency of the European Union, and UN Secretary-General Annan.[104]

Many of these declarations called for an investigation by the Office of the Prosecutor, and for the perpetrators to "be brought to justice."[105] Some declarations expressed outrage at claims by Mr. Milosevic that the OSCE Kosovo Mission impeded investigation of this crime, falsified evidence, and displayed partiality toward the KLA. Several declarations specifically called upon the Serbian regime to "publicly and unequivocally accept the jurisdiction of The Hague Tribunal for all of Kosovo . . . grant chief prosecutor Arbour and a [Yugoslav Tribunal] team immediate, unrestricted access to investigate this and other incidents, help identify those responsible for the Racak massacre and hand over any and all suspects to the [Yugoslav Tribunal] for prosecution, if the [Yugoslav Tribunal] requests."[106] General Clark and General Klaus Naumann appealed to Milosevic in person to grant access to Arbour.[107] Notably, the UN Secretary-General's statement was the only one which omitted a call for the Yugoslav Tribunal to be granted access to investigate the massacre.[108]

Before and immediately after the massacre, a number of prominent U.S. senators began to call for the use of force to promote the ends of justice. For instance, Senator Mitch McConnell declared, "[i]t is time for the United States to accept reality, recognize Kosovo's independence and provide Prishtina's leadership with the political and security assistance necessary to halt its genocidal war [and] demand a NATO vote to implement the Activation Order for air strikes."[109] Similarly, Senator Frank Lautenberg (D-N.J.) declared, "clearly Milosevic thinks he can get away with murder, literally, and NATO needs to send him a strong message. He is the Saddam Hussein of Europe, and force is the only language he seems to understand. NATO must follow through on its threats with air strikes to force the Serbs to respect their commitments."[110]

As a result of the Racak massacre, the collapse/nonimplementation of the Milosevic/Holbrooke deal, the apparent failure of the approach of accommodation, and mounting public pressure, the peace builders, led by the United States, modified their approach to include substantially increased reliance on the threat of the use of force, invocations of the norm of justice, and the introduction of direct mediation in the form of structured peace talks. This new policy came to be known as "diplomacy backed by the threat of force."[111]

To reinstitute the credible threat of the use of force, on 28 January 1999, NATO issued a declaration (1) indicating its full support for the conclusion of a political settlement under the mediation of the Contact Group, (2) demanding that the Serbian regime comply with their commitments to withdraw military forces under the 25 October 1998 agreement with NATO and with the obligations set forth in the agreement with OSCE, and (3) further demanding that the Serbian regime cooperate fully with the Yugoslav Tribunal by granting immediate and unrestricted access to its representatives to carry out their investigation of the Racak massacre and by ensuring the safety of the investigators.[112]

At this time, the Contact Group also demanded that the FRY cooperate fully with the Yugoslav Tribunal as required by numerous Security Council resolutions, that it conduct a full investigation of Racak with the participation of the Yugoslav Tribunal, and that it allow the prosecutor and Yugoslav Tribunal investigators to enter and work in Kosovo.

Subsequently, on 30 January 1999, the NAC reactivated the 13 October 1998 NATO activation order, and the member states declared that "the crisis in Kosovo remains a threat to peace and security in the region. NATO's strategy is to halt the violence and support the completion of negotiations on an interim political settlement for Kosovo, thus averting a humanitarian catastrophe." As such, NATO demanded that both parties attend the negotiations in Rambouillet and reach an agreement in the allotted time, and comply with the 25 October 1998 NATO-FRY agreement. If the parties failed to reach agreement, the NATO Secretary-General was authorized to order air strikes against the FRY.

The NAC also announced that it was prepared to take unspecified "appropriate measures" in the event of a failure by the Kosovo Albanian side to fully cooperate with the peace builders. For the first time, the NAC invoked the norm of justice and declared that "those responsible for the massacre at Racak must be brought to justice and that Serbian authorities must cooperate fully with [the] Yugoslav Tribunal."[113]

The motivations for a strategy of "diplomacy backed by force" included a mix of real-politik assessment of American and European security interests and the political need to save diplomatic face. As explained by President Clinton, "in this volatile region, violence we fail to oppose leads to even greater violence we will have to oppose later, at greater cost. There is a serious risk the hostilities [in Kosovo] would spread to the neighboring new democracies of Albania and Macedonia and re-ignite the conflict in Bosnia we worked so hard to stop. It could even involve our NATO allies, Greece and Turkey. . . . The time to stop the war is right now."[114]

With the April 1999 scheduled NATO fiftieth anniversary celebrations in Washington, D.C., rapidly approaching, many government officials and public commentators were keenly aware that NATO's credibility was being severely tested[115] in the same way the crisis of inaction in Bosnia from 1993 to 1995 substantially undermined the deterrent authority of NATO and sowed deep divisions within its political ranks.[116] As put bluntly by Jim Hoagland in *The Washington Post*,

> President Clinton and the other leaders can expect to be laughed off the stage if Rambouillet fails and ethnic war is raging on Europe's ragged southern fringe while they solemnly party at the [23-25 April NATO 50th] anniversary celebration. The road to a Washington summit that reflects glory on the good and great of the Atlantic community now passes through the police stations and city hall of the pitiable Kosovar capital of Prishtina. Stopping the bloodshed there and policing the peace is a mission Americans and Europeans should share equitably.[117]

Concerning the role of justice in the motivation for the new strategy of "diplomacy backed by force," casual observation would lead one to conclude that, while invocation of the norm was used to enhance public justification for the threat of the use of force, it did not appear to play a prominent role in motivating this new strategy. One must consider, however, the strong and unanimous public condemnation of the Racak massacre and its role in galvanizing the new approach. While the massacre did not pose a threat to American and European security interests, it did seem to permeate the policy debate and strike a moral cord in the peace builders, which supported their determination to halt an apparently never ending stream of atrocities in the former Yugoslavia for the simple reason that it would be the "right thing to do." The next chapter will explore whether this commitment to justice as an essential element of the peace-building process was maintained through the negotiations in the Rambouillet chateau.

Chapter 11

The Rambouillet/Paris Negotiations: From Coercive Appeasement to Humanitarian Intervention

Now, let me say this—we have looked at three scenarios here for the end of these meetings. One is that the talks end because the Serbs have walked out in which case the United States has said that NATO will bomb. The second scenario is that you all walk out of these talks. In which case you will lose our support. And not only that, we will make an effort to isolate you to make sure that you do not get outside assistance. Because we will feel that you are not really interested in the good of your people and self government, but that you're only interested in fighting. Or to change borders by force which is contrary to all the principles of the OSCE and international law. But the third scenario is obviously the best. The third scenario is that we come to an agreement here and that there will be an international implementation force.

—Madeleine Albright, U.S. Secretary of State[1]

To structure the negotiations called for in the 29 January 1999 Contact Group statement, and supported by the threat of the use of force in the NATO declaration of 30 January 1999, the Contact Group "proposed" that negotiations be held in a rather rundown chateau in Rambouillet, France, just outside of Versailles in early February. As these negotiations were inconclusive, a second round of negotiations were held three weeks later in Paris. Upon collapse of the talks, and in light of continued atrocities, NATO launched a strategic air campaign against Serbian forces in Kosovo and in the FRY. In early June the Serbian forces agreed to withdraw from Kosovo, and the UN Security Council adopted Resolution 1244, which provided for the interim administration of Kosovo by a collection of entities, including the UN, EU, OSCE, and NATO.

This chapter continues the inquiry begun in the last chapter concerning the role of justice in the mediation and negotiation phases of the peace-building process and in the post-negotiation/use of force phase by focusing on the Rambouillet/Paris talks, the subsequent NATO air campaign, and the UN creation of an international protectorate in Kosovo. As noted in the previous chapter, the primary question addressed is number eight, which concerns the extent to which the competition among the various approaches influenced the development of peace-building regimes. Other questions include numbers one, two, three, six, seven, nine, and ten. As such, the three primary areas of investigation include (1) the perceived inherent competition among various approaches and the efforts to meld their application, (2) the manner in which the norms and institutions of justice interacted with the other approaches to influence the use of mediation and negotiation as a means to build peace—including the efforts of key stakeholders, and (3) the extent to which the peace builders sought to weave the norms and institutions of justice into the agreements at hand, and thereby promote the implementation of those agreements and a lasting peace.

The parties to the peace conference included a Kosovo delegation, with representatives from the shadow government, the Kosovo Liberation Army, and the intelligentsia; a Serbian delegation, with representatives from the Serbian central government (two of which were subsequently indicted for war crimes committed before and during the Rambouillet/Paris peace process), members of the non-Serbian ethnic minority in Albania, and legal experts (notably, Slobodan Milosevic was not present at the negotiations); representatives of the Contact Group, including the United States, France, Germany, Russia, Italy, and Great Britain; and representatives of the European Union and OSCE. The Rambouillet/Paris negotiations were co-hosted by the French and British foreign ministers, and they were chaired by the United States, Russia, and the European Union.

The Constraints of Justice: With Whom to Negotiate and with What to Bargain?

[Response to query 'How can you trust President Milosevic?'] That's not my issue. That's for you guys. Our issue is to deal with the realities and do the best we can. As many of you know, you make the characterizations; we deal with realities. I've dealt with this extensively in my book, copies of which are on sale in the lobby, and there is no value in going down that route today. We are here to move forward.

—Richard Holbrooke, at Belgrade press
conference (13 October 1998)

The primary peace builders may have adopted a more aggressive approach to quelling the conflict in Kosovo in part because they believed it was the right thing to do—as announced in the Contact Group declaration of 19 January 1999. Putting this belief into practice, however, proved to be complicated. In order to convene proximity talks the peace builders naturally had to invite delegations from each of the parties. One of the first issues to arise regarded the role in the negotiations of individuals potentially responsible for the commission of war crimes.

In some instances, peace builders may claim there is significant doubt as to whether potential participants in the peace process are responsible for war crimes or other atrocities and thus there is no need to address the question of whether they should be excluded from the process. In the case of the Kosovo crisis, however, the culpability of the potential negotiators was quite clear. Since 1994 most commentators, and many former government officials, held the view that there existed a prima facie case for the indictment of Slobodan Milosevic for war crimes and crimes against humanity in Bosnia,[2] and the U.S. Congress had passed a resolution calling upon the U.S. government to share all necessary information with the Tribunal in order to promote his indictment. By the time of the Kosovo crisis, even the former prosecutor for the Yugoslav Tribunal was calling for Mr. Milosevic's indictment.

Similarly, many commentators believed the president of Serbia, Mr. Milutinovic, and Mr. Milosevic's senior adviser for Kosovo, Mr. Sainovic, were personally responsible for orchestrating the war crimes and crimes against humanity in Kosovo. In fact, a few weeks prior to the opening of the Rambouillet/Paris negotiations, *The Washington Post* reported on an intelligence intercept provided by the KVM detailing a conversation between Mr. Sainovic and Serbian military forces involved in the Racak massacre, wherein Mr. Sainovic discussed means for covering up the massacre and embarking on a campaign of disinformation designed to blame the KLA for the massacre. Even the Department of State acknowledged that the Serbian regime led by Mr. Milosevic openly harbored indicted war criminals and acted at all times to impede the operation of the Yugoslav Tribunal and the pursuit of justice.[3]

Absent the existence of a public indictment by the Yugoslav Tribunal, as with Ratko Mladic and Radovan Karadzic during the Dayton negotiations, the peace builders apparently believed that there was little practical value to be found in excluding from the peace process those generally believed to be responsible for orchestrating the atrocities which characterized the Kosovo crisis. If Milosevic, Sainovic, and Milutinovic were excluded from the process, the peace builders logically concluded that it would not be possible to conduct negotiations and arrive at a peaceful resolution of the crisis as no other Serb officials were capable of entering into an enforceable agreement.

However, by including those responsible for the commission of war crimes in the negotiation process, either as direct participants in the formal negotiation or by signaling that they were responsible for approving and guaranteeing any peace agreement, the peace builders legitimized those individuals and enhanced their ability to further the pursuit of their agenda. This concern in particular applied to Mr. Milosevic, who, although he did not attend the Rambouillet/Paris negotiations, was named by the peace builders as the individual responsible for guaranteeing the peace. As explained by Ognjen Pribicevic, a Serbian political analyst, the result was that "[Milosevic] has the West where he wants it. . . .

He's got Western representatives begging him to accept and acknowledging him as a key factor, as crucial to resolving this situation."[4] This in turn enhanced the status of Mr. Milosevic within Serbia, increasing the likelihood of further destabilization, which could undermine the efforts of the peace builders. As noted by Senator Richard Lugar (R-Ind.), "by creating the perception that he is a guarantor of the Kosovo agreement, Mr. Milosevic gained leverage at home and tolerance abroad to muzzle his democratic opposition and, if necessary, to plan the next Balkan crisis—in Montenegro perhaps."[5]

Herein lies a conundrum of peace-building: If you exclude those responsible for war crimes, then you are unlikely to secure a negotiated peace. If you include them in the process, you legitimize them as individuals as well as their agenda, and likely increase the possibility of continued atrocities or of a fundamentally flawed peace agreement which encourages additional ethnic aggression. One possible solution to this conundrum is to employ the use of force approach against those responsible for war crimes and to limit contact with these individuals to the extent necessary to secure the implementation of dictated terms of peace. As suggested by former National Security Council adviser Zbigniew Brzezinski during the course of NATO air strikes, "it follows that there cannot be any negotiations with Milosevic himself, except in order to implement the modalities of Serbian withdrawal following the imposition of NATO's terms."[6] Such action, however, requires significant political will, which generally does not coalesce until after some form of negotiations has been attempted.

If peace builders do decide to include in the negotiation process individuals reasonably suspected of responsibility for war crimes, the next question becomes whether those individuals might be offered immunity from prosecution as part of a strategy of accommodation designed to induce them into signing and implementing the agreement.

The perceived advantages of immunity are simply that it may be required by one or more of the opposing parties before they agree to sign a peace agreement. The disadvantages are essentially the same as those associated with including culpable individuals in the process, except more severe. In the case of the former Yugoslavia, as noted by a U.S. official in the intelligence community, actions taken that would inhibit the removal of Mr. Milosevic from power, such as a grant of immunity, would result in "continued power for Milosevic [and] an interminable U.S. presence in the region."[7]

With respect to the Rambouillet/Paris negotiations, the peace builders determined that it was appropriate for Mr. Sainovic and Mr. Milutinovic to attend the negotiations, despite their likely culpability, and for Mr. Milosevic to remain in Belgrade, but to be included in the process. Although U.S. government officials preferred that Mr. Milosevic attend the talks, it was rumored he believed there might be a secret arrest warrant issued by the Tribunal and was unwilling to risk possible arrest.

Although potentially culpable individuals were allowed to attend the Rambouillet/Paris negotiations, the existence of the Tribunal and the public pronouncements of government officials essentially precluded any discussion of de jure immunity for these individuals. There was, however, substantial speculation as to whether they might be provided de facto immunity. In fact, some government officials believed that Mr. Milosevic had been granted a de facto immunity for his agreement to the Dayton Peace Accord, and that he had "used up" this immunity by his actions in Kosovo and would seek to have it replenished during the Rambouillet process.

The concern was best articulated by *The Washington Post* editorial board, which declared, "now Mr. Holbrooke has returned to Belgrade for more talks with Mr. Milosevic. Since U.S. and European officials have all but assured the dictator that he no longer need fear a bombing campaign, there's reason to worry that Mr. Holbrooke will be offering rewards instead—assurances of immunity from war crimes prosecution for what's taken place in Kosovo so far, a lifting of economic sanctions, perhaps an increase in the already-too-high number of troops Mr. Milosevic would be permitted to station in Kosovo."[8]

In fact, Mr. Milosevic is reported to have declared to a high-level U.S. military official that Ambassador Holbrooke had already promised him immunity from war crimes prosecution in exchange for signature of the Milosevic/Holbrooke package. There is of course no way to confirm whether such a promise was in fact made, but it does demonstrate Mr. Milosevic's concern for possible prosecution and his interest in immunity.

Finding a Place for Justice in the Rambouillet/Paris Negotiations

Anybody who's dealt with [Milosevic] or watched him operate knows that agreement for him is about ten percent of your way to an objective. The other ninety percent is implementation, and if there are any discrepancies in the agreement or disagreements in how it's interpreted, he'll drive a truck through them.

—Warren Zimmermann,
former U.S. Ambassador to Yugoslavia [9]

Like the Dayton Accords, the final version of the Rambouillet/Paris Accords reflected only a minimal recognition of the obligation of the parties to employ the norm of justice. This was in large part a result of the tension during the negotiations between those participants who desired a quick peace deal in order to avoid the necessity of air strikes (most notably the French and German delegations), those who believed it might be possible to secure a deal if Serbian interests could be sufficiently accommodated (most notably the Russian delegation, and some members of the American delegation), and those who sought a peace package that is a structured set of commitments which, if fulfilled, could promote a meaningful peace in Kosovo (the Kosovar delegation, the European Union co-chair, and some members of the British delegation).

The Rambouillet/Paris negotiations were qualitatively different from the Dayton negotiations in that the work of the Tribunal had established a clear pattern of war crimes and genocide against the civilian population during the Bosnian war, and recent reports by the KVM credibly indicated a similar pattern was occurring in Kosovo. Another difference was that many members of the British political establishment, civilian and military leaders in the NATO chain of command, and a few American officials believed that it would be necessary to use force to stop continued ethnic aggression in Kosovo and that the peace talks were a necessary part of the political process prior to the initiation of air strikes.

In addition there were four other important differences. First, there had been a transfer of political power in the United Kingdom from the Tory Party to the Labour Party, accompanied by the emergence of a significantly stronger commitment to the norm of justice, and a lessening of allegiance to Serbia. Second, the talks were held in France, which gave the French government significantly more influence over the procedural aspects of the peace negotiations than during the Dayton negotiations. Third, the Russian delegation, while not necessarily exercising more influence over the substance of the negotiations, did exercise a higher political profile, and did manage to protect Serbian interests on a number of important matters. And fourth, the Serbian delegation adopted a strategy of presenting itself as unconcerned as to whether a negotiated settlement would be reached.

Just as at Dayton, the question of justice was not the only issue subject to intense difference of opinion. The parties also addressed issues concerning the withdrawal of Serbian military, police and paramilitary forces, the transformation/disarmament of the KLA, the nature of municipal and regional structures of government, the process for determining Kosovo's final status after the expiry of the three-year interim period, the nature and extent of any international peacekeeping force, the means for reconstituting the police force, the protection of minority rights, the protection of cultural property, Kosovo representation in the FRY's governing bodies, the economic powers of the Kosovo regional government, and the creation of a process for the return of property that had been nationalized by the Serbian regime.

War Crimes Provisions Proposed by the Contact Group

The initial proposal of the Contact Group presented to the parties on 27 January 1999, which addressed many of the issues mentioned in the preceding paragraph, contained a limited number of provisions designed to incorporate the norms and institutions of justice. Specifically, the draft accords provided that no individual who has been sentenced or indicted by the Yugoslav Tribunal could hold appointed or elected public office,[10] and that as a confidence-building measure, "all Parties shall comply with their obligation to cooperate in the investigation and prosecution of war crimes, crimes against humanity, and other serious violations of international humanitarian law." The parties were also obligated to provide complete access to international experts and Tribunal investigators.[11] The draft accords further provided that the human rights ombudsman would report to the Yugoslav Tribunal any evidence of war crimes, and the accords prohibited the parties from granting an amnesty for the commission of war crimes.[12]

War Crimes Provisions Proposed by the Kosovo Delegation Government

Early in the course of the Rambouillet/Paris negotiations, the Kosovo delegation proposed a number of additions to the draft text concerning the norm of justice and in particular the need to ensure the adequate investigation of war crimes and the subsequent apprehension and extradition of all indicted individuals.[13] Given the path of moral equivalence adopted by many members of the international community during the Bosnian conflict, the Kosovars also expressed concern about the necessity of creating an accurate historical record in order to deter the invocation of similar moral equivalence in their case.

To remove any ambiguity as to the responsibility of the parties to cooperate with the Yugoslav Tribunal and to arrest and extradite to The Hague all those indicted, the Kosovars proposed that the accords include language to the effect that "The parties to this agreement agree to discharge their obligation towards the International Criminal Tribunal for the Former Yugoslavia pursuant to all relevant Security Council resolutions. Consistent with these resolutions, the parties agree to arrest, detain, and transfer to the custody of the International Criminal Tribunal for Yugoslavia any and all persons indicted by the International Criminal Tribunal for the Former Yugoslavia who reside in or transit through or are otherwise present in Kosovo, Serbia and the Federal Republic of Yugoslavia."

Concerned about the nonimplementation of a general obligation to cooperate in the Dayton Accords, and the refusal of the Serbian government to date to cooperate with the Yugoslav Tribunal, the Kosovar delegation further proposed the inclusion of language stating that, "The parties further commit to provide any judicial assistance requested by the Tribunal, for example, taking of testimony, access to and production of evidence, access to any person, facility, document and area of territory, as well as the service of documents."

To create a benchmark for measuring cooperation with the Yugoslav Tribunal, to challenge the Serbian regime on a loophole in the Security Council resolutions which they frequently invoked to deny Yugoslav Tribunal investigators access to Kosovo to investigate crimes against both Kosovo Serbs and Kosovo Albanians, and to ensure security for the investigators, the Kosovar delegation proposed that "All Yugoslav Tribunal personnel shall be entitled to immediate and visa-free entry into Montenegro, Serbia and Kosovo, and shall be free to conduct unfettered investigations. NATO shall, where appropriate, escort Tribunal personnel."

To clearly establish that NATO possessed all necessary authority, and an obligation to implement the norm of justice, the Kosovar delegation further proposed that the accords clearly state, "NATO shall be responsible for the enforcement of these provisions, including the use of force under the NATO Activation Order."

Aware of the previous noncompliance with the Dayton Accords and relevant Security Council resolutions mandating cooperation with the Tribunal, the Kosovar delegation also proposed, "In the event a party fails to cooperate fully with the International Criminal Tribunal on the Former Yugoslavia and its organs in accordance with the Security Council resolutions, they shall be subject to economic and other sanctions as provided for by the Security Council. The application of such sanctions shall not prejudice states, acting individually or collectively, from imposing additional or supplemental sanctions on the parties for failing to comply with their obligations with respect to the arrest, detention, and transfer any and all persons indicted by the International Criminal Tribunal for the Former Yugoslavia."

Finally, the Kosovar delegation sought to significantly enhance the application of the norm of justice by providing the Yugoslav Tribunal with the authority to dictate when sanctions may be removed. Specifically, the delegation proposed, "existing sanctions may not be removed until the President of the Yugoslav Tribunal has certified that all parties are cooperating fully with the Tribunal and had accepted its jurisdiction, in principle and in practice, as demonstrated by the extradition to The Hague of all suspected war criminals indicted by the Yugoslav Tribunal who are present on the territory of the [the FRY], and that visa-free access has been provided to personnel of the Tribunal."

War Crimes Provisions Proposed by the Serbian Delegation

During the first week and a half of the Rambouillet/Paris negotiations, the Serbian delegation refused to engage on the substantive issues of the negotiation; rather, it raised a number of procedural concerns and objected to the fundamental structure and nature of the negotiations. When the Serbian delegation did begin to engage on the substantive issues, it set forth five primary objectives. The fifth of these was that there be no mention of the Tribunal in the accords. Subsequently, during the Paris phase of the negotiations, the Serbian delegation submitted a written counterproposal to the Contact Group proposal. The Serbian counter proposal contained a redlined deletion of the three paragraphs mentioning cooperation with the Tribunal and the paragraph prohibiting indicted or convicted war criminals from holding public office. The Serb proposal also deleted in their entirety the military, police, and humanitarian assistance annexes.[14]

The likely explanation for the rather severe reaction to the Yugoslav Tribunal by the Serbian delegation was that, as noted above, the chair and vice chair of the delegation, Mr. Milan Milutinovic, and Mr. Nikola Sainovic, respectively, were responsible for orchestrating much of the ethnic cleansing and attempted genocide in Kosovo, and they were in fact subsequently indicted by the Yugoslav Tribunal.[15] They were also named as defendants in a civil suit brought by Kosovar refugees in the United States charging the two men, among others, with conspiracy to commit genocide.[16]

Role of Nonstate Actors

During the Dayton negotiations, nonstate actors interested in the norms and institutions of justice, such as human rights NGOs, editorial boards, and individual representatives, generally observed and commented on the process, but they did not engage in any organized campaign to influence the extent to which the norm of justice was incorporated within the accords. During the Rambouillet/Paris negotiations, however, nonstate actors were significantly more involved and sought to employ a number of means to ensure the adequate representation of the norms and institutions of justice.

During the opening days of the conference, Human Rights Watch issued a number of important documents, including a detailed report on atrocities recently committed by Serbian forces in Drenica against Kosovar civilians,[17] and an accompanying press release calling upon the peace builders to ensure that justice was not traded for peace during the negotiations.[18] Upon the suggestion of international experts advising the Kosovo delegation, Human Rights Watch issued a second press statement on 9 February 1999 calling for the inclusion of specific language relating to the obligation to arrest and extradite war criminals and a rejection of the sufficiency of language merely calling upon the Serbian regime to "cooperate" with the Yugoslav Tribunal.

To buttress the efforts of Human Rights Watch, the Italian-based NGO No Peace without Justice created by EU commissioner Emma Bonito, issued a lengthy report detailing the responsibility of Mr. Milosevic for war crimes and crimes against humanity committed against the people of Kosovo through 1998.[19] These efforts were matched by the editorial board of the *New York Times* which tried to buttress those opposed to a grant of immunity by stating: "Mr. Milosevic senses that NATO countries are unenthusiastic about using air strikes. He expects he can divide the West and win concessions, among them the assurance that he cannot be prosecuted by the war crimes tribunal. The [Contact Group] should not let him dictate the terms of settlement for [the] conflict."[20]

A collection of NGOs in Washington, D.C., forming the Kosovo Action Coalition under the stewardship of John Fox, also prepared a steady stream of coalition letters to members of Congress, President Clinton, and other executive branch officials in an attempt to explain the practical benefits of incorporating the norm of justice and adopting provisions similar to those proposed by the Kosovo delegation and supported by the European Union co-chair. These efforts were supported by a letter to President Clinton from Senators Mitch McConnell and Gordon Smith (R-N.H.) advising that "there must be an immediate and complete withdrawal of all Serb police, security, army and paramilitary forces from Kosovo prior to any U.S. deployment a level of zero simplifies the monitoring task, reduces the threat of violence to U.S. troops and Kosovo's civilians, removes obstacles to the delivery of humanitarian relief, and opens access for . . . Tribunal investigations."[21]

While it is difficult to measure the actual impact of these efforts, they did have the effect of encouraging the Kosovo delegation to continue to strongly push for the inclusion of the norm of justice, and they undercut the ability of the

Contact Group to entirely dismiss the norm of justice or to engage in any de jure grant of immunity. These efforts may also have enhanced the ability of certain Contact Group members to advocate for the inclusion of the norm of justice and against immunity.

Response of the Contact Group

A few members of the Contact Group supported the proposals of the Kosovar delegation (in particular the European Union representative Wolfgang Petrich); others reacted coolly or dismissively (the German and American representatives); still others reacted harshly, accusing the Kosovar delegation of attempting to derail the peace process (the French and OSCE representatives); and finally, the Russians adopted the position of the Serbian delegation. At one point for instance, Femi Aghani, the member of the Kosovar delegation responsible for negotiating the constitutional aspects of the accords, requested that the term "genocide" be added to the list of matters on which the parties would have to cooperate with the Tribunal, as opposed to only war crimes and crimes against humanity. The Contact Group immediately dismissed this request on the basis that the Albanians were not being targeted for destruction as a group. In the following May, Aghani was hauled from a refugee train and executed by Serbian security forces as part of their plan to ethnically cleanse (arguably through genocide) Kosovo by executing Kosovar intellectuals.[22]

In response to the Kosovar delegation's proposals that the parties be obligated to arrest and extradite indicted war criminals and they cooperate on specific matters of interest to the Tribunal, the Contact Group proposed more vague language to the effect:

> All Parties shall comply with their obligation to cooperate in the investigation and prosecution of war crimes, crimes against humanity, and other serious violations of international humanitarian law.
>
> (a) The Parties will allow complete, unimpeded, and unfettered access to international experts including forensic experts and investigators from the International Criminal Tribunal for the Former Yugoslavia (Yugoslav Tribunal) to investigate such allegations.
>
> (b) Pursuant to the terms of UN Security Council Resolution 827 and subsequent resolutions, the Parties shall provide full support and cooperation for the activities of the Yugoslav Tribunal, including complying with its orders and requests for information, and facilitating its investigations.[23]

No rationale was given for this vaguely worded language other than to indicate that the Serbian delegation and the Russian representatives were opposed to any mention of the Tribunal and that this language was likely to be the best on which the parties could reach agreement. Subsequently this language was modified to provide:

> All Parties shall comply with their obligation to cooperate in the investigation and prosecution of serious violations of international humanitarian law.
>
> (a) As required by United Nations Security Council Resolution 827 (1993) and subsequent resolutions, the Parties shall fully cooperate with the International Criminal Tribunal for the Former Yugoslavia in its investigations and prosecutions, including complying with its requests for assistance and its orders.
>
> (b) The Parties shall also allow complete, unimpeded, and unfettered access to international experts including forensic experts and investigators to investigate allegations of serious violations of international humanitarian law.[24]

Although these changes were made at the request of the Serbian and Russian delegations, the American co-chairs strove to indicate that they were in fact improvements on the original language. In particular, they stressed that the revised language replaced the limited phrase "complying with its requests for information" with the more expansive formulation "complying with its requests for assistance and its orders." The new language, however, deleted reference to war crimes and crimes against humanity, continued to omit the reference to genocide, and deleted the specific obligation to cooperate with forensic experts and investigators from the Tribunal, while retaining only the vague commitment to "fully cooperate" with the Tribunal. The new language also deleted the obligation to comply with the Tribunal's request for information and to facilitate its investigations. The draft and final accords did, however, include the minimal provision which prohibited any person indicted by the Tribunal or serving a sentence from standing as a candidate or holding any office.[25]

Aware that the Serbians and Russians were mounting an attempt to delete any reference to the Tribunal, and that the European members of the Contact Group were relatively weak on the need to include reference to the Tribunal, let alone use the document as a means of enhancing the norm of justice, the president of the Tribunal, Gabrielle Kirk McDonald, sent a letter to the co-hosts of the peace conference, Foreign Minster Cook and Foreign Minister Vedrine, and she called a press conference, during which she expressly declared the need to reference the work of the Tribunal and to enhance the prospects for a meaningful role for the norm of justice. She declared in her letter that she was worried about reports that the draft text of the Rambouillet/Paris Accords did not contain provisions that would specifically "require [the parties] to recognize the competence of the International Tribunal (Tribunal) or to take specific measures to cooperate with the Tribunal," but would rather only require them to agree to "a general provision on cooperation."[26]

The president of the Tribunal then went on to explain that given the attitude of the FRY toward the Tribunal, "as demonstrated by its record of noncooperation with and obstruction of Tribunal requests and orders," she believed that "such a generic provision is not sufficient to ensure that the Tribunal will be able to discharge its mandate." She then invoked the commitment of France and the United Kingdom to an effective Tribunal to personally ask the foreign ministers to ensure that the accords contained express references to the obligation of the parties to recognize the jurisdiction of the Tribunal and to facilitate specific activities, including its legal right to access Kosovo and to conduct investigations there. The president of the Tribunal concluded with the declaration that "it is axiomatic that there can be no peace without justice," and that any agreement which failed to bind the parties to specific forms of cooperation "risks being perceived as sacrificing the principles on which the Tribunal is founded for short-term political interest."[27]

Paradoxically, the efforts of the president of the Tribunal were somewhat subverted by the deputy prosecutor, who, upon hearing that reference to the Tribunal might be deleted or weakened, reacted by sending a letter to the co-chairs of the conference. In this letter he declared he would prefer no reference to the Tribunal rather than some weakened reference which might constrain the operation of the Tribunal. He explained that in his view previous Security Council resolutions offered sufficient authority for the work of the Tribunal in Kosovo. At the time of the Rambouillet/Paris negotiations, however, the Security Council authorization, while legally sufficient, had not produced the desired compliance by the Serbian regime, and thus the negotiations provided a prime opportunity to improve upon the mandate of the Tribunal and partner organizations, such as NATO, and to more fully detail the obligations of the parties to the conflict. Notably, during this important time the prosecutor was in Africa.

All of the other proposed changes by the Kosovar delegation were expressly rejected. The provisions relating to the granting of visa-free access and escorts by NATO personnel were seen by representatives of the OSCE and German delegations as unnecessarily antagonistic to the Serbian regime and likely to produce a political backlash. Interestingly, the delegates who conveyed these messages seemed to be under the impression that the Serbian government did not intend meaningful cooperation with the Yugoslav Tribunal no matter which provisions were included in the accords, and thus it was unnecessary and inconvenient to propose such specific principles that would give the Serbian delegation an opportunity to object to the accords. This approach was reminiscent of the "peace deal" approach by some governments during the Dayton negotiations.

Concerning the proposal that NATO be specifically identified as possessing responsibility for enforcing the provisions of the accord relating to war crimes, the members of the Contact Group again objected on the basis that such a reference would unnecessarily antagonize the Serbian delegation. In fact, any references to NATO in Kosovar proposals, as well as repeated calls for a meeting with NATO officials, were rebuffed by the Americans, French, and British as NATO was not to be present during the Rambouillet/Paris negotiations out of deference to the wishes of the French hosts. Unfortunately, excluding NATO from the negotiations (until the last possible moment when the Kosovars refused to negotiate until they were briefed by General Wesley Clark) also affected the substance of the provisions of the accords relating to the operation of the norm of justice.

Similarly, the attempt of the Kosovo delegation to link sanctions to compliance with the norm of justice, and to essentially provide the Tribunal with veto authority over the lifting of sanctions was considered a policy "nonstarter" by the European governments who had grown tired of sanctions, and in particular the Italians who had invested heavily in Serbian infrastructure since the end of the Bosnia war and who intended, along with the Greeks, to continue such investment. Even the British government was reluctant to support the adoption of a program for automatic sanctions or for an enhancement of the power of the authority of the Yugoslav Tribunal out of deference to its European allies with more significant financial interests in Serbia. Moreover, certain members of the Contact Group, although not the United States, were quite interested in embarking on a program of positive economic inducements to encourage Serbia to comply with the Rambouillet/Paris Accords in the event of its signature.

Failed Negotiation and the Use of Force

Milosevic has made the horrors our parents saw in their youth part of our lives today. By doing so, he has inspired another generation to fight, in every way, to banish his tyranny from the Europe of the next millennium. We will win as our parents did 54 years ago.

—Tony Blair, British Prime Minister[28]

Despite the best efforts of the Contact Group members to induce the FRY into signing the Rambouillet/Paris Accords, the Serbian delegation refused to accept the terms of the agreement. The Kosovars too had difficulty accepting the agreement and required a two-week suspension of the talks in order to consult with the people of Kosovo. Upon returning to Paris for the second round of talks, the Kosovar delegation signed the accords, while the government of Serbia refused to sign them and continued to carry out its plan of ethnic cleansing against the Kosovo Albanians.

With the failure of the Rambouillet/Paris negotiations, the atrocities against Kosovar civilians intensified.[29] According to NATO spokesman Jamie Shea, speaking shortly after the collapse of the talks, "we have to recognize that we are now on the brink of a major humanitarian disaster the likes of which we have not seen in Europe since the closing days of World War II."[30] And according to British foreign secretary Robin Cook, "the victims herded by the thousands in the past few days onto overcrowded trains are not people fleeing from the regime, but people being forcibly evicted by that regime. What we are witnessing is mass deportation on a scale Europe has not seen since the days of Stalin and Hitler."[31]

NATO's Strategic Air Campaign

This escalation in ethnic aggression gave rise to calls for the Contact Group and for NATO to make good on their threat of force and seek to compel the Serbian regime's compliance with their demands. As described by the editorial board of *The Washington Post*, "towns are being burned, fathers executed in front of their children, thousands of people force-marched to unknown destinations, men separated en masse from women and children these are all too familiar indicators Mr. Milosevic has embarked on something close to genocide. NATO and President Clinton must not allow this to continue."[32] Even more pointed were calls for a military response by several U.S. senators, with Senator Joseph Lieberman (D-Conn.), for instance declaring, "we have been threatening [Milosevic] since Christmas of 1992 warning him that if he attacked Kosovo, we would respond with force. Great alliances and great countries don't remain great if they issue threats and don't keep them."[33]

President Clinton responded to the increasing atrocities and the intense pressure with a call to arms among the allies by declaring, "make no mistake, if we and our allies do not have the will to act, there will be more massacres. In dealing with aggressors in the Balkans, hesitation is a license to kill. But action and resolve can stop armies, and save lives."[34] Shortly thereafter, NATO began its strategic air campaign against Serbian forces wherein it launched a series of increasingly intense air strikes against Yugoslav forces in Serbia and Kosovo, as well as Serbia's civil and military infrastructure. In addition to a strategic air campaign, the peace builders agreed during the NATO Washington Summit from 23-25 April 1999 to impose enhanced sanctions, including the blocking of all property and interests in property of the FRY, and a general ban on all exports to and imports from the FRY, including specifically the export of petroleum and strategic goods.[35] Notably, until this time France had continued to export oil to the FRY.

Disillusionment with Accommodation and an Enhanced Role for Justice

With the turn to actual use of force, there developed a growing recognition among the peace builders that their efforts toward accommodation had failed, and might be deeply flawed. There were also increasing public calls for the Yugoslav Tribunal to make its presence felt in the conflict. While some of the enhanced rhetoric may have served as political cover for the use of force, it is likely the peace builders began to more deeply perceive the practical value of justice, or possibly that at this stage of the conflict, justice had more of a role to play.

Concerning the disillusion with accommodation, French president Jacques Chirac rebuffed calls in early May for renewed negotiations on the basis that, "one can have no faith today in the Belgrade authorities; with all conscience, as far as I am concerned, I see no reason to change strategy."[36] Even those most committed to accommodation, such as former secretary of state Warren Christopher, recognized the need to use force, when he declared in early April that "we—NATO and the United States—must prevail in Kosovo. We must do so unambiguously, using whatever force is necessary to accomplish the goal. Given the new facts on the ground, there is now no satisfactory alternative."[37]

The enhanced role of justice could first be recognized in the rhetoric of Western leaders. As declared by British prime minister Tony Blair:

> This is not a battle for NATO. This is not a battle for territory. This is a battle for humanity. It is a just cause. It is a rightful cause. And we will make sure that these people here are returned to their homes. I hope that the next time we meet going back across the border into Kosovo, allowing people the security and peace which is the right of any decent human being in the civilized world.[38]

Former British prime minister Lady Margaret Thatcher echoed Prime Minister Blair's position and further noted that the norm of justice dictated the necessity of a decisive victory for NATO when she declared, "we are not dealing with some minor thug whose local brutalities may offend our sensibilities from time to time. Milosevic's regime and the genocidal ideology that sustains it represent something altogether different—a truly monstrous evil. . . . And the only victory worth having now is one that prevents Serbia [from] ever again having the means to attack its neighbors and terrorize non-Serb inhabitants."[39]

The actual objectives of the air campaign did not necessarily coincide with the rhetoric used to justify the intervention. As an example of the incongruity can be seen by comparing the words of Tony Blair and General Charles Wald. On 18 April 1999, Tony Blair declared that while,

> there are real strategic interests at stake in the Balkans. . . . I believe that a real sense of moral purpose is also motivating NATO. We either allow ethnic cleansing to succeed, or we say that the world community has an obligation to stop this most violent form of nationalism. Our job is to go in there and reverse it and defeat it.[40]

Two days later General Charles Wald, speaking at the Pentagon, declared, "I don't know how prevalent [ethnic cleansing] is, and I don't think NATO's air [campaign] has stopped that at all. NATO's mission, once again, is to reduce Milosevic's army's capability."[41]

Similarly, while the Department of State publicly identified ten relatively low-level military commanders as potentially responsible for war crimes, the Press spokesman and secretary of state strictly avoided identifying Mr. Milosevic as legally responsible for the war crimes and atrocities carried out by Serbian forces in Kosovo.[42]

Notably, the perceived commitment to justice began to wane as it became more apparent that a strategic air campaign might not be sufficient to prevent the Serbian regime from carrying out the complete ethnic cleansing of Kosovo. As observed by Senator John McCain (R-Ariz.), "because the president has refused to consider ground troops, it has allowed Mr. Milosevic to be more efficient in

ethnic cleansing we're trying to win a war without waging one."[43] Similarly, as
noted by former Joint Chiefs chairman General Colin Powell, "the air campaign
may work. But the problem with this strategy is that it's up to Mr. Milosevic to
decide when he's had enough. . . . In Desert Storm, we took that decision away
from Saddam Hussein when we put in ground troops."[44]

With the anticipated failure of the air campaign, and the reluctance to discuss the deployment of ground troops, concern increased that it may be necessary to return to a process of negotiation, undermining NATO's deterrent capability, as well as the objectives of justice. As recognized by the *Financial Times*
editorial board,

> it is becoming painfully clear that bombing alone is not working NATO and
> above all President Bill Clinton's administration is guilty of a failure to use all
> necessary force. Mr. Clinton's prevarication about offering the U.S. troops that
> are vital to a successful outcome has left time on Mr. Milosevic's side. The
> window of opportunity is closing fast. . . . The alternative [is] a political settle-
> ment. There can be no pretense here that such a deal would be anything other
> than a terrible blow for the alliance.[45]

Even Western allies began to publicly worry, with, for instance, Jordan's
King Abdullah stating,

> as a friend of the United States, I think you have to be aware that the whole
> world is looking to see your commitment on this. If you step out of line and do
> this wrong, you will have a reaction. . . . There is a standard of values being ad-
> dressed here, and your success or lack thereof will either encourage radicals or
> give them the sense that they have to tow the line. There is a lot riding on this. I
> don't think people fully understand the implications, whatever the final solution
> is in Kosovo.[46]

At about this time, Russia reintroduced the approach of accommodation by
proposing settlement terms inconsistent with those set by NATO. From some
quarters negative reaction to the Russian proposal was strident, with former National Security Council adviser Zbigniew Brzezinski, for example, declaring,
"the alliance should reject the temptation to accept any deal contrived by Russia
that would grant Mr. Milosevic an easing of NATO's original terms. To do so
would mark the bombing as a tragically pointless failure, would reward Mr.
Milosevic for his ethnic cleansing, and would represent a great political success
for the Kremlin's anti-NATO posture."[47]

Indicting Mr. Milosevic

Just as Russia's attempt to reintroduce the approach of accommodation was
gaining support from some European states, a key senior State Department official met with Judge Arbour while she was visiting the United Nations for consultations and in very strong terms encouraged her to rapidly indict Milosevic.

The prosecutor was stunned as, without warning, the United States had apparently changed its stance from one of urging caution in pursuing Milosevic and withholding sensitive material that might further the case against him to an aggressive position favoring an immediate indictment.

While at the meeting the prosecutor rebuffed the State Department plea as an infringement upon her impartiality, shortly thereafter, on 27 May 1999, she indicted Mr. Milosevic, Mr. Sainovic, Mr. Milutinovic, and three other top Yugoslav officials for war crimes and crimes against humanity committed in Kosovo from January 1999.[48] The indictment of Mr. Milosevic put a quick end to the Russian efforts to return to accommodation. As noted by former senator Bob Dole, "the administration cannot reasonably expect the Kosovo Albanian deportees to return to Kosovo with an indicted war criminal and the very man who attempted to destroy them and their society as the guarantor of their security."[49]

While the State Department was encouraged by this development, according to General Clark, some Pentagon and White House officials were displeased with the indictment on the grounds that it would limit or preclude their ability to negotiate with Milosevic, and that it would strengthen his resolve to proceed with the ethnic cleansing of Kosovo.[50] These concerns were reminiscent of those of Secretary Christopher when he reasoned that labeling the Serbian atrocities in Bosnia as genocide would create a moral imperative to use force and would limit the ability of the United States to negotiate with Milosevic. Although in the case of Kosovo the threshold for the use of airpower had been crossed, some in the Clinton administration were concerned that the indictment of Milosevic would require NATO to actually defeat Milosevic, rather than wound his regime and then rely upon him to guarantee a negotiated settlement as was the case in the autumn of 1995 and the subsequent Dayton negotiations.

Despite these fears, the indictment had the positive effect of strengthening the resolve of America's European partners in the NATO air campaign, and it did not dissuade Russia from further engaging in the peace process.[51] The indictment also provided a legitimate basis for the peace builders to call for a regime change, something they had previously been reluctant to do because it would be perceived as a violation of the FRY's sovereignty and political independence. As detailed by British prime minister Tony Blair, "the world cannot help you [Serbs] rebuild your country while Mr. Milosevic is at its head. And nor will the world understand, as the full extent of these atrocities is revealed, if you just turn a blind eye to the truth and pretend it is nothing to do with you. . . . This evil was carried out by your soldiers and by your leaders."[52] Moreover, the indictment provided a basis for calls from within the FRY for a regime change. Serbian Orthodox bishop Artemije, for example, ventured that "there can be no solution under this regime, at least not a just and peaceful one. In Serbia as it is now, neither Serbs nor Albanians wish to live under this regime."[53]

The indictment alone, however, could not be sufficient in and of itself to propel Mr. Milosevic from power. As noted by General Wesley Clark, Slobodan Milosevic "has his hands still on the sinews of power in Serbia. He controls the army, he controls the police, including a very effective and brutal secret police network. He controls the media, and he controls the economy and finances. I think it's difficult at this point to predict with assurance that President Milosevic will be overthrown."[54]

Decreeing Peace: United Nations Security Council Resolution 1244

After over seventy days of air strikes and an increasing willingness of NATO forces to commit ground troops to the conflict, the government of Serbia agreed to peace. The terms of the peace were set out not within the Rambouillet/Paris Accords, but rather within United Nations Security Council Resolution 1244 adopted on 10 June 1999. Although the Rambouillet/Paris Accords never formally entered into force, they did provide the basis for the provisions of Resolution 1244.

During the course of negotiating Resolution 1244 there was much debate over the extent to which the norm of justice would be referenced in the resolution. Although neither of the parties were invited to comment on the substance of the resolution, the United States, France, and the United Kingdom supported the inclusion of at least a minimal reference to the Tribunal, while the Russians objected. The leadership of the Tribunal also conveyed a request to the Security Council that its authority be referenced, and that the parties be instructed to cooperate with the Tribunal.

After much negotiation, the resolution was drafted to include two references to the Tribunal. The first reference appears in the preamble and recalls "the jurisdiction and the mandate of the International Tribunal for the Former Yugoslavia." The second appears in paragraph 14 and "demands full cooperation by all concerned, including the international security presence, with the International Tribunal for the Former Yugoslavia." Although the nature of the security force envisioned by the Security Council removed the need to articulate specific details concerning the ability of Yugoslav Tribunal investigators to enter Kosovo without a visa and to obtain access to sites of suspected crimes, the Security Council missed an opportunity to craft a sanctions regime that would have empowered the Tribunal to compel compliance with its orders and to obtain access to Serbia proper. Again though, such a regime would have had little chance of being adopted given the Russian and French opposition.

As with the Dayton negotiations, the application of the norm of justice was eventually minimized in favor of a greater use of accommodation as it was feared that too much of a reliance on the norm of justice might derail the chances for a negotiated settlement. Importantly, the approach of force played a much more prominent role in the Kosovo crisis, but it was not necessarily linked to the norm of justice. As will be discussed in the next two chapters, the norm of justice was further retrenched during the implementation of the Dayton Accords, and it was only effectively linked to the approach of economic inducement near the end of the Yugoslav conflict.

Part V

The Role of Justice in the Implementation Phase of Peace Building

Chapter 12

Apprehending War Criminals: Mission Creep or Mission Impossible?

I think it's scandalous that those who have the responsibility for his arrest continue to fail to fulfill that obligation.

—Louise Arbour, prosecutor of
the International Tribunal[1]

There's no reason for my guys to get out of their vehicles and go over there to look for anything.

—Col. John Baptiste, U.S. commander in the Srebrenica area, on why
IFOR troops do not monitor suspected mass grave sites, which
apparently have been tampered with by Bosnian Serb forces[2]

Despite the creation of the Yugoslavia War Crimes Tribunal and the Western countries' repeated promises to support the Tribunal's mandate, NATO initially failed to use force to implement the norm of justice—by apprehending the most wanted indicted war criminals in its area of operations in Bosnia. To justify its inaction, the NATO commanders claimed that NATO's mandate in Bosnia did not permit use of force in aid of the norm of justice except under extremely limited circumstances (i.e., when indicted war criminals are "encountered in the course of its duties and if the tactical situation permits").[3] While there were legitimate concerns about the risks to NATO personnel involved in the arrests, as will be discussed, there was no legal basis for the assertion of a lack of mandate. As a result of the "no mandate" approach, until July 1997, NATO forces failed to apprehend a single war criminal. Later, NATO forces apprehended a handful of low- and mid-level indictees, while indicted Bosnian Serb leaders Radovan Karadzic and Ratko Mladic were given de facto immunity.

This chapter will thus examine why and how NATO member states sought to minimize the role of justice and accountability in the peace implementation process and some of the consequences of that policy. In so doing, questions one, six, seven, nine, and ten set out in chapter 1 will be addressed, in particular how the interests of NATO member states influenced its view of the role of justice, the extent to which the existence of the Yugoslav Tribunal affected the actions of NATO forces, to what degree were the approaches of accountability and force compatible, did the NATO forces undergo institutional learning as they reevaluated their approach to arresting war criminals, and to what extent did the initial exclusion of the norm of justice inhibit the effective implementation of the accords.

To order the discussion of the relationship between force and justice during the implementation phase, this chapter first examines NATO's legal obligation to arrest war criminals. The chapter then reviews NATO's initial policy on arresting war criminals, and the consequences for the peace process of the failure to arrest the most culpable criminals in a timely fashion.

NATO's Obligation to Arrest War Criminals

It would help a lot of people's tasks if [indicted Bosnian Serb war criminals Ravan Karadzic and Ratko Mladic] were gone, but I'm not authorized to do that. Hold those who signed Dayton responsible and get off IFOR's back.

—Admiral Leighton Smith, IFOR Commander[4]

The Dayton Accords

On 20 December 1995, a 60,000-personnel NATO Implementation Force known as IFOR (which a year later became the 30,000 strong Stabilization Force known as SFOR) was deployed in Bosnia.[5] One of the great debates surrounding the Bosnia peace settlement is whether IFOR's failure to arrest war criminals was a product of the way its mandate was drafted in the Dayton Accords and the related Security Council Resolution or the way its mandate was implemented by NATO commanders.

IFOR's mandate and mission were set forth in Security Council Resolution 1031, adopted on 13 December 1995, which authorizes "IFOR" to "take such actions as required, including the use of necessary force, to ensure compliance with Annex 1-A of the Peace Agreement." Article X of Annex 1-A provides inter alia that the parties undertake to "cooperate fully with all entities involved in implementation of this peace settlement," such as those authorized by the Security Council, "including the International Tribunal for the former Yugoslavia." Read together, these provisions give IFOR the authority to use force to ensure compliance with the Yugoslav Tribunal's arrest orders.

To the extent there was any ambiguity in this regard, it was eliminated by the statements made by the representatives of the United States, the United Kingdom, and France in the Security Council at the time Resolution 1031 was adopted. For instance, in her explanation of the vote, Ambassador Albright of the United States remarked:

> Let me emphasize that Annex 1-A of the Dayton Agreement obligates the parties to co-
> operate fully with the International Tribunal. The North Atlantic Council can now underscore
> this obligation by explicitly authorizing IFOR to transfer indicted persons it comes across to
> the Tribunal and to detain such persons for that purpose.[6]

Echoing this position, the U.K. representative stated:

> Should it be decided that, in the execution of its assigned tasks, the Implementation
> Force should detain and transfer to the appropriate authorities any persons indicted
> by the Tribunal who come into contact with it in Bosnia, then the authority to do so
> is provided by the draft resolution before us, read together with the provisions of
> the Peace Agreement.[7]

France, too, affirmed that paragraph 5 "recognizes the role that IFOR may play to ensure proper cooperation" with the Tribunal.[8] The other members of the Security Council did not make any specific statements concerning the role of IFOR in the arrest of suspects, but Russia did warn that it "will consistently defend the need to avoid unjustified use of force in the course of the operation."[9]

The attempt by the United States and its European allies to obfuscate and embellish the weak provisions in the Dayton Accords to create the impression they created a robust mandate for IFOR and would soon lead to the apprehension of indictees was transparent to the senior officials at the Tribunal. As explained by Grant Niemann, the Tribunal's senior trial attorney, to the authors, "[t]he Dayton Agreement doesn't seriously attempt to address the arrest and detention issue. Anyone who say's otherwise is deluded or lying."[10]

There are several limitations inherent in IFOR's mission statement as set forth above. First, IFOR was provided the "authority" but not the "responsibility" to arrest indicted persons. Had the Council wished to give IFOR this mandate, it would have used the phrase "calls upon" rather than "authorizes." Second, in accordance with the U.S. and British interpretive statements, this authority was limited to indicted war criminals that IFOR "comes across" or "comes into contact with"—providing support to those who would that it was inappropriate for IFOR to actively seek out such persons for arrest. Finally, Article XII of Annex 1-A provides that "the IFOR Commander is the final authority in theater regarding interpretation of this agreement on the military aspects of the peace settlement." Therefore, it was within the IFOR commander's complete discretion to determine whether or not action to arrest an indicted war criminal was warranted in the particular circumstances of a case.

In his recently published memoir, Ambassador Holbrooke describes the story behind the crafting of IFOR's limited mandate with respect to arresting indicted war criminals. Holbrooke maintains that he argued the Dayton Accords should explicitly have given the NATO force responsibility for arresting war criminals, but the Pentagon, supported by National Security Council adviser Tony Lake and Secretary of Defense William Perry, opposed expanding IFOR's mandate beyond disengaging the warring parties and force protection.[11] Military commanders were anxious to avoid a repeat of the disaster in Somalia, where eighteen American troops were ambushed and slaughtered while trying to apprehend the warlord Mo-hammed Farrah Aidid. Holbrooke recounts that, "as a result of the scars left over from the Mogadishu affair in Somalia, the [military] would not accept the assign-ment of search and capture of war criminals unless they had a force structure two or three or five times larger than the 60,000" envisioned in the Dayton Accords.[12] A week before the Dayton negotiations, a compromise was reached in which the Pentagon agreed to accept "the authority" to make arrests "but not the obligation."[13] In his memoir, Holbrooke laments, "had I known then how reluctant IFOR would be to use its 'authority,' I would have fought harder for a stronger mission state-ment."[14]

Richard Holbrooke claims that he told President Clinton on the eve of Dayton, "if we are going to create a real peace rather than an uneasy cease-fire Karadzic and Mladic will have to be captured. This is not simply a question of justice but also of peace. If they are not captured, no peace agreement we create in Dayton can ulti-mately succeed."[15] According to Holbrooke, President Clinton concurred saying, "It is best to remove both men."[16] But the president never gave the military a direct instruction to that effect, and as this book goes to press seven years after Dayton, the NATO forces have still taken no action to bring Karadzic and Mladic into cus-tody.[17] By the time they are arrested or extradited to The Hague, they will have already exercised the maximum destructive influence on the peace process.

While Holbrooke blamed the Pentagon and the president, others believe the failure to give NATO the responsibility of arresting war criminals may actually have been a quid pro quo countenanced by Holbrooke and the other Dayton nego-tiators in return for Slobodan Milosevic's support of the Dayton Accords.[18] Graham Blewitt, the Yugoslav Tribunal's deputy prosecutor confided that the Office of the prosecutor had continuing concerns about whether there were any side deals. Ac-cording to Blewitt, "To this day we don't know whether there were any. Maybe one day we will find out. But that is one of the concerns, that people were made prom-ises that even if they signed and agreed to certain things that they wouldn't be held accountable."[19]

At a minimum, Holbrooke had to have recognized that the Pentagon's insis-tence on a limited role for IFOR made his job as negotiator easier. On the eve of the Dayton talks, the posecutor of the Yugoslav Tribunal, Richard Goldstone, pressed the United States to beef up the provisions on arrests of war criminals. Holbrooke reportedly responded that he would not make the war crimes issue a "show stop-per" to the larger peace settlement.[20] It may be for this reason there was no further communication between Holbrooke and the prosecutor during the Dayton negotia-tions.

As noted above, under the Dayton Accords, the person responsible for deter-mining whether action by IFOR to arrest indicted war criminals was warranted was IFOR commander Admiral Leighton Smith. Smith literally interpreted away IFOR's limited mandate to arrest war criminals. Upon assuming his command in January 1996, Admiral Smith told the press, "One of the questions I was asked was, 'Admiral, is it true that IFOR is going to arrest Serbs in the Serb suburbs of Sara-jevo?' I said, 'Absolutely not, I don't have the authority to arrest anybody.'"[21] Ac-cording to General Clark, the NATO military leaders had decided, "they had wanted a 'clean' mission," and they were concerned that "arresting war criminals might mean taking sides and assuming additional risks."[22]

In February 1996, *The Washington Post* ran a story alleging that Karadzic had driven unchallenged through four NATO checkpoints—two of them manned by Americans—on a trip from Pale to Banja Luka. When confronted with the story, Admiral Smith reaffirmed that it was not the mission of his forces to go after indicted war criminals.[23] Since Article XII in Annex 1-A of the Dayton Accords provides that "the IFOR Commander is the final authority in theater regarding interpretation of this agreement," Smith's position was technically unassailable. This position significantly undermined the ability of the Tribunal to exert an impact on the implementation phase of the peace-building process, and it prompted the Tribunal's prosecutor to declare, "There is no moral, legal or political justification for a military authority to grant effective immunity to persons whom the prosecutor, on behalf of the Security Council, has determined should be brought to trial."[24]

Security Council Resolution 827

The Dayton Accords and Resolution 1031 were not the only source of law binding on the NATO force in Bosnia. In addition to being an enforcement measure of the Security Council under Chapter VII of the UN Charter, the Tribunal is also considered a subsidiary organ of the Security Council with delegated enforcement powers within the terms of Article 29 of the UN Charter.[25] The Tribunal's statute, approved by Security Council Resolution 827, grants the Tribunal the authority to issue international arrest warrants, which must be complied with "without undue delay."[26] Article 48(2) of the UN Charter requires member states to carry out the decisions of the Security Council (and its subsidiary bodies) under Chapter VII of the Charter "directly or through their action in the appropriate international agencies of which they are members," which would include NATO.

Colonel John Burton, the legal counsel to the chairman of the Joint Chiefs of Staff, explained the legal obligation that flows from such international arrest warrants in the following terms:

> The Yugoslavia War Crimes Tribunal has issued these orders. Now, orders can be issued to all the Member States who are going to play a part of this NATO force. And if those orders say not only in your territory, but in any jurisdiction under your control, would they apply in Bosnia? In other words, if the United States had such an order, that in Bosnia that the United States is charged to arrest and detain these people and turn them over, would we be bound? As far as a state obligation goes, I think that the answer is, "Yes." We view these orders, and literally the Statute of the Tribunal itself, as well as the United Nations Resolution under Chapter VII that set it up, as binding.[27]

Thus, according to the JCS Legal Counsel, IFOR would have to implement the Tribunal's arrest warrants provided (1) the orders were issued to the NATO states; and (2) the orders referred to making arrests in Bosnia.

On 11 July 1996, a trial chamber of the Yugoslav Tribunal issued an "International Arrest Warrant and Order for Surrender" in the cases of Radovan Karadzic and Ratko Mladic which met these two criteria.[28] By virtue of Security Council Resolution 1088 (1996), which establishes SFOR as the legal successor to IFOR, this directive applies with continuing effect to SFOR. Yet, instead of arresting Karadzic and Mladic pursuant to this international legal obligation, IFOR instituted a controversial policy of "monitor, don't touch."

NATO Policy on Arresting War Criminals

Of course, we'll arrest Karadzic. . . . But he may have some trouble getting past the guards at our front gate if he arrives without an appointment

—unidentified senior IFOR commander[29]

Phase I: Monitor, Don't Touch

When IFOR initially deployed in Bosnia "there was a perception that priority should be military disengagement," and that "the tenuous stability which had been created could be undermined if NATO became entangled in arresting indicted war criminals."[30] According to Richard Holbrooke, "the military viewed the Serbs as a potent military force that would threaten IFOR as it had the UN."[31] These fears were fanned by the incendiary statements emanating from the Serbian leaders. Mr. Milosevic warned that Bosnia "could blow up" if IFOR attempted to arrest the Bosnian Serb leaders who had been indicted by the Tribunal.[32] And General Mladic promised that the IFOR forces would pay heavily if they tried to arrest him. Mladic told an interviewer, "They have to understand one thing, that I am very expensive and that my people support me"[33]

Yet, according to General William Nash, the commander of IFOR's Task Force Eagle, "We overestimated the difficult task that we had in front of us."[34] The reality of the situation was that "the Bosnian Serbs were a spent force" and that Mladic and especially Karadzic were vulnerable targets.[35] According to a Yugoslav Tribunal official, in the months following Dayton, "it would have been possible to arrest Karadzic and Mladic with little consequences because the Bosnian Serbs were so demoralized. The failure to arrest them allowed them to once again consolidate their power and begin to cause problems for the NATO forces."[36]

Despite the menace posed by Karadzic and Mladic while they remained at large, according to General Nash, the rules of engagement permitted apprehending indicted war criminals only "if the risk was minimal and it would not result in a major fight."[37] In practice, "minimal risk" was interpreted as "zero risk."[38] Experts point to this so-called zero casualty doctrine as a significant reason why NATO failed to make any arrests in Bosnia for nineteen months following the deployment of IFOR.[39]

A second reason for NATO's failure was the requirement that IFOR act only when indicted war criminals are "encountered." In February 1996, State Department spokesman Nicholas Burns explained IFOR's narrow interpretation of the term, "in the interests of freedom of movement in Bosnia, U.S. troops are not intercepting civilian cars at checkpoints. If our troops encounter [indicted war criminals] walking around, though, they will be detained."[40] Thus one IFOR commander confirmed that his troops "would arrest suspects like Radovan Karadzic only if they literally stumble into an IFOR checkpoint." [41]

In fact, the record suggests that IFOR would not even arrest indicted suspects under these circumstances. In August 1997, when IFOR inspectors learned that General Ratko Mladic was inside a bunker they had planned to inspect, they rescheduled their visit rather than confront the indicted war criminal. Two days before the September 1997 elections in Bosnia, the United States commander of IFOR, Admiral Joseph Lopez, met with Serb officials in the headquarters of Radovan Karadzic, who was reportedly inside the building at the time. "And in a virtuoso display of IFOR's talent for not 'stumbling into' Mladic or Karadzic, none of the 53,000 IFOR troops deployed to provide security on election day in mid September had an arrest worthy encounter with these men, although both reportedly turned out to vote."[42]

IFOR officials concocted a litany of justifications for their policy of non-action, including: (1) arresting war criminals would jeopardize the fragile Bosnian peace; (2) arresting war criminals could damage NATO's image of impartiality among Bosnia's factions and invite retaliation against NATO troops; (3) arresting war criminals would disrupt municipal and federal elections in Bosnia; (4) arresting war criminals was the responsibility of governments in the region, not international troops; (5) the NATO forces did not have reliable intelligence information about the whereabouts of the war criminals; and (6) NATO troops were not trained to arrest criminal suspects.[43] While the legitimate concern over potential NATO casualties and the general lack of civilian implementation were reasonable and valid considerations, the pretexts listed above were generally without merit.

Phase II: Limited Case-by-Case Arrests

Consistent with IFOR's narrow interpretation of its mandate, in the first months after their deployment, IFOR personnel were not provided a list of names, let alone pictures of the persons indicted by the Yugoslav Tribunal.[44] Responding to public criticism of NATO troops for failing to apprehend Karadzic when he passed through NATO checkpoints, in February 1996 a new set of instructions were issued from NATO high command in Brussels. Pursuant to these instructions, "Most Wanted" posters featuring photographs and descriptions of the indicted war criminals were placed at IFOR checkpoints, headquarters, and barracks.[45]

While this might lead to more "encounters" at NATO checkpoints, the new policy did not mean that IFOR troops would actively seek out the indicted war criminals for arrest. John Shalikashvili, chairman of the Joint Chiefs of Staff, informed Congress that even if IFOR had orders to arrest the indicted war criminals who are at large in Bosnia, the NATO force just did not have enough intelligence information on their whereabouts.[46] To the embarrassment of the Clinton administration, Shalikashvili's assertion was countered by a Washington-based group called the Coalition for International Justice, which had been able to locate most of the indicted war criminals from telephone directories and news reports, and by *Boston Globe* journalist Elizabeth Neuffer who conducted in-person interviews with many of the indictees.[47] A year later, military officials acknowledged that the claim that they lacked intelligence information was largely false, and that Western military officials had long known where virtually all of the alleged criminals were located.[48]

With the election of Tony Blair as British prime minister, the United Kingdom began to press NATO for a more forceful policy on arresting indicted war criminals. But surprisingly, it was the United Nations peacekeeping force in Croatia, and not the NATO force, which made the first arrest. In June 1997, an agent of the Office of the Prosecutor lured indicted war criminal Slavko Dokmanovic out of Serbia and into Eastern Slavonia (Croatia), where he was apprehended by UN peacekeeping forces and delivered to the Yugoslav Tribunal.[49] Encouraged and slightly embarrassed by the success of the UN operation, a month later, on 10 July 1997, British IFOR troops arrested indicted war criminal Milan Kovacevic at his home in Republika Srpska and transferred him to the Tribunal.[50] That same day, British forces shot and killed indicted war criminal Simo Drljaca, the former police chief in Prijedor, when he fired upon them as they sought his arrest.[51]

Following Britain's lead, two months later, on 18 December 1997, Dutch IFOR troops, using tear gas and stun grenades, raided homes and arrested Vlatko Kupreskic[52] and Anto Furundzija.[53] The two had been indicted for raping and murdering civilians in the Lasva Valley area of Bosnia in 1993. Then, on 22 January 1998, American soldiers swept into the small town of Bijeljin and made their first arrest of an indicted war criminal in Bosnia: Goran Jelisic, a Bosnian Serb who liked to refer to himself as "the Serbian Adolf."[54] Jelisic commanded the Luka camp during May 1992, and he is charged with systematically killing Muslims and committing other atrocities at the Luka camp. U.S. IFOR forces undertook a second snatch operation on 27 September 1998, resulting in the apprehension of indicted war criminal Stevan Todorovic, formerly the Serb chief of police in.Bosanski Samac.[55] They undertook a third operation on 2 December 1998, resulting in the arrest of Radislav Krstic,[56] a Bosnian Serb general eventually convicted of genocide and sentenced to forty-six years in prison for his role in directing the 1995 attack on the "safe area" of Srebrenica, in which as many as 7,000 civilians were killed.[57]

On 20 December 1999, U.S. forces in Banja Luka, Bosnia, arrested retired Serb general Stanislav Galic,[58] who had commanded the Sarajevo Romanija Corps, which had subjected the civilian inhabitants of Sarajevo to continuous shelling and sniper fire from 1992 to 1995.[59] Following the apprehension of General Galic, U.S. ambassador at large for war crimes issues David Scheffer announced that "no more indicted men are living in the U.S. sector of Bosnia, though some may travel through the area unnoticed."[60] As of September 2001, SFOR troops had apprehended a total of seventeen indicted war criminals in Bosnia.

While Secretary of Defense William Cohen, asserted that these arrests were "in keeping with the rules we have had all along,"[61] none of the persons who were the subject of these NATO actions were encountered in public at the time of their arrests. Thus, NATO officials put a new gloss on the description of the NATO mission, saying "the policy is to apprehend suspects on a case-by-case basis *or* if NATO troops encounter them on patrols." Under its modified mission statement, officials said NATO's strategy was to concentrate on "plucking low-hanging fruit or capturing those war criminals that have the least protection and the most predictable daily routines."[62]

Payam Akhvan of the Office of the Prosecutor describes the reason for the July 1997 change in the NATO policy on arresting war criminals as follows:

> As time went on, as the immediate objective of military disengagement was achieved, it became clear that the NATO force was not going to achieve stability if the Serb warlords continued to exercise power. . . . While I'm not at liberty to disclose the details, I can say that much of the determination to arrest these people came from the soldiers on the ground and not from officials at NATO headquarters or distant capitals. There was a sense on the part of a lot of the soldiers on the ground that people like Milan Kovacevic and Simo Drljaca were one of the main destabilizing factors and they had to be removed one way or another. The fact that there were indictments on these two people became a very convenient pretext to get rid of them. So, I'm not saying that the impulse was to support justice but rather that the existence of the tribunal was very convenient.[63]

The new NATO policy came under criticism by Carl Bildt, the United Nations High Representative for Bosnia, who complained that going after minor figures served as "giving advanced warning" to the higher level indicted war criminals such as Karadzic and Mladic, and risked destabilizing the fragile peace in Bosnia.[64] But the arrests of Kovacevic, Kupreskic, Furundzija, Galic, Jelisic, Krstic, and Todorovic, and the killing of Drljaca had the effect of inducing other indicted war criminals to turn themselves in, less they be brought in by the NATO troops dead or alive. Thus, a dozen indicted war criminals surrendered to the Tribunal in the months after the British, Dutch, and American snatch operations.[65]

Not all of the segments of IFOR, however, adopted this more aggressive case-by-case approach to arresting indicted war criminals. The French, who command the NATO troops that patrol the Serb stronghold of Pale (where Karadzic is believed to reside) had expressed no enthusiasm for capturing war criminals. The French refusal to conduct arrests prompted Louise Arbour, the Tribunal's prosecutor, to complain to the press that "NATO's French sector in eastern Bosnia is a 'safe haven' for Serb war criminals."[66] An unnamed senior U.S. official told *The Washington Post* that

> France's inaction may be partly due to the trauma experienced by the French military command in May 1995, when Serb forces captured dozens of French officers employed as observers by the United Nations and chained them to bridges or radar sites that were prospective NATO bombing targets. They want no repeat of this and therefore no involvement with war criminals at all.[67]

France's reluctance was exemplified in March 1998, when a Serb named Dragoljub Kunarac, indicted in June 1996 on charges of gang rape, torture, and enslavement of Muslim women,[68] first offered to surrender to French military forces in the town of Pilipovic in eastern Bosnia. Nearly a week passed before the French concluded that "they couldn't avoid taking his surrender," said one U.S. official, who added that Washington had evidence the French military command deferred to several senior officials in the Bosnian Serb government. Only after the Serbs gave their private approval did the French take Kunarac into custody and transfer him to the Tribunal.[69]

The French problem came to a head in the summer of 1997, when, according to *The Washington Post*, the United States was forced at the last minute to abort plans for the apprehension of Radovan Karadzic when it was discovered that a senior French military officer held secret meetings with Karadzic. Afterward, senior Clinton administration officials acknowledged that "they were quite close to carrying it out, having determined how to arrange the capture and which troops would be involved." A senior official was quoted as saying he found the episode "despicable and appalling" and that "no trust" remained between the U.S. and French military forces in Bosnia, a development that led Washington to suspend virtually all consultations with the French about the possible capture of indicted war criminals.[70]

Afterward, the United States announced that it did not intend to renew the effort to apprehend Karadzic.[71] One can only guess whether the announcement accurately reflected American policy, was designed to keep Karadzic off guard, or was merely an effort to deflate public expectations. While seizing Karadzic would have been a public relations boon for the United States, by going public about the aborted operation and blaming the French for its failure, the United States succeeded in deflecting criticism of its anemic policy on arresting major indicted war criminals. In the four years since the aborted operation to seize Karadzic, the United States has made no overt effort to take the Bosnian Serb leader into custody.[72]

In response to intense international criticism over the botched operation to apprehend Karadzic and the continuing failure of the French SFOR troops to arrest other indicted war criminals in their area of operation in Bosnia, the French troops conducted a daring predawn raid on 3 April 2000 in order to seize Momcilo Krajisnik at the home of his father in Pale. Krajisnik had served as Radovan Karadzic's chief deputy during the conflict in Bosnia, he later replaced Karadzic as the leading Bosnian Serb political figure after the international charges against Karadzic forced him to go under ground. Krajisnik then served as the Bosnian Serb member of Bosnia's tri-partite presidency from 1996 to 1998. In a secret indictment issued on 26 February 2000, Krajisnik was charged with committing genocide, crimes against humanity, and war crimes in Bosnia. Emboldened by his troops' successful arrest of Krajisnik, French defense minister Alain Richard announced that "arresting Karadzic is now the French Army's prime objective."[73] For the next four years following Richard's announcement, no attempts were made to arrest Karadzic. When SFOR troops finally undertook two operations in the Spring of 2002 to arrest Karadzic, the operations were led by American special forces, with French forces excluded from the operation. Both attempts were, however, unsuccessful as Karadzic was not present at the site of the raids.

The Consequences of the Failure to Make Arrests

Indicted war criminals are having far too much influence on developments, particularly in the Republika Srpska, to be left at large.

—Kofi Annan, UN Secretary-General[74]

In December 1995, the *International Herald Tribunal* summarized the effect of the international indictments on Bosnian Serb leaders Radovan Karadzic and Ratko Mladic as follows:

General Ratko Mladic, the Bosnian Serbian warrior charged with the massacre of thousands of Muslim men, now spends much of his time isolated in a mountain bunker surrounded by a coterie of officers. His moods are said to swing from rage to uneasy calm. His partner, Radovan Karadzic, the psychiatrist-turned-politician, had his political program swept out from under him by the Bosnian peace accord. Those who have seen him say that his speech is often slurred, apparently the effect of medication, and his robust physique has been withered by anxiety as he faces an uncertain future that includes an indictment for war crimes. This is the picture acquaintances draw of the two men: beaten men desperately dealing to save their jobs and stay away from the International War Crimes Tribunal at The Hague.[75]

Based on this portrayal, Payam Akhvan of the Yugoslav Tribunal's Office of the Prosecutor argues that "absent their arrest and surrender to the Tribunal, the indictment of political and military leaders, and the consequent stigmatization, deprivation of liberty, and removal from public office has had the effect of an interim justice."[76]

But in the months to follow, buoyed by the NATO "monitor, don't touch" policy, Karadzic, Mladic, and their followers would completely rebound. Karadzic may have been forced to relinquish his official position, but like an evil puppet master he retained effective power in the Republika Srpska to the detriment of Bosnian peace. As one human rights monitoring organization concluded, Karadzic "still continues to exercise complete control over all events in the Republika Srpska."[77] From behind the scenes Karadzic continued to run the Serb nationalist-based party known as the SDS, which controls the Republika Srpska's police, court system, media, and major industries. He also dominated a network of underground Bosnian Serb paramilitary organizations, whose plans included destabilizing the peace process, creating opposition to IFOR and international agencies within the Bosnian Serb population in Republika Srpska, stirring up general animosity toward the Bosniac-Croat Federation, and destroying any moderate-line Serb elements.[78]

Emboldened by IFOR's inaction against him, Karadzic undermined virtually every major nonmilitary provision of the Dayton Accords. The first test came in February 1996, when Serb held neighborhoods in Sarajevo were transferred to the authority of the Bosniac-Croat government. Heading the calls of Karadzic, Serb paramilitary units set fire to Serb-occupied apartment buildings and forced the Serb residents to flee Sarajevo, rather than remain in an ethnically mixed neighborhood. Then in September 1996, Karadzic derailed the possibility of a credible voter registration process, leading to the postponement of municipal elections.[79]

For this reason, the United Nations High Representative for Bosnia has said, "as long as [the major indicted war criminals] are at large, there is not going to be a normal life in Bosnia, not only for rule of law reasons but also because of their influence in politics and economy in the country. . . . They have to go to The Hague."[80] Calling for NATO to take action, in particular to arrest Radovan Karadzic, then deputy high representative Jacques Klein stated, "Karadzic's presence still casts a cloud over what we do and it would be nice to have the political will to do what needs to be done because it poisons the atmosphere."[81] Canadian foreign minister Lloyd Axworthy was even more blunt in his assessment, "Without firm action on war crimes, reconciliation is doomed."[82] And without reconciliation, NATO troops will either be forced to remain in Bosnia indefinitely, or war will break out as they withdraw. As a senior NATO official acknowledged, "unless Karadzic and other war criminals are captured before our peacekeepers go home, there is a good chance that the war could return and all our good efforts would be in vain."[83]

In addition to damaging the goal of peace-building in Bosnia, the failure to make arrests substantially eroded the deterrent value of the Yugoslav Tribunal. Notwithstanding Akhvan's theory of "interim justice," international indictments alone have little value if they are not backed up with an expectation of consequences. While critics of the Tribunal point to the Srebrenica massacre in 1995 and ethnic cleansing in Kosovo in 1998-1999 as evidence that the existence of the Tribunal had no deterrent effect, the Yugoslav Tribunal's first prosecutor counters that the lack of deterrent was due to the failure of NATO to make arrests in Bosnia.[84] In addition to deterrence in the former Yugoslavia, Richard Goldstone believes, "the failure to make arrests also risks destroying the broader deterrent value of the Tribunal. Future tyrants will be given notice that they also have nothing to fear from international justice for as long as they are surrounded by armed guards."[85]

The failure to link the norm of justice with the use of force to arrest war criminals significantly undermined the implementation of the Dayton Accords and set back the peace-building efforts. While the initial reluctance to meld these two approaches was based on NATO strategic assessment of the risks both to soldiers and to the peace process, as well as the influence of key peace builders who believed that a combination of force and justice might undermine their entrenched approach of accommodation, eventually the NATO forces recognized that without some arrests, the credibility of NATO would be undermined and their long-term strategic interests might suffer. NATO and the peace builders have, to date, not yet found it imperative for their interests to arrest Karadzic or Mladic, and this has weakened the ultimate effectiveness of the regime created in Dayton. Similarly, as will be discussed in the next chapter, while the international community has at times successfully utilized the approach of economic inducement, the peace builders have not found it to be in their interest to apply sustained economic sanctions in support of an approach of accountability.

Chapter 13

Linking Justice and Economic Inducements: A Road to Peace

The potential benefits of the Tribunal's work can not be realized until the international community demonstrates the same commitment to empower the Tribunal as it had shown when it established it.

—fifth annual report of the Yugoslav Tribunal[1]

This chapter examines the relationship between the approach of financial inducement and the norm of justice. Financial inducement can be used as a carrot (as with the conditional promise of reconstruction aid or the offer of "rewards") or a stick (as with the threat or imposition of trade embargoes and the freezing of assets). Both forms of financial inducements are frequently invoked as a tool in the peacebuilding process.

At times the approach of financial inducement has a general relationship to or impact on the norm of justice. This was the case, for example, with the economic sanctions imposed on the FRY prior to the establishment of the Yugoslav Tribunal, the purpose of which was to "apply pressure on Serbia-Montenegro to meet UN demands to cease outside aggression and interference in Bosnia."[2] At other times, the approach of financial inducement and the norm of justice collide, as evidenced by the suspension of economic sanctions imposed by the UN on the FRY to reward Mr. Milosevic for the positive role he played at Dayton, thereby extinguishing any remaining financial incentive to cooperate with the Yugoslav Tribunal.[3] And at still others, the approach of financial inducement was invoked to support the application of the norm of justice, as when the United States threatened to veto IMF loans to Croatia unless it cooperated with the Yugoslav Tribunal and when the United States made hundreds of millions of dollars in reconstruction aid contingent on Serbia's surrender of Slobodan Milosevic.[4] Even when the intent was to employ financial inducements in aid of the norm of justice, the effort was not always successful.

Unilateral efforts were easily circumvented, and conflicting political interests often prevented the Security Council from taking the necessary action.

In examining the relationship between the norm of justice and the approach of economic inducement, this chapter seeks to contribute to an understanding of questions five, six, seven, and nine set out in chapter 1, in particular the utility of existing international sanctions regimes as a means of promoting peace and a vehicle for supporting the approach of accountability, the creation of additional sanctions or financial inducement regimes to promote the norm of justice, the extent to which the approaches of financial inducement and accountability were inherently compatible, and the extent to which the peace builders learned how better to use the approach of financial inducement over the course of its numerous applications during the Yugoslav conflict.

To structure this discussion this chapter will first review the nature and extent of sanctions imposed by the UN Security Council against the FRY. The chapter will then examine the use of conditional assistance as a means for enhancing compliance with the orders of the Tribunal, the targeting of assets and the provision of rewards to "personalize" the effects of the justice norm in order to induce greater compliance, and finally the use of aid conditionality to prompt the arrest and transfer to The Hague of Slobodan Milosevic.

Security Council Sanctions

My Government again stresses the importance of every country's obligation to co-operate with the Tribunal and to comply with its orders. Unless they comply with their obligations, the parties to the conflict cannot expect to reap the benefits of peace, [and] ensure the permanent easing of economic sanctions.

—Madeleine Albright, U.S. Secretary of State[5]

Article 41 of the United Nations Charter authorizes the Security Council to impose a range of sanctions in an effort to restore international peace and security, and Article 25 requires the members of the United Nations to comply with Security Council-imposed sanctions. On 30 May 1992, the Security Council adopted Resolution 757, imposing sweeping economic sanctions on the FRY and the Bosnian Serb entity. The sanctions regime established by this resolution, however, was littered with loopholes and contained no enforcement mechanisms.[6] As Serb atrocities continued unabated, the sanctions were later strengthened through the adoption of Security Council Resolution 787 in November 1992 and Security Council Resolution 820 in April 1993.

Collectively, these resolutions imposed an embargo on imports to and exports from the FRY and the Bosnian Serb entity, prohibited air flights to and from the FRY, called upon states to seize FRY-registered vessels and vehicles, froze the assets of the FRY government, and prevented representatives of the FRY from participating in international sporting events.[7] Most important, Resolution 820 authorized a multilateral interdiction unit to enforce the sanctions on the Adriatic

Sea, effectively imposing a naval blockade against the FRY. On land, enforcement of the sanctions was monitored by NATO Sanctions Assistance Missions, located on the borders of the frontline states. In Resolution 820 the Security Council made the phased lifting of sanctions conditional on the agreement of the leaders of the FRY and the Bosnian Serbs to the proposed European Union-United Nations peace plan and, after the adoption of Resolution 827, on their cooperation with the Yugoslav Tribunal.

Although the FRY asserted that its constitution prohibited the surrender of Serb nationals to the Yugoslav Tribunal, and that it otherwise lacked the necessary domestic legislation to comply with the Tribunal's orders, Resolution 827 specifically required all states to take any measures necessary under their domestic law to implement the provisions of the resolution. Under international law, a state has a duty to comply with its international legal obligations, including binding Chapter VII Security Council resolutions, which take precedence over all domestic legal obligations. A state may not legitimately assert that it is unable to fulfill its international legal obligations on the basis that it is prohibited from doing so by its constitution or domestic legislation, or that it lacks the necessary domestic authority.[8]

The sanctions were not immediately effective, but by 1994 they were beginning to have a significant impact on the FRY's economy. At that time, David Forsyth accurately predicted that if fighting in Bosnia were to cease, "outside interest in sanctions on states for not extraditing war criminals—sanctions that hurt the sanctioning states as well—would decline markedly."[9] Thus, following the initialing of the Dayton Agreement on 21 November 1995, the Security Council adopted Resolution 1022, whereby it decided to "suspend indefinitely with immediate effect" the economic sanctions which it had imposed against the FRY and the Republika Srpska beginning in 1992.[10] The representative of the United Kingdom explained the decision to lift sanctions in the following terms:

> In August last year, Belgrade took a significant step in deciding to close its border with the Bosnian Serbs until they were prepared to accept a negotiated settlement. This Council rightly responded by granting a limited package of sanctions relief, conditional on the border remaining closed. The existence of this Peace Agreement is the clearest possible vindication of the Council's use of economic sanctions to bring about change. It is therefore right that this Council should now reward Belgrade's contribution to the successful outcome of the Dayton negotiations by granting very substantial sanctions relief.[11]

As mentioned in chapter 9, Resolution 1022 contained a potentially important provision for the reintroduction of economic sanctions in the event of noncompliance with the Dayton Agreement. Paragraph 3 of the resolution provided, "if at any time, with regard to a matter within the scope of their respective mandates and after joint consultation if appropriate, either the High Representative [for civilian implementation] or the Commander of the international force informs the Council via the Secretary-General that the Federal Republic of Yugoslavia or the Bosnian Serb authorities are failing significantly to meet their obligations under the Peace Agreement, the suspension" of economic sanctions "shall terminate on the fifth day following the Council's receipt of such a report, unless the Council decides otherwise taking into consideration the nature of the non-compliance." Consequently, either High Representative for Civilian Implementation Carl Bildt or the IFOR commander, Admiral Leighton Smith, could trigger automatic reimposition of sanctions in the event of Serb noncompliance with the Dayton mandates.

On paper, Resolution 1022 seemed to create an ideal mechanism for inducing cooperation with the Yugoslav Tribunal. By making a report from Carl Bildt or Leighton Smith the automatic trigger, the resolution would avoid the need to seek Security Council approval for reimposition of sanctions in the event the FRY or the Bosnian Serbs breached their obligations under the Dayton Accords, thus depoliticizing the process (and circumventing an almost certain Russian veto).

In practice, however, there were three problems with the trigger mechanism. First, rather than providing for an incremental reimposition of sanctions, it made reimposition an all-or-nothing proposition, which would thus be psychologically difficult for Bildt or Smith to employ. Second, the resolution did not specifically define the term "significant failure" to include refusal to surrender indicted persons to the Tribunal, although that was the understanding of the United States and other members of the Council.[12] The third problem was that the trigger mechanism was placed in the hands of the two officials who, given their personalities and backgrounds, were least likely to use it. Carl Bildt, the leader of the opposition in the Swedish parliament, was the European Union's mediator in the last phase of the Bosnian conflict. As mediator, Bildt had a reputation for yielding to the Bosnian Serb aggressors. He came under criticism for opposing NATO air strikes when the Bosnian Serbs murdered thousands of civilians in the UN safe area of Srebrenica, and for refusing to reproach the Serbs for their actions at Srebrenica until three months after the massacre.[13] And as discussed in chapter 12, Admiral Smith, who was no fan of the Yugoslav Tribunal, had a penchant for narrowly interpreting the provisions of Security Council resolutions concerning the Tribunal.[14]

Despite the fact that the preamble of Resolution 1022 noted that, "compliance with the requests and orders of the International Tribunal for the former Yugoslavia constitutes an essential aspect of implementing the Peace Agreement," Carl Bildt and Admiral Smith did not view the refusal to arrest or transfer indicted persons to the Tribunal, or the continued presence of such persons in official positions in the Republika Srpska, as a "significant failure" to meet the obligations under the Dayton agreement within the meaning of Resolution 1022. Thus, no triggering report to the Security Council was forthcoming from either Bildt or Smith when the Tribunal informed them that the FRY and the Republika Srpska had refused to comply with the Tribunal's arrest warrants and that a number of persons publicly indicted by the Tribunal continued to hold official positions in Prijedor and Foca.[15] In May 1996, Bildt warned the FRY that its failure to cooperate with the Tribunal risked reimposition of the sanctions, but he never followed this up with any action.[16]

Then, over the strong objections of Alija Izetbegovic, the president of Bosnia's new coalition government, the ministers of the Contact Group on Bosnia (Germany, the United States, France, the United Kingdom, and Russia) decided to make the suspension of sanctions permanent.[17] In accordance with the approach of accommodation, this action was seen as an appropriate reward to the FRY for formally recognizing the new Bosnian government and for supporting democratic elections in Bosnia in September 1996. Consequently, on 1 October 1996, the Security Council adopted Resolution 1074, terminating the Yugoslav sanctions and disbanding the Sanctions Committee, thus giving away potentially the most effective mechanism for pressuring the Serbs to surrender indicted persons to the Yugoslav Tribunal.

Although Resolution 1074 warned that the Council would "consider the imposition of measures if any party fails significantly to meet its obligations under the Peace Agreement," it was clear that the Council would never be able to muster the necessary votes among the permanent members to reimpose such sweeping sanctions against the FRY. In particular, the period of sanctions on Yugoslavia had reportedly cost Russia approximately $2 billion, and immediately after the lifting of the sanctions, Russia moved to restore its economic and financial ties to the FRY.[18] Thus, it should have come as no surprise that in 1996 when the Yugoslav Tribunal reported that the FRY had repeatedly refused to comply with the orders of the Tribunal,[19] the Security Council condemned the failure to arrest and transfer the individuals involved, but it declined to reimpose any sort of sanctions to enforce compliance.[20] Graham Blewitt, the Tribunal's deputy prosecutor, lamented that the Security Council's position sent a signal to the Serbs that there would be no consequences for noncompliance with the Tribunal's orders, thereby encouraging their continued refusal to cooperate.[21] In fact, on 9 February 1999, the FRY formally announced that it would not extradite Mile Mrksic, Veselin Sljivancanin, and Miroslav Radic, whose extradition the Yugoslav Tribunal had requested to answer a 1995 indictment[22] on charges relating to their alleged involvement in the killing of 260 unarmed men at Ovcara farm near Vukovar in 1991.[23]

Three years later, in the midst of the Kosovo crisis, on 1 May 1999, the NATO allies collectively reimposed many of the sanctions which had been lifted in 1996.[24] But without universal application, which can be achieved only through a Security Council resolution, these sanctions had little more than a symbolic effect.

Targeting Individuals: Freezing of Assets and the Rewards Program

We have not put a price on Mr. Milosevic's head for someone to kill him.

—William Jefferson Clinton,
former President of the United States[25]

As mentioned above, one of the Security Council sanctions imposed on the FRY was the freezing of all government assets in foreign banks. In the context of the efforts by the United Nations to dislodge the military regime from Haiti in 1993, the Security Council adopted Resolution 841, which required UN member states to freeze the assets located within their jurisdiction of known supporters of the military regime. This was the first time the Security Council acted under Article 41 of the UN Charter to freeze the assets of private individuals rather than a government.

Drawing upon the Haiti precedent, in 1998 the authors of this book recommended in a widely disseminated study that the Security Council should pass a resolution requiring states to seize and freeze the assets of any person subject to an international arrest warrant who refuses to surrender to the Yugoslav Tribunal. Such action, we pointed out "would (1) further isolate persons indicted by the International Tribunal, (2) serve as an effective penalty even if such persons evade justice, and (3) induce such persons to surrender themselves to the International Tribunal."[26] Radovan Karadzic, in particular, was said to be protected by a small mercenary force which he paid for through funds on deposit in Cyprus.[27] Tying up Karadzic's offshore funds, therefore, would greatly facilitate his capture.

Because these sanctions would be targeted at specific individuals, not governments, we believed "it would be easier to gain support of the members of the Security Council for such a measure."[28] However, David Scheffer, the U.S. ambassador for war crimes issues, later informed us that he had circulated an assets freeze proposal along the lines we suggested to the members of the Security Council, and he had encountered stiff opposition to the idea.

When it indicted Slobodan Milosevic and four other Serbian officials on 27 May 1999, the Office of the Prosecutor of the Yugoslav Tribunal discovered a creative way to circumvent the problem of Security Council recalcitrance. Pursuant to Article 19(2) of the Tribunal's statute, the Milosevic indictment directed states to provisionally freeze any assets of the accused located in their territories until the accused are taken into custody.[29] The authority cited for this action, Article 19 of the Tribunal's statute, merely provides that "upon confirmation of an indictment, the judge may, at the request of the Prosecutor, issue such orders and warrants for the arrest, detention, surrender or transfer of persons, and any other orders as may be required for the conduct of the trial."[30] While it was not originally envisaged that Article 19 would be used as the basis for the freezing of the accused's assets, the prosecutor explained that the decision to request such an order "was taken in light of the consistent non-cooperation of [the FRY] with the Tribunal and the possibility that such assets be used to evade arrest."[31] Because the orders of the Tribunal are "considered to be the application of an enforcement measure under Chapter VII of the Charter of the United Nations," the Tribunal's order has the equivalent force of law of a binding Security Council resolution.[32]

While the assets freeze ordered by the Yugoslav Tribunal may have rankled some of the members of the Security Council who had opposed Ambassador Scheffer's proposal the year before, the order was timed to avoid any serious challenge. A month earlier, the European Union foreign ministers meeting in Luxembourg had decided to freeze the assets of Mr. Milosevic and his core associates in the territory of EU countries. Like Radovan Karadzic, Milosevic's fortune is reported to be held in Cypriot banks. Cyprus, which is one of five countries earmarked for accelerated accession to the European Union, decided to cooperate in the assets freeze.[33] For its part, the United States welcomed the decision of the Yugoslav Tribunal to require the freezing of the assets of the indicted Serb officials and announced that they had been pronounced "Specially Designated Nationals" whose property would be blocked pursuant to Executive Order 13088.[34]

Through an unexpected legal interpretation, the Tribunal managed to equip itself with a powerful new financial tool to induce compliance with its arrest warrants. Compared to other forms of financial inducement such as imposition of economic sanctions and conditionality of reconstruction aid which hurt the population at large, freezing the assets of indicted war criminals is a precision tool for promoting justice. Another mechanism also possessing this attribute is the offering of rewards for the arrest of indicted war criminals.

As with assassination, international law prohibits putting a price on an enemy's head.[35] But that does not mean that states cannot offer a reward for information or assistance leading to the arrest and conviction of indicted war criminals. On 24 June 1999, the United States announced that it was offering a reward of $5 million for such information and assistance.[36]

The U.S. rewards program was established by the 1984 Act to Combat International Terrorism, Public Law 98-533. Under the program, cooperating individuals and their immediate family members may be relocated to the United States, or elsewhere, and are assured complete confidentiality. To date, more than 6 million dollars have been paid out for help in twenty terrorism cases.[37] In October 1998, the U.S. Congress enacted legislation expanding the rewards program to cover war crimes, as well as terrorism.[38]

Thousands of flyers and posters, advertising the U.S. War Crimes Rewards program, were distributed throughout Europe and the former Yugoslavia. However, as of the time of this publication, this program has had no discernable impact, and no indicted individual has been transferred under the program.

The mixed approach of financial inducement and accountability proved to be effective in a number of instances, in particular with the Croatian governments transfer of a number of mid-level indictees and Serbia's surrender of Slobodan Milosevic in June 2000. The political will for a sustained imposition of economic sanctions in support of the approach of accountability, however, does not yet exist. While the conditioning of assistance or the provision of rewards produces results at limited cost to a state, the economic disadvantages experienced by states which impose economic sanctions currently seem to outweigh their perceived value of the role of justice.

Conditional Assistance

It is a simple proposition, but a critical one. The benefits of economic and financial assistance should not go to those who thwart the will of this Council's requirement to cooperate with the war crimes Tribunal.

—Madeleine Albright, U.S. Secretary of State[39]

Sanctions are punitive in nature and are politically difficult to impose and enforce. Conditionality of economic assistance, in contrast, creates a positive incentive for a particular course of conduct and does not require action by the Security Council.

Annually from 1996 to 1999, dozens of countries and international organizations met for a Bosnian aid summit to determine the amount and modalities of reconstruction assistance they would provide Bosnia. The top priority of the effort, however, was not inducing the parties to the Yugoslav conflict to cooperate with the International Tribunal, but rather to create a stable economy in which people could find work in order to allow for the return to Bosnia of 1.7 million refugees and displaced persons.[40]

At the 1996 London summit, donor nations vowed to increase pressure on authorities in the former Yugoslavia who had failed to extradite indicted war criminals. The donor nations issued a warning that reconstruction aid would be closely linked to cooperation with the Yugoslav Tribunal. Despite this warning, no action was taken to suspend the hundreds of millions of dollars in aid earmarked for the Republika Srpska when its president, Biljana Plavsic, in a letter addressed to the UN Secretary-General in early January 1997, stated that there will be no cooperation with the Yugoslav Tribunal, and warned that the arrest of suspects would cause "massive civil and military unrest."[41] A spokesman for the Office of the Civilian High Representative, entrusted with the task of implementing the civilian aspects of the Dayton Accords, expressed disapproval of Plavsic's letter, but indicated that "it makes no difference on the flow of reconstruction aid."[42] Plavsic was subsequently indicted by the Yugoslav Tribunal for her role in the Bosnian genocide from 1992 to 1995.[43]

The initial failure to actually condition aid reflected the prevailing view that the withholding of funds until a party complies with its obligation to cooperate with the Tribunal would undercut the goal of rapid economic revival and the positive incentive of commercial gain to entice nationalist groups to abandon their separatist interests. It was felt that steps to impose international economic isolation would only work in favor of extremists who have an interest in perpetuating the martyr complex among Bosnian Serbs.[44] Thus, the policy of conditional aid became de facto a policy of constructive engagement. This represented the temporary triumph of accommodation over the norm of justice.

But it soon became clear that the policy of constructive engagement was depriving the Yugoslav Tribunal of one of its few means of exerting pressure on recalcitrant authorities and that, with the indicted warlords still in control of Republika Srpska, the financial assistance was being diverted from its intended beneficiaries. Consequently, out of a total of 3.1 billion dollars pledged for Bosnian reconstruction in 1997, only 15 percent was earmarked to the Republika Srpska,[45] while the other 85 percent went to the Croat-Muslim Federation to reward it for its compliance with the Dayton Accords and its cooperation with the Yugoslav Tribunal.[46]

By the 1998 summit in Brussels, international aid donors were expressing confidence in the "new climate" in Bosnia. Under its new prime minister, Milorad Dodik, the Republika Srpska agreed to let the Yugoslav Tribunal open an office in Banja Luka, and convinced two Bosnian Serb indictees (Milan Simic and Miroslav Tadic) to turn themselves in to the Tribunal.[47] With these events as a backdrop, the donor nations pledged an additional 1.25 billion dollars in reconstruction aid for Bosnia and, noting with satisfaction the "efforts at reconciliation by the new Republika Srpska," they decided that the new aid package would be "more balanced than in the past."[48] But the Republika Srpska government continued to refuse to extradite the major Bosnian Serb indictees, including Radovan Karadzic and Ratko

Mladic.

The approach of financial inducement achieved a much greater measure of success with respect to Croatia. Croatia had allowed the international prosecutor to open an office in Zagreb in November 1994, but Zagreb had failed to execute the arrest warrants issued by the Tribunal. Under a plan crafted by Ambassador Gelbard, the United States threatened to veto substantial IMF and World Bank loans to Croatia, in April 1997 unless Croatia began to surrender indictees to the Tribunal. Croatia immediately surrendered indicted Bosnian Croat war criminal Zlatko Aleksovsk, who had commanded the notorious Kaonik detention facility, to the Tribunal.[49] That same month indicted Croatian general Tihomir Blaskic voluntarily surrendered to the Tribunal through the mediation of the Croatian government, and he was subsequently convicted of crimes against humanity and sentenced to forty-five years.

When it was disclosed that ten indicted Bosnian Croats had been given refuge in Croatia, the United States again moved to block a crucial IMF loan to Croatia. On 6 October 1997, Dario Kordic and nine other indicted Bosnian Croats "voluntarily" surrendered to the Tribunal under pressure from Zagreb. Kordic, the vice-president of the Croatian community of Herzeg-Bosna, is the highest-ranking indicted Croat war criminal.[50] The development took the Croat public by surprise as only two weeks earlier the Croatian prime minister, Zlatko Matesa, set a defiant tone on the subject of the extradition of war crime suspects, declaring, "we will not sell out our men in exchange for loans." Kordic explained his surrender as a patriotic act on behalf of the Croatian state, "which has been subjected to horrible pressures from the international community." The day that Kordic was surrendered, the World Bank approved the previously refused loan to Croatia.[51] In August 1999, a thirteenth indicted Croat war criminal (Vinko Martinovic) was transferred from Croatia to the Tribunal.[52]

The approach of conditional assistance ultimately achieved its greatest success with respect to the surrender of Slobodan Milosevic. In the aftermath of the 1999 NATO bombing campaign, Milosevic's local popularity dropped to just 20 percent, the lowest approval ratings in his thirteen-year rule.[53] Serbia's economic woes, brought on by years of international sanctions and exacerbated by the damage wrought by the NATO bombs, ultimately led to Milosevic's defeat in the Yugoslav presidential election on 24 September 2000.[54] When the federal election commission nevertheless declared there would be a run-off between Mr. Kostunica and Mr. Milosevic, Mr. Kostunica vowed to boycott a second round, and thousands of Serb civilians took to the streets in Belgrade, Novi Sad, Nis, Kragujevac, and Kraljevo in protest of Milosevic's perceived attempt to steal the election.[55]

As the throngs of protestors steadily grew outside the government offices in Belgrade, there was concern among the international community that Milosevic would quell the popular uprising by employing force, as he had done earlier. But rather than attack the protestors, the members of the local Serb army garrison joined them as they stormed various government buildings. Realizing that Milosevic's fate was now sealed, his confederates quickly scrambled for political cover. Subsequently, the Yugoslavia Constitutional Court ruled that

Milosevic's opponent, Vojislav Kostunica, had in fact captured over 50 percent of the vote.[56] This was followed by action by the Serbian parliament recognizing Kostunica's election as president. On 7 October 2000, Milosevic conceded defeat and turned the government over to Kostunica.

Although he relinquished his official position, Milosevic continued to reside in the presidential residence that had been his home for over a decade, and continued to serve as leader of the Yugoslav Socialist Party, perhaps contemplating a way to return to power. For his part, the new Yugoslav president, Vojislav Kostunica, made clear that he had no intention of turning Milosevic or any other indicted Serbs over to the Yugoslav Tribunal. Despite this announcement, the United States and European Union lifted their economic sanctions on the FRY to signal their support for the new Yugoslav regime.[57]

As a result of Kostunica's defiance of the Tribunal, Senator Mitch McConnell instructed his staff member, Robin Cleveland, on the Senate Appropriations Sub-committee on Foreign Operations to craft a provision conditioning further U.S. assistance to Serbia on compliance with its obligations under international law to the Tribunal. Together with a small group of NGO representatives including James Hooper of the Public International Law and Policy Group, Nina Bang-Jensen of the Coalition for International Justice, Susan Blaustein of the International Crisis Group, and John Fox of the Soros Foundation, Cleveland crafted section 594(a) of the 2001 Appropriations Act. This paragraph provided that the United States should cease all assistance to Serbia and seek to block international financial institution lending if by 31 March 2001 the FRY had not provided sufficient cooperation with the Tribunal, including access for investigators, provision of documents, and surrender and transfer of indictees or assistance in their apprehension. The provision also required the FRY to take steps consistent with the Dayton Accords to end Serbian financial, political, security, and other support which has served to maintain separate Republika Srpska institutions, and take steps to implement policies which reflected a respect for minority rights and the rule of law. The Clinton administration, and in particular the Department of State aggressively lobbied for the removal of this conditionality provision from the appropriations bill. But the provision was nevertheless enacted into law.

As 31 March 2001 approached, the new Bush administration began to signal to the Kostunica government that it was required to take at least some action to comply with the conditionality requirement. In response to continued attention to this issue by Senators McConnell and Patrick Leahey (D-Vt.), the Department of State in mid-March prepared a demarche for Ambassador Bill Montgomery to deliver to President Kostunica, which expressly made the "arrest" of Milosevic a condition of continuing assistance. The United States did not specify on what grounds Milosevic was to be arrested or whether it was necessary that he be transferred to The Hague, just that he be arrested. The demarche also included a number of other actions the FRY was to take in order to comply with the legislation. Reportedly the ambassador ended up under-emphasizing the requirement of arrest and emphasized other more easily attainable conditions. As a result, President Kostunica sought to comply with the conditions by turning over to the Tribunal a Bosnian Serb, Milomir Stakic, the former mayor of Prijedor, who was wanted under a sealed indictment issued to the FRY in March 1997 for atrocities allegedly committed in 1992 and 1993 at the Omarska, Keraterm, and Trnopolje camps in Bosnia.[58]

When, on the advice of Ambassador Montgomery, the State Department began to indicate that it would likely recommend that President Bush certify compliance and release the millions of dollars in aid funds despite the FRY's failure to arrest Milosevic or take any other meaningful steps to abide by the conditions, Senator McConnell, backed by Senator Leahey, publicly declared there had not been sufficient observance to warrant certification of compliance with the conditions and further assistance.[59] The Tribunal's prosecutor, Carla del Ponte, also added her voice to the chorus calling for the withholding of aid unless Milosevic was arrested and transferred to The Hague.

On 1 April 2001, Milosevic was arrested by Serbian security forces and charged with corruption, political assassination, and election fraud. On 3 April Secretary of State Colin L. Powell certified the FRY's compliance with the conditions, but he qualified the certification by noting that the United States support for up to $1 billion in additional international assistance to be pledged at a future international donors conference would be conditional on the FRY's full cooperation with the Tribunal. While much of the international community welcomed this development, the French objected to the use of economic conditionality to promote the arrest and the transfer to The Hague of Mr. Milosevic.[60]

While many Serbian government officials and NGOs made the claim that it was necessary first to try Milosevic in Serbia for economic crimes committed against the people of Serbia as they were the most serious victims of his actions, and only then transfer him to The Hague to face charges of crimes against humanity and possibly genocide, the United States led a campaign to condition international assistance on his transfer to The Hague. But when Prosecutor Del Ponte met with President Kostunica to work out arrangements for cooperating with the Tribunal, she found "he was absolutely [in denial], denying even the existence of the Tribunal—just accusing the Tribunal, because the Serbs are only victims."[61] During this time, half-hearted efforts of the FRY parliament to pass a law on extradition and cooperation with the Tribunal faltered, due in large part to the efforts of the pro-Milosevic Socialist People's Party from Montenegro, which, although delegitimized by the government of Montenegro, was frequently embraced and legitimized by Ambassador Montgomery and the Department of State.

As the 29 June 2001 deadline neared for the international donors conference in Brussels, all of the major European states agreed to attend despite the failure of the FRY government to act on the transfer of Milosevic to The Hague. In an interview with *Newsweek* magazine, in response to the question "What kind of pressure are the U.S. and other governments putting on Belgrade to hand him over?" Prosecutor Del Ponte replied, "the United States is giving very, very good support. I am very happy about that because the European Union support is low-level. The EU doesn't want to put conditions [on aid]. I am counting on the Americans. So aid must be conditioned? That is the only, only voice they hear.

. . . I am sure it is the only way to obtain what we need to make justice."[62] In the face of this failure of European resolve, and against the advice of career officers at the State Department, but under renewed pressure from McConnell and Leahey and other important senators, Secretary Powell declared that the United States would not be attending the conference unless Milosevic was extradited to the Hague.

On 28 June 2001, in the face of Kostunica's failure to comply with the conditions, Serbian prime minister Zoran Djindjic ordered the transfer of Milosevic to The Hague. While this act was welcomed by the international community, President Kostunica protested that the transfer of Milosevic was "illegal and unconstitutional," as well as "lawless and hasty."[63] Other members of Kostunica's cabinet resigned in dissent, throwing the fragile Belgrade government into turmoil. But the political crisis quickly faded when, two days later, Yugoslavia was awarded 1.28 billion dollars in aid by the United States and its European allies. The International trial of Slobodan Milosevic began on 12 February 2002, and is expected to last two years.

During the negotiation of the Foreign Appropriations bill for 2002 Senators McConnell and Leahey again proposed to condition aid to Serbia on its cooperation with the Yugoslav Tribunal. Despite the success of such conditionality in promoting cooperation the move was strongly opposed by the Department of State and America's European allies. Notwithstanding this opposition, Senators McConnell and Leahey again imposed the requirement that all non-humanitarian assistance be cut off to Serbia if it did not cooperate with the Yugoslav Tribunal by 31 March 2002. As a result of this legislation, the Serbian government for the first time issued arrest warrants for individuals indicted by the tribunal. Two prominent indictees voluntarily turned them selves over to the tribunal rather than face public arrest, and another committed suicide on the steps of the Serbian parliament. The Serbian government, however, continued to recognize the immunity of, and refused to issue an arrest warrant for, Mr. Milosevic who continued to serve as the president of Serbia despite his indictment for crimes against humanity committed in Kosovo. On 31 March 2002 economic assistance was cut off to Serbia by the United States and was set to resume only after Serbia had made further progress in arresting and extraditing indictees to The Hague.

Chapter 14

The Cohabitation of Justice and Peace: Concluding Observations

The utilization of the cognitive contextual process method for examining the role of justice in the peace-building process has produced a number of general conclusions concerning the employment of the norm and institutions of justice, the context in which this norm operates, and the evolving nature of the peace-building process and its affect on the norm of justice. These conclusions are organized according to the ten questions set forth in chapter 1.

1. *Who are the primary state, substate and nonstate actors, what are their geopolitical interests, and how did these interests influence their view of the norm of justice and its utility in the Yugoslav crisis?*

The primary state actors were the United States, United Kingdom, France, Germany, and Russia. Each of these states held a distinct set of interests, which significantly influenced their approach to peace-building and the role of justice in that process. The United States was at first primarily interested in deferring the responsibility for managing the Yugoslav crisis to the Europeans, but Washington was also concerned about domestic perceptions. By the time the United States began to assert a leadership role, many of the approaches had been tested and failed, and thus the United States found itself in the position of supporting the creation of the Yugoslav Tribunal; this action was also well received by the American political constituency, which generally favors the notion of international accountability. However, as the United States assumed the primary leadership role in resolving the conflict, it found that the institutions of justice could complicate its ability to accommodate, and at times appease, the Milosevic regime and thus it sought to minimize the role of justice in the peace-building process. As the American domestic constituency was in favor of a quick resolution to the conflict that did not involve use of U.S. military forces, this downplaying of accountability was politically expedient.

The United Kingdom sought to exert a leadership role both for itself and for the European Union, while simultaneously courting Russian participation and seeking to protect the interests of the United Kingdom's traditional allies. Because the British were leading the effort to employ the approach of accommodation, they were initially quite reluctant to utilize the norm of justice and the approach of accountability, and therefore they actively sought to delay the creation and implementation of the Tribunal. In more than one instance, British officers and diplomats sought to mischaracterize the facts on the ground in order to erode the moral imperative to rely more heavily on the norm of justice. With a change in government, however, the British became the most aggressive proponents of the accountability approach, and essentially pressed the Office of the Prosecutor into indicting Slobodan Milosevic for crimes against humanity in Kosovo. This then inhibited the ability of the peace builders to continue to resurrect the path of accommodation as a means for ending the NATO air campaign against Serbia.

France primarily sought to ensure a predominant role for the EU in resolving the crisis and a prominent role for France within those efforts. Although France was willing to support efforts at accommodating Mr. Milosevic in respect to Bosnia, it was quick to support the use of force and was not ideologically opposed to the norm of justice during the Kosovo crisis. Above all, however, France was interested in protecting its own interests, and thus Paris did not consistently or positively contribute to the development of an approach based on accountability. As a consequence, France was extremely reluctant to apprehend indicted war criminals present in its sector of control. On one notable occasion U.S. officials publicly announced that in 1997 they were forced to abort an attempt to apprehend Radovan Karadzic because the French military had leaked details of the plan to the Bosnian Serbs.

Germany, while taking an initial lead in the development of an EU policy toward the Yugoslav crisis—and one based on the intent to prevent crimes against humanity—was subsequently sidelined by the other European states and thus played a limited role in the development or implementation of EU policy. During the Kosovo crisis, however, Germany, like the United Kingdom, aggressively invoked the norms of justice as a rationale for the use of force. Although its EU allies frequently and publicly criticized German action in the region, Germany appeared to act on the belief that it held a special responsibility for preventing atrocities in the region given its actions during World War II.

Russia's approach to peace-building, and, in particular, the role of justice in that process, was directed almost entirely by self-interest and its perception that Serbia was its traditional ally. When the Security Council sought to create the Tribunal, Russia was deeply dependent on Western states for financial and political assistance and thus did not seek to prevent its establishment. However, as the crisis continued, Russia became more assertive about the need to limit the influence of the norm of justice, and Moscow sought to portray all sides as equally responsible for war crimes. Russia also sought to limit the use of force to apprehend indicted war criminals in Bosnia and the invocation of the norm of justice as a rationale for using force in Kosovo.

The UN Security Council, the EU, NATO, and the Yugoslav Tribunal were the primary nonstate actors to influence the peace-building process. The views and actions of the Security Council generally represented the lowest common denominator of the permanent five's interests. Despite this, the Security Council inadvertently became instrumental early on in the infusion of justice into the peace-building process—in large part through the creation of the War Crimes Commission, and subsequently the Yugoslav Tribunal. The Security Council, however, was never able to significantly promote the norm of justice through means such as sanctions or other enforcement mechanisms because of competing interests and the absence of a coherent understanding of the utility of justice by the permanent five. In addition, the bureaucratic nature of the United Nations Secretariat and its leaders' surprisingly anti-justice disposition inhibited the timely development of the Yugoslav Tribunal, and thus limited the role of justice in the Croatian and Bosnian conflicts.

The European Union, like the Security Council, reflected the lowest common denominator of the views of its members. Because of its initial and primary role in seeking a negotiated settlement based upon the accommodation of Mr. Milosevic's interests, the EU perceived of little or no role for the norm of justice and primarily left the matter to its individual members to pursue or support as they wished. In fact, it would be difficult to find even a minimum effort on the part of the European Union collectively to promote the role of justice in the peace-building process which was not directly attributable to significant pressure from one of its member states.

NATO, which was intently preoccupied by the redefinition of its mandate, plans for possible enlargement, and the search for a mechanism to constructively engage Russia, initially paid little attention to the conflict in the former Yugoslavia. Over time, NATO became aware that the war in Bosnia and the ineffective response of its member states—even under the umbrella of other organizations—was undermining its credibility. NATO thus undertook action to assist in the enforcement of Security Council-established no-fly zones and the protection of Security Council-established safe areas. NATO, however, did not initially perceive the norm of justice to serve its interests, and in fact actively avoided the possibility of arresting indicted war criminals in Bosnia. Eventually though, NATO recognized the value of the norm of justice both in terms of (1) providing a rationale for ridding Bosnia of war lords who threatened NATO's mandate, (2) identifying and characterizing its enemy (Mr. Milosevic) in a highly negative light, and thus aiding in the public and official support of its own initiatives, and (3) serving as a means for an exit strategy—by removing the most prominent war criminals from civil society and creating a basis for the establishment of a meaningful peace.

The Yugoslav Tribunal itself became an interested stakeholder over time. Naturally the norm of justice was the focus of the Tribunal's existence and from the beginning it sought to promote the relevance of the norm of justice and the perpetuation of its own existence. Over time, however, the Office of the Prosecutor came to espouse a narrow definition of justice, which encompassed only its existence and operation, and thus placed members of the Tribunal in the awkward position of seeking to squelch the development of other accountability institutions, such as domestic prosecutions and the establishment of a truth commission. The Office of the Prosecutor was also careful not to pursue the norm of justice to the point that it might undermine its own survival by causing the erosion of official support for the Tribunal. This was seen in its initial reluctance to indict Mr. Milosevic until it could assemble "an iron clad case" against him.

Finally, a number of individuals played an important role in the peacebuilding process, with their self-interest, worldview, and previous experience influencing their view of the utility of justice. The least supportive of the norm of justice would be UNPROFOR commander General Rose, peace negotiator David Owen, EU negotiator and high representative Carl Bildt, UN representative Yasushi Akashi, and U.S. secretary of state Warren Christopher—who actively sought to create a moral equivalence among the parties and thus erode public support for greater involvement in the crisis, thereby creating the maximum leeway for negotiations. Concerning the implementation of the norm of justice, Admiral Leighton Smith notably refused to trigger the reimposition of economic sanctions when Serbia failed to cooperate with the Tribunal, and he narrowly interpreted the IFOR mandate to exclude the arrest of war criminals. Other individuals such as Richard Holbrooke utilized the norm and institutions of justice as a tool to serve their objective of reaching a negotiated peace—at times promoting the norm, while at other times seeking to undermine it. There were also some officials, such as Prime Minister John Major, National Security Council advisers Sandy Berger and Anthony Lake, and Secretary of Defense William Cohen, who never seemed to quite grasp the function, or utility, of the norm of justice and thus minimized its impact on the decision-making process. Finally, there were individuals, such as Prime Minister Tony Blair, Secretary of State Madeleine Albright, Ambassador David Scheffer, and NATO commander Wesley Clark who viewed the norm of justice as playing a central role in the peace-building process and sought to promote its institutions, and invoke the principles of justice as a key element of the process.

2.   *Which approaches to peace-building did interested states initially employ to promote their objectives, and how did these evolve during the course of the conflict?*

The peace builders did not initially develop a strategy for conflict resolution which involved a strategic mix of approaches, but rather dealt with the crisis in an ad hoc manner, relying on additional approaches when the initial ones failed to yield meaningful results. The first approach was one of accommodation, by which the EU sent lawyers to the region to serve as mediators and to ascertain the interests of parties in order to craft a negotiated settlement. As these efforts bogged down, and credible reports emerged of atrocities, the EU sent monitors and elevated the level of mediation to more senior diplomats. The EU then employed economic sanctions, although it did not initially coordinate these measures with the United States and thus they were quite ineffective. Moreover, the initial level of sanctions was quite limited. Attempts to employ the norm of justice at this point were eschewed for fear that they would interfere with the process of accommodation.

As it pursued the primary approach of accommodation, the EU sought to entrench the approach by securing the deployment of UN peacekeepers, creating a formal negotiating process, and obfuscating the nature and extent of atrocities. The EU also sought to minimize the approach of force by actively arguing for the adoption of a UN Security Council arms embargo against all the parties. As the approach of accommodation failed to yield results, it was not abandoned or changed, but rather incrementally added onto with elements from the other approaches. Thus a War Crimes Commission was established to catalogue the atrocities, safe havens were created with light protection, and a no-fly zone was adopted but not initially enforced.

As this mélange approach failed to achieve a peaceful resolution to the conflict, still more elements of the other approaches were added. The Tribunal was created and began to issue indictments, the no-fly zone was enforced, and very limited air strikes were conducted to demonstrate the resolve of the international community and to bring the parties to the negotiating table. At this point the leadership of the peace-building process shifted to the United States.

With the limited success of the Dayton Accords, the policy of accommodation was resurrected, albeit with elements of the other approaches imbued within its structure. Thus, when the Kosovo crisis erupted three years later, the peace builders relied upon the new hybrid approach which primarily represented accommodation, with some elements of justice and the threat of the use of force. As this approach failed to yield results, a Dayton II was convened in Rambouillet and Paris under the threat of the use of force. When the hybrid approach failed to prevent further atrocities, the peace builders turned as a last resort to the tandem approach of the use of force and indictment of Mr. Milosevic.

Notably, the process of peace-building from 1991 to 1999 was characterized by a primary reliance on accommodation augmented by economic sanctions, justice, and the threat of force. As this approach failed each time, in Croatia, Bosnia, and then Kosovo, the peace builders turned to a greater use of justice and of force. Surprisingly there appeared to be little understanding or agreement on how best to employ the use of force, and what was the precise role or value of justice.

3. *During the peace-building process to what extent did the competing interests of relevant actors influence the selection of peace-building approaches and the application of other approaches in relation to the norm of justice? In what manner did states and substate stakeholders act to promote the role of justice and the other approaches?*

As noted in the discussions under questions one and two above, the interests of the stakeholders influenced their choice of approaches, and the success or failure of these approaches influenced the application of additional approaches.

With respect to the competition between interests and between approaches, the stakeholders engaged in what might be called second-tier positioning, wherein they sought to position themselves vis-à-vis other stakeholders and promote their interests through the different approaches to peace-building.

The European Union, for instance, was intent on maintaining a leadership position in the peace-building process—initially to signal the beginning of a new era of Common Foreign and Security Policy (CSFP), and subsequently to guard against claims that a CSFP could never materialize given the failure of the Yugoslav peace-building efforts. Thus, once the EU had settled on an approach of accommodation through EU-led mediation, it consistently pursued that approach even when it slid into appeasement. The EU attempted to deflect the adoption of the approach of justice and use of force as it would sidetrack its efforts at accommodation, and swing the leadership role to NATO and the United States. The UN also feared the use of force as it might endanger the peacekeepers—who were an integral part of the approach of accommodation—and would shift control from the UN, as happened in the Kosovo conflict. Correspondingly, some NATO and United States officials believed that an increased role for justice would limit negotiating options, and would compel the use of force, which the United States and NATO were not initially prepared to support.

Other actors, such as the United States, early in the Bosnia conflict, saw the approach of justice and the threat of force as a means to dilute the European Union control over what was perceived as a failed policy, while eschewing a primary role for the United States. The United States thus supported the creation of the War Crimes Commission and then the Tribunal, as well as the enforcement of the no-fly zone and protection of safe havens. When the United States assumed a leadership role in the negotiations, however, it became interested in minimizing the role of justice. While the United States took advantage of the Tribunal's indictments to exclude Karadzic and Mladic from Dayton, it rehabilitated Mr. Milosevic prior to the Dayton negotiations so that it could secure a peace, and Washington then relied upon him to aid in the implementation of the Dayton Accords. Similarly, the United States downplayed Mr. Milosevic's responsibilities for crimes against humanity in Kosovo while trying to negotiate an agreement. Notably, even during the first months of the air campaign the United States at times sought to minimize the culpability of Mr. Milosevic in order to maintain the option of accommodation. Only after the Tribunal indicted Mr. Milosevic for war crimes (at the urging of the United Kingdom and the U.S. ambassador) did the United States view the norm of justice as binding—and then only to the extent it limited direct American contact with Mr. Milosevic.

Other states and entities supported the creation of the Tribunal, but they failed to adequately appreciate the potential role of the Tribunal, or of other existing justice-based institutions, such as the International Court of Justice. In large part the failure to effectively utilize these institutions resulted from a general lack of understanding of the value of justice. Moreover, many of the primary actors in the peace-building process in the former Yugoslavia continued throughout the crisis to view the norm of justice as a hindrance to their efforts to achieve peace, and they sought to incorporate the norm into the process only as far as was required to justify their public rhetoric. In fact, it appears the primary factor supporting the inclusion of the norm of justice, or at least a reference to the institutions of justice, was that many public officials associated with the negotiations, or high-ranking members of their government, made public commitments to pursue justice in order to deflect public criticism of their policy of accommodation, and they then found themselves minimally bound to incorporate some role for justice in the process.

Finally, the likelihood of incorporating the norm of justice was enhanced when NGOs and the media highlighted justice-based concerns, and when representatives of justice-based institutions, such as the Yugoslav Tribunal, publicly called for a greater incorporation of the norm. Notably, however, even a press conference by the president of the Yugoslav Tribunal succeeded only in preserving a mention of the Tribunal in the Rambouillet/Paris Accords, and the action did not succeed in promoting the incorporation of provisions that would have enhanced the ability of the Tribunal to function in Kosovo.

4. To what extent did preexisting rules and norms influence the behavior of the relevant actors and the choice of peace-building approaches, and did the influence of specific rules and norms fluctuate over the course of the conflict?

Preexisting rules outlawing war crimes, crimes against humanity, and genocide and that required states to take action to prevent these crimes and to prosecute offenders were generally seen as impediments to the process of accommodation. The peace builders thus actively sought to characterize the conflict in terms which excluded the application of these norms for as long as possible. Yet, when the peace builders decided to take action deviating from the approach of accommodation, in particular when they invoked the use of force, they relied heavily on these norms to justify their action and build public support.

Overall, preexisting norms served less as a constraint on behavior and more as a tool to be utilized by peace builders at various points in the peace process to garner institutional or public support for their chosen course of action. As the primary objective of the peace builders throughout much of the conflict was to accommodate the interests of the aggressor parties, the peace builders sought to minimize the applicability of preexisting norms that might constrain their behavior. Thus, for example, they initially avoided labeling the systematic killings in Bosnia "genocide" or the ethnic cleansing in Kosovo as attempted genocide.

When the peace builders, however, sought to utilize the approaches of economic sanctions, use of force, and justice they were able to call upon provisions of international law such as Chapter VII authority under the UN Charter to compel compliance with an economic embargo, or to justify the use of force to protect safe areas and humanitarian convoys. Most important for the norm of justice, when the peace builders decided to create a Tribunal, the Security Council and then the judges of the Tribunal were able to draw from a wealth of norms relating to the substantive law of war crimes and crimes against humanity and historic precedent and procedures for prosecuting alleged war criminals to create relatively rapidly a generally fair and equitable means for ascertaining the responsibility of individuals for war crimes. It should be noted that the lack of preexisting norms, such as a clear legal justification for the use of force in Kosovo and Serbia, did not prevent the peace builders from engaging in the use of force to achieve their political objectives.

As the Tribunal operated throughout the Bosnian conflict it contributed to the norm of justice through the development of rules and precedent, and through the issuance of indictments. While these did not, to any appreciable degree, influence the initial approach of the peace builders to the Kosovo conflict—in large part because the Office of the Prosecutor had failed to take the important step of indicting Mr. Milosevic for his part in the Bosnian conflict—their existence enhanced the role of justice in the Kosovo conflict by providing a venue to delegitimize Mr. Milosevic, which by the time of the indictment had become a policy objective of some important peace builders.

5. *Which formal and informal regimes did the relevant states invoke to promote peace-building, and how did the nature of these regimes influence the ability of states to employ and evolve certain methods and norms?*

The peace builders invoked a number of formal regimes to promote their efforts at peace-building, including the UN Security Council, the UN Sanctions Committee, NATO, OSCE, and the International Court of Justice. The peace builders, in particular the European states, invoked the nascent regime of the Common Foreign Security Policy mechanism, which relied upon the EU Troika. To augment their efforts, the peace builders also created a number of regimes, such as an arms embargo, the Badinter Commission to make recommendations on applications for recognition by the EU, the EU/UN-hosted International Conference for the former Yugoslavia, the Dayton and Rambouillet/Paris negotiations, UN Protection Forces I and II, IFOR/SFOR, KFOR, the Contact Group, the Kosovo Diplomatic Mission, and the Kosovo Verification Mission. Most important for the norm of justice, the peace builders created the regimes of the War Crimes Commission and the Yugoslav Tribunal.

The peace builders also relied upon informal regimes such as the Perm-Three within the Security Council, the British-American special relationship, the emerging (and subsequently abandoned) British-Russian special relationship, the Franco-German EU axis, the British-French-Serbian relationship, and the Russian-Serbian partnership.

Most of these regimes were characterized by the domination of a few powerful states, but with a general practice of needing to reach consensus. This produced two dynamics which tilted the process in favor of accommodation and against other approaches. First, if a powerful state wished to block the adoption of other approaches, such as when the British sought to limit the use of force during the early and middle stages of the Bosnia conflict, it generally had the power to do so. Second, if a powerful state was interested in promoting the application of additional norms or approaches, it generally had to form a consensus within the organization, be it the Security Council, OSCE, or NATO, and this necessarily diluted the strength of the new or additional approach. The nature of these regimes also made it difficult to create a complex mix of norms and approaches as the value of these hybrid approaches was often difficult to comprehend by the necessary number of peace builders to forge a consensus, or inevitably prejudiced the related interests of a particular state—which then sought to inhibit the applicability of a particular norm or approach.

Importantly, however, the simple existence of these regimes did provide an opportunity to at least at times evolve the approach of accommodation and over time to slowly add in the elements of other approaches. Thus, while these regimes inhibited the timely adoption of more relevant and effective approaches, they did provide a mechanism for the slow evolution of the approach of accommodation, and its occasional augmentation with other norms and approaches.

6. *What regimes and institutions were created to aid in the incorporation of justice into the peace-building process and were they effective?*

The peace builders created a number of regimes and institutions to aid in the peace-building process. As noted immediately above, the peace builders created a War Crimes Commission and the Yugoslav Tribunal, which ended up playing a significant role in peace-building. Other institutions created by the peace builders, including the various forums for peace negotiation, IFOR/SFOR, the Kosovo Diplomatic Mission, and the Kosovo Verification Mission, also impacted the role of justice in the peace-building process.

The War Crimes Commission, although designed largely as a stalling tactic and public relations device, was exceptionally effective at promoting the role of justice as it clearly identified the nature of the acts being perpetrated in Bosnia and singled out the Serbian regime as the primary aggressor. The commission also made concrete recommendations for the creation of a Tribunal and thus created the necessary public exposure to enable those peace builders pushing for the creation of the Tribunal to create the necessary political will to accomplish that objective. The success of the commission in large part resulted from the efforts of its chair, Cherif Bassiouni, and from its dedicated staff, who were able to circumvent bureaucratic roadblocks, obtain funding outside the UN, and persuade the relevant states and international organizations to provide access to necessary documents and information to complete an accurate representation of the role of atrocities in the conflict.

The subsequent creation of the Yugoslav War Crimes Tribunal was in large part a response to the failure of other approaches—appeasement, economic inducements, and use of force. The members of the Security Council, moreover, had mixed motives for creating the Yugoslav Tribunal. While they justified their action in terms of achieving accountability, truth telling, deterrence, and reconciliation, the Tribunal was not perceived of solely (or even primarily) as a tool of justice, but as a public relations tool and as a potentially useful policy tool. The members of the Council knew that even if only low-level perpetrators were brought to justice, the existence of the Tribunal and the issuance of international indictments for the responsible leaders would deflect criticism from the major powers that they did not do enough to halt the bloodshed in the Balkans and would serve to isolate offending leaders diplomatically, strengthen the hand of domestic rivals, and fortify the international political will to expand economic sanctions or approve air strikes.

As a result of the nature of its creation, the Yugoslav Tribunal was initially much less effective than its historic predecessor—the Nuremberg Tribunal. During the early stages of its existence, the Yugoslav Tribunal was blessed with a highly capable prosecutor, but it was hampered by weak support from the peace builders, who had bought into the idea of war crimes prosecutions as an augmentation of the peace-building process, but who, when faced with its actual operation, became more hesitant and returned to their preference for an approach of accommodation. Moreover, the Tribunal rapidly became the victim of political rivalries between the Americans and the British, NATO member states and Russia, and developing and developed states.

Eventually, the Tribunal under the leadership of Prosecutor Goldstone was able to garner the necessary political support for its operation and to demonstrate it could play a role in the peace-building process—in large part by indicting Radovan Karadzic and General Ratko Mladic for genocide prior to the Dayton negotiations. Unfortunately, just as the Tribunal was garnering sufficient political support, there was a change in leadership in the prosecutor's office and a much more cautious approach was adopted, which was accompanied by a lower public profile. The passivity of the Office of the Prosecutor in many ways removed the norm of justice from any influence on the early stages of the Kosovo conflict, when it could have been most effective. Even when the Office of the Prosecutor did announce its indictment of Mr. Milosevic mid-way through the NATO air campaign, this was largely seen as a response to political pressure—which to some extent undermined the positive effect of the indictment. The indictment did, however, strengthen support within reluctant NATO countries for the continuation of air strikes, ultimately inducing Milosevic to agree to NATO's terms for Kosovo. Later, the Milosevic indictment facilitated the removal of the Serb leader from Serbia, ending his potential threat to the region.

A step back for the growing influence of the Tribunal came when the Office of the Prosecutor publicly declared its review of NATO actions for possible war crimes committed during its humanitarian intervention in Kosovo. Up until that time the Office of the Prosecutor had observed a strict code of not publicly commenting on ongoing investigations—a code which was frequently invoked to justify its lack of comment on Mr. Milosevic's potential responsibility for war crimes.

As will be briefly discussed below, justice was minimized during the various peace negotiations as it was perceived as inhibiting the ability to reach a negotiated settlement. But nonetheless the norm of justice was referenced in the Dayton and Rambouillet/Paris negotiations—in large part as a result of the public profile of the norm of justice created by the Tribunal and press attention as to whether it would be included. The IFOR/SFOR forces greatly assisted in promoting the role of justice by apprehending indicted war criminals, but also inhibited its full application by delaying the initiation of these arrests and by declining to arrest Karadzic or Mladic. The Kosovo Diplomatic Observer Mission and the Kosovo Verification Mission were instrumental in promoting justice by publicly declaring the nature of the atrocities and calling for an investigation by the Office of the Prosecutor. Ironically, the KDOM and the KVM were put in place as instruments of accommodation to forestall the use of force and create more time for engagement with Mr. Milosevic. By so publicly identifying the Serbian regime as responsible for crimes against humanity, the KVM unexpectedly played a key role in building the public support for the eventual use of force, while having the effect of creating public pressure on the Office of the Prosecutor to indict Mr. Milosevic and thus prevent resurgent efforts at accommodation by the peace builders.

7. *During the peace-building process to what extent did the various approaches and norms compete for primacy, and to what extent were certain approaches and norms compatible?*

During the course of the peace-building process there was fierce competition for primacy among the approaches, and on frequent occasion the approaches were interwoven into the process. From the objective perspective the most effective means at peace-building would entail a mix of approaches structured so as to promote a negotiated and peaceful resolution of the conflict. This would likely entail limited accommodation of all the parties insofar as possible as an initial starting point in order to induce interest in a negotiated settlement. If these efforts failed, economic sanctions and conditionality of aid could be employed as an additional inducement, coupled with the threat of the use of force against the aggressor party, and the employment of justice to set the parameters of a negotiation and to exclude those most culpable from the process. The exclusion would be key since it is nearly impossible to structure a lasting peace by accommodating the interests of an individual who relied upon crimes against humanity and genocide as his means for achieving his objectives.

Rather than undertaking such an approach, the peace builders adopted the approach of accommodation coupled with limited economic sanctions and eschewed the meaningful use of force and discounted any efforts to engage the norm of justice. As this approach failed to generate results, certain parties began to advocate for the incorporation of additional norms and approaches. At this point there was fierce competition between these approaches, with those in favor of accommodation believing that the inclusion of additional norms into the process would scuttle their efforts at accommodation which seemed perpetually poised to yield breakthrough results. Once these approaches were set against one another in this fashion the peace process took on two dimensions: One was between the peace builders and the parties to the conflict, while the other was between the peace builders themselves as they competed for the adoption of their respective approaches.

As the accommodation approach eventually became one of appeasement, and the United States assumed the leadership role, the process began to incorporate a diversity of approaches. Those in favor of creating conditions for a lasting peace—and the eventual withdrawal of NATO forces from Bosnia—began to understand the relationship between promoting justice through the arrest of war criminals and the creation of a stable peace. Similarly, as mentioned above, in the Kosovo context those in favor of the use of force found the Tribunal's indictment of Mr. Milosevic to serve their purpose of justifying enhanced air strikes, and in fact publicly called for the Tribunal to issue the indictment. Moreover, those who wished to exclude Karadzic and Mladic from the Dayton negotiations in order to promote their efforts to reach an accommodation with the parties found the indictments of the two Bosnian Serb leaders to be a useful basis for doing so. With respect to the implementation of the accords, the British, in particular, realized that the issuance of indictments by the Tribunal could serve as a useful justification for removing obstructionist individuals such as the mayors of Prijedor and Foca, and the former Serbian representative on the Bosnian presidency.

The conditioning of further financial assistance to Croatia and Serbia on their cooperation with the Tribunal led to impressive results, with Croatia surrendering over a dozen indictees to the Tribunal and Serbia eventually surrendering Slobodan Milosevic. As the Balkans experience has made clear, for a state faced with the tremendous costs of reconstruction after an armed conflict, conditionality of economic assistance can be a particularly compelling incentive.

Importantly, however, even this level of interrelationship fell short of what was possible and what could have produced a more timely and effective peace. During the Dayton negotiation, the peace builders could have melded the approaches of accommodation and justice and economic inducement by providing that economic sanctions would not have been lifted against Serbia or the Republika Srpska until all indicted war criminals had been turned over to the Tribunal. This would have likely led to the early apprehension of Karadzic and Mladic and would have radically improved the level of implementation of the Dayton Accords. Similarly, the peace builders could have explicitly provided in the IFOR annex and related Security Council resolution that NATO troops possessed the authority and mandate to apprehend war criminals, and this might have prevented the year-long delay in the apprehension of indictees while NATO and the international civilian administrators of Bosnia argued over whether NATO actually possessed the authority and mandate to do so. Moreover, if it were seriously committed to inducing compliance with the Tribunal's arrest orders, the Security Council could have placed the automatic trigger for reimposition of suspended sanctions in the hands of the Tribunal rather than the UN high representative and IFOR commander. In addition, during the early stages of the Kosovo conflict, the Security Council could have responded to the requests of the Tribunal to impose economic sanctions on Serbia for its failure to comply with its Chapter VII Resolution-based obligations to cooperate with the Tribunal, and the Council would have thus signaled its intent to take seriously any acts involving the commission of atrocities, and might have actually deterred some of these acts.

One of the primary concerns which led peace builders to eschew this additional integration of approaches was the fear that it would transfer the policy initiative from states to institutions over which they exercised limited or no control. Similarly there was the concern that, while institutions such as NATO and the Security Council seek to pursue a myriad of interests, institutions such as the Yugoslav Tribunal are more myopic.

8. *To what extent did competition between the various approaches and norms influence the development of new regimes, in particular during the Dayton and Rambouillet/Paris negotiations?*

On the whole, the norm of justice faired quite poorly in the give-and-take of international diplomacy. Both the Bosnian and Kosovar parties to the Dayton and Rambouillet/Paris negotiations made a number of detailed proposals concerning obligations to apprehend indicted war criminals and to cooperate with the Tribunal, and for the (re)imposition of sanctions for states and entities failing to do so. Other states predictably objected to the inclusion of these provisions in the end. The international community included just enough to meet the test of public scrutiny, but the actors did not consider it an essential element of the negotiation phase of the peace process.

Although the United States harshly criticized the Vance/Owen Peace Plan and UN/EU mediation efforts, when the United States took the lead in peace-building, it continued much of the UN and EU's policy of accommodation and in certain respects moved further in pursuit of a policy of appeasement.

The failure to incorporate the norms of justice into the negotiation process is largely the result of the failure of the peace deal-makers to acknowledge that their interlocutors may be responsible for war crimes, and that it is therefore nearly impossible to negotiate an agreement sufficiently imbued with the norm of justice to create a basis for a real or lasting peace. This lack of recognition of culpability or of the value of justice-based norms led to a minimization of the role of justice during the negotiation process. In hindsight, it can be seen that the general policy of appeasement represented by the "no one is innocent if everyone is to blame" line of argument came to fruition at Dayton—and again at Rambouillet/Paris. In effect, the peace builders forced Alija Izetbegovic to sit with Slobodan Milosevic, the man who had orchestrated the invasion of his country, and with sometimes enemy, sometimes ally, Franjo Tudjman, president of Croatia, and negotiate a peace deal with something in it for everyone.

Simply put, the negotiators may have found themselves compelled to mention the existence of the Yugoslav Tribunal and to urge cooperation with the Tribunal because of public pressure and scrutiny, but they were ultimately unwilling to employ the negotiation process as a means for enhancing the ability of the Tribunal to carry out its functions as this would have undermined their efforts at accommodation.

When the nature of the conflict pits a peace deal (as opposed to a meaningful platform for a lasting peace) against the norms of justice, the current prevailing perspective appears to be that it is better to negotiate a peace deal with those responsible for atrocities than to insist on the inclusion of the norm of justice which may derail the peace process, prolong the conflict, and limit foreign policy options to the use of force and economic sanctions. Even with the establishment and independent operation of justice-based institutions, the peace negotiators perceive these institutions to have value to the extent that they further the short-term policy objectives of the peace makers, with little recognition of their inherent value in sustaining a long-term peace.

In particular, the need to provide some benefit for each party under the approach of accommodation precluded the serious incorporation of justice during UN/EU sponsored mediations and the Dayton and Rambouillet/Paris negotiations. Thus during Dayton, the architects of the peace agreement sat down with Mr. Milosevic in a manner similar to Roosevelt's meeting with Stalin, drank to each other's health, and proceeded to come to an accommodation that would take into account the vested interests of every aggressor in the conflict as well as some of the bystanders. The Bosnians would stop dying in war thereby relieving the Clinton administration of the constant embarrassment of television images of dying or dead civilians in Europe during an election year. The Serbs would be granted half of Bosnia but, in a now typically American diplomatic strategy, it would be called Republika Srpska and would have its own "president" with a small "p" to allow the Serbs to act as if it was a separate state but it would be part of Bosnia to allow the Bosniacs to affirm their country had not been partitioned. Finally, Croatia would regain Vukovar, the last of its Serb-occupied territory, and would be placed on the track to joining European institutions. Bosnian Croats, the smallest minority in Bosnia, would be given an equal share in the Bosnian Federation with the majority Bosniacs. In such an arrangement there was little room for justice.

Importantly, the perceptions and commitments of individual peace builders made an important difference with respect to the role of justice, with Vance and Owen excluding any possible role, while Holbrooke and others used it to the extent that it promoted their interests. Interestingly, although the norm of justice was only minimally incorporated into the Dayton Accords, many government officials considered the norm to be well and adequately represented. This is an indication of both the extent to which it was difficult for U.S. government officials to compel certain parties and some European allies to accept inclusion of the norm and the relative lack of understanding among U.S. government officials as to the extent to which it might be necessary to weave the norm throughout the process in order to ensure that it would function properly to create a lasting peace.

According to many commentators, the failure to actually weave justice throughout the peace agreements sabotaged the possibility of a true peace. As noted by Ed Vulliamy, "the lie of equivalence between perpetrator and victim in a defiled but 'official' history of the Bosnian war" sabotages the prospect for true peace by avoiding a clear reckoning of the truth.[1]

9.   *To what extent did states "learn" during the process of peace-building, in particular to what extent did states re-evaluate the approaches of peace-building and the applicability of various norms?*

Throughout the decade of the 1990s, the peace builders, including the relevant institutions, seemed to be exceptionally slow at recognizing the limits of the various peace-building approaches and the ineffectiveness of certain combinations of approaches. In large part the peace builders were limited in their ability to take certain actions because of the lack of political will on the part of their allies. Despite this frequent justification for a lack of meaningful action, there is little indication that the peace builders actually sought to change the course of engagement.

Notably, throughout the Yugoslav crisis the United States and Europe clung to the failed policy of accommodation and appeasement, and only reluctantly did they draw on the approaches of economic inducements, use of force, and accountability to enhance that process. At all times, however, accommodation remained at the heart of the policy until the spring of 1999 when Mr. Milosevic and his regime were on the brink of another wave of ethnic cleansing. During the first year and a half of the Kosovo crisis, the United States and Europe employed almost the exact same approach as in Bosnia—an approach which they were fully aware had failed to halt genocide and crimes against humanity and by most public accounts was a failed peace process.

The time when the peace builders learned the most from their previous mistakes was when they were forced by actions of the institutions created to give effect to the norm of justice in the peace-building process. In particular, as the Tribunal began to take some action to influence the process, certain actors began to perceive value in the norm of justice and to modify their approach to the peace-building process. Once the Tribunal began to issue indictments, international arrest warrants, and, perhaps most important, press statements, even the most reluctant members of the peace-building process found themselves being pulled down the road toward enforcement, culminating with the NATO arrests beginning in 1997, and the successful application of aid conditionality which ultimately induced both Croatia to turn over thirteen indictees and Serbia, over objections of the FRY, to extradite Mr. Milosevic.

Although some individuals may have learned during the process to believe that force or justice or economic inducements should play a larger role in the process, they were reluctant to change their approach as this would have undermined their proclaimed success in earlier instances of peace-building. Some individuals not directly involved in the earlier negotiations were able to gain insights from the mistakes of others, and they therefore experienced more normative learning. This may explain the marked difference between Secretary of State Albright's belief in a strong role for justice and Ambassador Holbrooke's more utilitarian use of the norm.

In addition, there was also a certain amount of reverse learning in which public officials publicly proclaimed their interest in furthering the norm of justice, and then soon became quite reticent to invest significant political capital in order to ensure adequate inclusion of the norm. In many instances they openly acknowledged that the norm of justice, which they had previously supported, now interfered with their attempts to accommodate the interests of the opposing party in order to reach a "deal."

10. *To what extent did the eventual combination of approaches incorporated in the peace-building process create an effective foundation/framework for post-settlement implementation in Bosnia and Kosovo?*

As noted in the above paragraphs, since the creation of the Tribunal and the negotiation of the Dayton and Rambouillet/Paris Accords, only minimal progress has been made in the reconciliation between the quest for a negotiated peace and the norm of justice. The prevailing norm continues to be accommodation, and the prevailing state of implementation continues to be slow and mediocre.

Because of the need to accommodate the interests of the aggressors, the Dayton Accords created an arcane system of government which institutionalized ethnic identity and provided numerous ethnic vetoes. As a result, Bosnia remains a de facto divided state, with an ineffective central government and continued discrimination and "soft" ethnic cleansing on the local level, which prevents the meaningful return of refugees, freedom of movement, and economic development.

During the initial nineteen months of implementation of the Dayton Accords the IFOR and SFOR forces refused to effectively pursue war criminals as the peace builders were continuing their approach of accommodating the interests of the most powerful party, and the Tribunal because of various limitations was slow to issue further indictments. As a consequence, the indicted war criminals of Karadzic and Mladic, as well as a number of lower-level indictees, continued to exercise power and influence in Bosnia and to undermine the implementation of the accords. Because of this failure of the Office of the Prosecutor, Momcilo Krajisnik was elected as the Serbian representative on the Bosnian presidency and Biljana Plavsic was elected president of the Republic Srpska. It was not until after the conclusion of their terms in office—marked by numerous effective actions aimed at blocking the implementation of the Accords—that they were indicted for genocide against the people of Bosnia. In addition, the failure to arrest the major indicted war criminals also undermined the credibility of both NATO and the Yugoslav Tribunal and eroded any deterrent value they may have had in the early stages of the Kosovo conflict.

With the replacement of John Major by Tony Blair as British prime minister, the government of the United Kingdom began to advocate a more aggressive policy on arresting indicted war criminals. At the same time, IFOR commanders began to perceive some of the indicted war criminals as a threat to IFOR's mission and security. While promoting justice remained a low priority for the NATO troops, the existence of the Yugoslav Tribunal's arrest warrants became a convenient pretext to get rid of certain Bosnian Serb war lords. Thus, nineteen months after its deployment, the British, Dutch, and U.S. NATO forces in Bosnia instituted a new policy of arresting certain indicted war criminals. This not only resulted in several arrests and one death of an indicted war criminal but also induced a number of other indicted persons to turn themselves in. This enhanced mix to peace-building improved the level of Dayton implementation by removing many individuals who impeded its progress.

In the case of Kosovo, the indictment of Mr. Milosevic limited the peace builders' options for accommodation and forced them to give the Kosovars a de facto level of autonomy they might not otherwise possess. Unfortunately, the Office of the Prosecutor was slow to indicate that it continued to possess jurisdiction in Kosovo and thus did not deter crimes against Serbian civilians committed by extremist Kosovars. This reverse ethnic cleansing may undermine prospects for a long-term peace, and dampen the peace builders' willingness to permit Kosovo to attain the level of sovereignty necessary to finally establish peace in the former Yugoslavia.

By the end of 2001, the norm of justice and the approach of accountability had come to play an important part in efforts to resolve the Yugoslav conflict and bring peace to the region. An international tribunal had been created to prosecute those responsible for war crimes, two major peace agreements acknowledged the validity of the Tribunal and pledged all parties to cooperate with it, and the former head of state, as well as many other important war criminals, found themselves either convicted or awaiting trial in the Tribunal's detention center. Importantly, however, the actual effect of the norm of justice was limited by an outdated perception held by the peace builders of the relationship between justice and peace-building, the lack of experience of peace builders in creating and operating institutions of justice, and the lack of an understanding of the important role of justice by some of the key individuals tasked with operating the institutions of justice. In fact, although it is apparent that the rhetoric of justice has permeated the foreign policy-making community, the ability to adequately utilize the norm is inhibited by a prejudicial reliance on accommodation and a reluctance to integrate the various approaches to peace building.

As noted in the introduction, this book has sought to apply the cognitive contextual process method of inquiry to explain the functions of justice in the peace-building process and to ascertain the actual role played by the norm of justice in the Yugoslav peace process. In particular, this book has sought to identify circumstances that either promoted or inhibited the ability of the norm of justice to influence the peace process. As the Yugoslav conflict contained many cycles of violence and peace it provided an important and unique opportunity to examine how much states and institutions have learned during the peace-building process. Given the frequent dissipation of institutional memory of states and institutions involved in peace-building, we hope this book will aid foreign policymakers in ascertaining how best to integrate the norm of justice into future peace-building processes in order to construct a meaningful and durable peace.

Notes

Introduction

1. See Richard J. Goldstone, "The United Nations' War Crimes Tribunal: An Assessment," *Connecticut Journal of International Law* 12 (1997): 233.

2. For a detailed biography of Slobodan Milosevic, see Louis Sell, *Slobodan Milosevic and the Destruction of Yugoslavia* (Durham, N.C.: Duke University Press, 2002).

3. David Owen, *Balkan Odyssey* (New York: Harcourt Brace, 1995), 365.

4. See Fen Osler Hampson, "Can Peace-building Work?" *Cornell International Law Journal* 30 (1997): 701.

Chapter 1

1. Ambassador David J. Scheffer, Address at Dartmouth College, 23 October 1998.

2. Other methods employed by international legal scholars include the critical legal studies, feminist theory, and law and economics approach. For a review of the application of these methods to an assessment of international humanitarian law, see Anne-Marie Burley, "Symposium on Method," *American Journal of International Law* 93 (1993): 394-409.

3. The cognitive contextual process method also draws upon cognitive theory, which asserts that states and individuals can learn from previous experiences, and apply lessons learned to future situations. Cognitive theory assumes that learning from prior successes and failures are constant, and thus almost all elements of policy making are affected by the cognitive process.

4. See Lee Hockstader, "American Voids Order Barring Serb Candidates," *The Washington Post*, 17 September 1997, A1.

5. All policy making, to some degree, can be considered cognitive because states are constantly learning from past policy failures and successes. When studying the cognitive learning process, one must first examine the context in which decision making occurs, specifically whether or not it occurs in a crisis situation or is part of a long-term strategy. When examining foreign policy, cognitive theory scholars frequently choose among the several models of learning, such as causal, diagnostic, or analogical, and among the sev-

eral definitions of learning—what it means to learn and how learning is expressed. For our purposes, we have relied upon a number of different learning models and have applied the standard definition of learning, which can be described as the use of new information that leads to a change in means, but not ends, and involves "a recognition of conflicts among values [that] leads to a modification of goals as well as means." Jack Levy, "Learning and Foreign Policy: Sweeping a Conceptual Minefield," *International Organization* (spring 1994) 48: 279-312.

6. The most state centric international relations method is realism, which, as a political and doctrinal reaction to Wilsonian idealism or legal-moralism, maintains that states primarily behave as egoists, and the character and content of international relationships is therefore primarily determined by respective state power. See Hans Morgenthau, *Politics among Nations: The Struggle for Power and Peace* (New York: McGraw-Hill, 1993); Edward H. Carr, *The Twenty Years' Crisis 1919-1939: An Introduction to the Study of International Relations* (New York: HarperCollins Publishers, 1939); George Kennan, *American Diplomacy, 1900-1950* (Chicago: University of Chicago Press, 1951); See Kenneth N. Waltz, *Theory of International Politics* (New York: McGraw-Hill, 1979). With respect to international institutions or regimes, such as the Yugoslav Tribunal, realism posits that where an international regime is created by sovereign states, that regime may itself also exercise some degree of independent power, although it generally functions within the power matrix responsible for its creation.

7. In addition to being instructed by realism, these axioms are also deduced from game theory, which is a branch of applied mathematics concerned with modeling social and political interaction with game-like situations wherein participants seek to maximize some benefit or utility and their ability to do so is affected by the decisions of other players who also, cooperatively or uncooperatively, seek to maximize their own benefit or utility. In order to model a social or political interaction as a game, game theory requires the identification of the players, each of whom has a choice of strategies, the pursuit of which will lead to varying payoffs and the value of which is dependent upon the strategies selected by the other players. In making moves and choosing among strategies, players are considered to be acting in a rational manner for the purpose of achieving a set of ordered preferences. See generally, Peter Ordeshook, *Game Theory and Political Theory* (Cambridge: Cambridge University Press, 1986).

8. Not all scholars agree that governments, or even organizations, can learn. As Jack S. Levy argues, "the rectification of learning to the collective level—and the assumption that organizations or governments can be treated as organisms that have goals, beliefs, and memories—is not analytically viable. . . . They learn only through the individuals who serve in those organizations." Levy, "Learning and Foreign Policy," 287.

9. Although the subsequent development of neo-realism, often referred to as systems theory or structural realism, significantly modified the original school of realism, the basic premise of realism, that states will act to serve their self-interest, remains valid.

10. Support for the multidimensional nature of state players, the development of a state's ordered preferences, and the nesting of various related games can be found in game theory. See G. Schneider, "Getting Closer at Different Speeds: Strategic Interaction in Widening European Integration," in *Game Theory and International Relations: Preferences, Information and Empirical Evidence*, eds. P. Allan and C. Schmidt (Brookfield, Vt.: E. Elgar 1994), 128. See also R. Putnam, "Diplomacy and Domestic Politics," *International Organization* (1988): 427; K. Iida, *Two-Level Games with Uncertainty: An Extension of Putnam's Theory* (1991); V. Aggarwal and P. Allan, "Preferences, Constraints and Games: Analyzing Polish Debt Negotiations with International Banks." *Game The-*

ory and International Relations: Preferences, Information and Empirical Evidence. P. Allan and C. Schmidt eds. (Brookfield, VT.: E. Elgar, 1994), 10. Game theorists have attempted to integrate systematic and sub-systematic analysis by developing collective-choice models and multi level games. See Lars-Erik Cederman, "Unpacking the National Interest," in *Ordinal Games, Game Theory and International Relations: Preferences, Information and Empirical Evidence 50,* P. Allan and C. Schmidt eds. (Brookfield, Vt.: E. Elgar, 1994), 65-69; Schneider, "Getting Closer at Different Speeds," 126.

11. Legal theorists adopting the mantle of liberal theory have recently attempted to construct a theoretical framework to examine the creation and application of international law, providing due consideration of various factors they believe are excluded from traditional international relations theory and international law, including individuals, corporations, nongovernmental organizations, political and economic ideologies and interdependence. See Anne-Marie Burley, "International Law and International Relations Theory: A Dual Agenda," *American Journal of International Law* 87 (1993): 227. See also C. Chinkin and R. Sadurska, "The Anatomy of International Dispute Resolution," *Ohio St. Journal on Dispute Resolution* 7 (1991): 39.

12. Liberalism essentially parallels classical social liberalism/utilitarianism, analogizing states to people. Accordingly, individual state actors have preferences, and rationally adjust their means/policies to secure those preferences—a process which certain a priori rights allow them to pursue.

13. According to liberalism, structures of governance, such as norms and institutions of international law, exist to protect each state's rights, but also to prevent any state's pursuit of preference from compromising any other state's rights through acts such as invasion or restraint of trade.

14. This notion is well reflected in the traditional approach to international law which as articulated by George Schwarzenberger, views international law as "a body of mutually advantageous rules of social conduct," and by Hans Kelsen who elaborated that this body of rules of social conduct is broadly considered to constitute "a system of norms which prescribe or permit a certain conduct for states." G. Schwarzenberger, *The Frontiers of International Law* (1961), 41; Hans Kelsen, *Principles of International Law* (New York: Holt, Rinehart, and Winston, 1966), 17. This system of norms then "affords a framework, a pattern, a fabric for international society, grown out of relations in turn," which serves to guide and limit state action, but seldom controls their behavior. Consistent with the realist-based perspective, the primary function of international law is to promote stability and order between nation-states. Importantly, principles and norms are only imbued with the status of international law when they are agreed upon by states—either in the form of customary international law or through bilateral and multilateral treaties, or in rare instances as principles holding the status of jus cogens. Louis Henkin, *How Nations Behave: Law and Foreign Policy* (New York: Columbia University Press, 1979), 5, 24, 29, 41-47. See also J. Brierly, *The Law of Nations* (1963), 56.

15. Game theory, in particular, acknowledges the need to identify and enforce rules (i.e., norms) which govern the game of peace-building—such as the laws of war and the justifications for and limits on the use of force. Game theory further recognizes that participants in the game of peace-building may attempt to create additional rules (norms) in order to promote their self-interest and to achieve their short- and long-term objective—such as the more defined set of rules relating to the jurisdiction of and rules of procedure for the Yugoslav Tribunal. See generally, Ordeshook, *Game Theory and Political Theory.*

16. Of the various international relations theories, regime theory is the most preoccupied with the formation and operation of international structures or regimes operat-

ing to shape state behavior. For a concise review of the development of regime theory, see Burley, "International Law and International Relations Theory," 217-18 (referring to the early regime theorists as modified structural realists). For a more detailed examination of the development of regime theory and its limitations, see F. Kratochwill and J. Ruggie, "International Organization: A State of the Art on an Art of the State," *International Organizations* 40 (1986): 753.

17. Importantly, the constructivist approach seeks to promote an understanding of how policy, or what theorists call patterns of practice or social agency, plays a part in determining which behavioral norms actually constrain social behavior. Moreover, constructivism provides insight into how patterns of practice translate into a sense of which norms have priority and bind most firmly, a concept which has been described as norm salience.

18. The policy-oriented approach to international legal theory, also known as the New Haven School, supports the idea of examining in detail the context of the peace-building process as identity as it argues that the role of law is best understood by a comprehensive examination, from the perspective of the decision maker, of the nature and formation of international law in light of the process creating such law and the functions that it is intended to serve. In particular, the policy-oriented approach defines law as a process for social and political decision making, but limits that process to authoritative and effective decisions (e.g., those based on the principle of "rightness" and having actual effect). Since law is concerned with social choices determined by the perceptions of rightness or values of a particular community and is created from below (i.e., from the action of individual states), and not from above (i.e., from natural law or supranational organizations), the intellectual focus of the policy-oriented approach is on the myriad of social and political factors that should be considered by domestic policymakers confronted with international decisions. See M. Reisman, "The View from the New Haven School of International Law," *Proceed. ASIL* 86 (1992): 119-23. See also Harold Lasswell and Myers McDougal, *Jurisprudence for a Free Society* (New York: Kluwer Academic Publishers, 1992). Lung-Chu Chen, *An Introduction to Contemporary International Law: A Policy Oriented Perspective* (New Haven, Conn.: Yale University Press, 1989), 14-15; Myers McDougal and Associates, *Studies in World Public Order* (New York: Kluwer Academics Publishers, 1960); Myers McDougal, *International Law, Power and Policy: A Contemporary Conception* (RCADI, 1953), 137. For a review of the origins and subsequent development of the policy-oriented approach, See Burley, "International Law and International Relations Theory," 209-12.

19. Illustrative of the precedent for such inquiry is the international legal process method, which asserts an understanding of the role of international law can be discerned through the examination of the four questions: (1) in what manner is the authority to make foreign policy decisions allocated among competent authorities? (2) why has a particular regulatory arrangement been adopted for a specific subject-matter area as opposed to another regulatory arrangement or no arrangement at all? (3) how do particular institutions and the international legal system as a whole restrain and organize national and individual behavior? And (4) what are the elements of "the political, economic and cultural setting that predispose to success or failure in that development?" These four questions are paraphrased from Abram Chayes, Thomas Ehrlich, and Andreas Lowenfeld, *International Legal Process: Materials for an Introductory Course* (Boston: Little Brown, 1989) xii, cited by Mary Ellen O'Connell, "New International Legal Process," *American Journal of International Law* 93 (1999): 336-37.

20. The analogical reasoning approach, often used in cognitive theory, holds that

states and individuals draw upon past occurrences and experiences as a means of making decisions regarding current issues and problems, especially when there are structural similarities in the events. For the purposes of this study it thus becomes very important to determine how states use their past experiences as a reference point for analyzing and justifying their actions in current conflicts. Though it is difficult to define what exactly learning consists of, and whether or not it has in fact occurred, it is arguably the case that militaries analyze previous wars to better conduct future ones, and states search for lessons, such as those learned from Munich or Vietnam, in order to prevent repeating diplomatic or strategic mistakes. It is also fairly clear that the perceptions of states and their views of past events can cloud their analysis and decision-making choices.

21. Regime theory, in its contemporary form, posits that the use of power by states is constrained and shaped by interrelated international regimes, which are in effect sets of shared "implicit or explicit principles, norms, rules, and decision making procedures around which actors' expectations converge in a given area of international relations." S. Krasner, *Structural Causes and Regime Consequences: Regimes as Intervening Variables in International Regimes* (1983), 1, 2; See also Robert Keohane, *The Demand for International Regimes in International Institutions and State Power* (Boulder, Colo.: Westview Press, 1989), 101; Oran Young, *International Cooperation: Building Regimes for Natural Resources and the Environment* (Ithaca, N.Y.: Cornell University Press, 1989). For an overview of regime theory, See M. List and V. Rittberger, *Regime Theory and International Environment and Management, in the International Politics of the Environment: Actors, Interests, and Institutions,* ed. A. Hurrell and B. Kingsbury (Oxford: Oxford University Press, 1992). See Ethan Nadelman, "Global Prohibition Regimes: The Evolution of Norms in International Society," *International Organization* 44 (1990): 479; F. Kratochwill, *Rules, Norms, and Decisions: On the Conditions of Practical and Legal Reasoning in International Relations and Domestic Affairs* (1989).

22. For the element of process, the approach of constructivism is most relevant. Constructivism, a relatively new theoretical perspective, draws on the strengths of realism and liberalism while seeking to expand the theoretical horizon to encompass as many relevant variables of state and substate actor behavior as possible. Like the approach of realism, constructivism holds that political outcomes do correlate with actors' interests. However, constructivism departs from realism by holding that the principal constraint on actors' interests does not lie in "power," but rather in a system of necessary social norms which emerge from the patterns and substance of political interaction.

23. The international legal process approach, derived from the American legal process approach developed in the late 1920s and early 1930s to help ascertain the relationship between domestic law and society, in particular the role of law and how it operated, seeks to answer the same questions about international law, in particular how it operates within the international political system, and its relationship to other factors influencing the development of foreign policy. See Henry Hart Jr. and Albert Sacks, *The Legal Process: Basic Problems in the Making and Application of Law,* ed. Williams Eskridge, Jr. and Philip P. Frickey (Westbury, N.Y.: Foundation Press, 1994). For an application of the international legal process approach to international humanitarian law, see O'Connell, "New International Legal Process," 334-51. The founding text of the international legal process method is Chayes, Ehrlich, and Lowenfeld, *International Legal Process.*

24. Although constructivism relies on a description of agents constrained by structure to draw conclusions, it acknowledges that these agents are capable of altering structure through their actions. As such, constructivism may aid in the development of the necessary tools to draw a connection between human behavior, the frames with which

states and substate actors interpret their social and political world, and the social and political interaction which molds and conditions these interpretative frames. At its essence, constructivism might be characterized as explaining world politics from the perspective of a perpetually modified interactive causal loop:
Social interaction (Patterns of Practice) → Norms (Expectations about Behavior) →Actors' Identities (Who Am I?) →Actors' Interests (What Do I Want/Need?) → Social interaction (Patterns of Practice). See Peter Howard and Ramzi Nemo, "Norms of Denationalized Security in the New NATO" (Revised paper presented at 2001 Meeting of the International Studies Association, Chicago, Ill.: February 2001), relying upon Martha Finnemore, *National Interest in International Society* (Ithaca, N.Y.: Cornell University Press, 1996) and Alexander Wendt, *Social Theory of International Politics* (Cambridge, U.K.: Cambridge University Press, 1999).
25. Reuters, 11 December 1996.

Chapter 2

1. Interview with General William Nash, by Michael Scharf, Cambridge, Massachusetts, 29 September 1998.
2. Vulliamy, *The Crime of Appeasement*, 89 (quoting Justice Goldstone).
3. See Richard J. Goldstone, "Justice as a Tool for Peace-Making: Truth Commissions and International Criminal Tribunals," *N.Y.U Journal of International Law and Policy* 28 (1996): 486.
4. *"The War Crimes Commission's Final Report,"* U.N. Doc. S/1994/674 (27 May 1994).
5. U.S. Department of State, "Erasing History: Ethnic Cleansing in Kosovo," <http://www.state.gov/index.html> (1999). See also, James Rubin, "Responsibility of Individual Yugoslav Army and Ministry of Internal Affairs Commanders for Crimes Committed by Forces under Their Command in Kosovo," U.S. Department of State <http://www.state.gov/index.html> (1999); James Rubin, "Press Briefing on Massacre of Kosovar Albanians," U.S. Department of State <http://www.state.gov/index.html> (1999); Amb. David Scheffer, "On-the Record Briefing on Atrocities in Kosovo," *US Department of State* <http://www.state.gov/index.html> (1999); U.S. Department of State, "The Ethnic Cleansing in Kosovo: Fact Sheet Based on Information from U.S. Government Sources" <http://www.state.gov/index.html> (1999).
6. Karadzic and Mladic (IT-95-5) "Bosnia and Herzegovina," Initial indictment (July 1995), 24.
7. Hampson, "Can Peace Building Work?" 714.
8. Hampson, "Can Peace Building Work?" 714.
9. For a concise summary of the Milosevic propaganda campaign, see Georgie Anne Geyer, "How the Conscience of the West Was Lost," in *The Conceit of Innocence Losing the Conscience of the West in the War against Bosnia,* ed. Stjepan G. Meštović (College Station: Texas A&M University Press, 1997), 91-95.
10. For a review of the use of media by all three parties, see Mark Thompson, *Forging War: The Media in Serbia, Croatia and Bosnia-Herzegovina* (London: University of Luton, 1994), 271.
11. Warren Zimmermann, *Origins of a Catastrophe: Yugoslavia and Its Destroyers— America's Last Ambassador Tells What Happened and Why* (New York: Crown Publishing

Group, 1996), 120. According to Ambassador Zimmerman, "Those who argue that ancient Balkan hostilities account for the violence that overtook and destroyed Yugoslavia ignore the power of television in the service of officially provoked racism."

12. For a comprehensive refutation of the myth of the "bubbling over of ancient ethnic hatreds," see Donia and Fine, *Bosnia-Herzegovina*. For a more concise refutation, see Geyer, "How the Conscience of the West Was Lost," 91-95.

13. For example, according to Carol Hodge, in 1991, Robert Wareing, a member of the House of Commons Select Committee on Foreign Affairs publicly informed the House of Commons that the 1992 bread line massacre in Sarajevo, which killed 20 Muslim civilians, was carried out by Muslims to gain sympathy from the world community and increase antipathy toward Serbia. Carol Hodge, "The Serb Lobby in the United Kingdom," *12 Donald W. Treadgold Papers, Russian, East European, and Central Asian Studies* (September 1999), 13.

14. For examples of State Department reporting on Serbian propaganda, see Department of State Cable number Belgrade 01209 151953, 15 February 1994 (declassified 31 March 1997); Department of State Cable number Belgrade 01232 162107Z, 16 February 1994 (declassified 31 March 1997); Department of State Cable number Belgrade 05955 071806, October 1994 (declassified 17 February 1998).

15. For a dense, but useful, assessment of the extent to which Serbian misrepresentations found their way into the political decision-making process, see David Campbell, *National Deconstruction: Violence, Identity and Justice in Bosnia* (Minneapolis: University of Minnesota Press, 1998). See also, Rudi J. Rumiz, *Maschere per un Massacro: Quello che non Abbiamo Voluto Sapere della Guerra in Jugoslavia* (Rome: Editori Riunit, 1996), 166; see Kjell Arild Nilsen, *Europas Svik: Et Oppgjor med Vestlig Unnfallenhet I Bosnia* (Oslo: Spartacus, 1996). A typical example of the absorption of Serbian propaganda by government officials is former U.S. secretary of state Lawrence Eagleburger's statement in July 1995 just after the Srebrenica massacre that, "they have been killing each other with a certain amount of glee in that part of the world for some time now." Televised interview with Charlie Rose, 13 July 1995, Charlie Rose Transcript #1420, 1995 Thirteen/WNET, cited in Michael Sells, *The Bridge Betrayed: Religion and Genocide in Bosnia* (Berkeley: University of California Press, 1996), 124.

16. See for example, Secretary of State Warren Christopher at the opening statement at a news conference on 10 February 1993 entitled "New Steps toward Conflict Resolution in the Former Yugoslavia" where he proclaimed, "Those circumstances have deep roots. The death of [Yugoslav] President Tito and the end of communist domination of the former Yugoslavia raised the lid on the cauldron of ancient ethnic hatreds. This is a land where at least three religions and a half-dozen ethnic groups have vied across the centuries. It was the birthplace of World War I. It has long been a cradle of European conflict, [and] it remains so today." See also Interview of Secretary of State Warren Christopher by Mr. Roger Mudd, "MacNeil/Lehrer Newshour," 11 August 1993, where he declared, "In Bosnia, there are such ancient hatreds that evidently the ethnic groups want to try to divide it and be in separate enclaves. That will be a decision that they will have to make, and it's very hard to dictate that from a distance" and, Remarks by U.S. Secretary of State Warren Christopher at the Conference on Security and Cooperation in Europe Plenary Session on 30 November 1993, where he proclaimed, "We call upon all warring parties to stop their unconscionable conduct that blocks the delivery of critically needed supplies through [Tuzla airport]. We also call upon the warring parties to live up to their recently signed agreements to permit secure land access for relief convoys. The warring parties must see that this is in their best interests. Full access will serve the vital

needs of all Bosnia's factions." Even President Clinton found himself adopting the notions of warring factions and civil war in an exchange with reporters, where he declared, "But there will not be—the killing is a function of a political fight between three factions. Until they agree to quit doing it, it's going to continue. I don't think that the international community has the capacity to stop people within the nation from their civil war until they decide to do it." "Exchange with Reporters, 24 January 1994," *Public Papers of the Presidents of the United States*, William J. Clinton 1993, Book I, 122.

17. See Geyer, "How the Conscience of the West Was Lost," 91.

18. According to David Rohde, "A key element in Janvier's thinking was an apparent belief that he could do business with the Bosnian Serbs. Janvier may have turned down the crucial request for Close Air Support on the night before the town fell because he sincerely believed General Tolimir's promise the Serb attack had stopped. Janvier was quick to believe Serb propaganda and Mladic's complaints about Muslim provocations, according to aides. Janvier argued in the 9 June meeting in Split that the Serbs would no longer defy the UN if they were treated with respect." David Rohde, *Endgame the Betrayal and Fall of Srebrenica, Europe's Worst Massacre since World War II* (Boulder, Colo.: Westview Press, 1997), 367.

19. Wesley K. Clark, *Waging Modern War: Bosnia, Kosovo, and the Future Combat* (Reading, Mass.: Perseus, 2001), 68.

20. Department of State Cable number Belgrade 01232 162107Z, 16 February 1994 (declassified 31 March 1997).

21. Jurek Martin, "Holbrooke Sees 'Tough Slog' to Peace in Bosnia," *Financial Times*, 2 November 1995.

22. Robert Burns, "Clinton to Serbs: Rethink Milosevic," Associated Press, 27 June 1999).

23. *International Tribunal for the Former Yugoslavia, First Annual Report*, U.N. Doc. IT/68 (28 July 1994): para. 16.

24. Michael Walzer, *Just and Unjust Wars* (New York: Basic Books, 1979), 287-88.

25. Goldstone, "Justice as a Tool for Peace-Making," 490.

26. For an important discussion of how the citizens of Serbia have managed to psychologically shield themselves from the atrocities committed in their name, see Peter Morgan, *A Barrel of Stones: In Search of Serbia* (Aberystwyth, U.K.: Planet Books, 1997).

27. Graham Blewitt, deputy prosecutor of the International Criminal Tribunal for the Former Yugoslavia, Interview by Michael Scharf, The Hague, Netherlands, 25 July 1996.

28. Carlotta Gall, "Crisis in the Balkans: The Church," *New York Times*, 29 June 1999.

29. Department of State Cable number State 092092 080354z, April 94 (declassified 23 December 1996).

30. Warren Christopher, *In the Stream of History: Shaping Foreign Policy for a New Era* (Stanford, Calif.: Stanford University Press, 1998), 352.

31. See Hodge, "The Serb Lobby in the United Kingdom," 32.

32. Unnamed British UNPROFOR officer, Reuters, 10 November 1996. Not every military officer shared this view. As noted by General Clark in his memoirs, "[Mladic] carried a reputation among the UN forces for cunning and forcefulness, I found him coarse and boastful. He know far less than he thought about NATO, airpower, and the capabilities of the United States." Clark, *Waging Modern War*, 58

33. Michael Ignatieff, "Articles of Faith, Index on Censorship," (reprinted in 294 *Harper's Magazine*, 15 March 1997).

34. "Report to the President from Justice Robert H. Jackson, Chief of Counsel for the United States in the Prosecution of Axis War Criminals, 7 June 1945," *American Journal of International Law* 39 (Supp. 1945): 178.

35. See Neil J. Kritz, "The Rule of Law in the Postconflict Phase, *in Managing Global Chaos,* eds. Chester A. Crocker, Fenn Osler Hamson, and Pamela Aal, eds. (Washington, D.C.: U.S. Institute of Peace Press, 1996), 598-99.

36. Justice Richard Goldstone, *Healing Wounded People* (speech at the United States Holocaust Memorial Museum, 27 January 1997).

37. Michael Dobbs, "Serbs Shun Discussion of Atrocities," *The Washington Post,* 24 June 1999, A1.

38. Ambassador David Scheffer, Address at Dartmouth University, 23 October 1998.

39. Yugoslav Tribunal, *Joint Statement by the President and the Prosecutor,* U.N. Doc. CC/PIO/027-E (24 November 1995).

40. Richard Goldstone, "Fifty Years after Nuremberg: A New International Criminal Tribunal for Human Rights Criminals," in *Contemporary Genocides: Causes, Cases, Consquences,* ed. Albert J. Jongman (Ledien: PIOMM, 1996), 215.

41. President of the Tribunal, "First Annual Report of the International Criminal Tribunal for the Former Yugoslavia," para. 15.

42. BBC Broadcast, "Survivors Condemn 'Lenient' Verdict," 2 August 2001, 20:11 GMT 21:11 U.K.

43. Goldstone, "Justice as a Tool for Peace-Making," 499.

44. David J. Scheffer, "International Judicial Intervention," *Foreign Policy* 102 (1996): 34.

45. "War Crimes Prosecutor Says Tribunal May Have Deterred Violations," Deutsche Presse-Agentur, 26 January 1996.

46. Justice Richard Goldstone, Interview in Brussels, Belgium, by Michael Scharf, 20 July 1996.

47. See Payam Akhvan, "Justice in the Hague, Peace in the Former Yugoslavia?" *An Essay on the United Nations War Tribunal* (1997), 9.

48. William Horne, "The Real Trial of the Century," *American Lawyer* (September 1995): 5.

49. By rule of law, one generally assumes the presence of an independent judiciary that is transparent, predictable, and impartial to the parties involved. The rule of law also relies upon a legitimate, representative government to enforce the judiciary's decisions. This should be distinguished from rule by law, through which authoritarian governments often use the legal system to legitimate their oppression. See Kritz, *The Rule of Law in the Postconflict Phase.*

50. In the cases of Chile and Argentina, for example, "the prospect of trials for the gross violations of human rights perpetrated under the old regime provoked bald threats of military intervention." Kritz, *The Rule of Law in the Postconflict Phase,* 595.

51. The South African Truth Commission is the most successful example of this type of justice. Established with a two-year mandate, the commission has strict criteria for whether or not applicants qualify for indemnity in return for their testimony. There has to have been a political motive for the applicant to have committed human rights violations and there must be some degree of proportionality between that motive and the offenses committed. At the time of this writing over 4,500 applications for indemnity had been received by the commission. See Goldstone, "Justice as a Tool for Peace-Making."

52 For a detailed accounting of "Serbian rape warfare" constructed from interviews

with victims of mass rape, see Seada Vranic, *Breaking the Wall of Silence: The Voices of Raped Bosnia* (Zagreb: Izdanja Antibabarus, 1996). See also, Alexandra Stiglmayer, ed., *Mass Rape: The War against Women in Bosnia-Herzegovina* (Lincoln: University of Nebraska Press, 1994); Maria Von Welser, *Am Ende Wunschst du dir nur noch den Tod: Die Massenvergewaltigungen im Drieg auf dem Balkan* (Munich: Knaur, 1993); and Beverly Allen, *Rape Warfare: The Hidden Genocide in Bosnia-Herzegovina and Croatia* (Minneapolis: University of Minnesota Press, 1996).

Chapter 3

1. See Secretary-General, "Report Pursuant to General Assembly Resolution 53/35," *Srebrenica Report.*

2. Secretary-General, "Report Pursuant to General Assembly Resolution 53/35," *Srebrenica Report.*

3. Owen, *Balkan Odyssey,* 33.

4. See Yves Heller, *Des Brasiers mal éteints: Un reporter dans les guerres yougo-slaves 1991-95* (Paris: Le Monde, 1997). For a firsthand account by a British officer of the conflict resulting from the Vance Owen Peace Plan, see Colonel Bob Stewart, *Broken Lives: A Personal View of the Bosnian Conflict* (New York: HarperCollins, 1994).

5. See "Week in Review October 17-23," *Balkan Watch,* 24 October 1994.

6. According to David Rohde, "The series of statements and proposals made by Janvier before, during and after Srebrenica's fall indicate he may have intentionally allowed the safe area to fall." Rohde, *Endgame,* 364. Rohde acknowledges though that "Taking the extraordinary step of deciding to sacrifice a UN safe area on his own without the permission of his superiors does not fit into Janvier's character, according to supporters and detractors. 'This was a man who should've been selling roasted chestnuts on the streets of Paris,' said one former UNPROFOR official. 'Not making these kinds of decisions.'" Rohde, *Endgame,* 368. Rohde also noted that "Suspicions about what U.S. intelligence knew about the attack on Srebrenica and subsequent executions have been high. The CIA, the theory goes, knew of the pending attack and knew the town would fall. The United States then stood by as Srebrenica fell and an enclave that didn't fit into Anthony Lake's endgame strategy was eliminated. Aerial photos of suspected mass graves, according to the theory, were suppressed until after the executions were well over to avoid embarrassment and the United States being called on to stop the killing." Rohde, *Endgame,* 368-69.

7. Chuck Sudetic, "Why Is France Protecting Indicted War Criminals in the Sector of Bosnia It Controls?" *Atlantic Monthly,* (April 2000).

8. General Lewis MacKenzie, "Testimony before the U.S. House Armed Services Committee," Washington, D.C., 26 May 1993.

9. Sir John Nott, former British defense minister, *Reuters,* 26 November 1994, "Week in Review November 21-27," *Balkan Watch,* 28 November 1994.

10. Ed Vulliamy, *Bosnia: The Crime of Appeasement,* 81.

11. Geyer, "How the Conscience of the West Was Lost," 82-83.

12. For a detailed accounting of the constraints involved in the use of force, see Clark, *Waging Modern War.*

13. Walzer, *Just and Unjust Wars,* 62.

14. See generally Clark, *Waging Modern War*.

15. For a critical Secretary-General's UN report on the failure of UNPROFOR to prevent the Srebrenica massacre, see Secretary-General, "Report Pursuant to General Assembly Resolution 53/35," *Srebrenica Report*. For an edited diary recounting the activities of the UNPROFOR mission in Srebrenica, see Herman Veenhof, ed., *Srebrenica Oorlogsdagboek van Piet Hein Both*, (Barneveld: De Vuurbakk, 1995).

16. For a comprehensive critique of the arguments in favor of the arms embargo see Norman Cigar, *The Right to Defence: Thoughts on the Bosnian Arms Embargo* (London: Alliance Publishers, Ltd., for the Institute for European Defence and Strategic Studies, 1995).

17. "Week in Review November 28-December 4," *Balkan Watch* 1, no. 13 (5 December 1994).

18. Joshua Goldstein and John Pevehouse, "Reciprocity, Bullying, and International Cooperation: Time-Series Analysis of the Bosnia Conflict," *American Political Science Review* 91, no: 3 (September 1997): 527.

19. Goldstein and Pevehouse, "Reciprocity, Bullying, and International Cooperation," 527.

20. Radio Free Europe, *Only the Bombing Got Rid of Milosevic*, South Slavic Report, 8 February 2001, vol. 3, no. 5.

21. Bill Nichols, "For Clinton, Bosnia Offers Risky Move," *USA Today*, 9 December 1994; "Week in Review December 5-11," *Balkan Watch* 1, no. 14 (12 December 1994). For a discussion of the contradiction between the moralistic impulse and a lack of collective will to use (some) force on the part of the international community which led to the Srebrenica massacre, see Jan Willem Honig and Norbert Both, *Srebrenica: Record of a War Crime* (London: Viking Penguin, 1996).

22. For a first-hand account of the siege of Bihac see Brendan O'Shea, *Crisis at Bihać: Bosnia's Bloody Battlefield* (Stroud: Sutton Publishing, 1998).

23. Anonymous, "Human Rights in Peace Negotiations," *Human Rights Quarterly* (1997): 255.

24. Keith Doubt, "We Had to Jump over the Moral Bridge: Bosnia and the Pathetic Hegemony of Face-Work," in *The Conceit of Innocence Losing the Conscience of the West in the War against Bosnia*, ed. Stjepan G. Meštović (College Station: Texas A&M University Press, 1995), 121.

25. Doubt, "We Had to Jump over the Moral Bridge," 121.

26. See Vahakn N. Dadrian, "The Historical and Legal Interconnections between the Armenian Genocide and the Jewish Holocaust: From Impunity to Retributive Justice," *Yale Journal of International Law* 23 (1998): 503. Initially, the Allied Powers sought the prosecution of those responsible for the massacres. The Treaty of Sèvres, which was signed on 10 August 1920, would have required the Turkish government to hand over those responsible to the Allied Powers for trial. See "Treaty of Peace between the Allied Powers and Turkey (Treaty of Sèvres), 10 August 1920," reprinted in *American Journal of International Law* 15, no. 179 (Supp. 1921). The Treaty of Sèvres was, however, not ratified and did not come into force. It was replaced by the Treaty of Lausanne, which not only did not contain provisions respecting the punishment of war crimes, but was accompanied by a "Declaration of Amnesty" of all offenses committed between 1914 and 1922. See "Treaty of Peace between the Allied Powers and Turkey (Treaty of Lausanne), 24 July 1923, League of Nations Treaty Series 11," reprinted in *American Journal of International Law* 18, no. 1 (Supp. 1924).

27. See M. Cherif Bassiouni, *Crimes against Humanity in International Criminal Law* (Boston: Kluwer Law International, 1992), 228-30. During the war of Bangladesh's inde-

pendence, West Pakistan troops killed approximately one million East Pakistanis who supported efforts to establish the independent nation of Bangladesh. India and Bangladesh initially agreed to bring charges of genocide and crimes against humanity against 195 of the 10,000 Pakistani troops who had been captured by India. Meanwhile, Pakistan filed a case before the International Court of Justice to compel India to repatriate the Pakistani troops. Ultimately, political considerations prevailed and in 1973 Bangladesh and India agreed not to prosecute the Pakistani prisoners in exchange for political recognition of Bangladesh by Pakistan and the withdrawal of Pakistan's case against India before the International Court of Justice. See Bassiouni, *Crimes against Humanity*, 228-30.

28. See Naomi Roht-Arriaza, "State Responsibility to Investigate and Prosecute Grave Human Rights Violations in International Law," *California Law Review* 451 (1990): 451, 458-61, 484.

29. See Naomi Roht-Arriaza, *Conclusion: Combating Impunity, Impunity and Human Rights* (New York: Oxford University Press, 1995), 299-300.

30. See Adalbert Rückerl, *The Investigation of Nazi War Crimes 1945-1978* (Hamden, Conn.: Archon Books, 1980), 135 n. 6. The Nuremberg trials include the trial of the major Nazis before the International Military Tribunal and the twelve subsequent trials at Nuremberg (August 1946-April 1949) under the authority of Allied Control Council Law No. 10.

31. Peter Harlan Maguire, *Law and War: An American Story*, (New York: Columbia University Press, 2000), Chapter V, n. 93.

32. Anonymous, *Human Rights in Peace Negotiations*, 256.

33. See Jean E. Manas, "The Impossible Trade-off: 'Peace' versus 'Justice' in Settling Yugoslavia's War," in *The World and Yugoslavia's Wars*, ed. Richard H. Ullman. (New York: Council on Foreign Relations, 1996).

34. Akhvan, "Justice in the Hague," 1-2.

35. See Laurie Cohen, Application of the Realist and Liberal Perspectives to the Implementation of War Crimes Trials: Case Studies of Nuremberg and Bosnia." *UCLA Journal of International Law and Foreign Affairs* 2 (1997): 154 (citing Mirko Klarin, "The Moral Case for a War Crimes Tribunal," *Wall Street Journal Europe*, 17 March 1994).

36. Goldstone, "Justice as a Tool for Peace-Making," 488.

37. See Charles G. Boyd, "Making Bosnia Work," *Foreign Affairs* 77 (January/February 1998): 1.

38. Goldstone, "Justice as a Tool for Peace-Making," 488. See also Floyd Abrams and Diane F. Orentlicher, "In Cambodia, as in Bosnia, Issue Is Punish or Pardon," *Los Angeles Times*, 15 September 1996, 1M.

39. Department of State "Final Genocide q/a," Press Guidance, drafted 25 October 1993 (Released 13 December 1998).

40. See Richard Holbrooke, *To End a War* (Toronto: Random House, 1997), 367.

41. Holbrooke, "Hearing of the Senate Foreign Relations Committee Subject: Nomination of Richard Holbrooke as U.S. Ambassador to the United Nations," 24 June 1999.

42. Holbrooke, "Hearing of the Senate Foreign Relations Committee Subject: Nomination of Richard Holbrooke as U.S. Ambassador to the United Nations," 24 June 1999.

43. Brendan Simms, *Unfinest Hour: Britain and the Bosnian War* (London: Allen Lane, 2001). For a more detailed discussion of the approach of "saving lives" and the "man on the ground" argument, see chapter 5 entitled "The Men on the Ground."

44. Simms, *Unfinest Hour*.

45. Anonymous, *Human Rights in Peace Negotiations*, 256.

46. Anonymous, *Human Rights in Peace Negotiations*, 257.

47. Hampson, "Can Peace Work?" 712.

48. Hampson, "Can Peace Work?" 712 (citing generally William Zartman, ed., *Elusive Peace: Negotiating an End to Civil War* [Washington, D.C.: Brookings Institute, 1995]). See also, Donald Horowitz, *Ethnic Groups in Conflict* (Berkeley: University of California Press, 1985); Timothy Sisk, *Power Sharing and International Mediation in Ethnic Conflicts* (New York: Carnegie Corporation, 1996); David Lake and Donald Rothchild, "Containing Fear: The Origins and Management of Ethnic Conflict," *International Security* (fall 1996): 41; Neil J. Kritz, ed., *Transitional Justice: How Emerging Democracies Reckon with Former Regimes* (Washington, D.C.: U.S. Institute of Peace Press, 1995), 82-103, 292-334, 375-438. Cf. Timothy Mak, "The Case against an International War Crimes Tribunal for Former Yugoslavia," *International Peacekeeping* 2 (1995): 536.

49. Akhvan, "Justice in The Hague," 3-4.

50. Goldstone, "The United Nations' War Crimes Tribunals," 233-34.

51. For a review of the failings of amnesties, See Aryeh Neier, *War Crimes, Brutality, Genocide, Terror, and the Struggle for Justice* (New York: Random House, 1998), 96-107.

52. See Dadrian, "The Historical and Legal Interconnections between the Armenian Genocide and the Jewish Holocaust," 532.

53. Adolf Hitler, "Speech to Chief Commanders and Commanding Generals," 22 August 1939, quoted in Bassiouni, *Crimes against Humanity*, 176, n. 96.

54. David Matas, "Prosecuting Crimes against Humanity: The Lessons of World War I," *Fordham International Law Journal* 13 (1989-1990): 104.

55. See Michael Scharf, "The Case for a Permanent International Truth Commission," *Duke Journal of Comparative and International Law* 7 (1997): 398, n. 128.

56. For more on the increased demand for, and ability to provide, justice to those who have become victims of international war crimes, see Scheffer, "International Judicial Intervention," 34-51.

57. Goldstone, "Justice as a Tool for Peace-Making," 485, 486.

58. Interview with General William Nash, by Michael Scharf, Cambridge, Massachusetts, 29 September 1998.

59. Hampson, "Can Peace Building Work?" 705.

60. Elizabeth Cousens, "Making Peace in Bosnia Work," *Cornell International Law Journal* 30 (1997): 796.

61. Cousens, "Making Peace in Bosnia Work," 796.

62. U.S. Department of State, Information Memorandum, *Defense of the Safe Areas in Bosnia*, 19 July 1995 (declassified 17 February 1998).

63. For a more detailed description of the manner in which various norms operated at cross-purposes, See Cousens, "Making Peace in Bosnia Work," 793.

Chapter 4

1. Milovan Djilas, "War," *Encounters Magazine*, April 1962; quoted in Owen, *Balkan Odyssey*, 36.

2. For a comprehensive review of the crisis in the former Yugoslavia, see generally Mark Almond, *Europe's Backyard War* (London: Mandarin, 1994); Christopher Bennett, *Yugoslavia's Bloody Collapse: Causes, Course and Consequence* (New York: New York University Press, 1994); Steven Burg and Paul Shoup, *The War in Bosnia-Herzegovina:*

Ethnic Conflict and International Intervention (London: M.E. Sharpe, 1998); James Gow, *Triumph of the Lack of Will: International Diplomacy and Yugoslav War* (London: Columbia University Press, 1997); Reneo Lukić and Allen Lynch, *Europe from the Balkans to the Urals*; Branka Magas, *The Destruction of Yugoslavia and the Soviet Union* (Oxford: Oxford University Press, 1996); Noel Malcolm, *Bosnia: A Short History* (New York: New York University Press, 1994); Viktor Meier, *Wie Jugoslawien Verspielt* (Munich, 1995); Samantha Power, *Breakdown in the Balkans: A Chronicle of Events January 1989 to May 1993* (Washington, D.C.: Carnegie Endowment for International Peace, 1993); David Reiff, *Slaughterhouse: Bosnia and the Failure of the West* (New York: 1995); Carlos Taibo and Jose Carlos Lechado, *Los Conflictos Yugoslavos: Una Introducción*, 3rd ed. (Madrid: Fundamentos, 1995); Ed Vulliamy, *Seasons in Hell: Understanding Bosnia's War* (London: St. Martin's Press, 1994); Susan Woodward, *Balkan Tragedy: Chaos and Dissolution after the Cold War* (Washington, D.C.: Brookings Institute Press, 1996). For a comprehensive bibliography, see *Books on Bosnia: A critical bibliography of works relating to Bosnia-Herzegovina published since 1990 in West European languages,* eds. Q. Hoare, and N. Malcolm (London: The Bosnian Insitute, 1999).

3. *Reuters,* 5 November 1994.

4. For a more detailed review of the circumstances of the lesser known ethnic groups in the former Yugoslavia, see Noel Malcolm, *Kosovo: A Short History* (New York: HarperCollins, 1999), 202-16.

5. See Malcolm, *Kosovo: A Short History.*

6. George Kennan, ed., *The Other Balkan Wars* (Washington, D.C.: Carnegie Endowment for International Peace: Brookings Institution Publications, 1993), 151. (Originally published in 1914 as Report of the International Commission to Inquire into the Causes and Conduct of the Balkan Wars).

7. See Neier, *War Crimes,* 4-6.

8. Charles Lane, et. al., "Serbia's Ghosts: Why the Serbs See Themselves as the Victims, not the Aggressors," *Newsweek,* 19 April 1993.

9. Gregory Copley, "Hiding Genocide," *Defense and Foreign Affairs Strategic Policy* (Alexandria, Va.: International Media Corp., 1992), 5.

10. Copley, *Hiding Genocide,* 6.

11. See Neier, *War Crimes,* 113-14 (citing a 1941 SS report and Edmund Glaise von Horstenaur, the German plenipotentiary general).

12. See Malcolm, *Kosovo: A Short History,* 297-307.

13. Barbara Jelavich, *History of the Balkans* (Cambridge: Cambridge University Press, 1983).

14. See Neier, *War Crimes,* 116-18.

15. For a review of disputes relating to minority populations throughout Yugoslavia and the Balkans, see Hugh Poulton, *The Balkans: Minorities and States in Conflict* (London: Minority Right Publications, 1993).

16. For a detailed historical review of Tito's reign, see Sabrina Ramet, *Nationalism and Federalism in Yugoslavia 1962-1991,* 2nd ed. (Bloomington: Indiana University Press, 1994).

17. Patric Brogan, *The Captive Nations* (New York: Avon Books, 1990), 161.

18. For a review of the slow collapse of the Titoist political system after his death, see James Gow, *Legitimacy and the Military: The Yugoslav Crisis* (London: St. Martin's Press, 1992). For an interpretation of the Yugoslav crisis based upon economic determinants, see Woodward, *Balkan Tragedy.* For a narrative view of the final years of the Yugoslav federation, see Nicole L. Janigro, *L'esplosione delle Nazioni: Il Caso Jugoslav*

(Milan: Feltrinelli, 1993).

19. Laura Silber and Allen Little, *Yugoslavia: Death of a Nation* (New York: Penguin Books, 1997), 215.

20. See Neier, *War Crimes*.

21. For a well-researched review of the role of nationalism in the Yugoslav crisis, see Tim Judah, *The Serbs: History, Myth and the Destruction of Yugoslavia* (London: Yale University Press, 1997). See also, Jacques Julliard, *Ce Fascisme qui vient* (Paris: Seuil, 1994); Vesna Pešić, *Serbian Nationalism and the Origins of the Yugoslav Crisis* (Washington, D.C.: USIP, 1996).

22. Zimmermann, *Origins of a Catastrophe*, 138. For a discussion of the frequent revival of nationalism following the fall of communism, see Stefano Bianchini, *Sarajevo, Le Radici Dell'Odio. Identità e Destino dei Popoli Balcanici*, 2nd ed. (Rome: Edizioni Associate, 1996).

23. Ivo Banac, "The Fearful Asymmetry of War: The Causes and Consequences of Yugoslavia's Demise," *Daedalus*, (spring 1992): 141, 150-51.

24. Anthony Lewis, *War Crimes, the Black Book of Bosnia*, ed. Nader Mousavizadeh (New York: Perseus Books LLC, 1996), 58 (quoting James Ridgeway).

25. See Zimmermann, *Origins of a Catastrophe*, 413. See also interview with former NATO secretary-general Manfred Worner, in Geyer, "How the Conscience of the West Was Lost," 83.

26. Michael Libal, *Limits of Persuasion: Germany and the Yugoslavia Crisis, 1991-1992* (Westport, Conn.: Greenwood Publishing Group, 1997), 144.

27. See for example Owen, *Balkan Odyssey*, 10-13.

28. For a thorough critique of the Western policy response, see Stjepan Meštrovic, ed., *The Conceit of Innocence: Losing the Conscience of the West in the War against Bosnia* (College Station: Texas A&M University Press, 1997), 259.

29. *Reuters*, 21 January 1997.

30. For a detailed review of the breakdown of the federal structures in the 1980s, see Hans Stark, *Les Balkans: Le Retour de la Guerre en Europe* (Paris: La Découverte, 1991).

31. Silber and Little, *Yugoslavia: Death of a Nation*; Lewis, *War Crimes*, 61.

32. Zimmermann, *Origins of a Catastrophe*, 137.

33. For journalistic accounts of the early days of the Croatian and Bosnian conflicts, see Paul Harris, *Somebody Else's War: Frontline Reports from the Balkan Wars 1991-92* (Stevenage, U.K.: Spa Books, 1992); Alfonso Rojo, *Yugoslavia: Holocausto en los Balcanes* (Barcelona: Planeta, 1992).

34. See Blaine Harden, "Serbs Accused of '91 Croatia Massacre," *Washington Post*, 25 January 1993.

35. For a review of these efforts, see Henry Wynaendts, *L'engrenage: Chroniques yougoslaves juillet 1991—août 1992* (Paris: Denoël, 1993).

36. For an exhaustive collection of the documents produced by the ICFY, see B.G. Ramcharan, ed., *The International Conference on the Former Yugoslavia: Official Papers* (Dordecht: Kluwer Law International, 1997).

37. For Carl Bildt's memoirs, see Carl Bildt, *Peace Journey: The Struggle for Peace in Bosnia,* (London: Weidenfeld Orion, 1998).

38. For a well-documented critique of Thorvald Stoltenberg's basic misunderstanding of the crisis by a Norwegian academic, see Nilsen, *Europas Svik*. For Stoltenberg's memoirs, see Thorvald Stoltenberg and Kai Eide, *De Tusen Dagene: Fredsmeklere på Balkan* (Oslo: Gyldendal Norsk Forlag, 1996).

39. See UN Security Council Resolution 713.
40. See UN Security Council Resolution 727.
41. See UN Security Council Resolution 743.
42. The European Community announced recognition of Slovenia and Croatia on 15 January 1992. See Keesings, vol. 38, no. 1, p. 38703 (January 1992).
43. Silber and Little, *Yugoslavia: Death of a Nation*. For more information on the acts of Radovan Karadzic during the conflict, see Peter Köpf, *Karadžić: Die Schande Europas* (Düsseldorf: Econ Taschenbuch Verlag, 1995).
44. See Virginia Morris and Michael Scharf, *An Insider's Guide to the International Criminal Tribunal for the Former Yugoslavia* (New York: Transnational Publishers, 1995), 19.
45. See Zimmermann, *Origins of a Catastrophe*, 210.
46. The United States then recognized Slovenia, Croatia, and Bosnia as independent states on 7 April 1992. See Keesings, vol. 38, no. 4, p. 38848, April 1992.
47. On 16 December 1993, six members states of the European Union recognized Macedonia under the name Former Yugoslav Republic of Macedonia. Eventually, all the European Community member states, except Greece, recognized Macedonian independence. The United States recognized Macedonia on 9 February 1994. See "U.S. Recognition of the Former Yugoslav Republic of Macedonia," *White House Press Release* (9 February 1994).
48. For a critique of various actions of the Croatian and Bosnian governments which undermined the prospects for the continuation of a multiethnic Bosnia, see Vinko Puljić, *Suffering with Hope: Appeals, Addresses, Interviews* (Zagreb: HKD Napredak, 1995).
49. For a detailed firsthand account of the siege of Sarajevo see Zlatko Dizdarevic, *Sarajevo—A War Journal* (New York: Henry, Holt and Company Inc., 1994). See also, Janine Giovanni, *The Quick and the Dead: Under Siege in Sarajevo* (London: Phoenix House, 1994); and Adriano Sofri, *Lo Specchio di Sarajevo* (Palermo: Sellerio Editore, 1997).
50. See Norman Cigar, *Genocide in Bosnia: The Policy of 'Ethnic Cleansing'* (College Station: Texas A&M University Press, 1995), 48.
51. See Silber and Little, *Yugoslavia: Death of a Nation*.
52. See Cigar, *Genocide in Bosnia*, 49.
53. GAO Report, "Serbia-Montenegro: Implementation of UN Economic Sanctions," 4.
54. See generally, Michael Scharf and Joshua Dorosin, "Interpreting UN Sanctions: The Rulings and Role of the Yugoslavia Sanctions Committee," *Brooklyn Journal of International Law* 19 (1993): 781-88.
55. See generally, Scharf and Dorosin, "Interpreting UN Sanctions," 771-827.
56. See generally, Michael P. Scharf, "Musical Chairs: The Dissolution of States and Membership in the United Nations," *Cornell International Law Journal* 28 (1996): 30-69.
57. See UN Security Council Resolution 777.
58. See Carl-August Fleischhauer, under-secretary-general for legal affairs, "Letter to Kenneth Dadzie, Under-Secretary-General, United Nations Conference on Trade and Development," 29 September 1992
59. *Case concerning Application of the Convention on the Prevention and Punishment of the Crime of Genocide: Bosnia and Herzegovina v. Yugoslavia* (Serbia and Montenegro), 1993 I.C. J. 14 (April 8). In September 2000 the Federal Republic of Yugoslavia relinquished its claim to continue the international legal personality of the former Yugoslavia and was admitted to the United Nations as a new member.
60. On 14 September 1992, the Security Council adopted Resolution 776, authorizing

an expansion of UNPROFOR to protect relief convoys and, if necessary, respond in self-defense when attacked.

61. John Goshko, "Eagleburger Debuts on the Balkan Crisis," *The Washington Post*, 29 August 1992.

62. On 27 June 1992, the European Community issued a declaration stating that while all parties were responsible for the continuing violence, the greatest share of responsibility for the crisis fell on the Serbian leadership and the JNA controlled by it. See Keesings, vol. 38, no. 6, p. 38943, June 1992.

63. See UN Department of Public Information, *The United Nations and the Situation in the Former Yugoslavia* 13 (New York: UN Department of Public Information, 1993).

64. See Owen, *Balkan Odyssey*, 355.

65. For compelling accounts of the Srebrenica massacre, and the passive role of the international community, see Rohde, *Endgame*, and Chuck Sudetic, *Blood and Vengeance: One Family's Story of the War in Bosnia* (London: Simon and Schuster, 1998).

66. For more information on the Srebrenica massacre, see Laurence de Barros-Duchêne, *Srebrenica: Histoire d'un crime international* (Paris: L'Harmattan, 1996); Honig and Both, *Srebrenica*; Bob Van Laergoven, *Srebrenica: Getuigen van een Massamoord* (Antwerp: 1996); Rohde, *Endgame*; Eric Stover and Gilles Peress, *The Graves: Srebrenica and Vukovar* (Zurich: Scalo, 1998); Secretary-General, "Report Pursuant to General Assembly Resolution 53/35," *Srebrenica Report*.

67. Lewis, *War Crimes*, 175.

68. Credible reports exist that early in the conflict UN peacekeepers under the command of General Lewis MacKenzie actually participated in the commission of atrocities by frequenting the rape camp known as Sonja's Kon-Tiki, in the town of Vogosca near Sarajevo. According to author Michael Sells, "even after they learned that the women at the Kon-Tiki were Muslim captives held against their will, abused, and sometimes killed, UN peacekeepers continued to take advantage of the women there and to fraternize with their Serb nationalist captors. Only 150 yards away from Sonja's, scores of Muslim men were being held in inhuman conditions, but the peacekeepers took no notice." Sells, *The Bridge Betrayed*, 132-33. See also Roy Gutman, "Witnesses Claim UN Forces Visited Serb-Run Brothel," *New York Newsday*, 1 November 1993.

69. "Further Report of the Secretary-General Pursuant to Security Council Resolution 749," *U.N. Doc. S/23900* (1992), para 5.

70. "Prosecute Bosnia's War Criminals," *New York Times*, 4 January 1995, A18. See also, Tilman Zülch, ed., *Die Angst des Dichters vor der Wirklichkeit: 16 Antworten auf Peter Handkes Winterreise nach Serbien* (Göttingen: Steidl, 1996).

71. Silber and Little, *Yugoslavia: Death of a Nation*. For a detailed collection of reports concerning the concentration camps in Bosnia see Roy Gutman, *Witness to Genocide* (Longmeade, U.K.: Macmillan Publishing Company, 1993). For a comprehensive reporting of the extent of war crimes committed early in the war, see Helsinki Watch, *War Crimes in Bosnia* (New York: Helsinki Watch, 1992).

72. For a first hand account of a survivor of the Omarska death camp, see Hukanović, *Tenth Circle of Hell*.

73. Silber and Little, *Yugoslavia: Death of a Nation* (quoting Ed Vulliamy of *The Guardian*, who accompanied Penny Marshall to Omarska).

74. For additional information on the extent and nature of atrocities committed in the Yugoslav conflict see RenΠ Backmann, ed., *Le Livre noir de l'ex-Yougoslavie: Purification ethnique et crimes de guerre* (Paris: Arlia, 1993); Vahida Demirović, *Visages from the Wasteland: A Collection of True War Stories from Bosnia* (London: Genie Quest,

1999); Barros-Duchêne, *Srebrenica: Histoire d'un crime international*; Ilse Baumgartner and Wolfgang Baumgartner *Der Balkan-Krieg* (Berlin: VWF, Verlag für Wissenschaft und Forschung, 1997); Claire Boulanger, Bernard Jacquemart, and Philippe Granjon, *L'enfer Yougoslave: Les Victimes de la guerre témoignent* (Paris: Belfond, 1995); Nick Ceh and Jeff Harder, ed., *The Golden Apple: War and Democracy in Croatia and Bosnia* (Boulder, Colo.: Eastern European Monographs, 1996); Smail Čekić, *The Aggression on Bosnia and Genocide against Bosniaks: 1991-1993* (Sarajevo: Institute for the Research of Crimes against Humanity and International Law, 1995); Francois Chaslin, *Une Haine monumentale: Essai sur la destruction des villes en ex-yougoslavie* (Paris: Descartes and Cie, 1997); Božica Ercegovac-Jambrović, *Genocide: Ethnic Cleansing in North-Western Bosnia* (Zagreb: Croation Information Centre, 1993); Jean Hatzfeld, *L'air de guerre, sur les routes de Croatie et de Bosnie-Herzegovine* (Paris: L'Olivier, 1994); Honig and Both, *Srebrenica: Record of a War Crime*; Baukje Lieman, *Exit: Het Vluchtverhaal van Ibro Mensuri* (Amsterdam: Globe Pockets, 1993); Jan Stage, *Asken Braender: En Forfatter i Krig* (Copenhagen: Informations Forlag, 1994).

75. U.S. Department of State, *Bosnia Herzegovina Country Report 1993* (31 January 1994).

76. U.S. Department of State, *Bosnia Herzegovina Country Report 1993*.

77. See Michael Scharf, *Balkan Justice: The Story behind the First International War Crimes Tribunal since Nuremberg* (Durham, N.C.: Carolina Academic Press, 1997).

78. According to one commentator, "some safe areas, such as Srebrenica, Zepa, and Bihac, became abodes of misery, what one refugee worker called UN concentration camps." Sells, *The Bridge Betrayed*, 75.

79. Prutsalis, *Too Little, Too Late*, 84.

80. U.S. Department of State, *Bosnia Herzegovina Country Report 1993*.

81. See Gotovina (IT-01-45) "Krajina," initial indictment, 8 June 2001.

82. For an indictment of Bosnians and Croats for crimes committed against Serbs, see Delalic, Delic, Mucic, and Landzo (IT-96-21) "Celebici," initial indictment, 21 March 1996.

83. Department of State cable number Belgrade 01261 181728Z, February 1993 (declassified 17 February 1998).

84. Department of State Cable number Belgrade 02451 301209Z, March 1993 (declassified 18 February 1998).

85. Department of State Cable number Belgrade 02451 301209Z, March 1993 (declassified 18 February 1998).

86. See Galic (IT-98-29) "Sarajevo," initial indictment, 26 March 1999.

87. See Blaskic (IT-95-14) "Lasva Valley," initial indictment, 10 November 1995; Furundzija (IT-95-17/1) "Lasva Valley," initial indictment, 10 November 1995; Kordic and Cerkez (IT-95-14/2) "Lasva Valley," initial indictment, 10 November 1995; Z. Kupreskic, M. Kupreskic, V. Kupreskic, Josipovic, Santic, and Papic (IT-95-16) "Lasva Valley," initial indictment, 10 November 1995; Naletilic and Martinovic (IT-98-34) "Tuta and Stela," initial indictment, 21 December 1998; Rajic (IT-95-12) "Stupni Do," initial indictment, 29 August 1995; Aleksovski (IT-95-14/1) "Lasva Valley," initial indictment, 10 November 1995; Marinic (IT-95-15) "Lasva Valley," initial indictment, 10 November 1995; Delalic, Delic, Mucic, and Landzo indictment, IT-96-2; Hadzihasanovic, Alagic and Kubura (IT-01-47), initial indictment, 13 July 2001.

88. Christiane Amanpour, "Del Ponte Urges War Crimes Arrests," *CNN Web*, 27 April 2001.

89. Nikolic (IT-94-2) "Susica Camp," initial indictment, 4 November 1994.

90. Meakic, Gruban, and Knezevic (IT-95-4) "Omarska Camp," initial indictment, 13 February 1995.

91. B. Simic, M. Simic, M. Tadic, and Zaric (IT-95-9) "Bosanski Samac," initial indictment, 21 July 1995.

92. Sikirica, Fustar, N. Banovic, P. Banovic, Knezevic, Kolundzija, and Dosen (IT-95-8) "Keraterm Camp," initial indictment, 21 July 1995.

93. Karadzic and Mladic Indictments, IT-95-5, IT-95-18.

94. Martic (IT-95-11) "Zagreb Bombing," initial indictment, 25 July 1995.

95. Blaskic indictment, IT-95-14.

96. Mrksic, Radic, Sljivancanin and Dokmanovic (IT-95-13a) "Vukovar Hospital," initial indictment, 7 November 1995.

97. Jankovic, Janjic, Zelenovic, and Stankovic (IT-96-23/2), "Foca," initial indictment, 26 June 1999.

98. Krajisnik indictment, IT-00-39.

99. Plavsic indictment, IT-00-40.

100. Amnesty International, *All the Way Home: Safe 'Minority Returns' as a Just Remedy and for a Secure Future* (London: Amnesty International, 1998). Amnesty International "Who's Living in My House?" (London: Amnesty International, 1997); International Crisis Group "Going Nowhere Fast," (London: ICG, 1996) 74; International Crisis Group "Group, Minority Return or Mass Relocation," (London: ICG, 1998): 58; Michael O'Flaherty, and Gregory Gisvold, *Postwar Protection of Human Rights in Bosnia and Herzegovina* (The Hague: Martimus Nijhoff Publishing, 1998), 333; Erich Rathfelder, *Sarajevo und Danach: Sechs Jahre Reported in Ehemaligen Jugoslawien* (Munich: Beck, 1998).

101. See Malcolm, *Kosovo: A Short History*, 2736-76, 280-81. It is estimated that approximately 70,000 individuals settled in Kosovo as a result of the colonization program.

102. See Malcolm, *Kosovo: A Short History*, 283-86.

103. See Malcolm, *Kosovo: A Short History*, 289-93, 315-17.

104. See Malcolm, *Kosovo: A Short History*, 324-26.

105. For a comprehensive collection of the texts central to the operation of Serb nationalism, see Mirko Grmek, Marc Gjidara, and Neven Simić, eds., *Le Nettoyage ethnique: Documents historiques sur une Idéologie serbe* (Paris: Fayard, 1993).

106. See Malcolm, *Kosovo: A Short History*, 341-42.

107. See Malcolm, *Kosovo: A Short History*, 343-45.

108. See Malcolm, *Kosovo: A Short History*, 345-46.

109. See Malcolm, *Kosovo: A Short History*, 347.

110. For a review of the atrocities committed, See Human Rights Watch, and the reports of the Kosovo Verification Mission.

111. Robert Gelbard, "Press Conference," Special Representative of the President and the Secretary for Implementation of the Dayton Peace Agreement (Belgrade, Serbia and Montenegro, 15 January 1998).

112. See Richard Holbrooke and William Walker, "On-the-Record Briefing," Verification Mission (28 October 1998).

113. See Contact Group, "Statement on Kosovo," New York, 24 September 1997; Contact Group, "Statement on Kosovo," Moscow, 25 February 1998; Gelbard, "Press Conference," 15 January 1998.

114. See Contact Group, "Statement on Kosovo," London, 9 March 1998.

115. See North Atlantic Council, "Statement on Kosovo," Luxembourg, 28 May

1998.
116. North Atlantic Council, "Statement on Kosovo," issued at the Defense Ministers Session, 11 June 1998.

117. See Kris Janowski, "UN Warns of Further Bosnia-Type Horrors," *Irish Times*, 9 September 1998, UNHCR (spokesman commenting on Serbia's arrest of some 600 Kosovo Albanian men).

118. See Javier Solana, "Statement to the Press," NATO (Brussels, 13 October 1998).

119. See Agreement between the Minister of Foreign Affairs of the Federal Republic of Yugoslavia and the Chairman-in-Office of the Organization for Security and Cooperation in Europe (OSCE) signed in Belgrade on 16 October 1998.

120. See Agreement between the Chief of General Staff of the Federal Republic of Yugoslavia and the Supreme Allied Commander, Europe, of the North Atlantic Treaty Organization (NATO), signed in Belgrade on 15 October 1998.

121. See White House, "Statement by the President on the Massacre of Civilians in Racak," 16 January 1999.

122. See Albright, "Press Availability on Kosovo," 18 January 1999.

123. See Kai Eide, "Statement Issued at the Conclusion of the Special Meeting of the Permanent Council," *OSCE* (Vienna, 18 January 1999).

124. See Kofi Annan, "Statement on the Racak Massacre," United Nations (New York, 16 January 1999).

125. White House, Office of the Press Secretary, "Statement by the President on the Massacre of Civilians in Racak," Washington, DC, 16 January 1999; Madeleine Albright, "Press Availability on Kosovo following Volunteer Event at Children's Hospital," Washington, D.C., 18 January 1999.

126. See Javier Solana, "Statement to the Press," NATO (Brussels, 28 January 1999); North Atlantic Council, "Press Release," *NAC-(99)12*, 30 January 1999.

127. See North Atlantic Council, "Press Release," 30 January 1999.

128. See Madeleine Albright, "Statement on NATO Final Warning on Kosovo," Washington, D.C., 30 January 1999.

129. Secretary-General, "Report Prepared Pursuant to Resolutions 1160 (1998) and 1203 (1998) of the Security Council," 12 November 1998.

130. Secretary-General, "Report of the Secretary-General Prepared Pursuant to Security Council Resolution 1160 (1998)," 5 August 1998.

131. Secretary-General, "Report Prepared Pursuant to Resolutions 1160 (1998) and 1203 (1998) of the Security Council," 12 November 1998.

132. Secretary-General, "Report Prepared Pursuant to Resolutions 1160 (1998) and 1203 (1998) of the Security Council," 12 November 1998.

133. Milosevic, Milutinovic, Sainovic, Ojdanic, and Stojiljkovic (IT-99-37) "Kosovo," Initial indictment, 24 May 1999.

134. Milosevic, Milutinovic, Sainovic, Ojdanic, and Stojiljkovic Indictment, (IT-99-37).

135. For a review of the crimes against humanity and attempted genocide in Kosovo, see Human Rights Watch, *Humanitarian Law Violations in Kosovo* (New York, 1998); International Crisis Group, *Reality Demand: Documenting Viloations of International Humanitarian Law in Kosovo 1999* (London: International Crisis Group, 2000); and U.S. Department of State, *Erasing History: Ethnic Cleansing in Kosovo*.

Chapter 5

1. *Financial Times*, 26 October 1994.

2. For an assessment of how an international approach based less on accommodation might have ended the war in Croatia and possibly prevented the Bosnian conflict, see Christopher Cviić, *An Awful Warning: The War in Ex-Yugoslavia* (London: Centre for Policy Studies, 1994).

3. For an account of the Austrian policy with respect to the Yugoslavian crisis, see Alois Mock, ed., *Das Balkan-Dossier: Der Aggressionskrieg in Ex-Jugoslawien-Perspektiven für die Zukunft* (Wien: Signum, 1997).

4. For an assessment of U.S. interests in the former Yugoslavia, see Cohen, *Application of the Realist and Liberal Perspectives*, 150. For a European perspective on the development of U.S. policy, see Thomas Paulsen, *Die Jugoslawienpolitik der USA 1989-1994: Bergrenztes Engagement und Konfliktdynamik* (Baden-Baden: Nomos Verlagsgesellschaft, 1995).

5. See Ian Guest, *On Trial: The United Nations, War Crimes, and the Former Yugoslavia* (Washington, D.C.: Refugee Policy Group, 1995), 21.

6. Silber and Little, *Yugoslavia: Death of a Nation*, 29-30.

7. For a review of early U.S. policy toward Yugoslavia, see David Gompert, "The United States and Yugoslavia's Wars," in *The World and Yugoslavia's Wars*, ed. Richard H. Ullman (New York: Council on Foreign Relations, 1996); also, Richard Sobel, "U.S. and European Attitudes toward Intervention in the Former Yugoslavia: Mourir pour la Bosnie?" in *The World and Yugoslavia's Wars*, ed. Richard Ullman (New York: Council on Foreign Relations, 1996).

8. Silber and Little, *Yugoslavia: Death of a Nation*, 252 (quoting George Kenney).

9. Guest, *On Trial*, 33.

10. See Guest, *On Trial*, 35; See also Jacqueline Frank, "Former Department of State Aide Urges U.S. Intervention in Bosnia," Reuters, 28 August 1992.

11. Richard Johnson, "The Pinstripe Approach to Genocide," in *The Conceit of Innocence Losing the Conscience of the West in the War against Bosnia*, ed. Stjepan G. Meštović (College Station: Texas A&M University Press, 1997), 67.

12. Department of State Cable number State 015374 161706Z, January 1993 (declassified 17 February 1998).

13. Johnson, "The Pinstripe Approach to Genocide," 67.

14. See *Christian Science Monitor*, 26 May 1993, 18; For a description of the continued obfuscation of the genocide issue by the Department of State, see Saul Friedman, "Christopher Assailed; Official: U.S. Downplayed Bosnia Genocide," *Newsday*, 4 February 1994, 4.

15. Johnson, "The Pinstripe Approach to Genocide," 72, n. 13.

16. According to Geyer, the position of moral equivalence adopted by the British government served the position that "everybody's guilty, so we're not guilty for doing nothing." Geyer, "How the Conscience of the West Was Lost," 89.

17. U.S Department of State, Information Memorandum from (INR) Douglas P. Mulholland to (P) Mr. Kanter, "Bosnia: Actions Contributing to Genocide," 11 January 1993 (declassified).

For a well-documented account of the early stages of the campaign of genocide in Bosnia and the origins of this policy in the political and academic institutions of Serbia, see Cigar, *Genocide in Bosnia*, 48. For more information on the role of religion and myth in the Serbian nationalist movement, see Sells, *The Bridge Betrayed*.

18. Department of State, Information Memorandum, "Bosnia: Actions Contributing

to Genocide," 11 January 1993 (declassified).

19. Department of State, Information Memorandum, "Bosnia: Actions Contributing to Genocide," 11 January 1993 (declassified).

20. See "Papers Show U.S. Knew of Genocide in Rwanda," *New York Times*, 22 August 2001, A5. The article cites a number of recently declassified Department of State cables.

21. Department of State cable number Belgrade 02451 301209Z, March 1993 (declassified 18 February 1998).

22. Johnson, "The Pinstripe Approach to Genocide," 69-70.

23. See Gow, *The Triumph of the Lack of Will*, 213.

24. Chris Black, "U.S. Options Seen Fewer as Military Avoids Risk," *Boston Globe*, 23 July 1995, 12.

25. Johnson, "The Pinstripe Approach to Genocide," 70.

26. See Roger Cohen, "CIA Report Finds Serbs Guilty of Majority of Bosnia War Crimes," *New York Times*, 9 March 1995, A1.

27. For more information on the influence of Serbian propaganda on American and European policy, see Nilsen, *Europas Svik*.

28. Josip Zupanov, Dusko Sekulic, and Zeljka Sporer, "A Breakdown of the Civil Order: The Balkan Bloodbath," *International Journal of Political Culture and Society* 9 (1996): 401-401 (quoting Warren Christopher from a statement on 28 March 1993).

29. Zupanov, Sekulic, and Sporer, *A Breakdown of the Civil Order*, 405-07.

30. For more information on the failed Christopher visit, See Neier, *War Crimes*, 131.

31. Geyer, "How the Conscience of the West Was Lost," 117-19.

32. Cohen, *Application of the Realist and Liberal Perspectives*, 150.

33. For a rather unfair critique of the role of the United States in the Yugoslav peace process, see Bertrand de Rossanet, *Peacemaking and Peacekeeping in Yugoslavia. The Hague and London* (The Hague: Kluwer Law International, 1996), 127.

34. For more information on the various interests affecting U.S. policy toward the former Yugoslavia, see Wayne Bert, *The Reluctant Superpower: United States Policy in Bosnia 1991-95* (London: St. Martin's Press, 1997).

35. For more details, see Neier, *War Crimes*, 131.

36. See Serge Schmemann, "From Russia to Serbia, a Current of Sympathy," *New York Times*, 31 January 1993, A18.

37. Gwynne Dyer, "Russia Barks but Won't Bite in the Kosovo Crisis," *San Diego Union-Tribune*, 18 April 1999, G6.

38. See Guest, *On Trial*, 111. For a comprehensive assessment of Russian policy during this time, see Paul Goble, "Dangerous Liaisons: Moscow, the Former Yugoslavia, and the West," in *The World and Yugoslavia's Wars*, ed. Richard H. Ullman (New York: Council on Foreign Relations, 1996).

39. Department of State cable number Moscow 03705 091649Z, February 1994 (declassified 17 February 1998).

40. Department of State cable number Moscow 03705 091649Z, February 1994 (declassified 17 February 1998).

41. See Gow, *The Triumph of the Lack of Will*, 186.

42. See Cigar, *Genocide in Bosnia*, 145.

43. Mark Almond, "A Faraway Country," in *With No Peace to Keep: United Nations Peacekeeping and the War in the Former Yugoslavia* (London: Grainpress, 1995), 13.

44. Geyer, "How the Conscience of the West Was Lost," 87.

45. BBC Radio broadcast, 14 June 1999.

46. NewsHour with Jim Lehrer, 3 June 1999.

47. Almond, "A Faraway Country," 125, 133.

48. James Gow, *British Perspectives, in International Perspectives on the Yugoslavia Conflict* (New York: St. Martin's Press, 1996), 88.

49. For more information on the British approach to the conflict, see Thomas Cushman and Stjepan Mestrovic, eds. *This Time We Knew: Western Responses to Genocide in Bosnia* (New York: New York University Press, 1996).

50. Hodge, "The Serb Lobby in the United Kingdom."

51. See Gow, *The Triumph of the Lack of Will*, 176. See also Gow, *British Perspectives*, 90.

52. See Gow, *The Triumph of the Lack of Will*, 177.

53. Hans-Dietrich Genscher, *Rebuilding a House Divided*, translated by Thomas Thornton (New York: Broadway Books, 1997) 504.

54. See Lewis, *War Crimes*, 59, 60.

55. For a further assessment of British policy, see Jane Sharp, *Bankrupt in the Balkans: British Policy in Bosnia* (London: IPPR, 1993); Jane Sharp, *Honest Broker or Perfidious Albion?—British Policy in Former Yugoslavia* (London: 1997); Simms, *Unfinest Hour*.

56. For a review of the debate in Britain concerning intervention in Bosnia, see Philip Towle, "The British Debate about Intervention in European Conflicts," in *Military Intervention in European Conflicts,* ed. Lawrence Freedman (Cambridge, Mass.: Blackwell Publishers, 1994).

57. See Guest, *On Trial*, 100, 104.

58. Almond, "A Faraway Country," 131.

59. See Reiff, *Slaughterhouse*, 29 stating "about the worst of [the international negotiators] particularly at the most senior levels of the French and British governments and the United Nations Secretariat, who, sometimes publicly, sometimes stealthily, did whatever they could to ensure either a Serb victory or a Bosnian surrender, enough ill can never be said."

60. Almond, "A Faraway Country," 131.

61. Almond, "A Faraway Country," 131.

62. On at least one account a British officer was charged with passing NATO military secrets to the Bosnian Serb leadership during the war, severely damaging UNPROFOR's operational capability. For more information on the elements affecting British policy, see Sharp, *Honest Broker or Perfidious Albion?*; Sharp, *Bankrupt in the Balkans*; Simms, *Unfinest Hour*.

63. PBS interview, 14 June 1994.

64. See Vulliamy, *Seasons in Hell*.

65. For a review of the heroic efforts to provide humanitarian assistance to the victims of the conflict, see John Davies, Bob Myers, and Geoff Robinsone, eds., *Taking Sides—Against Ethnic Cleansing in Bosnia: The Story of the Workers Aid Convoys* (Leeds: Workers Aid for Bosnia, 1998). For a compilation of compelling advocacy designed to reorient British policy, see Adrian Hastings, *SOS Bosnia*, 3rd ed. (London: Alliance to Defend Bosnia-Herzegovina, 1994).

66. For a more detailed critique of General Rose's performance in Bosnia see Dizdarevic Zlatko and Gigi Riva, *L'ONU è Morta a Sarajevo* (Milan: Il Saggiatore, 1996).

67. Unnamed British UNPROFOR officer, Reuters, 10 November 1996.

68. Almond, "A Faraway Country," 131.

69. Almond, "A Faraway Country," 130.

70. Heller, *Des Brasiers mal éteints.*

71. Slaven Lepick, "French Perspectives," in *International Perspectives on the Yugoslav Conflict,* eds. Alex Danchev and Thomas Halverson (New York: Macmillan Press, 1996), 76.

72. John Laughland, "To Believe and to Dare," in *With No Peace to Keep: United Nations Peacekeeping and the War in the Former Yugoslavia* (London: Grainpress, 1995), 134-36.

73. Laughland, "To Believe and to Dare," 136.

74. For a journalistic commentary on the international dynamics of the conflict from the French perspective, see Daniel Vernet and Jean-Marc Gonin, *Guerre dans les Balkans— le Miroir brisé Yougoslave* (Paris, 1994).

75. See Laughland, "To Believe and to Dare," 136.

76. For a post hoc assessment of French policy in the former Yugoslavia, see Conference Proceedings, *L'ex-Yougoslavie en Europe.* See also, Bernad-Henri L9vy, *Le Lys et la Cendre: Journa; d'un Écrivain au Temps de la Guerre en Bosnie 1992-1995.*

77. Almond, *Europe's Backyard War,* xii.

78. For a detailed critique of the "false-blame" placed on the Germans by the French, see Daniele Conversi, *German-Bashing and the Break-up of Yugoslavia* (Seattle: Henry M. Jackson School of International Studies, University of Washington, 1998).

79. For a review of the debate in France concerning intervention in Bosnia, see Jolyon Howorth, "The Debate in France over Military Intervention in Europe," in *Military Intervention in European Conflicts,* ed. Lawrence Freedman (Cambridge, Mass.: Blackwell Publishers, 1994).

80. For an argument for early French intervention, see Gabriel Plisson, *Mourir pour Sarajevo* (Paris: Éditions In fine, 1994).

81. James Baker III, *The Politics of Diplomacy: Revolution, War and Peace* (New York: G. P. Putnam's Sons, 1995), 642.

82. For a critique of Mitterand's reluctance to support the use of force, see Alain Finkeildraut, *The Crime of Being Born,* translated by Graham McMaster (1997).

83. Lepick, "French Perspectives," 81.

84. Lepick, "French Perspectives," 81-82.

85. For an account by two French soldiers of the passivity of French forces in the face of Serbian defiance see Marc Benda and Francois Crémieux, *Paris-Bihać, Les Temps modernes* (Paris: Editions Michalon, 1995).

86. According to Chuck Sudetic, "in 1998 a French officer, a graduate of France's elite military academy, Saint-Cyr, was caught by the Americans and arrested by French authorities for allegedly passing information about likely NATO bombing targets to a Serb agent. *Le Monde* reported that the officer, Major Pierre-Henri Bunel, later confessed to disclosing the information out of sympathy for the Serb cause." Sudetic, "Why Is France Protecting Indicted War Criminals." Major Bunel subsequently argued at his hearing before a military tribunal in December 2001 that he was instructed to pass this information by a superior officer.

87. Sudetic, "Why Is France Protecting Indicted War Criminals."

88. Krajisnik and Plavsic (IT-00-39 and 40) "Bosnia and Herzegovina," Krajisnik: Amended indictment, 21 March 2000, Plavsic: Initial indictment, 7 April 2000.

89. Balkan Action Council, *Balkan Watch, Week in Review,* 22 December 1998—5

January 1999.

90. "French General at Fault in Srebrenica Massacre: Dutch Officers," Agence France-Presse, 19 April 2001. See also, "Hearing on Srebrenica Massacre Held," Associated Press Online, 26 January 2001, for a report on General Janvier's testimony. For a poignant testimony of the effect of Mr. Janvier's decision to withhold air strikes see Sudetic, *Blood and Vengeance.*

91. "Days of Slaughter: The Killing of Srebrenica," *New York Times,* 29 October 1995.

92. "Politics and Massacres: Did France Tacitly Trade a Bosnian 'Safe Haven' to the Serbs for the Return of Peacekeeper Hostages?" *Time,* international edition, 24 June 1996, 24.

93. "Hearing on Srebrenica Massacre Held," Associated Press Online, 26 January 2001.

94. Libal, *Limits of Persuasion* 5, 104.

95. For a review of the debate in Germany concerning intervention in Croatia and Bosnia, see Harald Mηller, "Military Intervention for European Security: The German Debate," in *Military Intervention in European Conflicts,* ed. Lawrence Freedman (Cambridge, Mass.: Blackwell Publishers, 1994).

96. Libal, *Limits of Persuasion,* 104.

97. Libal, *Limits of Persuasion,* 105.

98. Marie-Janine Calic, "German Perspectives," in *International Perspectives on the Yugoslav Conflict,* ed. Alex Danchev and Thomas Halverson (New York: McMillan Press, 1996), 58. For a German journalistic commentary on the early stages of the conflict arguing for swift and effective international intervention, see Johann Georg Reissmüller, *Die Bosnische Tragödie* (Stuttgart: Deutsche Verlags-Anstalt, 1993).

99. For a thorough review of German policy in the early years of the conflict by the head of the German Foreign Ministry's Yugoslav Department, see Libal, *Limits of Persuasion.*

100. Libal, *Limits of Persuasion,* 16.

101. Almond, *Europe's Backyard War,* 51.

102. See Genscher, *Rebuilding a House Divided,* 513-16.

103. See Libal, *Limits of Persuasion,* 4.

104. Beverly Crawford, "German Foreign Policy and European Political Cooperation: The Diplomatic Recognition of Croatia in 1991," *Geneva Politics and Society* 13, no. 2 (summer 1995): 18.

105. Calic, "German Perspectives," 61.

106. For more information on the effect of this decision on Germany's relations with its EU partners, see Crawford, "German Foreign Policy and European Political Cooperation."

107. Laughland, "To Believe and to Dare," 137.

108. Laughland, "To Believe and to Dare," 137.

109. Calic, "German Perspectives," 60.

110. See Crawford, "German Foreign Policy and European Political Cooperation," 1.

111. Calic, "German Perspectives," 56.

112. Richard Holbrooke, editorial, "Battles after the War," *New York Times,* 14 September 1999, A23.

113. For a concise review of early European political efforts to resolve the crisis, see Stanley Hoffmann, "Yugoslavia: Implications for Europe and for European Institutions,"

in *The World and Yugoslavia's Wars*, ed. Richard H. Ullman (New York: Council on Foreign Relations, 1996). See also, Sobel, "U.S. and European Attitudes toward Intervention in the Former Yugoslavia"; Jane Sharp, "Appeasement, Intervention and the Future of Europe," in *Military Intervention in European Conflicts*, ed. Lawrence Freedman (Cambridge, Mass.: Blackwell Publishers, 1994).

114. For a rare insight into the extent to which the approach of accommodation influenced by a perception of moral equivalence influenced the day-to-day operation of the EU Monitoring Mission and UNPROFOR, see O'Shea, *Crisis at Bihać*.

115. For a discussion of how the European focus on developing a CFSP and a security architecture clouded their approach to the conflict, see Jonathan Eyal, *Europe and Yugoslavia: Lessons from a Failure* (London: RUSI, 1993).

116. Alan Riding, "Conflict in Yugoslavia; Europeans Send High-Level Team," *New York Times*, 29 June 1991, A4.

117. Baker, *The Politics of Diplomacy*, 637.

118. Almond, *Europe's Backyard War*, 32-33.

119. Almond, *Europe's Backyard War*, 32-33.

120. See Mario Zucconi, *The EU in Former Yugoslavia in Preventing Conflict in the Post-communist World*, ed. Abram Chayes and Antonia Handler Chayes (Washington, D.C.: Brookings Institution, 1996).

121. See Crawford, "German Foreign Policy and European Political Cooperation," 6.

122. See Crawford, "German Foreign Policy and European Political Cooperation," 6.

123. Almond, *Europe's Backyard War*, xiii.

124. Baker, *The Politics of Diplomacy*, 645.

125. Department of State cable Belgrade 01232 162107Z, February 1994 (declassified 31 March 1997).

126. For a concise and compelling critique of the UN efforts to bring peace to Yugoslavia, see Thomas G. Weiss, "Collective Spinelessness: UN Actions in the Former Yugoslavia," in *The World and Yugoslavia's Wars*, ed. Richard H. Ullman (New York: Council on Foreign Relations, 1996).

127. For a complete collection of UN documents concerning the conflict, see Daniel Bethlehem and Marc Weller, eds., *The Yugoslav Crisis in International Law: General Issues, Part One* (New York: Cambridge University Press, 1997).

128. For a clear articulation of the doctrine of moral equivalence and its role in accommodation by a French military commander, see Commandant Franchet (with Fontenelle), *Casque Bleu pour rien* (Paris: J.C. Lattés, 1995). For a description of moral equivalence in action, see General Lewis MacKenzie, *Peacekeeper: The Road to Sarajevo* (Vancouver: Douglas and McIntyre, 1993). For a more balanced view from the perspective of a French general, see General Philippe Morillon, *Croire et oser: Chronique de Sarajevo* (Paris: Grasset, 1993).

129. For a critique of the performance of Secretary-General Boutros-Ghali see Dizdarevic and Riva, *L'ONU è Morta a Sarajevo*.

130. For a wide-ranging assessment of the UN efforts in the former Yugoslavia see Cohen and Stamkoski, eds., *With No Peace to Keep: United Nations Peacekeeping and the War in the Former Yugoslavia* (London: Grainpress, 1995).

131. For a comprehensive critique of the UN's mission in Bosnia see Reiff, *Slaughterhouse*.

132. For a candid interview with the Secretary-General concerning his preference

for a negotiated outcome and his aversion to the use of force, see Geyer, "How the Conscience of the West Was Lost," 107-108.

133. Geyer, "How the Conscience of the West Was Lost," 107-09.

134. Geyer, "How the Conscience of the West Was Lost," 109.

135. For a sobering account of the efforts of a Belgian UN officer to obstruct the exhumation of a mass grave near Vukovar, see Stover and Peress, *The Graves*.

136. See Williams and Scharf, "UN Mandates." See also, Richard Caplan, *Postmortem on UNPROFOR* (London: Brassey's for the Centre for Defence Studies, University of London, 1996).

137. For instance, after the Security Council adopted Resolution 770 empowering all states to use force to protect humanitarian convoys, the Secretary-General issued a report interpreting the resolution as providing that UNPROFOR had exclusive authority to use force. When the Security Council then adopted Resolutions 836 and 844 empowering UNPROFOR to use force to protect certain designated safe areas, the Secretary-General then issued a report interpreting the resolution to provide that UNPROFOR forces could use force only for their own self-defense and not for that of the safe areas. See Secretary-General's Report S/24540 submitted on September 1992, and Secretary-General's Report S/25939 submitted on 14 June 1993.

138. For a complete account of the failure of the UN to adequately carry out its obligations, see Roger Cohen, *Hearts Grown Brutal: Saga of Sarajevo* (New York: Random House, 1998); and Sudetic, *Blood and Vengeance*. For a pointed analysis of the failure of Mr. Akashi to fulfill his mandate, see Dizdarevic and Riva, *L'ONU è Morta a Sarajevo*, and Géneral Jean Cot, and Monnot, eds., *Dernière Guerre balkanique?—Ex-Yougoslavie: Témoignages, Analyses, Perspectives* (Paris: L'Harmattan, 1996).

139. Geyer, "How the Conscience of the West Was Lost," 99, quoting interview with Mr. Akashi.

140. Geyer, "How the Conscience of the West Was Lost," 113.

141. Geyer, "How the Conscience of the West Was Lost," 111, quoting interview with Mr. Akashi.

142. Sells, *The Bridge Betrayed*, 130-31.

143. Heller, *Des Brasiers mal éteints*. See Francis Briquemont, *Do Something, General! "Chronique de Bosnic-Herzégovine, 12 Juillet 1993— 24 Janvier 1994"* (Brusells: Labor, 1998).

144. Peter Maass, *Love Thy Neighbor: A Story of War* (London: Macmillan, 1996), 279, citing MacKenzie, *Peacekeeper: The Road to Sarajevo*, 255.

145. Geyer, "How the Conscience of the West Was Lost," 115-16.

146. Geyer, "How the Conscience of the West Was Lost," 96, quoting a Scandinavian UNPROFOR soldier.

147. Sells, *The Bridge Betrayed*, 133.

148. See "Yugoslavia Death of a Nation" (BBC, 1995), part IV.

149. See Ed Vulliamy, "How the CIA Intercepted SAS Signal," *The Guardian*, 29 January 1996. Cited in Sells, *The Bridge Betrayed*, 208, n. 42.

150. Rohde, *Endgame*, 24, 365, 366-67.

151. Rohde, *Endgame*, 193-94.

152. Geyer, "How the Conscience of the West Was Lost," 100-101.

153. For an assessment which discounts the roll of the CNN-factor in the foreign policy decision-making process, see Warren Strobel, *Late Breaking Foreign Policy* (Washington, D.C.: United States Institute of Peace Press, 1997), 122.

154. For insight into the difficulties of reporting in an unbiased, but not morally

equivalent, manner see Martin Bell, *In Harm's Way: Reflections of a War-Zone Thug* (London: Penguin, 1996).

155. Reiff, *Slaughterhouse*, 9.

156. For a personal account of Tom Gjelten's experiences in Sarajevo, see Tom Gjelten, *Sarajevo Daily: A City and Its Newspaper under Siege* (New York: Harper-Collins Publishers, 1995).

157. For a personal account of Janine di Giovanni's time in Sarajevo, Mostar, Travnik, Maglaj, and Tuzla from 1992 to 1994, see Giovanni, *The Quick and the Dead*.

158. For a personal account of Barbara Demick's time in Sarajevo from 1994 to 1995, see Barbara Demick, *Logavina Street: Life and Death in a Sarajevo Neighborhood* (Kansas City, Mo.: Andrews and McMeel, 1996).

159. Heller, *Des Brasiers mal éteints*.

160. Kemal Kurspahić, *As Long as Sarajevo Exists* (Stony Creek, Conn.: Pamphleteers Press, 1997).

161. For one account, see Sudetic, "Why Is France Protecting Indicted War Criminals."

162. Cigar, *Genocide in Bosnia*, 48; and Paul Williams and Norman Cigar, *War Crimes and Individual Responsibility: A Prima Facie Case for the Indictment of Slobodan Milosevic* (London: Alliance to Defend Bosnia-Herzegovina, 1996). See also, Nenad Stefanov and Michael Werz, eds., *Bosnien und Europa: Die Ethnisierung der Gesellschaft* (Frankfurt: Fischer Taschenbuch Verlag, 1994); Mark Mazower, *The War in Bosnia: An Analysis* (London: Action for Bosnia, 1992).

163. Malcolm, *Bosnia: A Short History*; Malcolm, *Kosovo: A Short History*.

164. Robert Donia and John Fine, *Bosnia-Hercegovina: A Tradition Betrayed* (London: Columbia University Press, 1994). For other competent historical reviews, see Mark Pinson, ed., *The Muslims of Bosnia-Herzegovina* (Cambridge, Mass.: Harvard University Press, 1993); Francine Friedman, *The Bosnian Muslims* (Boulder, Colo.: Westview Press, 1996); Paul Garde, *Vie et Mort de la Yougoslavie* (Paris: Fayard, 1992); Andreas Kappeler, Gerhard Simon, and Georg Brunner (ed. German edition 1989) and Edward Allworth (ed. English edition), *Muslim Communities Re-emerge: Historical Perspectives on Nationality, Politics and Opposition in the Former Soviet Union and Yugoslavia*, translated by Caroline Sawyer (Durham, N.C.: Duke University Press, 1994).

165. For an explanation of how "relativist assumptions" enticed many scholars into writing under the guiding principle of moral equivalence, see Thomas Cushman, *Critical Theory and the War in Croatia and Bosnia* (Seattle: Henry M. Jackson School of International Studies, University of Washington, 1997). For examples of the reliance upon relativism and the understatement of blame, see Lenard Cohen, *Broken Bonds: Yugoslavia's Disintegration and Balkan Politics in Transition* (Boulder, Colo.: Westview Press, 1995); Miron Rezun, *Europe and War in the Balkans: Towards a New Yugoslav Identity* (Westport, Conn.: Praeger, 1995); William Johnsen, *Deciphering the Balkan Enigma: Using History to Inform Policy*, 2nd ed. (Carlisle, Pa.: Strategic Studies Institute, 1995).

166. See M. Cherif Bassiouni, *The Law of the International Criminal Tribunal for the Former Yugoslavia* (New York: Transnational Publisher, 1996); M. Cherif Bassiouni, "Former Yugoslavia: Investigating Violations of International Humanitarian Law," *Fordham International Law Journal* 18 (1995): 1191; M. Cherif Bassiouni, *Commentaries on the International Law Commission's 1991 Draft Code of Crimes against the Peace and Security of Mankind* (Pau, France: Eres, 1993); Bassiouni, *Crimes against Humanity*; M. Cherif Bassiouni, *International Criminal Law* (New York: Transnatioanl Publishers, 1986-1987).

167. Theodor Meron, "International Criminalization of Internal Atrocities," *American Journal of International Law* 89 (1995): 554; Theodor Meron, "War Crimes in Yugoslavia," *American Journal of International Law* 99 (1994): 78; Theodor Meron, "The Case for War Crimes Trials," *Foreign Affairs* 72 (1993): 122; Theodor Meron, "Rape as a Crime under International Humanitarian Law," *American Journal of International Law* 87 (1993): 424; Theodor Meron, *Human Rights and Humanitarian Norms.*

168. For a review of the extent to which Serbian propaganda influenced Western media see Johannes Vollmer, ed., *Dass Wir in Bosnien zur Welt Gehören: Fŋr ein Multikulturelles Zusammanleben* (Solothum: Benziger, 1995).

169. For a detailed accounting of the extent to which "myths and mischaracterizations" were perpetuated by some journalists and academics, see Campbell, *National Deconstruction.* See also, Carole Hodge and Mladen Grbin, *Test for Europe* (Glasgow: IREES, University of Glasgow, 1996). For an at times candid assessment of the ethical dilemmas faced by journalists, see Maass, *Love Thy Neighbour.*

170. For example, see Misha Glenny, *The Fall of Yugoslavia: The Third Balkan War* (London: Viking Penguin, 1992), reportedly relied upon and praised by David Owen; John Lampe, *Yugoslavia as History: Twice There Was a Country* (Cambridge: Cambridge University Press, 1996), an influential CIA analyst; and Richard Kaplan, *Balkan Ghosts,* reportedly influential in President Clinton's early assessment of the crisis. (This story is recounted in Christopher, *In the Stream of History,* 347. See also, Edgar O'Ballance, *Civil War in Bosnia, 1992-94* (London: St. Martin's Press, 1995).

171. For example, see Marie-Janine Calic, *Der Krieg in Bosnien-Hercegovina: Ursachen, Konflikstruturen, Internationale Lösungsversuche* (Ebenhausen, Germany: Forschungsinstitut für Internationale Politik und Sicherheit, 1995); Woodward, *Balkan Tragedy.*

172. For a detailed tracking of the reflection of Serbian propaganda in the writings of Western academics and foreign policy experts, see Cushman, *Critical Theory and the War in Croatia and Bosnia.* For examples of work based in large part on Serbian propaganda see Yossef Bodansky, *Offensive in the Balkans: The Potential for a Wider War as a Result of Foreign Intervention in Bosnia-Herzegovina* (London: International Strategic Studies Association, 1995); Peter Handke, *Eine Winterliche Reise zu den Flüssen Donau, Save, Morawa und Drina: Oder Gerechtigkeit für Serbien* (Frankfurt am Main: Suhrkamp, 1996).

173. Johnsen, *Deciphering the Balkan Enigma,* 125.

174. James Sadkovich, *The U.S. Media and Yugoslavia 1991-1995* (Westport, Conn.: Praeger, 1998), 296.

175. For an in-depth critique of the pervasiveness of pro-Serb propaganda in Switzerland and France, see Yves Laplace, *L'Age d'Homme en Bosnie: Petit Guide d'une Nausée Suisse* (Lausanne: Editions D'en Bas, 1997).

176. See for example, Zarković Bookman, *Economic Decline and Nationalism in the Balkans*; Alex Dragnitch, *Yugoslavia's Disintegration and the Struggle for the Truth* (New York: Columbia University Press, 1995); Aleksandar Pavković, *The Fragmentation of Yugoslavia: Nationalism in a Multinational State* (London: Macmillan, 1997); Alex Dragnitch, *Serbs and Croats: The Struggle in Yugoslavia* (New York: Harcourt, 1992); Laslo ®ekelj, *Yugoslavia: The Process of Disintegration* (Boulder, Colo.: Westview Press, 1993); Svetozar Stojanović, *The Fall of Yugoslavia* (New York: Prometheus Books, 1997); Zametica, *The Yugoslav Conflict.* For a more moderate nationalist reconstruction of the conflict, see Mihailo Crnobrnja, *The Yugoslav Drama* (London: McGill-Queens University Press, 1994); Jasminka Udovicki and James Ridgway, eds., *Yugosla-*

via's Ethnic Nightmare: The Inside Story of Europe's Unfolding Ordeal (New York: Lawrence Hill Books, 1995).

177. Gregory Peroche, *Histoire de la Croatie et des Nations Slaves du Sud* (Paris: F.X. de Guibert, 1992); Marcus Tanner, *Croatia: A Nation Forged in War* (New Haven, Conn.: Yale University Press, 1997); Tvrtković, *Bosnia-Hercegovina—Back to the Future*.

178. Department of State Cable number Belgrade 01209 151953, 15 February 1994 (declassified 31 March 1997); Department of State Cable number Belgrade 01232 162107Z, 16 February 1994 (declassified 31 March 1997).

179. For an example of a Serb American lobby press release, see "Bosnian 'Genocide' Charges False Says Serbian-American Coalition, Assails Pro-intervention Propaganda," *SerbNet Media Center Press Release, 4* April 1995.

180. David Binder, "Bosnia's Bombers," *The Nation,* 2 October 1995, vol. 261, no. 10, 336.

Chapter 6

1. Anthony Lewis, editorial, "Abroad at Home; Then and Now," *New York Times,* 6 June 1997, A31.

2. Muhamed Sacirbey, *No Peace without Justice, International Campaign for the Establishment of the International Criminal Court* (1997), 54.

3. For a more detailed argument of the hypothesis that the Tribunal was established in part to relieve pressure to take more direct action to prevent atrocities, see Neier, *War Crimes.*

4. Representative of Spain, 6 October 1992.

5. Quoted in Scharf, *Balkan Justice,* 44-45.

6. Neier, *War Crimes,* 125.

7. Neier, *War Crimes,* 112, 125.

8. Editorial, "Halfway Responses to All-Out War," *New York Times,* 9 October 1992, A32.

9. Commission on War Crimes, "Interim Report."

10. Editorial, "Halfway Response to All-Out War," *New York Times,* 9 October 1992, A32.

11. Stephanie Nebehay, "Yugoslav War Crimes Body in Disarray on Anniversary," Reuters World Service, 6 October 1993.

12. John Pomfret, "War Crimes' Punishment Seem Distant; Balkan Probe Lacks Funds and Backing," *Washington Post,* 12 November 1993, 39A; M. Cherif Bassiouni, "The Commission of Experts Established Pursuant to Security Council Resolution 780: Investigating Violations of International Humanitarian Law in the Former Yugoslavia" (Occasional Paper No. 2), *International Human Rights Law Institute* (DePaul University College of Law, 1996), 13-14.

13. Bassiouni, "The Commission of Experts," 13-14.

14. Bassiouni, "The Commission of Experts," 31, 35-37.

15. UN War Crimes Commission, "Final Report."

16. Telephone interview with M. Cherif Bassiouni by Michael Scharf, 8 August 1996.

17. For a review of the funding difficulties faced by the Tribunal, see GAO Report,

"Former Yugoslavia: War Crimes Tribunal Workload Exceeds Capacity."

18. GAO Report, "Former Yugoslavia: War Crimes Tribunal Workload Exceeds Capacity," 8.

19. See Luc Huyse, "Justice after Transition: On the Choices Successor Elites Make in Dealing with the Past," in *Transitional Justice: How Emerging Democracies Reckon with Former Regimes*, ed. N. Kritz (Washington, D.C.: U.S. Institute of Peace Press, 1995). 490. See also "Ethiopia, Report of the Office of the Special Prosecutor," in *Transitional Justice*.

20. Roht-Arriaza, *Impunity and Human Rights*.

21. Geneva Convention for the Amelioration of the Condition of the Wounded and Sick in Armed Forces in the Field, 12 August 1949, art. 50, 75 UNTS 31; Geneva Convention for the Amelioration of the Condition of the Wounded, Sick and Shipwrecked Members of Armed Forces at Sea, 12 August 1949, art. 51, 75 UNTS 85; Geneva Convention Relative to the Treatment of Prisoners of War, 12 August 1949, art. 130, 75 UNTS 135; and Geneva Convention Relative to the Protection of Civilian Persons in Time of War, 12 August 1949, art. 147, 75 UNTS 287.

22. Convention on the Prevention and Punishment of the Crime of Genocide, 9 December 1948, 78 UNTS 277.

23. Commission on War Crimes, "Interim Report."

24. See Morris and Scharf, *An Insider's Guide*, 64-65.

25. See Article 51 of the Geneva Convention for the Amelioration of the Condition of the Wounded and Sick in Armed Forces in the Field, 12 August 1949, 6 UST 311, TIAS No. 3362, 75 UNTS 31; Article 52 of the Geneva Convention for the Amelioration of the Condition of the Wounded, Sick and Shipwrecked Members of the Armed Forces at Sea, 12 August 1949, 6 UST 3217, TIAS No. 3363, 75 UNTS 85; Article 131 of the Geneva Convention Relative to the Treatment of Prisoners of War, 12 August 1949, 6 UST 3316, TIAS No. 3364, 75 UNTS 135; and Article 148 of the Geneva Convention Relative to the Protection of Civilian Persons in Time of War, 12 August 1949, 6 UST 3516, TIAS No. 3365, 75 UNTS 287.

26. See Morris and Scharf, *An Insider's Guide* at 114 n. 356, 341 and accompanying text; see also Meron, *Human Rights and Humanitarian Norms*, 215 (Geneva Conventions not subject to derogation).

27. Article 4 of the Genocide Convention provides, "Persons committing genocide or any of the acts enumerated in article 3 shall be punished, whether they are constitutionally responsible rulers, public officials or private individuals." Article 5 requires states to "provide effective penalties" for persons guilty of genocide. Convention on the Crime of Genocide, 9 December 1948, 78 UNTS 277.

28. Convention on the Crime of Genocide, art. IX.

29. The UN Human Rights Commission has concluded that impunity is one of the main reasons for the continuation of grave violations of human rights throughout the world. United Nations Commission on Human Rights, "Report on the Consequences of Impunity." UN fact-finding reports on Chile and El Salvador indicate that the granting of amnesty or de facto impunity has led to an increase in abuses in those countries. Special Rapporteur on the Situation of Human Rights in Chile, "Report Prepared in Accordance with Paragraph 11 of the Commission on Human Rights Resolution 1983/38 of March 1983," para 341. (Impunity enjoyed by Chilean security forces "is the cause, and an undoubted encouragement in the commission, of multiple violations of fundamental rights."); see also Ed Broadbent, "Opinion," *The Toronto Star*, 20 October 1994, A27, (reporting that human rights groups have

documented an increase in the number of extra-judicial executions and death threats since the Salvadoran legislature voted in March 1993 for a "broad, absolute and unconditional amnesty.").

30. Elaine Sciolino, "U. S. Names Figures to Be Prosecuted over War Crimes," *New York Times*, 17 December 1992, A1. Other international experts who were calling for the creation of an international war crimes tribunal for the Balkans included the rapporteurs appointed by the Conference on Security and Co-operation in Europe under the Moscow Human Dimension Mechanism; the special rapporteur appointed by the United Nations Human Rights Commission to investigate the human rights situation in the former Yugoslavia, and Cyrus Vance and Sir David Owen, who were entrusted with conducting the peace talks on Bosnia. See Morris and Scharf, *An Insider's Guide*, 29.

31. See Michael Scharf, "The Politics behind U. S. Opposition to the International Criminal Court," *The Brown Journal of World Affairs* 6 (winter/spring 1999): 98-99.

32. Elaine Sciolino, "U.S. Names Figures to Be Prosecuted over War Crimes," *New York Times*, international edition, 17 December 1992, 1A.

33. See for example Carla Anne Robbins, "World Again Confronts Moral Issues Involved in War Crimes Trials," *Wall Street Journal*, 13 July 1993, 6A.

34. See Neier, *War Crimes*, 127-28.

35. The French report is reproduced in Morris and Scharf, *An Insider's Guide*, 327-75.

36. The record of debate leading to the adoption of Resolution 808 is reproduced in Morris and Scharf, *An Insider's Guide*, 159-75.

37. Payam Akhvan, "The Yugoslav Tribunal at a Crossroads: The Dayton Peace Agreement and Beyond," *Human Rights Quarterly* 18 (1996): 263.

38. David Forsyth, "International Criminal Courts: A Political View," *Netherlands Quarterly of Human Rights* 15 (1997): 9.

39. See Akhvan, "Justice in the Hague," 9.

40. D'Amato, "Peace vs. Accountability in Bosnia," 503-04.

41. David Forsyth, "Politics and the International Tribunal for the Former Yugoslavia," *Crim. L. Forum* 5 (1994): 401

42. Holbrooke, *To End a War*, 189-90.

43. Scharf, "The Politics behind U.S. Opposition to the International Criminal Court," 99.

44. See Neier, *War Crimes*, 129.

45. Forsyth, "Politics and the International Tribunal for the Former Yugoslavia," 401.

46. Rocco Cervoni, "Beating Plowshares into Swords—Reconciling The Sovereign Right to Self-Determination with Individual Human Rights through the International Criminal Court: The Lessons of the Former Yugoslavia and Rwanda," *St. John's J. Legal Comment* 12: 498.

47. President of the Tribunal, "First Annual Report of the International Criminal Tribunal for the Former Yugoslavia," 49.

48. See Secretary-General, "Report Pursuant to Paragraph 2 of Security Council Resolution 808 (1993)," para 34. Official Journal of the European Communities, Resolution on the Death Penalty, No. C 94/278, 12 March 1992; see also Secretary-General, "Report on Capital Punishment and Implementation of the Safeguards Guaranteeing the Protection of the Rights of Those Facing the Death Penalty," paras 5, 60.

49. The Nuremberg Tribunal was authorized to impose the death penalty or other just punishment in the event of a conviction. Nuremberg Charter, arts. 27-28, reprinted in Morris and Scharf, *An Insider's Guide*, 677. See Schabas, *War Crimes*, 766.

50. See the record of the debate leading to the adoption of Resolution 827, UN SCOR,

48th Sess., 3217th mtg., 16, UN Doc. S/PV.3217 (1993), reprinted in Morris and Scharf, *An Insider's Guide* 179, 188.

51. Interview with Payam Akhvan, legal adviser, Office of the Prosecutor of the Yugoslav Tribunal, by Michael Scharf, The Hague, Netherlands, 11 August 1998. Judge Abi-Saab resigned in 1995 and was replaced by Fouad Abdel-Moneim Riad, a professor of law at Cairo University.

52. Interview with Payam Akhvan, legal adviser, Office of the Prosecutor of the Yugoslav Tribunal, by Michael Scharf, The Hague, Netherlands, 11 August 1998.

53. Guest, *On Trial*, 131.

54. See Boris Krivoshei and Serbei Staroselsky, "Russia Will Obey Tribunal on War Crimes in Yugoslavia," *TASS*, 24 September 1993.

55. Guest, *On Trial*.

56. Guest, *On Trial*.

57. On 24 November 1993, the government of Bosnia sent a letter to the Security Council stating that it planned to institute such proceedings against Britain. The letter was published as Security Council Document S/26806, 26 November 1993. The Bosnian government dropped its case when Britain threatened to suspend its contribution to the Bosnian relief effort if the case proceeded.

58. President of the Tribunal, "First Annual Report of the International Criminal Tribunal for the Former Yugoslavia," para. 15, 20.

59. Horne, "The Real Trial of the Century," 5.

60. President of the Yugoslav Tribunal, "First Annual Report of the International Criminal Tribunal for the Former Yugoslavia," para 23.

61. Guest, *On Trial*.

62. James Bone, "U.K. Blocks Choice of War Crimes Prosecutor," *London Times*, 4 September 1993.

63. Guest, *On Trial*.

64. Guest, *On Trial*.

65. Stanley Meisler, "Jury Still Out on Bosnian War Crimes Tribunal Created by UN," *Los Angeles Times*, 25 December 1993, 5(A).

66. Guest, *On Trial*.

67. Geyer, "How the Conscience of the West Was Lost," 90.

68. Meisler, "Jury Still Out on Bosnian War Crimes," 5A.

69. Meisler, "Jury Still Out on Bosnian War Crimes, 5A.

70. Guest, *On Trial*.

71. "Venezuelan on War Crimes Panel; Tribunal Will Probe Atrocities in Former Yugoslavia," *Chicago Tribune*, 22 October 1993, 10N.

72. Roy Gutman, "Tribunal Setback: Prosecutor for War Crimes in Former Yugoslavia Quits," *Newsday*, 4 February 1994, 4.

73. Owen, *Balkan Odyssey*, 255.

74. Paul Lewis, "South African Is to Prosecute Balkan War Crimes," *New York Times*, 9 July 1994, 2.

75. Stephen Handelman, "Point of War Crimes Tribunal Is to Try Persons, Not Nationalities," *Toronto Star*, 10 July 1994, 9F.

76. Guest, *On Trial*.

77. S.C. Res. 936, UN SCOR, 49th Sess., 44, UN Doc. S/INF/50 (1996). See also UN Press Release DH/1682, 8 July 1994.

78. Meisler, "Jury Still Out on Bosnian War Crimes," 5A.

79. Handelman, "Point of War Crimes Tribunal Is to Try Persons," 9F.

80. Richard Goldstone, "The International Tribunal for the Former Yugoslavia: A Case Study in Security Council Action," *Duke Journal of Comparative and International Law* 6 (1995): 7.

81. Eduardo Cue, "Tough New War Crimes Prosecutor," *Christian Science Monitor*, 24 August 1999.

82. GAO Report, "Former Yugoslavia: War Crimes Tribunal Workload Exceeds Capacity."

83. Bruce Zagaris, "Milosevic Turned Over to the ICTY," *International Enforcement Law Reported* 17 (August 2001): 348.

84. In 1985, the United States enacted the "Kassebaum Amendment," which provided that the United States would withhold payments to the United Nations unless it began adopting budgets by consensus instead of the two-thirds vote provided for in Article 18 of the UN Charter. Faced with the prospect of bankruptcy, the United Nations made the change, and the United States began wielding a de facto U.S. financial veto. See Jose E. Alvarez, "Legal Remedies and the United Nations' a la Carte Problem," *Michigan Journal of International Law* 12 (1991): 229.

85. Interview with Tom Warrick, special counsel to the Coalition of International Justice, in Brussels, Belgium, by Michael Scharf, 20 July 1996.

86. See Statements of India, Brazil, Zimbabwe, Mexico, Ecuador, and Colombia. Summary Record of the 70th Meeting of the Fifth Committee, UN Doc. A/C.5/47/SR.70, 25 August 1993; Summary Record of the 72nd Meeting of the Fifth Committee, UN Doc. A/C.5/47/SR.72, 27 August 1993.

87. Secretary-General, "Report as Requested by the General Assembly in Resolution 47/235," 6.

88. General Assembly Resolution 48/241, 14 April 1994.

89. Secretary-General, "Report as Requested by the General Assembly in Resolution 47/235."

90. Thomas Warrick, special counsel, Coalition for International Justice before the House Committee on International Operations and Human Rights, *Federal News Service*, 26 October 1995.

91. Editorial, "Prosecute Bosnia's War Criminals," *New York Times*, 4 January 1995, A18.

92. Guest, *On Trial*.

93. According to the Secretary-General, "Report, Financing of the International Tribunal," 5 December 1994, 35, the voluntary contributions to the Tribunal for 1994-1995 were as follows: Cambodia: $5,000; Canada: $168,280; Hungary: $2,000; Ireland: $6,768; Liechtenstein: $2,985; Malaysia: $2 million; Namibia: $500; New Zealand: $14,660; Norway: $130,000; Pakistan: $1 million; Spain: $13,725; Italy: $1,898,049; United States: $3 million.

94. According to the Secretary-General, "Report, Financing of the International Tribunal," 5 December 1994, 30, the United States sent 22 lawyers and investigators, the United Kingdom 5, Sweden and the Netherlands each sent 3, and two each were sent from Denmark and Norway.

95. GAO Report, "Former Yugoslavia: War Crimes Tribunal Workload Exceeds Capacity."

96. GAO Report, "Former Yugoslavia: War Crimes Tribunal Workload Exceeds Capacity."

97. Marlise Simons, "Bosnian Rapes Go Untried by the UN," *New York Times*, 7 December 1994, 12A.

98. See Secretary-General, "Report Pursuant to General Assembly Resolution

53/35," *Srebrenica Report*.

99. Prepared Testimony of Thomas Warrick, Special Counsel, Coalition for International Justice before the House Committee on International Operations and Human Rights, Federal News Service, 26 October 1995.

100. Raymond Bonner, "UN Fiscal Woes Are Said to Threaten War Crime Tribunals," *New York Times*, 4 October 1995, 8A.

101. Bonner, "UN Fiscal Woes Are Said to Threaten War Crime Tribunals," 8A.

102. General Assembly Resolution 49/242, 7 August 1995.

103. After the Security Council decides to establish a peacekeeping mission, the UN's Department of Peacekeeping Operations prepares an implementation plan and the UN's Field Operations Division prepares the mission's budget and deployment plan. The mission's budget is then sent to the UN's Advisory Committee on Administrative and Budgetary Questions, the Fifth Committee, and finally the General Assembly for approval. See GAO Report, "UN Peacekeeping: Lessons Learned in Managing Recent Missions," December 1993, 16.

104. Bulletin of the International Criminal Tribunal for the Former Yugoslavia, No. 18.

105. GAO Report, "Former Yugoslavia: War Crimes Tribunal Workload Exceeds Capacity."

106. Meisler, "Jury Still Out on Bosnian War Crimes," 5A.

107. Bob Dart, "Defense Cost Cap Weighed, Okla. Bombing Trials May Top $50 Million," *Denver Post*, 15 June 1997, 14A.

108. Bassiouni, "Remarks at the Annual Meeting."

109. GAO Report, "Former Yugoslavia: War Crimes Tribunal Workload Exceeds Capacity."

110. GAO Report, "Former Yugoslavia: War Crimes Tribunal Workload Exceeds Capacity."

Chapter 7

1. Colum Lynch, "Departing War Crimes Tribunal Chief Assails UN Inaction," *Washington Post*, 9 November 1999, A26.

2. Chris Hedges, "First Hague Trial for Bosnia Crimes Opens on Tuesday," *New York Times*, 6 May 1996, A1.

3. Goldstone, "The International Tribunal for the Former Yugoslavia," 7.

4. Minna Schrag, "The Yugoslav Crimes Tribunal: A Prosecutor's View," *Duke Journal of Comparative and International Law* 6 (1995): 191.

5. See D. Tadic Indictment, IT-94-1.

6. John Lichfield, "Sharks Escape as the Hague Tries a Minnow," *The Independent*, 12 May 1996, 14.

7. Schrag, "The Yugoslav Crimes Tribunal," 193.

8. See Scharf, *Balkan Justice*, 213-14.

9. Robert Block, "First Catch You a War Criminal," *The Independent*, 30 April 1995, 4.

10. Justice Richard Goldstone, interview in Brussels, Belgium, by Michael Scharf, 20 July 1996.

11. Erdemovic Indictment, IT-96-22. Drazen Erdemovic was found guilty on 14 January 1998, and sentenced to a five-year prison term.

12. Delalic, Delic, Mucic, and Landzo Indictment, IT-96-21. Hazim Delic was found

guilty and sentenced to a twenty-year prison term. Esad Landzo was found guilty and sentenced to a fifteen-year prison term.

13. Anto Furundzija was found guilty on 10 December 1998, and sentenced to a ten-year prison term.

14. See Mrksic, Radic, Sljivancanin, and Dokmanovic Indictment, IT-95-13a.

15. Delalic, Delic, Mucic, and Landzo Indictment, IT-96-21.

16. See Blaskic Indictment, IT-95-14.

17. Secretary-General, "Report on the Activities of the Office of Internal Oversight Services," para. 55-56.

18. Secretary-General, "Report on the Activities of the Office of Internal Oversight Services," para. 55-56, 59.

19. Tom Hundley, "A Prosecutor's Viewpoint," *Chicago Tribune*, 19 July 1998, 3.

20. Martin, "Holbrooke Sees 'Tough Slog' to Peace Business in Bosnia," 3.

21. Milosevic, Milutinovic, Sainovic, Ojdanic, and Stojiljkovic Indictment, IT-99-37.

22. Forsyth, "International Criminal Courts," 11.

23. See Scharf, *Balkan Justice*, 90.

24. See Scharf, *Balkan Justice*, 150-55.

25. See Scharf, *Balkan Justice*, 154.

26. Ed Vulliamy and Patrick Wintour, "War in the Balkans: Hawks Smell a Tyrant's Blood," *The Observer*, 30 May 1999, 15.

27. Vulliamy and Wintour, "War in the Balkans," 15.

28. See for example Albright, "Statement to the Ministerial Meeting of the North Atlantic Council," 12 April 1999.

29. Albright, "Statement to the Ministerial Meeting of the North Atlantic Council," 12 April 1999.

30. Milosevic, Milutinovic, Sainovic, Ojdanic, and Stojiljkovic Indictment, IT-99-37.

31. See Williams and Cigar, *War Crimes and Individual Responsibility,* which was reportedly used as a research template for the indictment.

32. Fionnuala Ni Aolain, "The Fractured Soul of the Dayton Peace Agreement: A Legal Analysis," *Michigan Journal of International Law* 19, no. 957 (1998): 995.

33. Third Annual Report of the Yugoslav Tribunal, U.N. Doc. S/1996/665, 16 August 1996, at para. 80.

34. Ni Aolain, "The Fractured Soul of the Dayton Peace Agreement," 999.

35. President of the Tribunal, "Third Annual Report of the International Criminal Tribunal for the Former Yugoslavia," para 82.

36. Ni Aolain, "The Fractured Soul of the Dayton Peace Agreement," 999.

37. Graham Blewitt, deputy prosecutor of the International Criminal Tribunal for the Former Yugoslavia, interview by Michael Scharf, The Hague, 11 August 1998.

38. Graham Blewitt, deputy prosecutor of the International Criminal Tribunal for the Former Yugoslavia, interview by Michael Scharf, The Hague, 11 August 1998.

39. "Fifth Annual Report of the Yugoslav Tribunal," U.N. Doc. S/1998/737, 10 August 1998, at para. 129.

40 Ni Aolain, "The Fractured Soul of the Dayton Peace Agreement," 995.

41. Ni Aolain, "The Fractured Soul of the Dayton Peace Agreement," 1000-1001.

42. Reuters, 18 November 1999.

43. Daniel Jonah Goldhagen, *Hitler's Willing Executioners* (New York: Alfred A. Knopf, 1996).

44. See Scharf, *Balkan Justice,* 216-17.

45. Krajisnik and Plavsic Indictments, IT-00-39 and 40.

46. See "Report to the President from Justice Robert H. Jackson, Chief of Counsel for the United States in the Prosecution of Axis War Criminals, June 7, 1945," reprinted in *American Journal of International Law* 39, 178 (Supp. 1945): 184.

47. Priscilla Hayner, "Fifteen Truth Commissions—1974 to 1994: A Comparative Study," *Transitional Justice* (1994) 225-62.

48. Anne L. Quintal, "Rule 61: The "Voice of the Victims" Screams Out for Justice," *Columbia Journal of Transnational Law* 36 (1998): 723.

49. Charles Trueheart "Charges against Milosevic Detailed: Yugoslav, Top Aides Face Counts Rooted in Purges, Slayings," *Washington Post,* 28 May 1999.

50. Robert Pollock, "A Milosevic Indictment May Be Drawing Near," *Wall Street Journal,* 19 April 1999, A22.

51. Interview with Fred Graham, by Michael Scharf, New York City, 20 August 1996.

52. *Prosecutor v. Slavko Dokmanovic,* Decision on the Motion for Release by the Accused Slavko Dokmanovic, No. IT-95-13a-PT, T. Ch. II, 22 October 1997.

53. N. Miletich, "UN Court to Try Suspect in Biggest Croatian Massacre," *AAP Newsfeed,* 18 January 1998.

54. Yugoslav Tribunal Press Release, "Completion of the Internal Inquiry into the Death of Slavko Dokmanovic," U.N. Doc. CC/PIU/334-3, 23 July 1998.

55. For a review of the human rights abuses committed before and after the Dayton Accords in Foca, see Human Rights Watch, *Bosnia and Herzegovina—'A Closed, Dark Place': Past and Present Human Rights Abuses in Foca* (London: Human Rights Watch, 1996), 67.

56. See Mrksic, Radic, Sljivancanin, and Dokmanovic Indictment, IT-95-13a.

57. Zeliko Raznatovic "Arkan" Indictment, IT-97-27.

58. Meakic, Gruban, and Knezevic Indictment, IT-95-4.

59. Kovacevic, Drljaca, and Stakic Indictment, IT-97-24.

60. Christiane Amanpour, "Del Ponte Urges War Crimes Arrests," *CNN Web,* 27 April 2001.

61. See Krstic Indictment, IT-98-33.

62. "Survivors Condemn 'Lenient' Verdict," BBC Broadcast, 2 August 2001, 20:11 GMT 21:11 U.K.

63. Nick Thorpe, "Special Report: War Crimes in the Former Yugoslavia," *The Guardian,* 2 May 2001.

64. Karadzic and Mladic Indictment, IT-95-5; See Zeliko Raznatovic "Arkan" Indictment, IT-97-27; and Milosevic, Milutinovic, Sainovic, Ojdanic, and Stojiljkovic Indictment, IT-99-37.

65. Petar Lukovic, "Vote for Your Favourite War Criminal: Why Do Serbs Still Regard Milosevic and His Cronies as National Heroes?" *Institute for War and Peace Reporting* <info@iwpr.net> 8 June 2001.

66. See Letter dated 29 November 1995 from the Permanent Representative of the United States of America to the United Nations addressed to the Secretary-General, UN Doc. A/50/790, S/1995/999, 30 November 1995, 4 (General Framework Agreement for Peace in Bosnia and Herzegovina), 63 (Constitution of Bosnia and Herzegovina).

67. Tribunal spokesman Paul Risley, Associated Press, 3 April 2000.

68. See Krajisnik and Plavsic Indictments, IT-00-39 and 40.

69. See Associated Press, 3 April 2000.

70. See Krajisnik and Plavsic Indictments, IT-00-39 and 40.

71. See International Crisis Group, *War Criminals in Bosnia's Republika Srpska: Who Are the People in Your Neighborhood* (ICG Balkans Report No 103, Brussels, 2 November 2000).

72. Statute of the Yugoslav Tribunal art 24(3).

73. See Crook, "The United Nations Compensation Commission."

74. The judges provided in their rules of procedure a victim compensation mechanism based on national proceedings. Under Rule 106 of the Tribunal's rules, the registrar is to transmit any judgment containing a specific finding that the convicted person caused injury to a particular victim or victims to the competent authorities of any states in which the victim may file a claim against the individual perpetrator. Rules of Procedure and Evidence of the Yugoslav Tribunal (as amended), Rule 106, UN Doc. IT/32/Rev.10. As a consequence of the primacy of the Yugoslav Tribunal, the national court is bound by the finding contained in the judgment of the Tribunal to the effect that the convicted person is guilty of the crime which resulted in injury to the victim. Unfortunately, the courts of Serbia and Republika Srpska have so far not been receptive to awarding victim compensation pursuant to the Tribunal's findings. Thus, the Rule 106 procedure has been a failure.

75. "NATO's 17-Point Statement on Kosovo," Associated Press, 24 April 1999.

76. Martin, "Holbrooke Sees 'Tough Slog' to Peace Business in Bosnia," 3.

77. Charles Trueheart, "War Crimes Panel Gathers Evidence against Milosevic," *Washington Post*, 11 May 1999, A13.

78. Trueheart, "War Crimes Panel Gathers Evidence against Milosevic," A13.

79. Trueheart, "War Crimes Panel Gathers Evidence against Milosevic," A13.

80. Trueheart, "War Crimes Panel Gathers Evidence against Milosevic," A13.

81. Statute of the International Tribunal, art. 1.

82. Robert L. Pollock,"A Milosevic Indictment May Be Drawing Near," *Wall Street Journal,* 19 April 1999, A22.

83. Yugoslav Tribunal press release, "Prosecutor Seeks Assurance from President Milosevic Regarding Kosovo Investigations," The Hague, 15 October 1998. <http://www.Un.org/Yugoslav Tribunal/pressreal/p.353-e.htm, 3 September 2001.

84. Yugoslav Tribunal press release, "Statement on behalf of Louise Arbour, Prosecutor International Criminal Tribunal for the Former Yugoslavia," The Hague, 24 July 1999. <http://www.un.org/Yugoslav Tribunal/pressreal/p.422-e.htm, 3 September 2001.

85. Vladimir Javanovski, "The Crimes of Ljuboten," *Institute for War and Peace Reporting Balkan Crisis Report*, No. 276, 31 August 2001.

86. Balkan Action Council, *Balkan Watch, Week in Review*, 28 April-5 May 1998.

87. "It is that sort of deterrence that is important," stated Goldstone, Balkan Action Council, *Balkan Watch, Week in Review*, 28 April-5 May 1998.

88. Balkan Action Council, *Balkan Watch, Week in Review*, 20-27 October 1999.

89. Yugoslav Tribunal press relase, "Statement by the Office of the Prosecutor: The Prosecutor Does Not Accept the Refusal by [the FRY] to Allow Kosovo Investigations." The Hague, 7 October 1998, http:// www. Un.org/Yugoslav Tribunal/presreal/p351-e.Htm, 3 September 2001. See also Yugoslav Tribunal press releases, "Prosecutor Seeks Assurance from President Milosevic Regarding Kosovo Investigations" The Hague, 15 October 1998. http://www.un.org/Yugoslav Tribunal/presreal/p353-e. Htm, 3 September 2001.

90. Yugoslav Tribunal press release, "Prosecutor Seeks Assurance from President Milosevic Regarding Kosovo Investigations," 15 October 1998.

91. Yugoslav Tribunal press release, "Statement by Justice Louise Arbour, Prose-

cutor of the Yugoslav Tribunal," 5 November 1998.

92. Yugoslav Tribunal press release, "The Prosecutor Does Not Accept the Refusal by [the FRY] to allow Kosovo investigations," 7 October 1998.

93. Milosevic, Milutinovic, Sainovic, Ojdanic, and Stojiljkovic Indictment, IT-99-37.

94. Justin Brown, "Facing Up to Atrocities?" *Christian Science Monitor*, 16 February 1999, 6.

95. Yugoslav Tribunal press release, "Statement by the Prosecutor," 31 March 1999. See also Charles Trueheart, "UN Investigating Milosevic for War Crimes; Prosecutor says Yugoslav Leader and Aides May Have Known of Atrocities," *The Washington Post*, 1 April 1999, A24.

96. Yugoslav Tribunal press release, "Statement by the Prosecutor," 31 March 1999.

97. Trueheart, "UN Investigating Milosevic for War Crimes," A24.

98. Pollock, "A Milosevic Indictment May Be Drawing Near," A22.

99. Pollock, "A Milosevic Indictment May Be Drawing Near," A22.

100. Trueheart, "War Crimes Panel Gathers Evidence Against Milosevic," A13

101. Balkan Action Council, *Balkan Watch, Week in Review*, 17-24 November 1998.

102. Statement by the president of the Security Council, 19 January 1999, <http://www. Un.org/peace/kosovo/sprst992.htm> 3 September 2001.

103. Gabrielle McDonald, "The Government of the Federal Republic of Yugoslavia Has Become a Rogue State," *Yugoslav Tribunal*, <http://www.un.org/YugoslavTribunal/presreal/p.359-e.htm> (3 September 2001).

104. Yugoslav Tribunal press release, "The Tribunal for the Former Yugoslavia Seeks the Assistance of the Security Council," The Hague, 9 September 1998, <http://www.un.org/Yugoslav Tribunal/pressrel/p/344-e.htm> (3 September 2001).

105. Yugoslav Tribunal, "The Tribunal for the Former Yugoslavia Seeks the Assistance of the Security Council."

106. William Branigan, "U.S. Classified Data Placed Milosevic in Chain of Command," *Washington Post*, 28 May 1999, A30.

107. Branigan, "U.S. Classified Data Placed Milosevic in Chain of Command," A30.

108. Pollock, "A Milosevic Indictment May Be Drawing Near," A22.

109. Balkan Action Council, *Balkan Watch, Week in Review*, 24 November - 1 December 1998.

110. NATO and U.S. in the Dock over Depleted Uranium Weapons, Agence France Presse, 8 January 2001.

111. Betsy Pisik, "Tribunal Holds Off on Investigating Kosovo Bombing: Prosecutor Weighs Probe of NATO," *Washington Times*, 9 March 2000, 13A.

112. Charles Trueheart, "Taking NATO to Court: Tribunal Reviews Professors' Charges That Alliance Committed War Crimes," *Washington Post*, 20 January 2000, 15A.

113. See Final Report to the Prosecutor by the Committee Established to Review the NATO Bombing Campaign against the Federal Republic of Yugoslavia, 8 June 2000.

114. Steven Erlanger, "Rights Group Says NATO Bombing in Yugoslavia Violated Law," *New York Times*, 8 June 2000, 7A.

115. For a copy of the report submitted to the Tribunal, see Williams and Cigar, *War Crimes and Individual Responsibility*.

Chapter 8

1. For the relevant court documents and orders in this case, see www.icj-cij. org/icjwww/idocket/ibhy/ibhyframe.htm, 25 August 2001.

2. See Application of the Convention of the Prevention and Punishment of the Crime of Genocide *(Croat. v. Yugo.),* www.icj-cij.org/icjwww/idocket/icry/icryframe.htm, 10 August 2001.

3. Case concerning Legality of Use of Force *(Yugoslavia v. United States).* The transcript of the oral arguments are available at http://jurist.law.pitt.edu/kosovo.htm.

4. Michael Dobbs, "Limit on GI Stay Tested in Bosnian Border City: U.S. Force's Year Tour Looking Untenable," *Washington Post,* 24 June 1996, A1. For an accounting of Serb atrocities in Brcko, see Jusuf Kadrić, *Brcko: Genocide and Testimony,* translated by Saba Risaluddin and Hasan Roncevic (Sarajevo: Institute for the Research of Crimes against Humanity and International Law, 1999).

5. For a complete accounting of the preliminary hearings in the case and a review of relevant evidence from Bosnia's attorney, see Francis Boyle, *The Bosnian People Charge Genocide: Proceedings at the International Court of Justice concerning Bosnia v. Serbia on the Prevention and Punishment of the Crime of Genocide* (North Hampton, Mass.: Aletheia Press, 1996).

6. For a schedule of the various court actions concerning the case, see www.icj-cij.org/icjwww/idocket/ibhy/ibhyframe.htm, 25 August 2001.

7. For a review of the legal debate concerning humanitarian intervention, see Richard B. Bilder, "Kosovo and the 'New Interventionism': Promise or Peril?" *Journal of Transnational Law and Policy* 9 (1999): 153; Bartram Brown, "Humanitarian Intervention at a Crossroads," *William and Mary Law Review* 41 (2000): 1683; Julie Mertus, "Reconsidering the Legality of Humanitarian Intervention: Lessons from Kosovo," *William and Mary Law Review* 41 (2000): 1743; Laura Geissler, "The Law of Humanitarian Intervention and the Kosovo Crisis," *Hamline Law Review* 23 (2000); Dr. Klinton Alexander, "NATO's Intervention in Kosovo: The Legal Case for Violating Yugoslavia's National Sovereignty in the Absence of Security Counsel Approval," *Houston Journal of International Law* 22 (2000); Abraham D. Sofaer, "International Law and Kosovo," *Stanford Journal of International Law* 36 (2000): 1.

8. For the a review of the legal arguments made by the NATO member states, see Legality of Use of Force *(Yugo. v. Belgium),* CR/99/15 (10 May 1999) and CR/99/26 (12 May 1999) at www.icj-cij.org/icjwww/idocket/iybe/iybeframe.htm, 3 September 2001; Legality of Use of Force *(Yugo. v. Canada),* CR/99/16 (10 May 1999) and CR/99/27 (12 May 1999) at www.icj-cij.org/icjwww/idocket/iyca/iycaframe.htm, 3 September 2001; Legality of Use of Force *(Yugo. v. France),* CR/99/17 (10 May 1999) and CR/99/28 (12 May 1999) at www.icj-cij.org/icjwww/idocket/iyfr/iyfrframe.htm, 3 September 2001; Legality of Use of Force *(Yugo. v. Germany),* CR/99/18 (11 May 1999) and CR/99/29 (12 May 1999) at www.icj-cij.org/icjwww/idocket/iyge/iygeframe.htm, 3 September 2001; Legality of Use of Force *(Yugo. v. Italy),* CR/99/19 (11 May 1999) and CR/99/30 (12 May 1999) at www.icj-cij.org/icjwww/idocket/iyit/iyitframe.htm, 3 September 2001; Legality of Use of Force *(Yugo. v. Netherlands),* CR/99/20 (11 May 1999) and CR/99/31 (12 May 1999); at www.icj-cij.org/icjwww/idocket/iyne/iyneframe.htm, 3 September 2001; Legality of Use of Force *(Yugo. v. Portugal),* CR/99/21 (11 May 1999) and CR 99/32 (12 May 1999) at www.icj-cij.org/icjwww/idocket/iypo/iypoframe.htm, 3 September 2001; Legality of Use of Force *(Yugo. v. Spain),* CR/99/22 (11 May 1999) and CR/99/33 (12 May 1999) at www.icj-cij.org/icjwww/idocket/iysp/iyspframe.htm, 3 Sep-

tember 2001; Legality of Use of Force *(Yugo. v. U.K.)*, CR/99/23 (11 May 1999) and CR/99/34 (12 May 1999) at www.icj-cij.org/icjwww/idocket/iyuk/iyukframe.htm, 3 September 2001; Legality of Use of Force *(Yugo. v. U.S.)*, CR/99/24 (11 May 1999) and CR/99/35 (12 May 1999) at www.icj-cij.org/icjwww/idocket/iyus/iyusframe.htm, 3 September 2001.

9. See public sitting held on Monday, 10 May 1999, the Peace Palace, Vice-President Weeramantry, Acting President, presiding in the case concerning Legality of Use of Force *(Yugoslavia v. Belgium) (Yugoslavia v. Canada) (Yugoslavia v. France) (Yugoslavia v. Germany) (Yugoslavia v. Italy) (Yugoslavia v. Netherlands) (Yugoslavia v. Portugal) (Yugoslavia v. Spain) (Yugoslavia v. United Kingdom) (Yugoslavia v. United States of America)*, <html://www.icj-cij.org/icjwww/idocket/iyus/iyusframe.htm> (10 August 2001).

10. Convention on the Crime of Genocide, 9 December 1948, 78 UNTS 277.

11. Oppenheim's International Law 7-8 (9th ed., 1992). The rule against the use of force, however, has also been recognized as "a conspicuous example of a rule of international law having the character of jus cogens" Case Concerning Military and Paramilitary Activities in and against Nicaragua *(Nicaragua v. United States)*, ICJ Reports 1986, p. 100, para. 190.

12. Holbrooke, "Hearing of the Senate Foreign Relations Committee Subject: Nomination of Richard Holbrooke as U.S. Ambassador to the United Nations," 24 June 1999.

13. See See Oscar Schachter, "The Right of States to Use Armed Force," *Michigan Law Review* 82 1620 (1984): 1628-33.

14. See Scharf, "Musical Chairs," 29, 57.

15. Brownlie, *Principles of Public International Law*, 513, 515.

16. Antonio Cassese, *Self Determination of Peoples* (1995), 151.

17. Case concerning Military and Paramilitary Activities in and against Nicaragua *(Nicaragua v. United States)*, 1986, IC J 14, 133.

Chapter 9

1. Doubt, "We Had to Jump over the Moral Bridge," 121, citing *New York Times* article by Roger Cohen quoting unnamed Western official.

2. Helen Fein, "Genocide as State Crime: Examples from Rwanda and Bosnia" (Paper prepared for the annual meeting of the American Sociological Association, Toronto, 9-13 August 1997): 10, 11.

3. For a review of the general challenges faced in the implementation of the Dayton Agreement, see GAO Report, "Bosnia Peace Operation."

4. Owen, *Balkan Odyssey*, 365.

5. Vulliamy, *Bosnia: The Crime of Appeasement*, 80.

6. Rohde, *Endgame*, 440.

7. Department of State cable number Belgrade 01268 171941Z, 17 February 1994, (declassified 31 March 1997).

8. Department of State cable number Belgrade 01268 171941Z, 17 February 1994, (declassified 31 March 1997).

9. Vulliamy, *Bosnia: The Crime of Appeasement*, 80.

10. Speech delivered by Assistant Secretary John R. Bolton at the UN Human Rights Commission Session on the Situation in the Former Yugoslavia, 13 August 1993, http://foia.state.gov/Documents/foiadocs/2af8.PDF.

11. Owen, *Balkan Odyssey*, 236.

12. For a comprehensive assessment of the effect of these proposals, see Bunyan Bryant, *The Betrayal of Bosnia*. For a review of the numerous proposals for the territorial division of Bosnia, see Mladen Klemenčić, *Territorial Proposals for the Settlement of the War in Bosnia-Herzegovina* (Durham, N.C.: International Boundaries Research Unit, University of Durham, 1994).

13. For a pointed critique of the Vance-Owen peace plan, see Reneo Luki□, *The Wars of South Slavic Succession: Yugoslavia 1991-93* (Geneva: Graduate Insitute of International Studies, 1993).

14. Balkan Action Council, *Balkan Watch Week in Review*, 14-23 July, vol. 2.29.

15. David Rieff, "Almost Justice" (Review of Holbrooke's *To End a War*) *The New Republic*, 6 July 1998, 30.

16. See for example, Secretary of State Warren Christopher at the opening statement at a news conference, "New Steps toward Conflict Resolution in the Former Yugoslavia" (Washington, D.C.) 10 February 1993; Interview of Secretary of State Warren Christopher by Mr. Roger Mudd, "MacNeil/Lehrer Newshour" (Washington, D.C.) 11 August 1993; Remarks by U.S. Secretary of State Warren Christopher at the Conference on Security and Cooperation in Europe Plenary Session, "Remarks at CSCE" Speech as Delivered (Rome, Italy), 30 November 1993. See also, "Exchange with Reporters, 24 January 1994," *Public Papers of the Presidents of the United States*, William J. Clinton 1993, Book I: 122 (1 January 1994 to 31 July 1994).

17. For a comprehensive account of both the siege and massacre of Srebrenica and the international response, see Rohde, *Endgame*, 440; Secretary-General, "Report Pursuant to General Assembly Resolution 53/35," *Srebrenica Report*.

18. Clark, *Waging Modern War*, 67-68.

19. Holbrooke, *To End a War*, 135, where Holbrooke notes, "We may also have underestimated the strength of our negotiating hand on that day, when the bombing had resumed," and considers that he should have sought more meaningful concessions from the Serbian regime during the bombing campaign.

20. For an insightful review of the Contact Group negotiations leading up to the Dayton Accords, see Francine Boidevaix, *Une Diplomatie informelle pour l'Europe* (Paris: Fondation pour les études de défense, 1996).

21. Reiff, "Review," 38.

22. Nikolic Indictment, IT-94-2.

23. Holbrooke, *To End a War*, 233.

24. Reiff, "Review," 33.

25. Holbrooke, *To End a War*, 226, 316.

26. Holbrooke, *To End a War*, 279.

27. Holbrooke, *To End a War*, 237; Christopher, *In the Stream of History*, 353.

28. Holbrooke, *To End a War*, 147-49.

29. Yugoslavia Tribunal Press Release, CC/PIO/027-E, 24 November 1995. See also Scharf, *Balkan Justice*, 221-222.

30. For the Nikolic indictment and a summary of the Rule 61 hearing, see http://www.un.org/icty/glance/nikolic.htm (25 August 2001).

31. Interview with General William Nash, by Michael Scharf, Cambridge, Massachusetts, 29 September 1998.

32. Reiff, "Almost Justice," 33. If the world were a moral place," Reiff argues, "the Dayton Agreements would never have been allowed to come into effect."

33. For review of the aims of Bosnians, Serbs, and Croatians, as well as the interna-

tional community, see Paul C. Szasz, "The Dayton Accord: The Balkan Peace Agreement," *Cornell International Law Journal* 30 (1997): 776.

34. Doubt, "We Had to Jump over the Moral Bridge," 123-24.

35. Christopher, *In the Stream of History*, 353.

36. See for instance Warren Christopher's speech during the initialing of the Accords, Christopher, *In the Stream of History*, 366.

37. See Dayton Peace Accords, Annexes 3, 4, 6, 7, and 11.

38. See for instance Warren Christopher's speech during the initialing of the Accords, Christopher, *In the Stream of History*, 366.

39. Doubt, "We Had to Jump over the Moral Bridge," 125.

40. See also, Szasz, "The Dayton Accord," 762.

41. Bosnian Delegation Proposed Amendments to the General Framework Agreement, 12 November 1995.

42. *Balkan Watch Week in Review*, 20 November 1995.

43 Bosnian Delegation Proposed Amendments to the Constitution of Bosnia and Herzegovina, 9 November 1995.

44. Bosnian Delegation Proposed Amendments to the Constitution of Bosnia and Herzegovina.

45. Bosnian Delegation Proposed Amendments to Annex 1, the Agreement on the Military Aspects of the Peace Settlement, 17 November 1995.

46. Bosnian Delegation Proposed Amendments to the General Framework Agreement.

47. Szasz, "The Dayton Accord," 762.

48. This letter was never produced, and it is unclear whether this representation was intentionally made to mislead the Bosnian delegation or whether it was an honest mistake.

49. Clark, *Waging Modern War*, 63.

50. Holbrooke, *To End a War*, 320.

51. See International Crisis Group, "War Criminals in Bosnia's Republika Srpska."

52. Holbrooke, *To End a War*, 271.

53. The Bosnian delegation was skeptical of the actual breadth of this provision and proposed that if IFOR was intent on providing itself with the maximum possible authority to protect its forces from imminent or potential threats, that it insert into the accords a provision to the effect that IFOR was authorized to use all necessary force to ensure the implementation of any provision of the accords if IFOR perceived that a failure to implement such provision would have negative consequences for the ability of IFOR to carry out its mandate. This proposal was not accepted by the military representatives at Dayton.

54. The obligation to cooperate also appears in Annex 9 concerning the establishment of public corporations, The Human Rights Annex, Annex 10 concerning civilian implementation, and Annex 1-4 concerning military matters. The norm of justice also appears in a number of other narrow provisions which prohibit indicted war criminals from serving on the Joint Military Commission, require the parties to turn over to The Hague any prisoners of war in their custody who are indicted by the Tribunal, and requires the International Police Task Force to share information with the Tribunal. For a more detailed review of the details of these provisions Paul C. Szasz, "The Protection of Human Rights through the Dayton/Paris Peace Agreement on Bosnia," *American Journal of International Law* 90 (1996): 313.

55. General Framework Agreement, Article IX.

56. Article IX of Annex 4 to the General Framework Agreement.

57. Szasz, "The Dayton Accord," 764.

58. Christopher, *In the Stream of History*, 366-67.

59. Szasz, "The Protection of Human Rights."

60. Szasz, "The Protection of Human Rights."

61. International Crisis Group, "War Criminals in Bosnia's Republika Srpska," 2, 68, 69, 78. According to the ICG, the municipal council in Srebrenica has changed the name of Tito Street to Karadzic Street.

62. Krajisnik and Plavsic Indictments, IT-00-39 and 40.

63. International Crisis Group, "War Criminals in Bosnia's Republika Srpska," 69.

64. International Crisis Group, "War Criminals in Bosnia's Republika Srpska," iii.

65. International Crisis Group, "War Criminals in Bosnia's Republika Srpska," 77.

66. International Crisis Group, "War Criminals in Bosnia's Republika Srpska," 77.

67. See International Crisis Group, *Is Dayton Failing? Bosnia Four Years after the Peace Agreement* (Sarajevo, Washington, Brussels: International Crisis Group, 1999).

68. International Crisis Group, "War Criminals in Bosnia's Republika Srpska," 77.

69. International Crisis Group, "War Criminals in Bosnia's Republika Srpska," 2.

70. Nick Thorpe, "Special Report: War Crimes in the Former Yugoslavia."

71. See "An Editor Pays the Price in Republika Srpska," *Institute for War and Peace Reporting Crisis Report*, no. 86 (23 October 1999), cited in International Crisis Group, "War Criminals in Bosnia's Republika Srpska," 3.

Chapter 10

1. Ambassador David Scheffer, Address at Dartmouth University, 23 October 1998.

2. Christine Spolar, "Serbs Intensify Attack on Ethnic Albanians; Border Villages in Kosovo Are Targeted," *The Washington Post*, 30 May 1998, A13.

3. Editorial, "Shock and Dismay," *The Washington Post*, 13 August 1998, A20.

4. Reuters, 30 October 1998.

5. Jane Perlez, "Massacres by Serbian Forces in 3 Kosovo Villages," *New York Times*, 30 September 1998, A1.

6. *New York Times*, 11 June 1998. A similar comment was made by a Serbian police major commenting on plans to clear KLA roadblocks: "fifteen days ago we should have begun our operation to free the road, but our politicians have been keeping a low profile because of Mr. Holbrooke and the West. But if diplomacy does not work soon, we will have to begin a cleansing operation like the one in Decane. These people are terrorists, pure and simple."

7. Tom Walker, "Serbs Step Up Hunt for Rebel Cells in Kosovo," *Times* (London), 9 March 1998.

8. *Newsday*, 28 June 1999.

9. See interview with Zoran Djindjic, head of Serbia's Democratic Party, proclaiming, "there are no institutions to guarantee any kind of relationship between Serbia and the ethnic Albanians . . . Milosevic is destroying those institutions so there cannot be any negotiations." Justin Brown, "Will Serbs Fight for Kosovo?" *Christian Science Monitor*, 18 March 1998, 1.

10. Marie Colvin, "Kosovo Guerillas Flock to the Flag," *Sunday Times* (London), 22 March 1998.

11. U.S. Department of State, "Secretary Albright Announces $1.075 Million to Support Yugoslav War Crimes Tribunal Investigations in Kosovo," Press Statement by James P. Rubin (13 March 1998).

12. As eventually described by EU humanitarian aid commissioner Emma Bonino in October 1998, "the situation [in Kosovo] is really very bad. Security has not improved. These people had their homes burned down. Now it's snowing. The real problem is to get compliance from Milosevic. Humanitarian aid can provide a lot, but it cannot provide security." Reuters, 26 October 1998.

13. Holbrooke and Walker, "On-the-Record Briefing," 28 October 1998.

14. Holbrooke and Walker, "On-the-Record Briefing," 28 October 1998.

15. Gelbard, Robert, "Press Conference," 15 January 1998.

16. Contact Group, "Statement on Kosovo," 24 September 1997; Contact Group, "Statement on Kosovo," 25 February 1998.

17. Contact Group, "Statement on Kosovo," 8 January 1998.

18. Contact Group, "Statement on Kosovo," 24 September 1997; "Contact Group Statement on Kosovo," 8 January 1998; Contact Group, "Statement on Kosovo," 25 February 1998.

19. See for example, UN Security Council Resolutions 1160, 1199, 1203, 1244.

20. UN Security Council Resolution 1239.

21. Gelbard and Greenstock, "Press Conference," 26 March 1998.

22. Gelbard, "Statement before the House International Relations Committee," 23 July 1998.

23. Contact Group, "Statement on Kosovo," 24 September 1997.

24. Contact Group, "Statement on Kosovo," 25 February 1998.

25. See for example, UN Security Council Resolutions 1160, 1199, 1203.

26. Gelbard, Robert, "Press Conference,"15 January 1998. As cynically observed by Serbian political journalist Stojan Cerovic, in response to a question concerning Gelbard's labeling of the KLA as terrorist, "Maybe Mr. Gelbard Had a Twitch, so Milosevic Thought It Was a Wink to Go Ahead." *New York Times*, 13 March 1998.

27. Gelbard, "Press Conference," 22 February 1998. In a subsequent question from a journalist concerning implementation of the previous agreements, such as the Education Agreement, Gelbard declared, " We strongly feel that it is imperative that all democratically oriented groups here come out very strongly meanwhile and condemn terrorism. I consider that the UCK is a terrorist group by its actions. I used to be responsible for counter-terrorist policy in the American government. I know them when I see them. And I think is important to draw the line between groups that are democratic versus groups that are anti-democratic through their use of terrorist means." Gelbard, "Press Conference," 22 February 1998

28. Associated Press, 8 July 1998.

29. Contact Group, "Statement on Kosovo," 9 March 1998.

30. Contact Group, "Statement on Kosovo," 9 March 1998. Some confusion was caused with respect to the imposition of sanctions. Just when the Contact Group was announcing these relatively weak sanctions, Ambassador Gelbard announced that as "in recent months we've seen some positive actions by the government of [the FRY]" on matters in Bosnia it might be possible to begin the lifting of sanctions if Serbia were to demonstrate "forward movement on Kosovo." Gelbard, "Press Conference," 22 February 1998. Ambassador Gelbard did indicate that if there was no forward movement then sanctions may be intensified.

31. UN Security Council Resolution 1160, para. 18.

32. Albright, "Statement at the Contact Group Meeting on Kosovo," 25 March 1998.

33. The impact of the potential arms embargo was minimized as Serbia possessed significant weaponry, and it did not apply to open-ended contracts between Serbia and Russia concluded prior to the Contact Group announcement. See Cook's response to question concerning application of the arms embargo, Secretary Albright and the Ministers to the Contact Group, "Press Conference," 9 March 1998.

34. UN Security Council Resolution 1160, preamble, para. 8.

35. Reuters, 29 March 1998.

36. According to one British official, "we and the Americans will argue that we should stick to the logic of our strategy and that the credibility of the Contact Group is at stake. The logical conclusion is that we impose further measures, but it may be difficult to achieve that." Reuters, 28 April 1998.

37. The foreign ministers of the countries of south-eastern Europe requested the Contact Group take only political and not economic sanctions given the impact such sanctions would have on their economic development. Ministers of Foreign Affairs of the countries of southeastern Europe, "Joint Statement on Kosovo," 25 March 1998.

38. Contact Group, "Statement on Kosovo," 9 March 1998.

39. UN Security Council Resolution 1160, para. 16.

40. Ministers of Foreign Affairs of the countries of southeastern Europe, "Joint Statement on Kosovo," 25 March 1998.

41. Contact Group, "Statement on Kosovo," 9 March 1998.

42. Secretary Albright and the Ministers to the Contact Group, "Press Conference," 9 March 1998.

43. Secretary Albright and the Ministers to the Contact Group, "Press Conference," 9 March 1998.

44. Secretary Albright and the Ministers to the Contact Group, "Press Conference," 9 March 1998. In the question and answer session Robin Cook even declared, "we are insisting on the right of the international community to police international law and that means that we have a perfect right to express concern as we have done today at extra judicial killings and the death of eighty people without any trial or any judicial process." Secretary Albright and the Ministers to the Contact Group, "Press Conference," 9 March 1998.

45. UN Security Council Resolution 1160, para 17.

46. UN Security Council Resolution. 1160, para 9.

47. Albright, "Statement at the Contact Group Ministerial on Kosovo," 9 March 1998.

48. Albright, "Statement at the Contact Group Ministerial on Kosovo," 9 March 1998.

49. Rubin, "Secretary Albright Announces $1.075 Million to Support Yugoslav War Crimes Tribunal Investigations in Kosovo."

50. Commenting on the softening of U. S. policy toward Belgrade and the squandered opportunity to prevent the Kosovo conflict, a Western diplomat stated in May 1998, "Milosevic has agreed only to talk not to strike an agreement on the future of Kosovo. The Americans have used our leverage to get the dialogue going, rather than to get somewhere." *New York Times*, 28 May 1998.

51. Voice of America, 5 June 1998.

52. Robert Anderson, "Havel Urges Slovak EU Entry," *Financial Times* (London), 19 October 1998, 2.

53. Jane Perlez, "Serb Pullback May Forestall NATO Attack," *New York Times*, 5

October 1998, A1.

54. James Morrison, *Washington Times*, 24 September 1998, A19.

55. Editorial, "Action Not Activation," *Times* (London), 25 September 1998.

56. R. Jeffrey Smith, "U.S. Criticizes Yugoslavia on 'Dangerous' Military Buildup," *The Washington Post*, 7 May 1998, A28.

57. Reuters, 30 April 1998.

58. As noted by Adem Demaci, Kosovo Albanian leader, on Ibrahim Rugova's decision to hold political discussions with Mr. Milosevic without international mediation, "All of Milosevic's conditions have been accepted and none of the Albanians'. It is an unpardonable step by Mr. Rugova." *Reuters*, 13 May 1998.

59. Michael J. Jordan, "Kosovo, the Next Generation," *Christian Science Monitor*, 14 May 1998, 1.

60. Tom Walker, "Serb Units Take Their 'Cleansing' Fire to Kosovo," *Times* (London), 25 May 1998.

61. Steven Lee Myers, "U.S. Urging NATO to Step Up Plans to Act against Yugoslavia," *New York Times*, 24 September 1998, A8.

62. In resolution 1199, the Security Council underlined the need for Serbian authorities to bring to justice those members of the security forces involved in the mistreatment of civilians and the deliberate destruction of property. UN Security Council Resolution 119, para 14. In resolution 1203, para 7, the Security Council called for the prompt investigation of all atrocities committed against civilians and full cooperation with the Yugoslav Tribunal.

63. Draft Kosovo Agreement, 29 October 1998, part IV, para. 11(c).

64. Draft Kosovo Agreement, 29 October 1998, Part VI, para. 1(b).

65. Draft Kosovo Agreement, 29 October 1998, Part IX, para. 7 and 8.

66. Draft Kosovo Agreement, November 1998, Section II, Part I, para. 6.

67. Draft Kosovo Agreement, November 1988, Part VIII, para. 8 and 9, Annex 1, para. 9.

68. North Atlantic Council, "Statement on Kosovo," 11 June 1998.

69. While not adopting the threat of the use of force, the Contact Group in its 12 June 1988 meeting did imply such a threat by declaring that if the Serbian regime did not cease their aggression, "there will be moves to further measures to halt the violence and protect the civilian population, including those that may require the authorisation of a United Nations Security Council resolution." It must be noted, however, that this phrase could also be taken to refer to economic sanctions, and did not necessarily imply the threat of the use of force. Contact Group, "Statement on Kosovo," 12 June 1998.

70. See comments of Kris Janowski, UNHCR spokesman, commenting on Serbia's arrest of some 600 Kosovo Albanian men, *Irish Times*, 9 September 1998. During the summer of 1998, the Serbian regime did allow the deployment of a Kosovo Diplomatic Observer Mission (KDOM) to observe events in Kosovo and promised to permit the return of refugees and internally displaced persons. The movement of the KDOM, however, was strictly limited and the promised return of refugees did not occur. Rubin, "Milosevic Assurances of Access and Refugee Returns."

71. Senior NATO diplomat, *The Washington Post*, 17 September 1998.

72. According to a senior Western diplomat, "the negotiating track is a very difficult one when villages are being burned and aid workers are being killed." Reuters, 26 August 1998.

73. Clark, *Waging Modern War*, 125-26, 128.

74. Editorial, "A Massacre without Knives," *Washington Post*, 16 September 1998.

75. See Editorial, *New York Times*, commenting on American plans to finance Serb run "humanitarian centers" for displaced Kosovo Albanians. Editorial, "Helping Kosovo's Displaced," *New York Times*, 7 September 1998.

76. *USA Today*, 25 September 1998.

77. Solana "Press Statement," 13 October 1998.

78. See Clark, *Waging Modern War*, 137-38.

79. See Agreement between the Minister of Foreign Affairs of the Federal Republic of Yugoslavia and the Chairman-in-Office of the Organization for Security and Cooperation in Europe (OSCE), Belgrade, 16 October 1998.

80. Agreement between the Chief of General Staff of the Federal Republic of Yugoslavia and the Supreme Allied Commander, Europe, of the North Atlantic Treaty Organization (NATO), Belgrade, 15 October 1998.

81. North Atlantic Council, "Statement on Kosovo," 16 October 1998.

82. Holbrooke and Walker, "On-the-Record Briefing," 28 October 1998. In connection with the agreement, NATO decided to deploy a rapid reaction force in neighboring Macedonia—although the force was never given a clear mandate as to what might be its responsibilities.

83. Clark, *Waging Modern War*, 138-40.

84. On this point, see former ambassador Morton Abramowitz commenting: "The durability of the agreements depends on what the Kosovo Albanians got politically after seven months of destruction. If they got less than the pre-1989 autonomy they had and the Administration promised, then I'm afraid we're in for long-term trouble." Steven Erlanger, "Conflict in the Balkans: In Washington, Clinton Presses Yugoslavs as NATO's Role Is Hailed," *New York Times*, 14 October 1998.

85. KVM Chief William Walker, Reuters, 4 March 1999.

86. See interview with Veton Surroi, editor, Koha Ditore, *Daily Telegraph* (London), 21 October 1998.

87. Editorial, "Appeasement in Kosovo," *The Washington Times*, 14 October 1998.

88. Solana, "Press Statement," 27 October 1998.

89. According to General Wesley Clark, "[Milosevic] is bringing in reinforcements continually. If you actually added up what's there on any given day, you might actually find out that he's strengthened his forces in there. And that's going to be a phenomenon until we can further cut the lines of supply and go more intensively against his forces." Craig R. Whitney, "Crisis in the Balkans: NATO Chief Admits Bombs Fail to Stem Serb Operations," *New York Times*, 28 April 1999.

90. For a general sense of the criticism of the U.S. government during this time, see Editorial, "Kosovo," *Washington Post*, 14 December 1998, which states, "From some of the self-congratulations circulating among U. S. and European officials, you might assume that the peace deal they brokered in Kosovo is working out. Unfortunately, that's not the case. It was a weak deal to begin with, and now Serb strongman Slobodan Milosevic is flouting it. Without NATO ground forces in Kosovo or democratization in Serbia, peace in Kosovo remains unlikely."

91. Voice of America, 29 October 1998.

92. When pressed by the American Albanian community during a meeting in New York on 19 October 1998 as to why the norm of justice was excluded from the deal, Holbrooke argued that as the deal referenced an obligation to comply with Security Council Resolutions 1160 and 1199, and as these resolutions referenced the authority of the Tribunal in paragraphs 17 and 13, respectively, Milosevic had in fact committed to fully cooperate with the Tribunal. The American Albanian community was not persuaded by

this line of reasoning.

93. Fred Hiatt, "Phony Deal in Kosovo," *The Washington Post*, 18 October 1998.

94. Holbrooke, Richard, "Press Conference," 13 October 1998.

95. Holbrooke and Hill, "Round-Table Discussion with Representatives of the Serbian Independent Media," 15 December 1998. Ambassador Holbrooke was responding to the question, "Ambassador Holbrooke, you have been exposed to critics for dealing only with Milosevic, neglecting democratic institutions, opposition, and independent media. Will you change that attitude and do you see Mr. Milosevic as a trouble-maker or someone who is the guarantor of stability in the Balkans?"

96. Holbrooke and Hill, "Round-Table Discussion with Representatives of the Serbian Independent Media," 15 December 1998. Ambassador Holbrooke was responding to the question, "Ambassador Holbrooke, maybe that question should be put this way: Do you see any change in the official attitude of, let's say, Department of State toward President Milosevic in the last 10 days or so, having in mind some very rough and tough statements about his personality?"

97. Holbrooke and Hill, "Round-Table Discussion with Representatives of the Serbian Independent Media," 15 December 1998.

98. 8 September 1998 (S/1998/839), 22 October 1998 (S/1998/990), and 6 November 1998 (S/1998/1040).

99. In particular, in para. 2 the resolution called upon all states to "to comply with requests for assistance or orders issued by a Trial Chamber under Article 29 of the Statute, to execute arrest warrants transmitted to them by the Tribunal, and to comply with its requests for information and investigations."

100. Veton Surroi, "Token Sanctions Won't Help Kosovo," *New York Times*, 14 March 1998.

101. White House, "Statement by the President on the Massacre of Civilians in Racak," 16 January 1999.

102. Albright, "Press Availability on Kosovo," 18 January 1999. See also Johnson, "Statement at the Extraordinary OSCE Permanent Council Meeting on Kosovo," 18 January 1999.

103. Eide, "Statement issued at the conclusion of the Special Meeting of the Permanent Council," 18 January 1999.

104. Annan, "Statement on the Racak Massacre," 16 January 1999.

105. White House, "Statement by the President on the Massacre of Civilians in Racak," 16 January 1999; Albright, "Press Availability on Kosovo," 18 January 1999.

106. Johnson, "Statement at the Extraordinary OSCE Permanent Council Meeting on Kosovo," 18 January 1999.

107. Clark, *Waging Modern War*, 159-60.

108. Annan, "Statement on the Racak Massacre," 16 January 1999. The Secretary-General merely called for "a full investigation by the competent authorities."

109. Senator Mitch McConnell, Editorial, *The Washington Post*, 22 January 1999.

110. Senator Frank Lautenberg, 19 January 1999. See also Editorial, *New York Times*, 20 January 1999, "NATO should give Mr. Milosevic a short deadline to comply with his promises, including a pullout of his forces and full cooperation with international monitors, humanitarian agencies and the war crimes tribunal. If he refuses, it should pull out the monitoring force and bomb selected Serbian military targets. If, as has been his habit, he promises compliance but then reneges, NATO must immediately resume the threat."

111. Albright, "Statement on NATO Final Warning on Kosovo," 30 January 1999.

112. Solana, Javier, NATO Secretary-General, "Statement to the Press," Brussels, Belgium, 28 January 1999.

113. North Atlantic Council, "Press Release," 30 January 1999.

114. President Bill Clinton, "Weekly Radio Address," 13 February 1999. See also Open letter to President Clinton signed by a bipartisan group of twenty-one prominent former government officials, which declared, "Mr. President, all eyes are turned to Washington. Only forceful U. S. leadership can stop Milosevic from continuing with this new round of ethnic cleansing. As a newly expanded NATO approaches its 50th anniversary in Washington, the savagery in Kosovo endangers more than civilian life and regional stability. It threatens the interests of the United States, the credibility of NATO and the gains we have achieved in Bosnia," *New York Times*, 29 January 1999.

115. As noted by Senator Joseph Lieberman, "the credibility of the United States and NATO are at stake here. We must act forcefully. Unless Milosevic immediately comes into the ceasefire agreement by returning his troops to barracks and drastically lowering the number of police operating in Kosovo, NATO, under the leadership of the United States, should take military action to force the Serbs to abide by the agreement." Sen. Joseph Lieberman, 19 January 1999. See also, Clark, *Waging Modern War*, 130-33.

116. According to former American ambassador to NATO Robert Hunter, "during 1993-95, NATO was nearly destroyed by its inability to act in the Bosnian war. . . . Today, the alliance faces a similar moral and political challenge in Kosovo, but once again, it stands by as Serb forces trample on human rights and take the lives of people who are 'different.'" *The Washington Post*, 1 September 1998.

117. Jim Hoagland, Editorial, *The Washington Post*, 14 February 1999.

Chapter 11

1. Introductory remarks to the Kosovo Albanian delegation to the Rambouillet negotiations.

2. Williams and Cigar, *War Crimes and Individual Responsibility*.

3. McClenny, "Press Statement," December 1998. Specifically, the Department of State charged that the failure to turn over three indicted war criminals was the "latest act of defiance is just another in a long series of violations by [Serbian] authorities, who have failed to comply with the Tribunal's orders: they have failed to transfer or even facilitate the surrender of a single Serb indictee to the Tribunal; they have failed to issue visas to allow Yugoslav Tribunal investigators into Kosovo (and into the rest of [the FRY], including for investigations of crimes committed against ethnic Serbs); they have failed to adopt implementing legislation that would allow full cooperation with the Tribunal; and they are now openly harboring indicted war criminals. McClenny, "Press Statement," December 1998.

4. Reuters, 10 March 1999.

5. Senator Dick Lugar, Editorial, *Washington Post*, 30 November 1998.

6. *National Review*, 3 May 1999.

7. *Observer*, 29 November 1998.

8. Editorial, "Modest Assaults Only, Please," *Washington Post*, 10 March 1999.

9. *NewsHour with Jim Lehrer*, 3 June 1999.

10. Draft Rambouillet/Paris Accords, Part II, 27 January 1999, para. 6.

11. Draft Rambouillet/Paris Accords, Part VIII, 27 January 1999, para. 8.

12. Draft Rambouillet/Paris Accords, Part VIII, 27 January 1999, para. 9.

13. See Proposed Changes to the Rambouillet/Paris Accords, Kosovar Delegation, February 1999.

14. Serbian Counterproposal to the Rambouillet/Paris Accords, 15 March 1999.

15. Milosevic, Milutinovic, Sainovic, Ojdanic, and Stojiljkovic Indictment, IT-99-37.

16. John Doe I and John Doe II vs. Milosevic and Others, No. 99 (D. Mass. Filed 23 May 1999). Available at http://www. Balkanaction.org/pubs/complaint. Html, 3 September 2001.

17 Human Rights Watch, "Federal Republic of Yugoslavia: A Week of Terror in Drenica" (New York, 6 February 1999).

18. Human Rights Watch, "Settlement without Accountability for War Crimes," Press Release on Kosovo, 6 February 1999.

19. No Peace without Justice, "Report on the Responsibilities of the Belgrade Regime to the Special Representative of the European Union for Kosovo, M. Wolfgang Petrich," 18 February 1999.

20. Editorial, "Peace Equations in Kosovo," *New York Times*, 13 March 1999.

21. Letter to President Clinton from Senators Mitch McConnell and Gordon Smith, 1 February 1999.

22. For an accounting of the assassination of Professor Fehmi Agani, see Melissa Eddy, "Kosovars Mourn Death of Agani," Associated Press, 27 June 1999.

23. Draft Rambouillet/Paris Accords, Framework Agreement, 27 January 1999, para. 14.

24. First included in Draft Rambouillet/Paris Accords, Framework Agreement, 18 February 1999, para. 11. Included in final Rambouillet/Paris Accords, Framework Agreement, March 1999, para. 13.

25. Rambouillet/Paris Accords, Constitution, March 1999.

26. McDonald, "Letter to Foreign Ministers Vedrine and Cook."

27. McDonald, "Letter to Foreign Ministers Vedrine and Cook."

28. "It Will Be Peace, on Our Terms," *Times* (London), 7 May 1999.

29. Some commentators even noted that the ethnic aggression surpassed that even of the Bosnian and Croatian conflicts, "the refugees' stories do seem to be consistent and credible. If they are to be believed, we are now seeing, in scale and ferocity, the worst 'ethnic cleansing' of any of the Balkan conflicts of the past decade." BBC correspondent Paul Wood, reporting from Macedonia, BBC television broadcast, 29 March 1999.

30. Peter Finn, "Refugees Flee across Border by Thousands," *The Washington Post*, 29 March 1999.

31. *Times* (London), 5 April 1999.

32. Editorial, "The Ground War," *The Washington Post*, 28 March 1999.

33. Senator Joe Lieberman, Editorial, *New York Times*, 22 March 1999.

34. President Bill Clinton, 19 March 1999.

35. White House, "New Sanctions against the Federal Republic of Yugoslavia Fact Sheet," 1 May 1999. See also Exec. Order No. 13,088 (1999).

36. French president Jacques Chirac, in a televised address to France, *The Washington Post*, 4 May 1999. See also John F. Harris and Charles Babington, "Despite Peace Push Bombing Continues: Clinton Demands Yugoslav Retreat," *The Washington Post*, 4 April 1999.

37. Warren Christopher, Editorial, "Whatever It Takes," *The Washington Post*, 4 April 1999.

38. British prime minister Tony Blair, Voice of America, 3 May 1999.

39. Lady Margaret Thatcher, Editorial, *The Washington Post*, 5 May 1999.

40. Interview by columnist Jim Hoagland with British prime minister Tony Blair, *Washington Post*, 18 April 1999.

41. General Charles Wald, Editorial, *Washington Times*, 20 April 1999.

42. Secretary of State Madeleine Albright, *NBC 'Meet the Press.'*

43. Senator John McCain, Fox Television, 16 May 1999.

44. Former Joint Chiefs of Staff chairman General Colin Powell, *NBC 'Meet the Press,'* 19 May 1999.

45. Editorial, *Financial Times* (London), 17 May 1999.

46. Nora Boustany, "Jordan's King Says Stakes High for U.S. in Kosovo," *Washington Post* 18 May 1999.

47. *National Review*, 3 May 1999.

48. Milosevic, Milutinovic, Sainovic, Ojdanic, and Stojiljkovic Indictment, IT-99-37.

49. Bob Dole, "No Deals with Milosevic," *Washington Post*, 1 June 1999.

50. Clark, *Waging Modern War*, 325-26.

51. Clark, *Waging Modern War*, 325-26.

52. *Financial Times* (London*)*, 22 June 1999.

53. Serbian Orthodox Bishop Artemije, Associated Press, 14 June 1998.

54. *The Washington Post*, 2 July 1999.

Chapter 12

1. Lee Hockstader, "Letter from Bosnia: The Rumor Heard Around the World," *The Washington Post*, 27 September 1997.

2. *New York Times*, 4 April 1996.

3. Press Briefing by National Security Adviser Berger on Bosnia, U. S. Newswire, Thursday, 10 July 1997.

4. Tracy Wilkinson, "Serb Leaders Seen as Barriers to Peace," *Los Angeles Times*, 29 April 1996.

5. See Peace Agreements Bring a 'Long-Delayed Birth of Hope': Multinational Force Set Up in Bosnia to Replace UNPROFOR, 33(1) UN Chronicle 25, 26 (Spring 1996).

6. UN SCOR, 3607th mtg. at 19, UN Doc. S/PV.3607 (1995), reprinted in Morris and Scharf, *An Insider's Guide*, 179.

7. UN SCOR, 3607th mtg. at 19, UN Doc. S/PV.3607 (1995), reprinted in Morris and Scharf, *An Insider's Guide*, 179.

8. UN SCOR, 3607th mtg. at 19, UN Doc. S/PV.3607 (1995), reprinted in Morris and Scharf, *An Insider's Guide*, 179.

9. UN SCOR, 3607th mtg. at 19, UN Doc. S/PV.3607 (1995), reprinted in Morris and Scharf, *An Insider's Guide*, 179.

10. Interview with Grant Neimann, senior trial attorney in the Yugoslav Tribunal's Office of the Prosecutor, by Michael Scharf, The Hague, 11 August, 1998.

11. Holbrooke, *To End a War*, 216-18.

12. Louis Freedberg, "Talking Your Way Out of Hell," *San Francisco Chronicle*, 7 April 1996 (quoting Richard Holbrooke).

13. Holbrooke, *To End a War*, 222.

14. Holbrooke, *To End a War*, 223.

15. Holbrooke, *To End a War*, 226, 315.

16. Holbrooke, *To End a War*, 315.

17. Holbrooke, *To End a War*, 316.

18. Forsyth, "International Criminal Courts," 11.

19. Graham Blewitt, deputy prosecutor of the International Criminal Tribunal for the Former Yugoslavia, Interview by Michael Scharf, The Hague, 11 August 1998.

20. Stephen Engelberg, Panel Seeks U. S. Pledge on Bosnia War Criminals, *New York Times*, 3 November 1995, A1.

21. Quoted in Holbrooke, *To End a War*, 226, 315.

22. Clark, *Waging Modern War*, 73.

23. Holbrooke, *To End a War*, 339.

24. Jon Swain, "Serb War Criminals Flaunt Their Freedom," *Sunday Times* (London), 23 June 1996.

25. Secretary-General, "Report Pursuant to Paragraph 2 of Security Council Resolution 808 (1993)," para. 28.

26. Statute of Yugoslav Tribunal, articles 29 and 61.

27. John Burton, "War Crimes during Military Operations Other than War: Military Doctrine and Law 50 Years after Nuremberg and Beyond," *Military Law Review* 149 (1995): 203-04.

28. International Arrest Warrant and Order for Surrender, Case Nos. IT-95-5-R61, IT-95-18-R61 (11 July 1996), reproduced in Walter Gary Sharp, Sr., "International Obligations to Search for and Arrest War Criminals: Government Failure in the Former Yugoslavia," *Duke Journal of Comparative and International Law* 7 (1997): 411, 448.

29. Colin Soloway and Stephen J. Hedges, "How Not to Catch a War Criminal," *U. S. News and World Report*, 9 December 1996, 63.

30. Interview with Payan Akhvan, legal adviser, Office of the Prosecutor, International Criminal Tribunal for the Former Yugoslavia, The Hague, Netherlands, by Michael Scharf, 11 August 1998.

31. Holbrooke, *To End a War*, 218.

32. Jane Perlez, "War Crimes Prosecutor Vents Frustrations," *New York Times*, 22 May 1996, A8.

33. "Shrugging Off Indictment, Bosnian Serb General Skis," *New York Times*, Monday, 11 March 1996, A3.

34. Interview with General William Nash, by Michael Scharf, Cambridge, Massachusetts, 29 September 1998.

35. Holbrooke, *To End a War*, 218.

36. Interview with Payan Akhvan, legal adviser, Office of the Prosecutor, International Criminal Tribunal for the Former Yugoslavia, The Hague, Netherlands, by Michael Scharf, 11 August 1998.

37. Interview with General William Nash, by Michael Scharf, Cambridge, Massachusetts, 29 September 1998.

38. As the Yugoslav Tribunal's deputy prosecutor, Graham Blewitt, explained, "if the NATO forces think there is any risk of casualties then they won't move." Graham Blewitt, deputy prosecutor of the International Criminal Tribunal for the Former Yugoslavia, Interview by Michael Scharf, The Hague, 11 August 1998.

39. Interview with Payan Akhvan, legal adviser, Office of the Prosecutor, International Criminal Tribunal for the Former Yugoslavia, The Hague, Netherlands, by Michael Scharf, 11 August 1998.

40. Barry Schweid, "U. S. Warns War Crimes Suspects to Avoid Traveling in Bosnia,"

Associated Press, 14 February 1996.

41. Diane F. Orentlicher, "Swapping Amnesty for Peace and the Duty to Prosecute Human Rights Crimes," *ILSA Journal of International and Comparative Law* 3 (1997): 713.

42. Orentlicher, "Swapping Amnesty for Peace."

43. Kenneth Roth, "Why Justice Needs NATO," 265(8) *The Nation* 21, 22 September 1997 (Roth provides detailed responses to each of these excuses for non-action).

44. Interview with General William Nash, by Michael Scharf, Cambridge, Massachusetts, 29 September 1998.

45. "All Things Considered," National Public Radio, 12 February 1996.

46. Colon Soloway and Stephen J. Hedges, "How Not to Catch a War Criminal," *U. S. News and World Report*, 9 December 1996, 63.

47. Stephen L. Myers, "Rights Group Says Bosnian Suspects Flaunt Freedom," *New York Times*, 26 November 1996, A11.

48. Jeffrey Smith, "Secret Meetings Foiled Karadzic Capture Plan; U. S. Says French Jeopardized Mission," *Washington Post*, 23 April 1998, A1.

49. See "Decision on the Motion for Release by the Accused Slavko Dokmanovic," IT-95-13a-PT, T. Ch. II. Dokmanovic was mayor of Vukovar, the capital of Eastern Slavonia, and administrator of the Ovcara area at the time of the massacre. He was charged with six counts of grave breaches of the Geneva conventions, violations of the laws or customs of war, and crimes against humanity for his role in the massacre.

50. Press Briefing by National Security Adviser Berger on Bosnia, *U. S. Newswire*, 10 July 1997. See Kovacevic, Drljaca, and Stakic Indictment, IT-97-24.

51. Press Briefing by National Security Adviser Berger on Bosnia, *U. S. Newswire*, 10 July 1997

52. See Z. Kupreskic, M. Kupreskic, V. Kupreskic, Josipovic, Santic, and Papic Indictment, IT-95-16.

53. Furundzija Indictment, IT-95-17/1.

54. Holbrooke, *To End a War*, 339.

55. Robert MacPherson, Bosnian Serb Snatched in NATO Operation, Agence France Presse, 27 September 1998.

56. See Krstic Indictment, IT-98-33.

57. Office of the Prosecutor, "Statement Regarding the Detention of Radislav Krstic," 2 December 1998; Steven Erlanger, "Bosnian Serb General Is Arrested by Allied Force in Genocide Case," *New York Times*, 3 December 1998, A1.

58. See Galic Indictment, IT-98-29.

59. "Bosnian Serb General Arrested on War Crimes Charges," Agence France Presse, 20 December 1999.

60. Sudetic, "Why Is France Protecting Indicted War Criminals," 91.

61. Jeffrey Fleishman, "U. S. Forces Make First Bosnian War-Crimes Arrest," *Fresno Bee*, 23 January 1998, A14.

62. Smith, "Secret Meetings Foiled Karadzic Capture Plan," A1.

63. Interview with Payan Akhvan, legal adviser, Office of the Prosecutor, International Criminal Tribunal for the Former Yugoslavia, The Hague, Netherlands, by Michael Scharf, 11 August 1998.

64. Batuk Gathani, "Most Notorious War Criminals at Large," *The Hindu*, 15 July 1997.

65. Ewen Allison, "News from the International War Crimes Tribunals," 5(2) *Human Rights Brief* 3 (winter 1998).

66. Sudetic, "Why Is France Protecting Indicted War Criminals," 91.

67. Smith, "Secret Meetings Foiled Karadzic Capture Plan," A1.

68. Kunarac and Kovac Indictment, IT-96-23, IT-96-23/1.

69. Smith, "Secret Meetings Foiled Karadzic Capture Plan," A1.

70. Smith, "Secret Meetings Foiled Karadzic Capture Plan," A1.

71. Associated Press, "U. S. Reportedly Ends Plan to Catch Bosnia War Criminals," *Boston Globe*, 26 July 1998, A14.

72. Richard J. Newman, "Hunting War Criminals," *U. S. News and World Report*, 6 July 1998, 45.

73. Kevin Cullen, "War Crimes Tribunal Wins New Esteem," *Boston Globe*, 17 April 2000, A1, A14.

74. Reuters, 1 September 1997.

75. Jane Perlez, "Karadzic and Mladic: No More Swagger for 2 Losers," *International Herald Tribunal*, 16 December 1995.

76. Akhvan, "The Yugoslav Tribunal at a Crossroads," 273.

77. Human Rights Watch, "Bosnia-Hercegovina: The Continuing Influence of Bosnia's Warlords," December 1996.

78. Human Rights Watch, "Bosnia-Hercegovina."

79. Orentlicher, "Swapping Amnesty for Peace."

80. John Pomfret, "In Bosnia, a War Crimes Impasse: NATO Differences with UN Tribunal Mean Few Are Arrested," *The Washington Post*, 9 December 1997.

81. Reuters, 22 November 1998.

82. Fred Barbash, "Conference Hints Cutoff of Aid to Bosnian Rivals, Serbs Considered Main Target of London Warning," *Washington Post*, 5 December 1996.

83. John Drodziak, "NATO Chief's Block Call for Pursuit of War Criminals," *Washington Post*, 13 June 1997.

84. Albright and Arbour, "Joint Press Conference on the International Criminal Tribunal for the Former Yugoslavia," 30 April 1999.

85. Commentary by Richard Goldstone, "Bosnia-Herzegovina: The Responsibility to Act," *Inter Press Service*, 27 June 1996.

Chapter 13

1. President of the Tribunal, "Fifth Annual Report of the International Criminal Tribunal for the Former Yugoslavia," para. 276.

2. "Report: Serbia-Montenegro: Implementation of U.N. Economic Sanctions," *U.S. General Accounting Office* (April 1993), 4.

3. UN Security Council Resolution 1022, para. 1.

4. Chris Hedges, "10 Bosnian Croats Surrender to War Crimes Tribunal," *New York Times*, 7 October 1997, A3; Louis-Marie Tattavin, "Ten Bosnian Croat War Crimes Suspects Surrender to UN," Agence France Presse, 6 October 1997.

5. UN SCOR, 3607th mtg. at 20, UN Doc. S/PV.3607 (1995).

6. Scharf and Dorosin, "Interpreting UN Sanctions," 771-827.

7. Scharf and Dorosin, "Interpreting UN Sanctions," 771-827.

8. See Articles 25 and 103 of the United Nations Charter, and Article 46 of the Vienna Convention on the Law of Treaties.

9. Forsyth, "Politics and the International Tribunal," 415.

10. See para. 1.

11. UN SCOR, 3595th mtg., 3, UN Doc. S/PV.3595 (1995).

12. UN SCOR, 3607th mtg. at 20, 30, UN Doc. S/PV.3607 (1995).

13. Anthony Lewis, "Early Signs of Progress in Bosnia Are Far from Encouraging," *Seattle Post-Intelligencer*, 12 December 1995, A16.

14. Holbrooke, *To End a War*, 226, 315, 339.

15. See President of the Tribunal, "Third Annual Report of the International Criminal Tribunal for the Former Yugoslavia," para. 167-69. Following Rule 61 hearings in the cases of Nikolic, Karadzic, and Mladic, and Rajic, the President of the Yugoslav Tribunal notified the Security Council of the refusal of the Republika Srpska, the Federal Republic of Yugoslavia, and Croatia, respectively, to surrender the accused to the Tribunal. See President of the Tribunal, "Letter to the President of the Security Council (Karadzic and Mladic case);" President of the Tribunal, "Letter to the President of the Security Council (Rajic case);" President of the Tribunal, "Letter to the President of the Security Council (Nikolic case)."

16. "Bildt Urges Bosnian Serb War Criminals Be Turned In," Deutsche Presse-Agentur, 20 May 1996.

17. "Bosnia Opposes End to Sanctions against Serbs," *European Report*, " 28 September 1996.

18. Cohen, *Application of the Realist and Liberal Perspectives*, 153.

19. Following Rule 61 hearings in the cases of Nikolic, Karadzic, and Mladic, and Rajic, the President of the Yugoslav Tribunal has notified the Security Council of the refusal of the Republika Srpska, the Federal Republic of Yugoslavia, and Croatia, respectively, to surrender the accused to the Tribunal. See President of the Tribunal, "Letter to the President of the Security Council (Karadzic and Mladic case);" President of the Tribunal, "Letter to the President of the Security Council (Rajic case);" President of the Tribunal, "Letter to the President of the Security Council (Nikolic case)."

20. Shraga and Zaklin, "The International Criminal Tribunal for Rwanda," 517.

21. Graham Blewitt, deputy prosecutor of the International Criminal Tribunal for the Former Yugoslavia, Interview by Michael Scharf, The Hague, 11 August 1998.

22. Mrksic, Radic, Sljivancanin, and Dokmanovic Indictment, IT-95-13a.

23. "Croatia Arrests Croatian Serbs Suspected of War Crimes While Yugoslavia Rejects War Crime Tribunal Extradition Requests," *International Law Enforcement Rptr.* 15 (1999):128.

24. White House, "New Sanctions against the Federal Republic of Yugoslavia Fact Sheet," 1 May 1999.

25. Christopher Boian, "Clinton Tells Serbs to 'Come to Grips' with Milosevic," Agence France Presse, 26 June 1999.

26. Paul Williams, Michael Scharf, and Diane Orentlicher, *Making Justice Work* (New York: The Century Foundation, 1998), 50.

27. Smith, "Secret Meetings Foiled Karadzic Capture Plan," A1.

28. Smith, "Secret Meetings Foiled Karadzic Capture Plan," A1.

29. See Office of the Prosecutor, "President Milosevic and Four Other Senior FRY Officials Indicted for Murder, Persecution and Deportation in Kosovo," 27 May 1999, 3.

30. Statute of the Yugoslav Tribunal, art. 19.

31. See Office of the Prosecutor, "President Milosevic and Four Other Senior FRY Officials Indicted for Murder, Persecution and Deportation in Kosovo," 27 May 1999, 3.

32. Secretary-General, "Report Pursuant to Paragraph 2 of Security Council Resolution 808 (1993)."

33. "Cyprus Vows to Honour Tighter EU Sanctions on Yugoslavia," Agence France Presse, 27 April 1999.

34. Rubin, "Daily Press Briefing," 2 June 1999.

35. Dep't of the Army, The Law of Land Warfare, art. 31 (1956), Army Field Manual No. 27-10, Washington, D.C.

36. Peter Almond, "U.S. Puts $5m Price on the Head of War Criminal Milosevic," *Evening Standard* (London), 25 June 1999, 2.

37. Almond, "U.S. Puts $5M Price on the Head of War Criminal Milosevic," 2.

38. "U. S. Will Offer Bounties for Bosnian War Crimes Suspects," 15 *International Law Enforcement Reporter*, 39 (1999).

39. UN SCOR, 3607th mtg. at 20, UN Doc. S/PV.3607 (1995).

40. Stephane Barbier, "Bosnia to Get 1.25 Billion Dollars in Aid in 1998," Agence France Presse, 8 May 1998.

41. Dan De Luce, "Bosnian Serb Defiance Won't Affect Aid—Official," Reuters, 10 January 1997.

42. De Luce, "Bosnian Serb Defiance Won't Affect Aid."

43. Krajisnik and Plavsic Indictments, IT-00-39 and 40.

44. Susan Woodward, "Implementing Peace in Bosnia and Herzegovina: A Post-Dayton Primer and Memorandum of Warning," Discussion Paper (Washington, D.C.: Brookings Institute, 1996), 37.

45. Stephane Barbier, "Bosnia to Get 1.25 Billion Dollars in Aid."

46. See President of the Tribunal, "Third Annual Report of the International Criminal Tribunal for the Former Yugoslavia," para. 167.

47. Misha Savic, "Two Serbs Suspected of War Crimes Surrender Voluntarily to Tribunal," *San Diego Union-Tribunal*, 15 February 1998, A24.

48. Stephane Barbier, "Bosnia to Get 1.25 Billion Dollars in Aid."

49. Yugoslav Tribunal press release "Accused Aleksovski Turned Over to the Tribunal," 28 April 1997.

50. See Kordic and Cerkez Indictment, IT-95-14/2.

51. Tattavin, "Ten Bosnian Croat War Crimes Suspects Surrender to UN."

52. Yugoslav Tribunal press release, "Vinko Martinovic ("Stela") Surrendered to Yugoslav Tribunal by the Republic of Croatia," 9 August 1999.

53. See opinion poll taken by the Independent Center for Political Studies and Public Opinion Research at the Institute of Social Sciences, Belgrade 1999, http://www.cpijm.org.yu.

54. National Democratic Institute, "Serbia Post-Election Poll," 6 October 2000.

55. Steve Erlanger, "After Yugoslavs Celebrate, Belgrade Orders a Runoff," *New York Times*, 28 September 2000.

56. Erlanger, "After Yugoslavs Celebrate," A1.

57. Michael Ignatieff, "The Right Trial for Milosevic," *New York Times*, 10 October 2000, A27.

58. Jane Perlez, "U.S. Set to Finesse Tribunal Issue and Allow Belgrade Aid," *New York Times*, 29 March 2001.

59. Perlez, "U.S. Set to Finesse Tribunal Issue."

60. From the newsroom of the BBC World Service B-92, 5/3, France opposes bid to swap Milosevic for cash 17:01 Paris, Thursday.

61. Roy Gutman and Daniel Klaidman "Tracking War Criminals Del Ponte Says NATO Troops Are 'Doing Nothing,'" *Newsweek International*, 21 May 2001.

62. Gutman and Klaidman "Tracking War Criminals."

63. Marlise Simons with Carlotta Gall, "The Handover of Milosevic: The Overview; Milosevic is Given to UN for Trial in War-Crime Case, *New York Times*, 29 June 2001.

Index

Abi-saab, Georges, 105
Abramowitz, Morton, 181, 300n84
accommodation; Bosnia and, 44, 96;
conflict with justice, 29-35, 113,
235-36; constructive engagement,
230; Dayton negotiations and, 151-
52, 167; definition of, 24-26;
European Union and, 80-81, 247;
examples of, 24-25; exposed by
Commission of Experts, 96; failure
to indict Milosevic, 120, 127; immunity from prosecution, 194;
Kosovo crisis and, 204-5; mixing of
approaches, 33-35, 245, 250;
peacebuilders and, 82; perception
of failure of, 180; pressure on Bosnia to drop ICJ Genocide Case,
140-42; risks of, 25; refusal to recognize genocide, 144; refusal to
release classified information, 133;
Secretary General and, 82; Security
Council and, 82; suspension of
sanctions, 226-27; UN/EU Peace
Conference and, 153-55; United
Kingdom and, 71, 72, 236; United
States and, 235, 240, 249; use of
force verses, 156; Vance/Owen
peace process and, 108, 153-55
Activation Order. *See* NATO
Additional Protocols of 1977. *See* Geneva conventions
adversarial approach, 105
Advisory Committee on Administrative
and Budgetary Question (ACABQ).

See budget of the ICTY
Aegon Insurance Company Building,
111
Aghani, Femi, 200
aid conditionality. *See* conditionality of
economic assistance
airstrikes, 25, 27, 28, 29, 54, 71, 81, 82,
83, 84, 153, 156, 181, 183, 239.
See also NATO
airtight case. *See* indictments
Akashi, Yasushi, 24, 82, 83, 239
Akhvan, Payam, 30, 100, 219, 221
Albania, 68, 185, 186, 190
Albright, Madeleine, 28, 59, 65, 68, 91,
117, 127, 173, 174, 177, 179, 180,
181, 190, 191, 212, 224, 229, 238,
249
Aleksovsk, Zlatko, 231
Algerian war, 34
Almond, Mark, 70, 71, 72, 73, 80, 81
Amerasinghe, Christopher, 108
American Bar Association's Central and
Eastern European Law Initiative,
119
Amin, Idi, 32
amnesty, 20, 29, 33, 97, 183, 197
Amnesty International, 48, 133
analogical reasoning approach, 256n20
Anderson, Betsy, 129
Annan, Kofi, 59, 188, 221
annual budget. *See* budget
anonymous witnesses, 106
antijustice, 14-16, 152, 157
appeasement, 26, 71, 91, 111, 127, 154,

311

275n66
Roth, Kenneth, 142
Ruff, Charles, 108
rule of law, 261n49
Rule 61 hearing. *See* ICTY
Rules of the Road Agreement, 118-19, 125
Rules of Procedure. *See* ICTY
Russia, 69-70, 99, 100, 105, 176, 184, 195-96, 206, 213, 226, 235, 236, 274n38; Russian media, 69; Security Council veto, 73
Russian-FRY Joint Declaration, 182
Rwanda, 66
Rwanda Tribunal, 115

SAAS Memorandum, 43
Sacirbey, Mohamed, 93, 138
Safe Areas, 28, 34, 48, 50, 83, 156, 185, 237, 239, 240
Sainovic, Nikola, 60, 130, 193, 194, 198, 207
Salam, Ramon Escovar, 108
sanctions, 27, 46-47, 224-27; automatic trigger, 166-67, 225-26, 246; cooperation with ICTY and, 164; Kosovo and, 175, 198, 203, 211; Sanctions Committee, 254; suspension of, 242; termination of, 226-27; transshipments and, 47
Santayana, George, 19
Santer, Jacques, 80
Sarajevo, 46, 48, 84, 140, 154, 268n49
Sarajevo Marketplace massacre, 15, 54, 81, 86, 108, 156
Savic, Ljubisa, 167
Scheffer, David, 3, 21, 171, 218, 228,
Schrag, Minna, 114-15
Schwarzenberger, George, 255n14
sealed indictments, 166
second-tier positioning, 240
Secretary-General. *See* Annan, Kofi; Ghali, Boutros Boutros
Security Council, 249; authorization for use of force, 27, 93, 143; Chapter VII decisions, 101; failure to act, 43; interests of members, 98; Kosovo agreement, 208. *See also* sanctions; arms embargo
self-defense, 27, 146

self-determination, 146
Sell, Louis, 253n2
Sells, Michael, 83, 84
Serbian Academy of Arts and Sciences, 43, 56
Serbian misrepresentations. *See* propaganda
Serbian Orthodox Bishop Artemije, 20+
Seselj, Vojislav, 178
SFOR. *See* IFOR/SFOR
Shalikashvili, John, 217
Shattuck, John, 34
Shea, Jamie, 203
shuttle diplomacy, 182
Sidhwa, Rustam, 105
Sikirica, Dusko, 52
Simic, Milan, 51, 230
Simic, Blagoje, 51
Simms, Brendan, 31
Sljivancanin, Veselin, 53, 227
Smith, Gordon, 199
Smith, Leighton, 212, 214, 226, 238
Smith, Rupert, 84
snatch operation. *See* arrests
Solana, Javier, 60
Soreabjee, Soli Henhangir, 108
Soros Foundation, 95, 122, 232
South Africa, 17
South African Truth and Reconciliation Commission, 17, 18, 261n51
Specially Designated Nationals, 228
Srebrenca, safe area, 48; massacre, 28, 30, 48, 52, 153, 156
Stakic, Milomir, 233
Stalin, Joseph, 42
Stankovic, Radovan, 53
Stephen, Ninian, 105
Stern, Brigitte, 138
Stojilkovic, Vlajko, 60
Stoltenberg, Thorvald, 24, 45
Strategic Air Campaign. *See* NATO intervention; airstrikes
structural realism approach, 254n9
Sudetic, Chuck, 74
suicides and indicted war criminals, 123
Surroi, Veton, 181, 188
Susica camp, 49, 51, 157
Szas, Paul, 167

Tadic, Dusko, 114-15

About the Authors

Paul R. Williams is the Rebecca Grazier Professor of Law and International Relations at American University, where he holds a joint appointment in the School of International Service and the Washington College of Law, and directs the MA/JD Joint Degree Program. He has also taught at the University of Georgetown and the University of Paris. Professor Williams has previously served as a senior associate with the Carnegie Endowment for International Peace where he directed the Public International Law and Policy Program, and as the managing director of the Public International Law & Policy Group, which provides pro bono legal assistance to developing states and states in transition. He has also held the position of a Fulbright research scholar at the University of Cambridge and has served in the U.S. Department of State's Office of the Legal Adviser for European and Canadian Affairs.

During the course of his legal practice, Professor Williams has advised the Macedonia-Albanian delegation to the Skopje/Lake Ohrid peace talks, advised the Montenegrin government during the Belgrade/Podgorica talks on the future status of the FRY, served on the Kosovar delegation to the Rambouillet/Paris peace talks, on the Bosnian delegation to the Dayton negotiations, and as an adviser to Armenian delegation to the Key West negotiations. He has also advised the president of Estonia on territorial negotiations with Russia, the president of Macedonia on matters relating to state sovereignty, the president of Bosnia on the implementation of the Dayton Peace Accords, and the foreign minister of Montenegro on state secession. He has also testified as an expert on the crisis in the former Yugoslavia before the Sub-Committee on European Affairs of the U.S. Senate Foreign Relations Committee, and before the Joint Senate/House Helsinki Committee.

Professor Williams earned his Ph.D. from the University of Cambridge, his J.D. from Stanford Law School, and his B.A. from the University of California at Davis. He has authored books entitled the *Treatment of Detainees*, the *Role of International Law in the Resolution of Central and East European Transboundary Environmental Disputes*, and *Indictment at The Hague: The Milosevic Regime and Crimes of the Balkan Wars*. In addition, he has authored a number of articles concerning public international law which have appeared in law reviews such as the *International and Comparative Law Quarterly*, the *Denver Journal of International Law and Policy*, the *Georgetown International Environmental Law Review*, and the *Harvard International Law Journal*. He has also authored policy-oriented editorials which have appeared in the *International Herald Tribune*, *Los Angeles Times*, *Le Monde*, and the *Christian Science Monitor*, and he is frequently interviewed on matters relating to war crimes and public international law by major networks and newspapers.

Michael P. Scharf is professor of law and director of the War Crimes Research office at Case Western Reserve University School of Law. During the George H.W. Bush Administration and the Clinton administration. He served in the Office of the Legal Adviser of the U.S. Department of State, where he held the positions of Counsel to the Counter-Terrorism Bureau, Attorney-Adviser for Law Enforcement and Intelligence, Attorney-Adviser for United Nations Affairs, and delegate to the United Nations General Assembly and to the United Nations Human Rights Commission. In 1993, he was awarded the State Department's Meritorious Honor Award "in recognition of superb performance and exemplary leadership in support of U.S. policy initiatives regarding the former Yugoslavia."

Since leaving the state department Scharf has served as professor of law and director of the Center for International Law and Policy at New England School of Law, and as a visiting professor at the Fletcher School of Law and Diplomacy, the University of Paris X, the National University of Ireland in Galway, and the Australian National University in Canberra. He teaches criminal law, criminal procedure, public international law, international criminal law, the law of international organizations, and international human rights law. Since 1996, under a unique arrangement with the prosecutor of the Yugoslavia and Rwanda Tribunals funded by a multi-year grant by the George Soros Foundation, Scharf and his students have provided over ninety legal memoranda and hundreds of thousands of pages of supporting research material to the Office of the Prosecutor on issues pending before the Tribunals.

A graduate of Duke University School of Law, Scharf is the author of numerous articles and several books, including *Balkan Justice*, which was nominated for the Pulitzer Prize in 1998, and *The International Criminal Tribunal for Rwanda*, which was awarded the American Society of international law's Certificate of Merit for the outstanding book in International Law in 1999. Scharf has testified as an expert on war crimes issues before the U.S. Senate Foreign Relations Committee, and has appeared as a frequent commentator on CNN's *Burden of Proof*, *Court TV*, the BBC's *The World*, and *National Public Radio*.

A past chairman of the D.C. Bar's International Law Section, Scharf is currently chairman of the American Bar Association's International Institutions Committee, chairman of the American Society of International Law's International Organizations Committee, chairman of the Board of Directors of the International Law Students Association, a member of the Executive Committee of the American Branch of the International Law Association, a member of the

Board of Directors of the International Legal Assistance Consortium, and executive director of the Public International Law and Policy Group—a nonprofit corporation and official UN nongovernmental organization that provides pro-bono international legal services to foreign governments and international organizations.

Other Books by the Authors

Paul R. Williams

Indictment at the Hague: The Milosevic Regime and Crimes of the Balkan Wars (with Dr. Norman Cigar)

International Law and the Resolution of Central and East European Transboundary Environmental Disputes

Treatment of Detainees: Issues of Detention as Examined by the United Nations Human Rights Committee

Michael P. Scharf

Slobodan Milosevic on Trial: A Companion (with William Schabas)

The Law Of International Organizations: Problems and Materials

The International Criminal Tribunal for Rwanda (with Virginia Morris) (Winner of the 1999 American Society of International Law Certificate of Merit for the Outstanding Book in International Law)

Balkan Justice: The Story behind the First International War Crimes Trial since Nuremberg (nominated for a Pulitzer Prize in Letters)

International Criminal Law: Cases and Materials (with Jordan Paust et. al)

An Insider's Guide to the International Criminal Tribunal for the Former Yugoslavia (with Virginia Morris)